World without End

The twenty-eighth volume in the series
RELIGION IN NORTH AMERICA
Catherine L. Albanese and Stephen J. Stein, editors

World without End

MAINSTREAM AMERICAN PROTESTANT VISIONS

of the

LAST THINGS, 1880–1925

⁂

JAMES H. MOORHEAD

*Indiana
University
Press*

BLOOMINGTON AND INDIANAPOLIS

This book is a publication of
Indiana University Press
601 North Morton Street
Bloomington, IN 47404-3797 USA

http://www.indiana.edu/~iupress

Telephone orders 800-842-6796
Fax orders 812-855-7931
Orders by e-mail iuporder@indiana.edu

*The paper used in this publication meets the minimum
requirements of American National Standard for Information
Sciences—Permanence of Paper for Printed Library
Materials, ANSI Z39.48-1984.*

MANUFACTURED IN THE UNITED STATES OF AMERICA

Library of Congress Cataloging-in-Publication Data

Moorhead, James H.
World without end : mainstream American Protestant visions of the last things, 1880–
1925 / James H. Moorhead.
p.   cm. — (Religion in North America)
Includes bibliographical references and index.
ISBN 0-253-33580-9 (alk. paper)
1. Eschatology—History of doctrines—19th century. 2. Protestant churches—
Doctrines—History—19th century. 3. Protestant churches—United States—History—
19th century. 4. Eschatology—History of doctrines—20th century. 5. Protestant
churches—Doctrines—History—20th century. 6. Protestant churches—United States—
History—20th century. I. Title. II. Series.
BT819.5.M66   1999
236′.9′0973—dc21   99-24448

1 2 3 4 5 04 03 02 01 00 99

For Cynthia

CONTENTS

FOREWORD

IN THIS VOLUME, James H. Moorhead, who is arguably the most perceptive interpreter of American postmillennialism today, carries his historical analysis of the development of that influential eschatological tradition to the time of its serious erosion in the opening decades of the twentieth century. In earlier publications, he examined the religious and social uses to which Northern Anglo-Protestants in mainstream churches applied postmillennial notions. Powerful reform movements, in times of both war and peace, drew religious energy from the eschatological vision of a this-worldly Kingdom of God and from the related concept of unending progress that was the product of human enterprise. Inauguration of a future millennial age, whether literal or figurative, rested on the shoulders of those working to improve society, whether by religious, social, or political means.

But the decades surrounding the turn of the twentieth century, the time period that Moorhead examines closely in this volume, witnessed the demise of religious postmillennialism among "mainstream" northern Protestants. His narrative therefore describes the end of the idea of "the End of History" among middle-of-the road liberal religious communities, those denominations where this progressive outlook had previously dominated. This is the story of the loss of faith in predictive prophecy and of a corrosive ambiguity toward eschatology among moderate to liberal Protestants. Some commentators may be tempted to describe this change as simply the inevitable result of the process of secularization, but Moorhead's analysis is far more subtle and probing than any such reductionist proposal.

Moorhead contextualizes his account by reminding us that millennialism, or religious apocalypticism of whatever stripe, needs to be understood as an effort to use biblical prophecy as a way to make sense of human experience. Postmillennial thinkers traditionally spoke of sacred and profane forces advancing together in harmony into the future, a judgment that was premised on a residual faith in the value of predictive prophecy. It was the loss of that faith that seriously eroded the postmillennial outlook. Even the rearguard efforts of some to retain belief in a possible Second Advent of Christ, while at the same time resorting to metaphorical interpretations of other traditional eschatological elements, failed to change what to Moorhead appears the inevitable destruction of postmillennial apocalypticism among mainstream Protestants.

Moorhead's account of these intellectual changes demonstrates clearly how they were bound up with acts and deeds. His authorial stance is intrinsically a subtle critique of the kind of social-science reductionism that would relegate ideas to intellectual attics that have little to do with the life that unfolds on lower floors. Moorhead shows how postmillennial developments within Protestantism undermined the developers in the end. Protestant assertions of thisworldliness and unending progress, along with a waning sense of apocalyptic terror, took away a sense of transcendence as well as of meaningful confrontation with primal human fears. The specter of hell as an eternal night faded. By contrast, the notion of heaven became continuous with the present life, specifically, with the depiction of it as an ideal home. These changes inevitably resulted in a different view of the primary Christian eschatological text—the biblical book of Revelation.

Moorhead's account adeptly chronicles the ways in which crusading, kingdom-building Protestantism was influenced by what he calls a "secular Great Awakening," the insight and knowledge available through the new social sciences. Scientific planning, rational organization, business management, professional standards, a preoccupation with efficiency—these replaced theological principles or religious traditions in this new "eschatological" world. Such new measures energized the relentless drive by liberal Protestants in these decades to reshape the nation and the world. The attempt to bring to fruition their liberal vision of the kingdom of God had increasingly little in common with earlier eschatological ideas.

By the end of the second decade of the twentieth century, the divide between the progressive heirs of the postmillennial tradition and the conservatives (a.k.a. the fundamentalists) who were watching and waiting for an imminent catastrophic end to history was immense. Moorhead depicts that gap as the contrast between naturalism and supernaturalism. Liberals saw no end in sight; for them the "Second Coming" was a continuous process throughout history. Conservatives anticipated a very different endtime scenario; in their scheme, Christ's physical return was to be instrumental in the denouement of history. Moorhead's volume is a masterfully written argument for the self-inflicted nature of the mainstream-Protestant wound in the Gilded Age and the Progressive Era. His work also adds up to a trenchant critique of the mainstream Protestant church as a church of order but of only lukewarm supernaturalism.

Catherine L. Albanese
Stephen J. Stein, Series Editors

PREFACE

In 1907 the British literary critic and essayist Edmund Gosse recalled the moment when he began to lose the faith of his childhood. Alone at school on a summer afternoon, the other students having gone on a walk, Gosse looked out from the schoolhouse upon trees and gardens which sloped down to the sea. "There was," he wrote, "an absolute silence below and around me; a magic of suspense seemed to keep every topmost twig from waving." For one reared in a Plymouth Brethren home where he had been taught to await the imminent return of Jesus, the summer stillness was a sign of the End.

> Over my soul there swept an immense wave of emotion. Now, surely, now the great final change must be approaching. I gazed up into the tenderly-colored sky, and I broke irresistibly into speech. "Come now, Lord Jesus," I cried, "come and take me to be for ever with Thee in Thy Paradise. . . . " I waited awhile, watching, and then I felt a faint shame at the theatrical attitude I had adopted, although I was alone. Still I gazed and still I hoped. Then a little breeze sprang up and the branches danced. Sounds began to rise from the road beneath me. Presently the colour deepened, the evening came on. From far below there rose to me the chatter of the boys returning home. The tea bell rang,—last word of prose to shatter my mystical poetry. "The Lord has not come, the Lord will never come," I muttered, and in my heart the artificial edifice of extravagant faith began to totter and crack.[1]

The American Protestants whom this book examines did not experience a tottering and cracking of faith as obvious or as datable as Gosse's. Unlike him, they did not expect the early return of Jesus. As postmillennialists, they believed that time would have an ultimate closure at the coming of Jesus, but this event would not occur until *after* the millennium or thousand years of earthly bliss foretold in the twentieth chapter of Revelation. Thus they assumed that the world had yet a long run and that history would in the meantime carry humanity toward ever greater triumphs. Those who held this hope had no reason to surrender it because Jesus failed to return on a particular summer afternoon.

Their hope, however, did totter and crack in other ways. As a distinct biblically grounded eschatology, postmillennialism ebbed away during the decades after the Civil War. In 1859, one writer called postmillennialism "the commonly received opinion" among American Protestants; by the early twentieth century it had largely vanished. With only slight partisan exaggeration, one author could claim in 1936 that it was without "living voice." In part this change resulted from the defection of some conservatives to the expanding premillennial ranks, but most leaders of American Protestantism did not become premillenarians. Among the moderate to liberal mainstream Protestants with whom this study is chiefly concerned, postmillennialism was not rejected outright; it eroded into something more amorphous: a decisively this-worldly hope for limitless spiritual improvement and temporal progress.[2]

The transformation, while more prolonged and subtle than Gosse's single moment of truth, had a similar outcome. The rise of the wind, the chatter of the boys, and the sound of the tea bell convinced Gosse that time might simply amble on without denouement. Erstwhile postmillennialists also lost the sense of a definitive End. They retained the confidence that God was present in the struggles of humanity and was guiding it ever upward—at least they maintained this confidence until after World War I and the onset of the Great Depression. But this process no longer had a clear End, a moment of ultimate completion and fulfillment. The Second Coming was reduced to a metaphor of perpetual improvement. Eternal progression was a goal unto itself, and the human pilgrimage through time lacked a final destination. The old liturgical formula "world without end" received an ironic new meaning.

This development had immense significance, for the notion of an End addresses a basic need. Human beings, Frank Kermode remarks in *The Sense of an Ending*, are born and die *in medias res*, "and to make sense of their span they need fictive concords with origins and ends." By setting their lives— whether as individuals or groups—within a narrative having both a beginning and a terminus, they are thus doing more than asserting that time will have a conclusion (though they are affirming that, too); they are asserting that time has a goal or purpose. History is not, in the famous line of Arnold Toynbee, simply "one damned thing after another."[3]

Although other cultures have had different ways of framing the idea of an End, apocalypticism has decisively shaped notions of an ending in Western civilization. In Greek, "apocalypse" means unveiling or revealing and has been used to denote both a literary genre and a set of ideas generally (though not uniformly) associated with it. As a literary type, apocalypses flourished in Judaism and later in Christianity from the second century B.C.E. to the end of the first century C.E. These writings, often written pseudonymously and cloaked in dramatic imagery, revealed heretofore hidden knowledge about human destiny. Usually they depicted a sharp struggle of good versus evil, cast history into a predetermined pattern of crisis, judgment, and vindication, and asserted that these final events were at hand. Vindication often entailed the violent destruction of the current order and a renovation of the cosmos so total that the new age following judgment would be radically discontinuous with the present. In the Christian tradition, notions about the millennium, the Second Coming of Jesus, the resurrection of the dead, the Last Judgment, the great beast or dragon (often identified with the Antichrist), heaven, and hell are all deeply informed by the apocalyptic tradition which is manifest most obviously in the biblical books Daniel and Revelation. In Western culture, to speak of the End has been almost inevitably to call upon these images.[4]

To speak of the End has also been to make assertions about the fate of good and evil, for apocalypticism is in the final analysis a theodicy. Time, according to the apocalypticist, will have a conclusion that is morally satisfying. There will be a final reckoning when all accounts are squared and every debt paid, the good and the wicked receiving their appropriate recompense. Accordingly, apocalyptic literature often trades in images of lavish reward and savage punishment. Its vivid pictures—on the one hand, of a city paved with gold, a place where death is no more, and on the other hand, of a world awash in blood risen to the height of a horse's bridle or of a lake of fire burning forever—awaken both elemental dreams and fears. All of this adds up to what one student of contemporary apocalyptic movements calls "a remarkable myth of violence, revenge, and renewal."[5]

Given the primal terrors and fantasies simultaneously evoked by the apocalyptic vision, it is little wonder that the notion of the End has elicited profound ambivalence. If, as Kermode would have it, human beings need to relate themselves to an End in order to make sense of their little span of time, they also may turn from such notions, fearful of their mortality and of final reckonings and of all the images of disintegration and doom associated with endings. The biblical writers themselves voice alternate sentiments. The book of Revelation closes with a cry of longing, "Come, Lord Jesus!" (Rev. 22:20); but the Old Testament book of Amos expresses greater hesitancy: "Woe unto you that desire the day of the Lord! The day of the Lord is darkness and not light" (Amos 5:18).

Much of the subsequent history of Christianity has been an effort to maintain a sense of the End while keeping it at a seemly distance. One such effort was postmillennialism. During its heyday in the mid-nineteenth century, postmillennialism represented a compromise between an apocalyptic and evolutionary view of time, between a history characterized by dramatic upheavals and supernatural events and one governed by natural laws of organic development. For postmillennialists, time was bounded by a transcendent End beyond itself and yet was capable of generating almost limitless improvement. The theory postponed history's cataclysmic end until after the millennium and thereby allowed the temporal interval necessary for the gradual evangelical conquest of the world and the triumph of secular progress. Nevertheless, a hard residue of apocalypticism survived in postmillennial thought. Committed to the premise of a thoroughly dependable Bible, Protestants could not discount predictions of an eventual supernatural Second Coming. Thus that end, though delayed to the far side of the thousand years, had to come. Moreover, views of individual destiny underscored this theme. In a time when most Protestants still believed, in the words Philippe Ariès applied to an earlier period, that "death was a moment of tragic confrontation between heaven and hell," the Last Judgment acquired a fearful imminence; and conversion, the center of evangelical piety, became an anticipation of the final battle of Christ and Antichrist.[6]

This book is, in the first instance, an account of the way in which these varied commitments ceased to hold together. In the late nineteenth and early twentieth centuries, the triumph of the so-called higher criticism undermined the biblical basis of millennialism. Moreover, liberal and moderate Protestants reconfigured piety in significant ways. They stopped depicting hell in lurid detail, participated in the growing denial of death, displaced conversion from the center of the spiritual life in favor of nurture and development, stressed the natural over the supernatural, and generally emphasized this life rather than the life to come. All of these changes weakened motifs that had kept nineteenth-century postmillennialists at least partially rooted in the apocalyptic mentality. By 1915, one theological professor was thus prepared to write the obituary of postmillennialism. It was, he said, a futile "attempt to unite a modern spirituality with a primitive view."[7]

This transformation was more than a bit of theological arcana; it influenced the way in which Protestants grappled with deep anxieties, and there were many of these during the decades that postmillennialism was subsiding into hope for an immanent kingdom of God. Protestant hegemony was assaulted on many fronts. After 1880, waves of new immigrants, mostly Catholics and Jews from eastern and southern Europe, weakened the numerical majority of Protestants. Dislocations wrought by urban growth and by the expansion of industry, technology, finance capitalism, and large corporations prompted serious unrest and disrupted church leaders' aspirations for an harmonious society. As large numbers of workers and farmers arose to protest their loss of self-mastery to impersonal banks, railroads, and industries, they became symbols of disorder to the more comfortable (and Protestant churchgoing) classes. Yet even among the latter groups, the technology and corporate organizations, so often celebrated as engines of progress, sometimes threatened to make people cogs in a machine-like society, to destroy the sense of personal autonomy, and to drain the wellsprings of human vitality. To these anxieties was added the uncertainty of changing gender roles as the Victorian ideology of separate spheres for men and women became problematic.

The new eschatology had difficulty in addressing these fears. In eliminating the idea of a definitive End, it had also gotten rid of the darker biblical themes associated with the End. Visions of the last things no longer had room for the blood of the apocalypse, the terror of the final judgment, or the fearsomeness of the lake of fire. Yet these were the very images by which primal fears could be named, objectified, and endured. Without them, eschatology could not fully acknowledge deeper anxieties or had to convert them into problems awaiting rational solution. But in the final analysis, these concerns involved existential issues that would not fully yield to logical resolution. Since the new eschatology had scanty resources with which to address matters at this level, it could do nothing other than return again and again to the quest to subject time to rational mastery. Kingdom building encouraged a frenetic, never-ending activism. Kinesis, not telos, was its prescription for the human condition.

The older postmillennialism had, of course, likewise encouraged activism. From the early nineteenth century, postmillennialists had invoked their eschatology for unabashedly promotional purposes. They used it to advance revivals and to enlist support for a vast panoply of benevolent causes designed to Christianize the nation. Postmillennialism, in short, was part of a culture-molding project aimed at asserting Protestant hegemony over American life. As postmillennialism gave way to the newer theology of the kingdom, this activism intensified, but the rationale changed. Whereas the older postmillennialism treated the secular fruits of the millennium as by-products of conversion, the newer theology of the kingdom increasingly sought them as objects worthy of direct pursuit in their own right. The advocates of the new view regarded the kingdom as a present ethical reality growing to fulfillment in every facet of *this* world. Through the foreign missions movement, the Social Gospel, and attempts at church federation, many Protestants sought to build such a kingdom. To create the reign of God in this world, they employed worldly instruments: denominational and ecumenical bureaucracies patterned on business, new forms of professional expertise drawn from the social sciences, and efficiency programs fashioned in accord with then current theories of scientific management.

The use of worldly instruments was not intended to secularize Christianity but to conform the world to faith. Yet as the perception of the End receded, so, too, did the sense of a transcendent bar of justice before which these activities might be brought to judgment. Unceasing activity virtually became a goal in its own right; and kingdom-building theology offered meager resources for a critique of this self-referential motion, for at the heart of the kingdom was the notion of never-ending process. The process of the kingdom was the goal of the kingdom. This view of history fit into a larger pattern of pragmatic thought common in both Europe and America after 1870. Central to that outlook was, in James T. Kloppenberg's words, an understanding of "knowledge as an unending experiment whose results can be validated only in activity rather than reflection, and whose conclusions are at best provisional and subject always to further testing in practice." Or one might point to the description of that temper by John Patrick Diggins. "With pragmatism in particular," Diggins argues, "the use of experience only prepares us for further experience, without experience itself being immediately self-illuminating or self-rewarding. The assumption that truth and value are produced in future action rather than revealed in present reflection holds out the promise of success, and as such pragmatism becomes not so much a philosophy as a story of the upward movement of life, a hopeful vision that appeals to America's romantic imagination." It is a story, Diggins argues, captured well in F. Scott Fitzgerald's lines in *The Great Gatsby:* "Gatsby believed in the green light, the orgiastic future that year by year recedes before us. It eluded us then, but that's no matter—to-morrow we will run faster, stretch out our arms farther. . . . [8]

This open-ended process also corresponded to the emerging ethos of consumerism which, with its dread of stasis, encouraged people to define themselves by ever-expanding, never-satiated longings—or, in Jackson Lears's expressive phrase, "the quiverings of continuous desire." Yet the new eschatology was not simply about limitless dreams and possibilities. It was also about control. Having largely banished from history notions of supernatural coups de main, liberal Protestants were eager to assert that people could exercise rational mastery over time to create an ever-improving society. With this double-sidedness—unlimited longing and the rage for order—the notion of a world without end became a mighty engine promoting restless activity, as desire and mastery chased one another in an ascending spiral. [9]

My account of this eschatology, of its setting, and of its implications is in large measure a story about mainstream Protestantism. I use the term "mainstream" and (more occasionally) "mainline" with trepidation. The terminology did not gain widespread currency until the second half of the twentieth century and is thus somewhat anachronistic when applied to the years of this study. Yet no other terms convey my meaning quite so well. By them, I mean to denote certain major northern religious bodies: Congregationalists, Baptists, Presbyterians, Methodists, Episcopalians, and the Disciples. These groups provided much of the leadership for various interdenominational ventures, understood themselves in varying degrees as custodians of a common

American Protestantism, and were often so regarded by others. How much influence they actually wielded in American life is an open question, but it is clear that they believed themselves called to exercise a moral proprietorship over the nation. Although I emphasize chiefly the moderate to liberal elements within this mainstream, it would be erroneous to portray these denominations as unequivocally modernist in theology. As William R. Hutchison has recently observed, they are more properly designated as broad or inclusive churches making room for a variety of theological persuasions. Moderate to liberal views, however, were especially well represented among denominational leaders, prominent pastors, and seminary professors. These people did much to set the official tone of mainstream Protestantism. Accordingly, they loom in the foreground of my account.[10]

This book, then, does not attempt to present a comprehensive history of American Protestantism from 1880 to 1925. It is limited by its focus upon liberal revisions of eschatology and their outworking in Protestant life and institutions. It is also bounded by its concentration upon leaders of mainstream Protestantism. Given the nature of the structures of power in the major Protestant churches, the result is a narrative in which males, tracing their lineage chiefly to the British Isles, are the major actors. People of different ethnic origin, women, theological conservatives, and nonmainstream Protestants do not occupy center stage in the pages that follow. But neither are they entirely offstage, for their presence and activities shaped the realities—and the fantasies—with which the leadership of mainstream Protestantism had to cope.

I do not claim that this account provides the master narrative into which every other chronicle of the period's religious history must be folded. The story *is*, however, an important one. From one perspective, it is an account of success. During the years of this study, the explosive energies released by mainstream Protestantism's search for the kingdom produced impressive results. Major denominations created agencies to address the ethical implications of a modern industrial society, innovative forms of ministry from settlement houses to institutional churches were established, creative alliances with the social sciences were explored, and a major effort to export Christianity through foreign missions took shape. All of these things occurred in the context of the continuing numerical growth of Protestantism. Yet one could also make the case that this activity and motion were ineffectual. Increasing numbers of conservative Protestants in the mainstream churches themselves were unconvinced by the vision of a world without End and turned to premillennialism. They envisioned a future, in Timothy Weber's words, of "angels, demons, lakes of fire which burned forever, and a personal Son of Man . . . coming soon on the clouds of heaven." In short, they believed in a future with a very definite End and a quite supernatural one at that. Their eschatology registered, as Paul Boyer has noted, a deep protest against notions of time without a definitive goal. Nonmainstream Protestants, particularly Pentecostals, flourished after 1906, and most of them came to share the premillennial eschatology. Moreover, by the early twentieth century, many of the secular allies upon whom Protestants had counted to help bring in the kingdom were going their own way. Divided within itself and deserted by erstwhile partners, mainstream Protestantism was experiencing what Robert Handy has called a "second disestablishment," a significant diminution of its power to shape American life.[11]

Explanations of this situation often turn on developments outside the churches: for example, growing religious pluralism, industrialization, or the rise of Darwinism. There is undeniable merit to such explanations, for external changes massively altered the world of American Protestants. The story of postmillennialism's transformation does not contradict those accounts; but it does frame them in a different perspective, one suggesting that at least in part the mainstream churches inadvertently contributed to their own dilemmas.

My conclusions bear similarity to those of James Turner. In an often-quoted passage from his *Without God, Without Creed,* Turner remarks on nineteenth-century unbelief: "If anyone is to be arraigned for deicide, it is not Charles Darwin but his adversary Bishop Samuel Wilberforce, not the godless Robert Ingersoll but the godly Beecher family." If I read Turner correctly, he is arguing that by their efforts to conform ideas of God to contemporary notions of reason and morality, nineteenth-century defenders of the deity stripped away much of the awe and mystery essential to the survival of faith. I would contend that the loss of a distinct sense of the last things was part of the process that Turner describes. To be sure, there was a positive side to what the moderate to liberal Protestants achieved. In espousing a theology that exalted eternal becoming over the sense of an End, that eliminated the more somber elements of eschatology, and that valued this world over the next, mainstream Protestants succeeded in promoting a crusading activism, many of whose goals and results were laudable. But in the process, they may also have lost the capacity to address humanity's more primal fears and longings and to provide symbols of a transcendent resolution and closure of these issues. For many decades, this result remained hidden by the cultural and religious optimism dominant within many sectors of the Protestant mainstream. But after the fundamentalist controversy of the 1920s and once the religious mood turned more somber in the 1930s, the hints of what had happened began to emerge. Yet in point of fact what a recent historian has called "the travail of the Protestant establishment" in the twentieth century had already been aborning for a number of decades. To illumine that process from the perspective of liberal revisions of eschatology—from the perspective of a world without End—is the goal of the pages that follow.[12]

A few words on the method governing these pages are perhaps also in order. What ensues is partly an intellectual history. Basing my research on the published works of mainstream Protestant figures, I have sought to trace the development of a set of interrelated ideas about the last things. The book is not, however, a story of ideas in isolation. That approach to intellectual history, while valuable, is not the one followed here. My goal is to show that the transformations in Protestant eschatology had consequences. Ideas and deeds went together. Moreover, liberal revisions in eschatology stood in intimate connection with a host of other matters: to name only a few, urban and technological growth, the expansion of the consumer economy, the bureaucratization of large segments of American life, the changing place of Protestantism vis-à-vis other religious groups whose numbers were expanding rapidly. In relating liberal eschatology to such issues, I seek to navigate between two extremes which I find equally unacceptable: a reductionism that views ideas as mere foam on the waters of social change and an intellectual isolationism that treats ideas as if they existed in a realm of pure essences. My goal is to demonstrate something of the interaction of idea and act, text and context. This approach probably leaves *World without End* open to criticism across a wider academic front. I hope that it also makes the account fuller and more illuminating.

Several readers of the manuscript have pressed me to speak more openly of my own opinions. How, they have asked, do I personally view the matters here discussed? From what standpoint do I approach the issues? I am a member of a so-called mainstream Protestant body, and my commitments have been profoundly shaped by the moderate to liberal tradition I have described. To the extent that my account exposes the tradition's weaknesses and the ironic outcomes of the decisions its adherents made, the critique comes from an insider and represents, I suppose, a lover's quarrel. Nevertheless, this book is *not* an attempt to define a normative view of the last things. *World without End* is neither a polemic nor an exercise in constructive theology. It is an historical analysis of the way in which one group of American Protestants used—or more accurately, largely ceased to use—the idea of the End.

ACKNOWLEDGMENTS

DURING THE FAR too many years that *World without End* was in process, it sometimes appeared that project without end might prove to be the more apt designation. The book would still be without termination were it not for the support of many people. Of these my family deserves first notice. By sharing their lives and their love with me, Cynthia Stephens Moorhead and our children—Evan, Stefan, and Olivia—have sustained me and given richness to my days. To Jean Stephens, I am indebted for the love of a mother from whom the suffix "in-law" has, in my estimation, long since disappeared.

My debts extend to colleagues at the two schools where I have taught. At North Carolina State University, James C. VanderKam (now of the University of Notre Dame) helped me put my research in larger historical perspective by sharing his knowledge of apocalypticism in a period much earlier than my own. To Jim I am also grateful for a friendship stretching back more than two decades. At Princeton Theological Seminary, I have likewise incurred many debts. President Thomas W. Gillespie and the trustees of the seminary have nourished an environment supportive of scholarship—not the least of these encouragements being a generous policy of sabbatical leaves. Karlfried Froehlich, who chaired the search committee that brought me to Princeton, provided the inspiration of his devotion to rigorous scholarship and also commented on ideas developed in chapter 2. Richard K. Fenn read the entire manuscript and managed to believe in it even on those days when I did not. Over numerous meals and cups of coffee, Dick has provided a friendship that is one of the most notable gifts of my life in Princeton. At various times, Daniel L. Migliore and John W. Stewart commented on portions of the argument. I am also grateful to a host of students who by their reactions to the ideas in this book sharpened my thinking. Without the facilities and staffs of several libraries—D. H. Hill Library at North Carolina State University, the Speer and Luce Libraries at Princeton Theological Seminary, and Firestone Library at Princeton University—*World without End* could not have been written.

Others outside my two schools deserve mention. The late Sydney E. Ahlstrom, esteemed mentor and friend, offered encouragement when this book was only an idea. Grant Wacker tendered characteristically witty and perceptive comments on early portions of my research. Some years ago Albert J. Raboteau, John Wilson, and Princeton University Ph.D. candidates in religion devoted an afternoon seminar to my work. Also, the National Endowment for the Humanities provided the funds for a leave in the beginning stages of the project. Stephen J. Stein and Catharine L. Albanese, editors of the series in which this volume appears, improved the manuscript by their suggestions. W. Clark Gilpin likewise offered useful commentary. I am also grateful to Robert J. Sloan, Jane Lyle, and Marilyn Grobschmidt of Indiana University Press for their assistance during the editorial process. Copy editor Ruth Barzel honed my prose.

Portions of my argument appeared earlier in somewhat different form in articles published in *Church History, The Journal of American History, Soundings,* and *The Princeton Seminary Bulletin.* I have also drawn upon the argument developed in my essay published in *Biblical Hermeneutics in Historical Perspective: Studies in Honor of Karlfried Froehlich on His Sixtieth Birthday,* edited by Mark S. Burrows and Paul Rorem and published by Eerdmans Publishing Company.

World without End

INTRODUCTION

The Postmillennial Tradition, 1800–1880

IN 1870 Professor Samuel Harris of Yale Divinity School journeyed to Massachusetts to address the faculty and students at Andover Theological Seminary. His theme was a large one—the Kingdom of Christ on earth. Throughout his lecture series, he asserted that a proper understanding of the last things required delicately counterpoised affirmations. On the one hand, the kingdom bore an organic relationship to history. The kingdom was not "something outside of . . . and above" time, nor would the kingdom be "consummated at last in a violent disruption of that history." "Human agency" would play a vital role in "the slow progress of Christ's kingdom." No eschatology suggesting interference in the orderly unfolding of human events was "a true and satisfactory philosophy of human history." No Kingdom of God arbitrarily imposed was morally acceptable. And yet Harris also insisted that the kingdom would not evolve according to an automatic law of progress inherent in the scheme of things or from unaided human striving. It required "a divine energy supernaturally flowing into the history of man." Miracles had attended the birth of the kingdom, providence had smoothed its forward movement, and an event far removed from naturalistic progress would mark its culmination: the return of Jesus to judge the quick and the dead. In prefiguration of that final act, the earth would in the meantime be the "battleground for the soul of man between the powers of heaven and hell."[1]

Harris's lectures epitomized the complexity of the postmillennial vision that had taken shape during the nineteenth century. Friends of modern progress, postmillennialists gloried in the advances of their age and expected far greater triumphs to come. They often asserted that the tokens of that happy future would not be (at least until the far-distant end of the world) graves supernaturally opened and Jesus returning on the clouds. History would spiral upward by the orderly continuation of the same forces that had promoted revivals, made America a model Republic, and increased material prosperity. But the theory had another side whose features included supernatural judgment and overturning. If postmillennialists had one foot in the world of steamships and the telegraph, the other was still firmly planted in the cosmos of John's Revelation—a universe where angels poured out vials of wrath, the dead would rise again, and the wicked would be cast into a lake of fire burning forever.[2]

Although this union of progress with the symbols of the Apocalypse may strike most late-twentieth-century people as awkward or quaint, it offered a powerful fusion of commitments deeply held by many nineteenth-century Protestants. To understand why the synthesis was credible and how it functioned is to grasp central features of the mid-nineteenth-century Protestant mind.

An Ordered Millennium

Postmillennialism antedated the nineteenth century. Some credit Daniel Whitby, a liberal English theologian, with initiating the view in *A Paraphrase and Commentary on the New Testament* (1703), and others contend that Jonathan Edwards introduced this "new departure in eschatology" in America in the 1730s and 1740s. The claims are exaggerated, for these men merely stated more systematically what had been implicit in certain earlier theories. Moreover, one must not attach greater significance to the early manifestations of postmillennialism than contemporaries did. The position of the Second Coming relative to the millennium was only one of many disputed eschatological questions and not necessarily the one on which exegetes placed the greatest weight. The fact that the term "postmillennialism" was not used before the nineteenth century—even among those who held the view—underscores the point. Postmillennialists prior to that period did not make the time of Jesus's return the key to a consistent view of the meaning of time. But in the 1790s this situation began to change. Postmillennialism started to become more than a matter of dating the Second Advent. It came to denote an understanding of history as gradual improvement according to rational laws that human beings could learn and use. It was becoming a faith in an orderly ascent of history into the golden age—a hope, as Perry Miller once said aphoristically, that America might find the "the way, without any Fifth-Monarchy nonsense, into the millennium."[3]

There was much irony in the timing of the emergence of this faith. The decades from the mid-eighteenth to the mid-nineteenth century were anything but orderly. The transition from colonial status to nationhood brought intense political factionalism and disputes over the allocation of power. These political dissensions reflected a deeper sea change taking place in American thought, a transformation that Gordon S. Wood has called a "democratization of mind." Harrison Gray Otis summed up the results of the change in an address at Harvard in 1836: "Everywhere the disposition is found among those who live in the valleys, to ask those who live on the hills, 'How came we here and you there?' accompanied with intelligible demonstrations of a purpose in the former, to partake of the benefits of the mountain air." Evidences of that determination appeared in the popular assault against professional elites, in the extension of suffrage to the vast majority of white males, and in the conversion of politics into a form of popular mobilization and entertainment. An economic transformation—a market revolution, gaining force in the several decades after the end of the war with Britain in 1815—profoundly altered human relations. In the Northeast, the growing scarcity of land tore young men and women loose from the ties of blood, place, and prescribed social roles and hurled them westward or into the towns and cities. In the urban areas, artisans who had previously enjoyed some degree of status and independence were subjected to the more impersonal regime of wage earning. Among the growing middle classes, the nature of work tended to separate production from the home and produced a major rethinking of the proper roles of men and women. As Robert Wiebe has written, it is little wonder that many observers professed to see in the young nation "only bursts of atomized behavior, a kinetic confusion that was undermining the last pillars of an old order."[4]

Yet alongside fragmentation there was a search for a new basis of order. Its foundation lay in the ideal of the self-disciplined individual, whose internal moral compass enabled him or her to achieve proper equilibrium and thus contribute to the right ordering of society. The home provided that gyroscope, and mothers, now confined (at least in theory) to the "woman's sphere" of domesticity, were to be its chief guarantors. Schools, churches, and various voluntary societies likewise aided in instructing the individual. Whether in school or at home or in church, order was to be promulgated chiefly through influence or persuasion, not arbitrary power. The new ideal was, of course, largely the creation of the middle classes (though other groups could use it to their own ends) and met considerable resistance in important subcultures of the nation. It represented an effort to tame antinomian impulses, the surging popular passions that democratization evoked, in the service of a new form of order. The coalescence of the so-called "second party system" in the 1830s symbolized a similar move toward order. The Whig Party in particular represented the political expression of emerging middle-class notions of discipline.[5]

The same dynamics of fragmentation and the search for order played themselves out in the domain of religion. Splintering was everywhere in evidence. By the early nineteenth century, popular denominations such as the Baptists and Methodists were surging numerically far ahead of the Episcopalians, Presbyterians, and Congregationalists who had been the "big three" of the colonial era. Moreover, new religious bodies—for example, the Mormons

and various "Christian" movements, some of which coalesced into the Disciples of Christ—were flourishing. Even the older churches experienced fragmentation within themselves as Presbyterians, for example, endured a seces-
sion of members in Kentucky in 1810 and then a major rupture of the entire
denomination in 1837. Protestantism itself, it might be argued, was being
democratized, and a new kind of leader came to the fore. Often lacking formal education and contemptuous of both creeds and learned ministers, that
leader mobilized popular support by encouraging others to thumb their noses
at ancient authority, to think for themselves, and to examine the scriptures directly. The new leader's power came from an ability to identify with the common people and to speak to their concerns in a direct, pungent style. Such
leaders created a new sermonic genre characterized by pithy colloquialisms,
popularized a new hymnody whose roots were sunk deep in folk culture, and
pioneered a religious journalism which sought to express the thought of the
masses.[6]

Yet something much more complex than an undifferentiated process of
democratization was taking place in American religion. The popular movements could be exceedingly authoritarian: witness the atavistic patriarchy of
Mormonism, the hierarchical structure of Methodism with its bishops rigidly
controlling circuit riders, and the rigorous communal discipline that characterized many Baptist congregations and Methodist class meetings. Moreover,
by the 1830s and 1840s many so-called popular denominations were imitat-
ing the style of the more genteel churches as they founded colleges, seminaries, and literary journals or built more tasteful houses of worship and began
celebrating middle-class domesticity as an ideal. For their part, leaders of the
older denominations learned to use the instruments of mass persuasion effectively. Through the so-called voluntary societies, organized first at the local
level, there emerged in the early nineteenth century a national network of benevolent institutions—known collectively as the Evangelical United Front—
which included organizations to disseminate tracts and Bibles, to promote
temperance, and to sponsor home and foreign missions as well as numerous
other causes.[7]

As in the nation at large, a new sense of order was emerging out of the
wreckage of the old. Sometimes consciously and often by inadvertence, important segments of Protestantism were generating what Donald M. Scott has
called "a whole new social grammar—a new and distinctive way of perceiving
how the social order was composed, operated, and maintained." That new
grammar contained the vocabulary of the order characteristic of the middle
classes: emphasis upon the self-disciplined individual, upon domesticity, and
upon persuasion as the instrument for the extension of that order. The parallel
between Protestant visions and those of the culture is not surprising, for evan-

gelical Protestants more than any other group helped to shape the new national ethos. Yet this consensus was always a tenuous one beset by critics who did not accept it and by rival interpretations. From Mormons to various "plebeian" expressions of Christianity, the new order—or at least, the mainstream version of it—was anathema. At best, it exercised a presumptive hegemony which required militant offensive action if dreams of its dominion were to be realized.[8]

Crucial to that quest—and to the emergence of a postmillennial perspective—were the religious revivals that rumbled intermittently across the American landscape from the eighteenth to the nineteenth century. Initially deemed a surprising work of God, these outpourings of the spirit recurred with such frequency as to appear, especially after the Second Great Awakening, the normal state of the church. "They have become," said Robert Baird in his influential study of American religion in 1844, "a constituent part of the religious system of our country." Calvin Colton, a noted apologist for revivals who later became one of their most acerbic critics, made the same point. So numerous and regular were the awakenings that they disclosed "the probabilities of a perpetual *revival* of religion—a revival without a consequent decline." At first, many Protestants still in the grip of a predestinarian theology regarded the revivals as something to be awaited "as men are wont to wait for showers of rain." (At least this posture was the official one, despite the fact that George Whitefield, the folk hero of the Great Awakening, had achieved his triumphs in large part through careful advance publicity and self-promotion.) But as Calvinistic doctrine was attenuated, the theory of revivals began to resemble the practice. Awakenings became consciously an "object of systematic effort," or "matters of human calculation." By studying the laws underlying that spiritual renaissance, persons could use—indeed, God expected them to use—means that could produce revivals at will. Such promotional tactics were legion. They included techniques of mass persuasion—the anxious bench, the protracted meeting, and the newly emerging popular press—as well as the host of voluntary societies organized to extend the sway of the gospel. Those associations ranged from the churches planted in the frontier back country by Methodist itinerants and Baptist farmer-preachers to the numerous tract, missionary, education, and other societies of the so-called Evangelical United Front. Widespread revivals, in short, were the matrix from which emerged the conviction that a wondrous new day was at hand and that the systematic labors of the saints would help bring it to pass.[9]

Postmillennialism was an expression of this ethos. Jonathan Edwards, the putative father of American postmillennialism, was among the many who saw tantalizing signs of the approaching millennium in the Great Awakening. Although Edwards may have later retreated from that optimistic assessment, others soon reiterated his hope and made it the basis for a far more programmatic approach to evangelical activity. As Protestants began aspiring to the conquest of the world through revivals, missions, and voluntary societies, postmillennialism provided a rationale and motivation to sustain the imperial vision. Dilating on the glories of the millennial era, writers held out the carrot of success as an inducement to action. Triumph was certain; the labors of the saints would lead inevitably to the millennial glory. As a report of the American Tract Society observed in 1823, "preachers of righteousness [will] go forth and speak each one to an individual, a family, a neighbourhood, till they shall have no need to say any more, 'Know ye the Lord, for all shall know him from the least to the greatest; and the whole earth be filled with the knowledge of the glory of the Lord, as the waters fill the sea.'" And yet the underside of those visions of glory was always a reminder that triumph was conditional on vigorous human exertion. Since the Kingdom of God would not arrive by a supernatural destruction of the world, only the labors of believers could bring it about. If they proved laggard in their task, the millennium would be retarded. From the divine point of view, certain, and from the human perspective, contingent on the saints, the Kingdom of God thus combined in delicate balance hope and anxiety to induce maximum evangelical exertion. William Cogswell of the American Education Society succinctly captured both aspects of postmillennial motivation when he declared in 1833: "Soon the whole earth will chant the praises of the Redeemer, and the song of salvation will echoe from shore to shore. But in order to [do] this, there must be more fervent prayer, more abundant labors, more enlarged charities. In this conquest of the world to Christ, the church must become a well-disciplined army, and every member of it must know her place and duty." "All this," Cogswell insisted, is to be accomplished "not by miracles, but by the blessing of God accompanying the use of suitable means." In the hands of such people, postmillennialism functioned as a synergistic theology ready-made for the crusading and voluntaristic evangelicalism of the antebellum period.[10]

The emphasis on human cooperation as an instrument of the Kingdom of God fit into a larger Protestant desire to portray God's purpose in a way defensible to enlightened reason. Although the orthodox clergy battled the supposed excesses of rationalism, they had absorbed much of the spirit of the Enlightenment, especially as mediated through the Scottish Common Sense Philosophy. The most telling evidence of that preoccupation was the extent to which antebellum thinkers made the moral government of God a central theme of theology. That theory depicted the purpose of God in terms of moral law binding on the Creator and creature alike. Usually defining that law as benevolence, or the intention to seek the greatest good of the universe, theologians then sought to demonstrate that God ordered affairs in such a way as to benefit the vast majority of sentient beings. Far from being capricious, his government was thus defensible on rational utilitarian principles. Moreover, because his government was moral and rational, God exercised his dominion chiefly through persuasion rather than by arbitrary interference in human affairs.[11]

Postmillennialism was the moral government of God stretched out on the frame of time. In one sense, of course, millennial schemes of all sorts are efforts to justify the ways of God to man by showing that, at the last, good will win over evil. But postmillennialists wished a theodicy written in a grander key. It was not enough to demonstrate that light would eventually triumph over darkness. In order to vindicate the government of God, the temporal process *as a whole* had to yield far more happiness than woe. Postmillennialism, as generally interpreted, guaranteed a favorable balance. It assured that history would not be terminated at a time when most of the human race, living and dead alike, had already gone or were destined to hell. Beginning with Joseph Bellamy and Samuel Hopkins, a number of commentators suggested that during the millennium massive increases in population coupled with nearly universal conversions would enable the census of the redeemed to catch up with and then far surpass the number of the damned. The evangelist Charles Finney, so different from Hopkins and Bellamy in many respects, concurred fully at that point. If the world, he asked, "should now be swept out of the universe [by a premillennial Second Coming], could we suppose that it was created with a benevolent design?" Since "a great majority of those who have inhabited the earth, have gone to hell," a premature end to the world would impeach the rational order and benevolence of its Creator. Therefore, this earth must "not be destroyed till its work is fully done"—that is, until after the kingdom had been attained and the total amount of sin and unhappiness reduced to a minuscule spot.[12]

Postmillennialism also guaranteed the rationality of the universe by asserting that God would win his dominion by persuasion. To those enamored with reason and law, it was offensive to suggest that God had to subject the world by legions of angels or by other supernatural legerdemain. As the nineteenth century wore on and as postmillennialism became increasingly stylized, a frequent objection to the premillennial alternative was that it made Jesus into a warrior chieftain who would eventually launch a celestial army of invasion to conquer by force a world he could not win by persuasion. "Is this our idea of the King of kings," asked Methodist Bishop Thomson, "after eighteen hundred years of Christian progress?" A kingdom of brute strength was "such a one that the devil desired our Lord to establish." The world, in short, had to be allowed to run its course until its goals were achieved by moral and rational means. Thus postmillennialists envisioned an essentially voluntaristic kingdom—one is tempted to say Republic—bound together by allegiance freely given and expanding its domain by its persuasive power.[13]

This similarity sheds light on the tendency of Protestants to make the Republic itself an object of eschatological fulfillment. Although all millennialists did not find the Redeemer Nation in John's predictions, that reading was, in J. F. Maclear's words, "so common as to be almost canonical." That such conflation of the religious and the profane should occur is not entirely surprising. In whatever form, millennialism looks forward to an ultimate merger of the sacred and the secular, for it envisions a time when "the kingdoms of this world are become the kingdoms of our Lord." Moreover, so many of the symbols of the Apocalypse describe political and social upheavals that even relatively apolitical millennialists—Jonathan Edwards, for example—have usually been compelled, at least in an external fashion, to relate wars and the rise and fall of empires to the history of redemption. For many Protestants, however, prophecy and nationalism were more integrally related. America was not merely an extrinsic token of the impending millennium but an intrinsic instrument of its coming. Students of American culture have suggested various origins of that "civil millennialism": Puritan typology, the mid-eighteenth-century infusion of libertarian or Radical Whig concepts into eschatological thought, the Great Awakening, American religious pluralism. At the level of the history of ideas, one can make a case for each of those interpretations, but from another perspective the question of formal intellectual origins is an issue of secondary importance, for millennialism was not in the first instance a matter of abstract theory. It was an effort to use enigmatic biblical prophecies to make sense out of experience, and from that experience Protestants discerned instinctively a bond, a symbolic unity, between their lives as evangelicals and their lives as citizens.[14]

That sense of affinity can be read in countless texts from the nineteenth century. A Fourth of July oration delivered by Samuel Harris in Bangor, Maine, during the first year of the Civil War illustrates the point. Discussing the essence of American nationality, Harris explained:

> It is the embodiment of our great American idea into our institutions which constitutes us a nation. This is indeed the Saviour's teaching, loosely interpreted and applied, that a man is not a Jew because he is descended from Abraham, but only because, whatever his descent, he has the faith of Abraham. He who is not in sympathy with the American idea that breathes in our political institutions, is an alien unworthy to bear the name of American citizen. But . . . everyone who seeks the protection of our government, intelligently sympathizing with its idea and spirit, he is an American, a native "to the manor born" by a new political birth, and entitled in due form of law to become a citizen.

If one substituted "Protestant" for "American" and "church" for "nation" and altered a few other words accordingly, this remarkable passage could read equally well as a definition of the evangelical conception of the church. In both cases community is attained voluntarily—that is, by a "new birth" in which citizens or church members freely commit themselves to the common values. That perceived congruence between national ideals and religious ones, far more than any formal theory, contributed to the tendency to accord the Republic an important role in the inauguration of the Kingdom of God.[15]

This affinity could be—and, of course, often was—spelled out explicitly. The terms of the synthesis were simple: Civil liberty created conditions favorable to the flourishing of the gospel, and the gospel in turn secured the voluntary order without which society—religious or secular—could not long endure. As the Reverend Erskine Mason explained in an 1848 address to the American Home Missionary Society, the absence of external coercion placed Americans in ideal circumstances to demonstrate "the power of an untrammeled Gospel." But that principle of freedom "can never be seen as a true and safe one, except as the influence of the Gospel prevents its perversion and defines its proper limitations." In tandem, however, freedom and voluntary submission would "revolutionize the globe" and bring down the latter-day glory. Again one must note that not all millennial treatises explicitly connected the Republic with the Kingdom of God, but they did not need to do so. The notes of Gabriel's trumpet resonated with national values in such a way that millennial symbols could shift, almost effortlessly, from a religious to a political context as the needs of the moment dictated.[16]

Nor was the Republic the only secular harbinger of the kingdom. As early as 1793, Samuel Hopkins in his *A Treatise on the Millennium* (1793) was arguing that the golden era would be marked by improved material and technological conditions. He envisioned labor-saving devices reducing work to two or three hours a day, printing innovations rendering books cheaper, and a communications revolution enabling "correspondence . . . with much less expense of time and labour, perhaps a hundred times less, than that with which men now correspond." Although Hopkins did not make these improvements instruments for the advance of the kingdom, later postmillennialists amid the nineteenth century's scientific advances and market revolution took that step. Increasingly, millennialists enumerated more sophisticated technology, greater prosperity, and the flourishing of the arts and sciences as signs of the millennium. Just as the polity of the Republic bore an intimate relationship to evangelicalism, so, too, other secular advances went hand in hand with the triumph of Christianity. Thus when one group of Protestants received word in 1858 that the transatlantic cable had been completed, they

rejoiced by breaking into song: "Jesus shall reign where e're the sun. . . . "
Eight years earlier a writer for a Methodist women's magazine had drawn even
more explicitly millennial conclusions from telegraphic communication:
"This noble invention is to be the means of extending civilization, republican-
ism, and Christianity over the earth. . . . Then shall come to pass the millennium." Protestant experience by midcentury lent considerable plausibility to
that heady dream. Improvements in printing had permitted the inundation of
the nation with religious tracts and newspapers; the steamboat and the merchant opened the doors of foreign lands to the missionary; and affluence
made possible the host of Christian colleges from which evangelical influences
emanated. The list could be extended indefinitely. Protestants did carp periodically about the spiritual dangers inherent in such material advances, but
despite such protests they were ardent promoters of modernity. Rightly understood, secular improvements had, in words Presbyterian Albert Barnes uttered several years after the Civil War, "an essential connection with Christianity. They become incorporated with it. They carry Christianity with
themselves wherever they go."[17]

This variety of postmillennialism readily became, in Charles Sellers's
words, a charter for "cultural imperialism." Speaking to a foreign missions
society in New York City in late 1860, a Presbyterian minister enunciated the
implications of that quest for dominion. "For eighteen centuries," said the
Reverend Walter Clarke, "the saints have been gradually getting possession of
the world, of its intelligence, of its arts, of its property, of its positions of
power and influence. . . . Project this Church into the future now! Let the
saints of God go on for the centuries to come, acquiring and accumulating as
they have done in times gone by; and is not here an argument to attest what
the prophet [Daniel] foresaw? That the kingdom and dominion, and the
greatness of the kingdom under the whole heaven, shall be given at length
to the people of the saints of the Most High God?"[18]

The Millennium and the Apocalypse

Such paeans resemble a theological gloss on J. B. Bury's famous definition
of progress, that "civilisation has moved, is moving, and will move in a desir-
able direction," and some have argued that by the nineteenth century millennial imagery had been translated "from its meaning within the closed system
of sacred history into a metaphor for limitless secular improvement." On
many occasions the symbolism was indeed hazy and deracinated from
specifically biblical and religious meaning. One might point, for example,
to the historian George Bancroft, for whom a vaguely millennial statement
about "God . . . visible in history" meant little more than "humanity itself
engaged in formative efforts, constructing sciences, promulgating laws, orga-

nizing commonwealths and displaying its energies in the visible movement of its intelligence." Sometimes even fuzzy clerical pronouncements suggested that the fulfillment of John's Apocalypse would derive less from divine activity than from the fact that the nineteenth century was "an age of steam, of electricity, [of] greatest and most wonderful invention." It would be a serious error, however, to equate postmillennialism with faith in progress if one means by the latter a serene confidence in the automatic, uninterrupted improvement of the human condition. Although evangelicals often spoke in that fashion, they also adopted another vocabulary, one characterized in Mark Hanley's words by the "withering fire of salvation messages [and] . . . final judgment scenarios." Even for postmillennialists the future was latent with a sense of the final End, of transcendent judgment and calamity.[19]

That note of judgment and overturning is usually associated more with pre- than with postmillennialism, and the former usually did pronounce a harsher indictment against the present age. For example, the Presbyterian premillennialist George Duffield asserted that the world was too sinful for one to suppose that the Kingdom of God was "now in the progress of its expansion," and he asserted categorically that his nation had no reason to suppose that it could "escape the disaster and ruin which had befallen the highly civilized nations of antiquity." While few postmillennialists would have painted so gloomy a picture, their stress on judgment and cataclysm differed only in degree from Duffield's fulminations. When the Reverend Leonard Woods preached the ordination sermon commissioning Luther Rice and Adoniram Judson, among others, as missionaries, he noted the "civil revolutions and convulsions, and the desolating wars of the present day." He concluded that the Lord "has arisen now to shake terribly the earth: and that such terrors had to come to pass before "the spiritual coming of Christ, and the millennial glory of the church." The children of Lyman Beecher recalled how their famous father daily prayed: "Overturn and overturn till He whose right it is shall come and reign, King of nations and King of saints." The overturning for which he prayed was not merely a gradual mushrooming of evangelical influence; it included wars and upheavals "such as shall veil the sun, and turn the moon into blood, and shake the heart with the violence of nation dashing against nation, until every despotic government shall be thrown down and chaos resume its pristine reign." Because of the unique position that many Protestants believed America to occupy, those darker contours of millennialism were sometimes blurred. The model Republic, its religion pure and its democracy strong, might escape the catastrophes that would cast down anciens régimes elsewhere. "We had flattered ourselves," wrote an editor during the Civil War, when the hope appeared illusory, "that we should escape the desolating wars which have marked the fluctuating fortunes of European Empire, and that in a pathway of unbroken peace we should sweep forward into the cloudless splendors of the Millennial era." Yet that hope of an unimpeded ascent to the millennium had always been more an expression of American exceptionalism than a general rule of history, and even the Redeemer Nation enjoyed at best a provisional exemption from travail—an exemption conditional on the continued righteousness of the American people. Judgment hung precariously over the nation, and whenever strains or conflict did erupt within the Republic, the stark categories of apocalyptic judgment were available to render those problems intelligible.[20]

Indeed, nineteenth-century Americans may have stood in especial need of the clarity with which apocalypticism endowed history. Relative geographic and social mobility, growing ethnic heterogeneity, weak and diffuse centers of government, and the absence of state-supported churches, a monarch, or a clearly fixed class structure removed many of the landmarks by which Western societies had traditionally been bounded. Moreover, the national faith in liberty, which supposedly knit Americans together in ideological unity, tended to exalt that boundlessness into a virtue and was susceptible to a profoundly asocial, disintegrative interpretation. Despite the fact that postmillennialists often celebrated the new order, they also felt a measure of uncertainty in the face of its poorly defined boundaries. Under those circumstances apocalyptic images performed a useful function. The dualistic struggle of good against evil reduced an amorphous social reality to an intelligible pattern and focused vaguely understood anxieties on specific foes. In more extreme cases that symbolism contributed to what Richard Hofstadter called the "paranoid style" or more particularly to the various countersubversive campaigns described by David Brion Davis. Thus nineteenth-century Americans espied numerous supposed conspiracies—the Illuminati, Mormonism, Roman Catholicism, abolitionism, the slave power, Freemasonry, to name only a few—and that conspiratorial mode of analysis was frequently cloaked in apocalyptic language. Although premillennialists' usually greater sense of impending doom may have lent itself more readily to the paranoid style, their postmillennial counterparts were certainly not immune to it. From Timothy Dwight's portrayal of the radical Enlightenment as a plot of the dragon down to the Civil War writer who saw Transcendentalism, Robert Owen's philosophy, and the slaveholders' rebellion as marks of the beast, postmillennialists also used the simplistic categories of the Revelation to define more precisely the uncertain limits of American identity.[21]

It would, however, be too reductionistic to attribute the persistence of apocalypticism solely to social strain. One must also note the unwavering commitment of Protestants to the Bible. A terrible day of wrath, a literal Second Coming, and a dramatic overturning of the present age were motifs deeply embedded in the scriptures, and since evangelicals believed the Bible to be God's authoritative word, they could not dismiss such themes. Biblical predictions, declared the *Biblical Repertory and Princeton Review,* "were real disclosures of future events, and must therefore of necessity always be accomplished." Thus mid-nineteenth-century expositors could not take the approach characteristic of more liberal, twentieth-century commentators—namely, to view apocalyptic scriptures as tracts for their own times and to deny that they foretold either accurately or in detail the far-distant future. There were, to be sure, divergent interpretations about how many vials had been poured out, whether the Man of Sin was Papal Rome or a sinister figure yet to be revealed, when the travail of the witnesses would end. Likewise, some voices urged caution, reminding others how enigmatic biblical predictions were and how frequently persons had made fools of themselves trying to extrapolate a time-specific chronology from Revelation. That exegetical wrangling, however, testified to a consensus taken for granted by the disputants: the Bible did contain a unified and accurate set of predictions.[22]

Postmillennialists felt an especial need to assert the accuracy of biblical predictions, since premillennialists charged them with being soft on that issue. According to premillennialists, one ought to interpret prophecies literally except where language is self-evidently figurative. Thus New Testament passages promising the return of the Son of Man like a thief in the night or enjoining believers to await "the day of the Lord wherein the heavens being on fire shall be dissolved" foretold precisely what the words implied—a Second Coming terminating this world violently and without warning. Postmillennialists, influenced by the historic Protestant bias in favor of literal exegesis, could not ignore the force of this argument. They walked a precarious tightrope. Anxious to avoid chiliastic literalism with its implication that the curtain of history might abruptly descend, they also felt constrained to agree that "every jot and tittle of prophecy" would come to pass. Postmillennialism resolved the problem by delaying the supernatural destruction of this age until after the millennium—that is, until after the gospel and secular progress had run their appointed courses without unseemly intrusion. But the End, though postponed, had to come, for the Bible had foretold it, and the Bible was the word of God. Like marine navigators, Protestants could tack across apocalypticism, but they could not sail directly against it.[23]

The final judgment was thus conveniently delayed, but apocalyptic terrors were by no means held in complete abeyance until the end of time. As ministers such as Woods and Beecher suggested, it was possible to read the portents of this bouleversement in contemporary events as well. The paradox becomes intelligible when one remembers that the majority of millennialists viewed Revelation as an encoded history of the church from the Incarnation (or sometimes earlier) to the end of the world. Thus the sharply dualistic struggle of good against evil, the pouring of the vials of wrath, the earthquakes, wars, and famines were not merely reserved to the End; they constituted the fabric of all history. Christ might not return in person for many centuries, but in the interim the rise and collapse of kingdoms would portend that final event. And even if one denied that the Apocalypse contained a detailed chronology, the present relevance of apocalyptic categories was not thereby refuted. The Revelation, said biblical scholar Moses Stuart, "is a τύπος [type] of all that is to happen in respect to the church. I regard the whole book as particular illustrations of a general principle"—the principle that God shall overthrow his foes and establish his perfect kingdom. These prophecies, then, had perennial relevance, for they not only embraced specific occurrences but also provided models of the way in which God would always act and posited a view of history as a succession of fulfillments, each prefiguring some aspect of the last things. In that sense, every era was contemporaneous with the End, and in the words of a Civil War editor, prophecy is "fulfilled anew from age to age . . . in all these great events that baffle human foresight."[24]

Apocalyptic themes were credible because they constituted more than a grand interpretation of history. Their roots were also sunk deep in the biographies of individual Protestants. At the heart of evangelicalism was the believer's intense struggle to pass from sin to holiness. That stress on conversion and sanctification established a complex symbolic linkage between each person's destiny and the millennial sense of history. In some ways, the emphasis reinforced the hope of gradual temporal improvement. For example, after 1830 a crescendo of perfectionism—or belief that the saints could eradicate sin—merged with postmillennialism in some quarters, most notably in the theology of the Methodists and of Finney. The result was a vision of humanity, individually and collectively, surging forward to a happier future. (One must not, however, push this correspondence too far. All postmillennialists did not adhere to perfectionism, and sometimes holiness advocates—the Keswick Movement of the late nineteenth century is a case in point—joined the search for holiness to a premillennial view of a deteriorating world.) But if the evangelical's warfare against sin sometimes awakened bright pictures of progress, it also evoked simultaneously the darker, more catastrophic side of the apocalyptic view of history. The psychological upheaval often associated with conversion illustrates the point. Conversion, along with the accompanying dreams of the heaven or hell into which death would shortly usher each person, constituted a miniature apocalypse paralleling the historical scenario of the book of Revelation. Just as the Kingdom of God arrived only through overturning and judgment, so, too, believers achieved assurance of salvation only after a season of terror, sometimes prolonged, during which they knew themselves to be destined to hell. Indeed, the two processes were one, for the history of redemption was only the aggregation of the stories of countless men and women fleeing the wrath to come. The Reverend M. T. Adam made the connection explicit in an 1837 treatise. As the millennium approached, increasing numbers of people would endure that preconversion anxiety until "every one will feel himself to be lost, and as standing on the brink of destruction, and as not having a moment to lose without fleeing to the Saviour."[25]

The case can be framed more sharply still. The quest for personal salvation not only recapitulated the apocalyptic pattern of history. It also provided an imaginative participation in the last things. The agony of the unregenerate carried them forward to the hour of death, when they would be hurled into the flames of hell, and that terrifying moment in turn prefigured the day when all people would stand before Jehovah's awful throne. In a word, the struggle surrounding each believer's conversion was for the believer a proleptic enactment of the final battle between Christ and Antichrist. Regardless of the number of years that might separate the eschaton from the present, a person *now* confronted the decision that would seal his or her fate when the last day dawned. Through conversion and the subsequent struggle for holiness it was as if time were collapsed and the saint projected forward to the judgment. Postmillennialists especially emphasized this theme in response to William Miller, whose predictions that Christ would return around 1843 generated widespread interest and a popular movement in the early 1840s. Henry Cowles of Oberlin College, for example, argued vigorously against an early Second Coming and for an indefinite extension of the present age, but that perspective did not lull him into complacence. Leaping ahead in an anticipation of the final judgment, he asked: "Will the eye of one enemy of God read these pages? Let that reader understand his controversy with God. It hastens to its issue. The day of conflict draws nigh. And will you choose to meet the Man of Calvary a foe and not a friend?" Baptist minister John Dowling of Providence, Rhode Island, made the same point more emphatically as an aside in his book refuting the Millerite brand of premillennialism.

> Before closing this chapter, let me address a word to my *unconverted readers*. I cannot make the supposition that the coming of Christ to judgment will occur in 1843, as Mr. M[iller] does, a basis for my exhortation to you, to prepare to meet your God, because I do not believe such a supposition is sanctioned by the bible. Yet I can tell you that in three years, *eighty millions* of the inhabitants of this earth will have been summoned to give up their account; and they will know their eternal destiny as surely as if the Judge were to come in the clouds, seated on his great white throne. Beloved reader, whose eye now rests upon this page, THOU MAYST BE ONE OF THEM! Art thou prepared?

From that perspective it mattered not "whether the Judgment shall set tomorrow, or thousands of years to come." For each person the struggle determining that judgment was today, and its outcome could, if unpredictable death intervened, be known as early as the morrow.[26]

By the 1830s and 1840s, that model of evangelical piety had, of course, begun to change in some quarters. With the subversion of predestinarian views, preconversion terrors of hell were ceasing to be a period of indefinite duration, suffered until God deigned to grant salvation, and became instead a brief crisis that the sinner could resolve by accepting Christ. Among some Protestants gradual Christian nurture displaced the *Sturm und Drang* of conversion as the expected path to salvation, and the tender love of God superseded his judgment as a theme of pulpit declamation. Visions of death were likewise undergoing a metamorphosis in those same circles. That awesome moment of truth, the instant wherein eternal destiny would become manifest, was becoming a return home—a transformation of attitude that may be traced in the rise of the rural cemetery movement, in funerary art, and in consolatory literature.[27]

To the extent that these new perceptions triumphed, they diminished apocalyptic referents in popular piety, but at least until the post–Civil War period their victory was far from complete. Most Protestants were still reared in churches or Sunday schools that pressed for their conversion; denominations and colportage societies issued tracts warning the sinner of the horror awaiting at death, and not a few persons heard, as did the young Washington Gladden, vivid pulpit descriptions of "the writhings of the lost in that pit of flame." Even in the pronouncements of those who propagated the gentler views, a somber note often intruded. Thus the future Methodist bishop Gilbert Haven, who quoted sentimental poems about death, also warned of a hell so terrible that "Byron's dream is only a faint conception of that state where sun and moon are orbs of blackness and every flame intensifies the gloom." As long as such notions remained prominent in Protestant thought, evangelical piety lent an experiential immediacy to apocalyptic categories and counterbalanced assertions that the day of wrath was many centuries removed. Writing years later of his antebellum boyhood, the liberal theologian William Newton Clarke gave pointed expression to that ambivalence. "The theory [postmillennialism]," he said, "put the end indefinitely far away, and yet I listened trembling for the trump of God in every thunder-storm."[28]

The Place of Postmillennialism in American Thought

Given Clarke's confusions, we must ask about the extent of postmillennialism within American Protestantism. Among leading clerical figures, it was clearly the dominant view, but how widespread was the eschatology among the rank and file in the pews? A definitive answer is impossible to give, but there are tantalizing hints. Surveying numerous diaries and letters of obscure Americans in the antebellum period, Lewis Saum has found little evidence of an explicit postmillennialism. "When millennial intimations surfaced in the writings of the common folk," Saum writes, "they often did so as little more than predictions of cataclysmic retribution"—in other words there was little of the genial hope of gradual progress usually associated with postmillennialism. Similarly, William J. Gilmore, after an extensive canvass of personal libraries recorded in the estates of persons in Vermont during the early nineteenth century, has noted that premillennial works tended to outnumber postmillennial ones. Moreover, postmillennialism lacked the sharp clarity and cosmic drama of the premillennial hope. It is difficult to imagine a postmillennialist movement exciting the fervor or even the curiosity that the Millerites aroused when they predicted that Christ would return around 1843. Perhaps Ruth Bloch is correct when she writes: "On the level of popular culture, the image of Christ appearing in the flesh had probably always dominated over the idea of a purely spiritual coming, both because of its greater dramatic power and because of its greater faithfulness to the literal biblical word."[29]

To make these observations is not to suggest that the so-called average person was either a confirmed post- or premillennialist. Most persons probably had not sorted out their views clearly but lived with a mental hodgepodge of images of the last things, which they had not ordered into a distinct or coherent theory. They might alternately hope for the gradual conquest of the world to Christ and the sudden return of the Lord. Many were no doubt like Clarke, who awaited an "end indefinitely far away and yet . . . listened trembling for the trump of God in every thunder-storm."[30]

The genius of postmillennialism was that it made room for both perspectives. The postponement of the final judgment assured the temporal interval necessary for the gradual evangelical conquest of the world, the fulfillment of America's providential mission, and the triumph of secular progress. Postmillennialism assured that the golden age would be a rational continuation of the best features of the present; its synergism enlisted the efforts of the saints to create that future; and its ideal kingdom of voluntary persuasion resonated with—indeed, helped to create—the values of the American republic. Postmillennialism was an appropriate eschatology for activistic Protestants who aspired to subject themselves and their culture to a rational evangelical order. Yet postmillennialism also retained more than a vestige of the apocalypticism to which Protestants were committed by reason of their doctrine of the Bible and by virtue of a piety centered on conversion, death, and the choice of heaven or hell. Much of postmillennialism's power came from its evocation of these cataclysmic images of the End and its ability to harness their power in service to the building of an evangelical empire.

That synthesis was credible in large measure because of the peculiar historical position of Protestantism in the late eighteenth and early nineteenth centuries when the American republic was born and reached its brassy adolescence. The great modernizing forces—the Enlightenment, independence from the British Crown, democratization, and the market revolution—did not arrive in America as strident opponents of traditional religion. By contrast to their impact in much (though not all) of Europe, these changes possessed no sharp antiecclesiastical or heterodox edge, forcing persons to choose between the new order and faith. In fact, much of the initial thrust toward a modern America came from the Protestant churches, which prospered and enjoyed considerable cultural eminence. Under these circumstances, it was plausible to invest secular changes with positive religious meaning and to use traditional eschatological symbols—the millennium, the Second Coming, and the Last Judgment—to depict a future in which sacred and profane forces would advance in harmony, a future over which the saints would enjoy mastery.[31]

When Confederate forces fired on Fort Sumter in April 1861, this hope would appear to have suffered refutation. After decades of evangelical enterprise, Americans had not been persuaded to move toward an orderly millennium. They marched instead into the four bloodiest years of American history. Yet postmillennial dreams, filled with the images of apocalyptic judgment as well as with pictures of peaceful progress, adapted remarkably well to the new context. Northern clergy for the most part argued that the war was a struggle to realize the orderly millennium, and the North's success on the field of battle apparently vindicated their hope. Indeed, paradoxical as it might seem, the war itself probably saved the postmillennial tradition from a premature demise. In the closing years of the antebellum era, intractable moral confusions over slavery, ecclesiastical schisms, and sectional animosity belied the hope of an orderly millennium. It took the harsh discipline of an unprecedentedly large military establishment—and the burnished rows of steel it sent into the field—to restore the hope of orderly progress.[32]

Yet after it won its seeming confirmation, the postmillennial hope soon waned. Perhaps the deepened emphasis upon institutional loyalty and the incipient bureaucracy generated by the northern war effort began to shatter the tenuous balance of rational order and supernatural overturning, of nearly unbounded time and the sense of a definitive End. In any event, the balance began shifting toward rational order and continued to do so at an accelerated rate after 1880. The shift was most evident at the intellectual foundations of postmillennialism—in attitudes toward the Bible itself—and to that subject we turn.

1

Prophecy, the Bible, and Millennialism

❧❧❧

LIKE OTHER Christian visions of the last things, postmillennialism claimed its authority from the Bible. To be sure, not everyone invoking eschatological images or themes offered a thorough exegesis of scripture. During the Civil War, shortly after the Battle of Antietam, for example, Theodore Tilton, who edited the *Independent,* published a hymn expressing his hopes for the conflict's outcome:

> By the great sign, foretold, of Thy Appearing,
> Coming in clouds, while mortal men stand fearing,
> Show us, amid this smoke of battle, clearing,
> Thy chariot nearing![1]

Tilton's poetry vividly affirmed the eschatological significance of the struggle for the Union, but he made no effort to ground his hope in a detailed interpretation of the Bible. Throughout the nineteenth century, hundreds, if not thousands, of other Protestants often limned pictures of millennial glory or of apocalyptic judgment without stopping to provide systematic scriptural warrant. Yet even when its texts were not carefully plumbed, the Bible loomed in the background. Allusions to biblical prophecy carried weight because men and women assumed that biblical predictions would in fact come to pass. Lines from the *Princeton Review* summarized the prevailing view:

> The predictions uttered by the prophets were real disclosures of future events, and must therefore of necessity always be accomplished. . . . Prophecy . . . came not in old time by the will of man, but holy men of God spake as they were moved by the Holy Ghost. It proceeded from Him to whom the future equally with the present, is naked and opened, and whose word cannot return to him void. This removes it entirely out of the region of vague anticipations, the forebodings of hope or fear, shrewd conjectures.[2]

Formal consensus on the authority of prophecy did not, of course, yield unanimity as to its meanings. Millennial interpretations assumed kaleidoscopic variety. Because biblical prophecies were simultaneously canonical and obscure, they offered an authoritative language through which diverse and changing meanings might be expressed. But that language remained authoritative only insofar as people believed that the predictions of the scripture were "real disclosures of future events." Without this conviction, millennialism had no firm basis.[3]

In the decades after the Civil War, many discarded that conviction and with it the cornerstone of millennialism. A 1919 book by Kemper Fullerton, professor of Old Testament Language and Literature at the Oberlin Graduate School of Religion, epitomized the change. In *Prophecy and Authority: A Study in the History of the Doctrine and Interpretation of Scripture,* Fullerton argued that contemporary biblical studies had demolished the notion that the prophets uttered errorless predictions, often of events far from their own time. Modern scholarship, he asserted, demonstrated that the prophets were primarily preachers of righteousness. To the extent that they offered prognostication, it related to their own era, and even then they sometimes "failed in their predictions." A modern understanding of prophecy "does not concentrate its attention upon a series of unconnected predictions whose truth depends upon their minute, literal fulfillment." Rather it stressed the ethical vision of the biblical authors and looked for its development in subsequent history. Did the Bible, then, contain anything which could enable Christians to tell the future? Fullerton replied bluntly that the Bible was not a blueprint for the ages ahead. Aside from a hope "for a spiritual consummation of this world order which will be satisfying to the moral demands of the conscience of the race," one could extrapolate nothing about the future from the scriptures. This fact meant that "the various Millennialist attempts to read the signs of the times are so much labor wasted, and the peculiar forms which the Millennialist hope takes must be relegated to the place where they properly belong—the sphere of Christian mythology."[4]

The story of the loss of faith in predictive prophecy is multifaceted. It is an account of (1) the unfolding of ambiguities or tensions within postmillennial exegesis, of (2) changing understandings of the Bible and its authority, and of (3) the scholarly reevaluation of prophetic and apocalyptic literature. Taken together, these developments constituted a major revolution in religious consciousness—a transformation in which the contours of mid-nineteenth-century postmillennialism blurred into a more amorphous vision of the last things.

Postmillennial Exegesis

To understand why postmillennialism was vulnerable to erosion, one must grasp the ways in which its adherents interpreted biblical texts. What principles governed their reading of the Bible? The diversity of their approaches has prompted one scholar to rule out the possibility of an unequivocal answer to the question. Postmillennialism, Robert Whalen contends, was "a collection of various optimistic eschatologies, sacrificing uniformity to popularity, complex but without leadership or accepted traditions, and forming no integrated system or philosophy." Although Whalen overstates the case, he is correct in emphasizing the assortment of opinions which flourished under the rubric of that eschatology.[5]

At one extreme, postmillennialists included precursors of modern critical scholarship. Moses Stuart, professor of Sacred Literature at Andover Theological Seminary from 1810 until his death in 1852, provides the most notable case in point. A self-taught philologist who read German biblical scholarship with avidity (though seldom with complete approval), Stuart applied critical principles to apocalyptic and prophetic scriptures. For example, in *A Commentary on the Apocalypse* (1845), Stuart concluded that the Revelation was a tract for its own time. John wrote to the victims of persecution, probably under the reign of the Emperor Nero, in order to shore up their courage by telling them of things which would shortly come to pass. Therefore, to regard the Apocalypse as a "Syllabus of history" or "to look for the Pope, or the French Revolution, or the Turks, or the Chinese in it" was patently absurd. Yet while asserting that the events foretold in the first nineteen chapters of Revelation had been accomplished in the first century, Stuart also insisted that chapter 20 and following—the portion of the book dealing with the millennium and the final consummation—did predict future events which, even in the nineteenth century, had yet to occur: a spiritual reign of Christ on earth, then a final unleashing of evil once again, and the raising of the dead for the Last Judgment. Stuart in effect had made the Apocalypse a postmillennial drama whose middle portion was missing. The book contained a first act detailing events of the early Christian era and a final scene explaining how the play would turn out. No one, however, could say how many intervening acts John had omitted or what would transpire during them.[6]

What then could nineteenth-century Protestants, who lived somewhere in the midst of the missing acts, learn from the Revelation of John? Could they discover anything about the coming millennial glory? "My answer to the question . . . would be," Stuart replied, "that *it will speedily take place, when all Christians or at least the great body of them, come up to the standard of duty, or come very near to this standard, in their efforts to diffuse among the nations of the earth the knowledge of salvation.* The divinely appointed means will secure the end, because God will bless them. Every Christian, then, and every Society for propagating the knowledge of Christianity, is helping to usher in the millennial day, when they ply this work to the best of their ability." In the explosion of evangelical benevolent activity in the antebellum era, Stuart saw hopeful "signs that such a day is approaching." Nevertheless, he insisted that contemporary Christians had no biblical warrant for establishing precise events or dates which would augur that happy time. At best they could derive from the Revelation a "generic truth"—that is, the general knowledge that in all eras "*Christ will reign until all enemies are put under his feet.*" Stuart intended to take the Apocalypse away from "the dreams and phantasies [*sic*] of ancient or modern Millenarians"—he had contemporary premillennialists in mind—who arrogantly presumed to locate the present moment in the timetable of the Apocalypse, but he also wished to affirm the reliability of apocalyptic forecasts and to assert the reality of those great eschatological events so dear to mid-nineteenth-century Protestants: the millennium, the Second Coming, and the Last Judgment. He succeeded in this endeavor, but at the cost of severely delimiting the sphere within which predictive prophecy operated.[7]

At Princeton Theological Seminary, the bastion of Old School Presbyterianism, a similar caution toward apocalyptic and prophetic scriptures reigned. Charles Hodge, who was the commanding eminence at the school from mid-century to his death in 1878, affirmed a postmillennial hope "that before the second coming of Christ there is to be a time of great and long continued prosperity." In many respects, Hodge's scheme resembled Stuart's, but there were important differences. Unlike the Andover professor, his Princeton counterpart believed that specific events, institutions, and persons between the first century and the millennium were foretold in scripture. He supported, for example, the traditional Protestant notion that the papacy was the Antichrist. Still, Hodge was exceedingly diffident about precise identifications of historical events with particular biblical predictions. That reticence reflected no suspicion that prophecy was in any sense flawed or inaccurate. Interpretation demanded caution because the prophecies were frequently enigmatic, sometimes telescoped widely separated events into a single portrait, and often dealt with whole classes of similar events under a single figure. Biblical prediction was "not intended to give us a knowledge of the future analogous to that which history gives us of the past . . . prophecy makes a general impression with regard to future events, which is reliable and salutary, while the details remain in obscurity." Thus prudence demanded that one abstain from overly precise prophetic schemes and allow future events to supply the interpretation.[8]

Not all postmillennialists were as unwilling as Stuart and Hodge to posit contemporary events as the fulfillment of specific biblical predictions. In two extended analyses in 1856 and in 1859, the Reverend Joseph Berg, one of the leading ministers of the Dutch Reformed Church, sought to correlate particular biblical passages with events then in process. Among his numerous conclusions were that the power of Louis Napoleon signified the pouring of the seventh vial of the Apocalypse, that contemporary evangelical efforts to convert sailors fulfilled prophecies in Isaiah (chapter 24) concerning those who "go down to the sea," and that the appearance of the United States in world history clearly corresponded to Daniel's prediction of an enduring fifth world kingdom. Several years later, during the Civil War, a postmillennialist writing in the Methodist weekly *Christian Advocate and Journal* argued that the scriptures foretold the American Civil War. The Apocalypse's twelfth chapter, recounting the celestial battle of the Archangel Michael, was fulfilled in the Southern rebellion, and the dragon's expulsion from heaven signified the Confederacy's defeat. But the forces of tyranny would regroup among the tottering regimes of Europe, and these corrupt powers would ally to confront the United States, probably on the field of battle. That future conflict, as prophesied in the thirty-eighth and thirty-ninth chapters of Ezekiel, would eventuate in American victory. Then as a result of the triumph over European despotism, the way would be clear "for the universal spread of the Gospel, and the sublime realization of self-government among all people . . . That long cycle of ages called the millennium will then be ushered in."[9]

In view of these diversities (and many more could be cited), one may be tempted to echo Whalen that postmillennialism indeed offered "no integrated system or philosophy," but the conclusion would be premature. That eschatology acquired a unity as it defined itself against competing premillennial views. Of these the theories of the Baptist William Miller constituted a notable instance. Predicting that Christ would return around 1843, Miller generated a mass movement which at its height rated front-page coverage in the newspapers. Although the Millerites provided an easy mark for scoffers (at least after the time of Jesus's supposed advent had gone by), the popular interest they aroused forced postmillennialists to define themselves against the movement.[10]

Nor did the challenge end once the Millerite excitement abated. Within the major denominations, vocal advocates kept premillennialism before the public. While eschewing the setting of specific dates, these people nevertheless expected an early end to the present world order and an imminent Second Coming. They won relatively few prominent Protestants to their cause prior to the 1870s, but thereafter their numbers grew dramatically through yearly Bible conferences, two major prophecy conferences, and through the numerous Bible institutes created to train Christian workers. A new variant of premillennialism gradually took shape in these years. Before the 1860s, most premillennialists adhered to an historicist interpretation asserting that the Bible contained predictions of the church throughout the ages, but after that decade, a futurist interpretation gradually replaced its rival. The latter position is so named because it maintained that none of the prophecies concerning the latter days had yet been fulfilled. The foremost proponent of that view was John Nelson Darby (1800–1882), an unofficial leader of a British sectarian movement known as the Plymouth Brethren. His futurist view received the name dispensationalism and soon overflowed the banks of its sectarian origins to win adherents among premillennialists in many American denominations.[11]

According to most dispensationalists, the key to the interpretation of prophecy was the timetable in Daniel 7–9. Purportedly written in the sixth century B.C.E. after the capture of Jerusalem by the Babylonians, the text predicted the rebuilding of the holy city and the restoration of the Jewish people to their homeland. Daniel described 70 weeks (in the Hebrew, 70 "sevens") at the end of which God would act "to bring in everlasting righteousness, and to seal up the vision and prophecy, and to anoint the Most Holy" (Daniel 9:24). The text further subdivided the seventy weeks. Sixty-nine would elapse prior to the coming of "Messiah the Prince" who would be "cut off" shortly after his appearance (Daniel 9:26). Only at the end of the seventieth week would restoration finally occur. For dispensationalists, the seeming obscurity of the prophecy disappeared once one understood that the Hebrew "sevens" referred to years, not weeks. Sixty-nine weeks—that is, 483 years—passed, according to their reckoning, between the decree permitting the rebuilding of the Jerusalem temple and the time of Christ. Prophecy had received indisputable confirmation.

This computation left a crucial question: why had Jesus not returned seven years after the crucifixion to complete his work? Dispensationalists explained that God had temporarily stopped the clock of biblical prediction when the Jews rejected Jesus. With prophecy postponed, the risen Christ commissioned his disciples to gather a people from among the Gentiles. To this people (the church), Christ had not given—as postmillennialists wrongly supposed—the task of building the kingdom on earth. That task he himself would perform once the fulfillment of prophecy resumed. In the interim, the church had the more modest task of proclaiming the gospel to all nations and of summoning individuals to faith. At the close of the age of the church, true Christian believers would be literally "caught up in the clouds, . . . to meet the Lord in the air" (I Thessalonians 4:17). Most dispensationalists believed that this event, known as the Rapture, would transpire prior to the tribulations foretold at the end of history. Then, the church having been taken from the earth, the clock of prophecy would tick off the final seven years of Daniel's prophecy. The Jews would be restored to Palestine, the dreadful wars and desolations of the Book of Revelation would take place, and finally Jesus would establish the thousand-year kingdom. According to dispensational theory, no one could predict with certainty the time of the Rapture—after all, the church existed in a prophetic hiatus for which no prediction had been given—but signs indicated the nearness of the great day.

Not all premillennialists accepted dispensationalism, but it illustrated in extreme form several themes common to most millenarian tracts of the nineteenth century: a refutation of the postmillennial view that the thousand years would be merely a perfection of the current age, a concomitant belief that a supernatural abrogation of the present declining order was necessary, and hence an expectation that Jesus would return on the clouds of heaven to establish his kingdom. Undergirding all of these millenarian motifs was a self-proclaimed adherence to a literal exegesis of God's inerrant word.

Millenarians claimed, as if it were their special property, the historic Protestant bias in favor of the plain meaning of the biblical text—a meaning which they generally identified with the literal sense. Premillennialists also shared the prevailing commitment to the Scottish Common Sense Philosophy, which dominated much of American thought until after the Civil War. That philosophy glorified the empirical method, shunned metaphysical speculation, and stressed that the common sense of humanity offered a sure guide to truth. When the scriptures were viewed through this philosophical lens, it was assumed that they offered a source of pure, hard "facts"—facts to be taken at face value and requiring no elaborate theory to explain them. Thus any biblical interpretation that seemed to deviate from a straightforward, factual reading of the text was at a severe disadvantage.[12]

George Duffield, a nondispensational premillenarian, provided a graphic case in point in his *Dissertation on the Prophecies* (1842). Duffield claimed to bring no preconceptions to his study. A common-sense man of no metaphysical presumptions (or so he styled himself), Duffield merely turned to the text to derive its plain meaning. "Theory is out of place and unallowable in the study of prophecy. . . . It is a simple question that in all cases must be asked, what is the fair and legitimate meaning of the words—a matter-of-fact investigation—no theorising, no speculations." This common-sense literalism did, of course, allow for metaphor in many instances. No millenarian was fool enough, said Duffield, to think that when the Apocalypse spoke of a woman who "appeared in heaven clothed with the sun, having the moon under her feet, and upon her head a crown of twelve stars, there ever, literally or in reality, was such a thing." But the burden of proof always rested on those who wished to make prophecy metaphoric. A prediction was always presumed literal unless good common sense dictated that it had to be read in a nonliteral or spiritual fashion. By this standard, he reasoned, there was nothing in human consciousness which logically forbade a supernatural rending of the present age and a premillennial coming of the Lord. Failure to take those predictions of the miraculous literally was prima facie evidence of religious unbelief, and Duffield implied with only slight qualification that some post-millennial views were verging dangerously close to infidelity.[13]

The issue of literal versus spiritual exegesis was particularly troublesome for postmillennialists. On the one hand, they did indeed argue for a spiritual reading of prophecies relative to the millennial kingdom. Hodge, for example, asserted: "This whole theory of a splendid earthly kingdom is a relic of Judaism, and out of keeping with the spirituality of the Gospel." Likewise, Moses Stuart insisted that the Gospel itself, through its persuasive power, would bring about the Kingdom of God on earth. He mocked the "modern enthusiastic interpreters, who find in our text [Rev. 20] a temporal and visible reign of Christ on earth." Such carnal fantasies Stuart thought scarcely worth refuting. Similarly, Joseph Berg insisted that scriptural images of Christ's rule ought not to be read as descriptive of an actual physical or temporal sovereignty; they were symbols of a "spiritual reign" which Christ would exercise. Yet at the same time, postmillennialists were by no means willing to cede literalism to the opposition. They, too, had inherited the historic Protestant bias toward the literal sense of the biblical text and likewise had felt the influence of the Scottish philosophy. Thus postmillennialists, even as they proposed spiritual readings of prophecy, insisted that they had in no way departed from the plain or literal interpretation of scripture.[14]

Indeed postmillennialists often insisted that they, not their millenarian counterparts, held clear title to common sense, literal exegesis. Thus in January 1843, a writer in the *Methodist Quarterly Review* insisted: "We claim to be, not only rigid literalists, but unsparing iconoclasts—ruthless demolishers of all theories. We wish to strip the passage [concerning the millennium] of all the superincumbent strata which ingenious men have deposited all round it, and come down to the plainest and most obvious literal reading of the text. The advocates of Chiliasm boast of being, by eminence, *the literalists;* if therefore we detect them in unnatural figure, and show them both a more natural and more literal mode, they are bound either to give up their boast or adopt our exposition." The postmillennial attack enumerated instances in which millenarians allegedly departed from their own vaunted adherence to "matter of fact investigation—no theorising, no speculations." That assault took the form of interminable arguments over the proper exegesis of a wide range of biblical verses and issues. Had Jesus already taken the throne of his kingdom, or was that event yet future? Did the great commission—Jesus's command to go unto all nations and make disciples of them—imply the eventual conversion of the world or rather a witness to all peoples? Did the description of the raising of the martyrs at the outset of the millennium portend an actual resurrection of some of the dead or merely a revivifying of the martyrs' values? If the former, were there, then, two resurrections—one at the beginning of the millennium and another at the end—and could one square a double resurrection with numerous scriptures appearing to recognize only one? In the matter of the political restoration of the Jewish people, which biblical verses should receive greater weight: those which promised a new Jewish kingdom or those which asserted that the old covenant had been fulfilled in the new? One could continue to list, to the point of tedium, other matters of contention. To today's readers, perhaps less familiar with the Bible than their nineteenth-century ancestors were, such disputes may appear to resemble disorganized house-to-house combat in which clearly defined battle lines have dissolved, but a common front can be discerned in most of these skirmishes. Postmillennialists insisted that the major referent of prophecy was the triumph of Christ's kingdom, a kingdom which was moral or spiritual in character. To make this assertion was not to abandon the plain meaning of scripture but rather to affirm it. In a word, the spiritual reading of the text was the literal one.[15]

The Reverend E. Benjamin Andrews, president of Denison College and later of Brown University, presented one of the sharpest and most succinct examples of this principle at work in an 1875 essay in the *Baptist Quarterly.* In Old Testament prophecy, Andrews noted that one could find two basic sets of images: first, predictions of a time of spiritual peace, plenitude, and prosperity; second, passages describing "the Messianic victory . . . as coming by force, strife, or bloodshed." One must not suppose that these latter verses dealt chiefly with "judgments and victories of a physical kind," although no one would deny that some of these predictions were in fact "fulfilled in wars and judgment" experienced by the Hebrew people. However, the primary referent of both the sanguinary and peaceful prophecies was the same: the moral triumphs of Christ's kingdom. Thus Andrews posited a fundamental hermeneutical principle: "When pictures of physical victory constitute the prophecies, spiritual and saving victories are to be the corresponding fulfillment." As if in anticipation of millenarian protests that he had illicitly "spiritualized" the literal meaning of God's word, Andrews asserted that the New Testament itself sanctioned this interpretation. Christ taught that the kingdom was a spiritual reality, not a geographic or political one, and Paul used military imagery as a symbol of spiritual rather than military crusading. Moreover, Peter's sermon on the day of Pentecost asserted that the prophecy of Joel—a prophecy speaking not only of the pouring out of the Spirit but also of terrible supernatural portents of blood, fire, and darkness in the heavens—was fulfilled on that occasion. Similarly, the Book of Revelation depicted the conquering Christ subduing the world with the sword which was in his mouth—in other words, via the proclamation of the Gospel. How baseless, then, was the millenarian expectation that Christ would return in a carnal or literal sense in order to inaugurate the millennium.[16]

According to postmillennialists, their opponents' alleged literalism was a false one, resting upon a retrograde exegetical principle. Millenarians read the New Testament through the eyes of the Old, rather than vice versa. To long for a thousand years during which King Jesus literally occupied a throne in Jerusalem was to confound the carnal types of prophecy with their spiritual antitype, to confuse shadow with substance. In so doing, millenarians made Jesus conform to the erroneous conceptions of his first-century contemporaries. That view, said a writer in the *Methodist Quarterly Review* in 1843, "violates the true nature of Christ's moral government." It is a return to "fables of Jewish dotage." Or as a writer in the same journal declared more than thirty years later: "After we have seen the sad and fatal mistake of the Jews in *literalizing* and *secularizing* the reign of Christ, until they have judged themselves unworthy of eternal life, is it not strange that we should swing back through the *spiritual* life and power of Christianity for eighteen hundred years, and seek to take the Son of man by force and make him an earthly king?"[17]

Deciding who came away victor in these exchanges is not an easy task. Each side scored telling points against the other. Postmillennialists could justly claim that their opponents' "literal" exegesis often pulled verses out of historical context, produced logical muddles, and subverted traditional Protestant hermeneutics in favor of rules of interpretation so novel that, in the words of the *Princeton Review* in 1853, "the Bible may almost be said to wear a new visage and speak with a new tongue—a tongue not very intelligible, in many of its utterances, to the uninitiated." Yet quite apart from the merits of its specific arguments, millenarianism accurately perceived that important parts of the New Testament vibrated with apocalyptic urgency. Jesus, for example, warned his disciples that they should be prepared for the coming of the Son of Man at an unexpected hour. How, on the basis of a postmillennial eschatology, could one account for this admonition? In an article in 1875, Methodist minister Daniel D. Buck pressed this point vigorously:

> Indeed, assuming that the advent is post-millennial, unto whom do these warning appeals apply? Do they intend to excite apprehensions without the slightest reason to expect what is apprehended? Certainly, if the advent is post-millennial, no one who lives before the beginning of the millennium, and no one who lives during the first nine tenths of it, can have the slightest reason to apprehend the coming of the Lord. . . . Can a post-millennialist, with any show of sincerity, or any appearance of propriety, pray, preach, and exhort as our Lord did, with reference to the uncertainty, imminency, or the immediate practical use of the advent of the Lord?"

(The argument, of course, cut two ways: if the postmillennialist was embarrassed by the prominence of the apocalyptic hope, the millenarian had to explain why it was so long deferred. Upon the latter's hypothesis, said postmillennialists, the New Testament taught more than eighteen hundred years ago the possibility of an imminent advent, and therefore its writers either were in error or misled their readers—suppositions no devout Christian could accept.) Nevertheless, the millenarian critics exposed a fundamental weakness in postmillennial eschatology: how could the hope of an imminent apocalyptic overturning remain a vital one within a system which postponed such fulfillment by centuries?[18]

Yet this exegesis suffered from an even deeper problem. At its heart, the postmillennial hermeneutic was profoundly ambiguous. It wanted to treat the hope of the Apocalypse partly as figurative truth and partly as literal. Against the millenarians, for example, postmillennialists fought verse by verse, insisting that prophecy had spiritual rather than carnal fulfillment. Prophecies of a political kingdom for the Jews were types of Christianity's religious influence, the promise of a special resurrection of the martyrs was a metaphor for the resurgence of their values, and the picture of Christ reigning in the millennium was only an emblem of his presence in the hearts of all men and women. Yet when postmillennialists came to the passages speaking of a Second Coming in which Christ would raise the dead and subject them to judgment, figurative and spiritual interpretation ceased. These prophecies were deemed literal descriptions of future events, albeit events which would occur after the thousand years. Given the basic principle of interpretation postmillennialists had enunciated, it was not clear why such predictions should be exempt from a spiritual reading. If descriptions of an earthly millennium required a spiritual interpretation, why should not the same hermeneutic dissolve the literal factuality of a postmillennial Second Coming and end of the world?

But postmillennialists were not prepared for a step so radical. A future day of judgment, a literal Second Coming, a dramatic overturning of the present age, and the resurrection of the dead—these were motifs too deeply embedded in the scriptures and in the Protestant tradition to permit their transmutation into metaphor, at least for persons still deeply committed to the notion of an inerrant Bible whose literal sense was authoritative. The postmillennial compromise was to spiritualize those prophecies having to do with the advent of God's kingdom on earth, but to keep as nonmetaphoric or literal truths those which were expected to transpire (conveniently) many centuries hence. As Methodist Bishop S. M. Merrill summarized in an 1879 book, a proper interpretation of the Apocalypse had simultaneously to avoid two extremes: the millenarian notion that Jesus might return at any moment "to wield an earthly scepter over the nations" and a "liberalist" view that denied altogether a literal Second Advent and Last Judgment. Merrill had, in effect, stationed the postmillennialist on a precarious exegetical tightrope.[19]

By the late nineteenth century, there were signs that this tenuous exegetical balancing act could not be maintained indefinitely. In the same year that Bishop Merrill's book appeared, Israel Warren, a Maine Congregationalist of some eminence within his denomination, published an immensely learned work entitled *Parousia*. Warren argued that there would be no future millennium, Second Coming, end of the world, or Last Judgment. He did not derive these conclusions from religious skepticism. An orthodox Congregationalist, he was firmly committed to an inerrant Bible and saw himself as one who interpreted that authoritative Word according to the principles of Moses Stuart. His starting point in the endeavor was a massive catalogue of New Testament verses demonstrating that Jesus and the early Christians expected the parousia (the Greek word usually translating as "appearing," or "coming") in the near future. Warren ridiculed the usual devices by which orthodox interpreters obviated the natural meanings of these tests—for example, the one which made the destruction of Jerusalem in about 70 C.E. into a type of the end of the world. The plain meaning of the New Testament indicated that Jesus and his disciples expected an imminent parousia. Unwilling to admit that inspired writers could have been in error, Warren then looked for evidence that the so-called Second Coming of Christ did occur. He acknowledged that the chief obstacle to his interpretation lay in the vivid imagery used by the New Testament to describe eschatological events. Planets reeling in their courses, the heavens rolled up like a scroll, or the earth consumed with fire—these were not events which appeared to have already transpired, but the problem was obviated when one realized that the ancients used such dramatic imagery to describe political and religious upheavals. Thus all of the great eschatological events foretold in the Bible—including the Second Coming—could be attributed to historical events early in the Christian era. Nineteenth-century Protestants need expect no future return of Christ on the clouds, and the world moved toward no future smashup at which time the dead would be raised and judged. Each person experienced resurrection and judgment at the moment of death, and the physical universe would go on indefinitely—perhaps forever. Lest anyone think these conclusions overly radical, Warren hastened to assure his reader that they were the results of interpretive principles sanctioned by the New Testament itself:

> The material type is never fulfilled in a material antitype; bloody rite has no bloody rite as its counterpart; no Christian altar answers to Hebrew altar, no earthly Jerusalem to the Jerusalem that then was. . . . And so, by all the principles of analogy, as the ancient ritual dispensation was in all its parts symbolical of the new, which is spiritual, so [images of] its inauguration with material splendors ought to find its fulfillment in one that is spiritual. To look for one appealing to

the senses is to reverse all the laws of progress and development in God's revelation to man.

Few postmillennialists could have taken exception to the principle, but many must have squirmed when they saw the rigor with which Warren applied it.[20]

Warren's theory disclosed the ambiguous and fragile nature of the biblical interpretation postmillennialists had created. Uncomfortable with elements of the apocalyptic mentality, they could not repudiate it entirely lest they call into question biblical inspiration as they understood it. What they did, in effect, was to spiritualize a significant portion of the Apocalypse while retaining as literal truth a Second Advent, the end of the world, and the final resurrection to judgment. Thus postmillennialism was a theological and exegetical Janus—one face looking toward the literal accomplishment of apocalyptic hopes, the other turned away, slightly embarrassed by such crudities. Warren had demonstrated how difficult it might be to maintain that dual orientation.

The debates over proper millennial interpretation might have an even more radical outcome. William Newton Clarke described the impact that these debates had upon his views.

> During the Seventies I was usually in attendance upon a weekly conference of ministers living in and about a city, at which all sorts of religious and theological topics were discussed. More than once in the decade the advent question was taken up . . . , and on both sides of it I heard as able advocates as our denomination contained. The premillennial and postmillennial views of the advent were presented, elaborated, and defended, sometimes with conspicuous power. . . . The first thing I observed was that neither of the two theories could be better defended from the Bible than the other. Either could be defended perfectly well, by making proper selection of proof-texts. The Bible contained the confident prediction of an early advent, and at the same time it contained an outlook upon the future that neither included an early advent nor had place for one. . . . At first I did not see how much this meant, but gradually it came to me, and a very important change in my convictions was a necessary result. It was borne in upon me that the Bible contains material for two opposite and irreconcilable doctrines about the early return of Christ to this world. . . . Whatever its nature may be, the book in which these facts are found cannot have been given me by God as a book that bears his own authority in support of all its statements. The book from which these two theories can be drawn is of necessity a different book from that. Thus the Bible itself, upon examination, shows me that it is not a book infallible throughout, in which error does not exist, and that I am not required to say that it is.[21]

What Is the Bible?

Clarke's comments indicate that a fundamental issue was at stake in debates over the Second Coming and the millennium. Nothing less than the nature of the Bible and its authority was in question. For some decades, European scholars, especially in Germany, had advanced a new biblical scholarship, often called the higher criticism. The new scholarship was not so much a set of agreed-upon conclusions—critics debated the "assured results" of their craft—as it was a new and sometimes disturbing angle from which to view the scriptures. Basic to that perspective was a commitment to analyze the Bible in the same fashion in which other documents were analyzed, and traditional interpretations were frequent casualties of such investigations. Although one can find earlier instances of biblical criticism, the movement flowered in the nineteenth century, especially in the German universities. For example, D. F. Strauss argued in 1835 that the Gospels were largely myth, and, in the same year, F. C. Baur analyzed the pastoral epistles and concluded that primitive Christianity, far from being monolithic, contained divergent viewpoints which contended for mastery. In 1878, Julius Wellhausen presented his famous documentary hypothesis, arguing that Moses had not written the Pentateuch, which was instead the product of a much later editor who had assembled several diverse traditions. At about the same time that Wellhausen was announcing his conclusions, the Dutch scholar Abraham Kuenen published several works which explained the growth of ancient Hebrew religion solely in terms of naturalistic development.

Not everyone who professed the new learning automatically derived radical conclusions from it. German scholars such as Ernst Wilhelm Hengstenberg, Franz Delitzsch, Johan Friederich Keil, and Johan Peter Lange departed only minimally from received opinions. Their use of higher criticism represented, in T. K. Cheyne's expressive phrase, "a brave attempt to save the citadel of orthodoxy at the cost of some of its outworks." Yet even in the hands of conservatives eager to restrict demolition of traditional views, the critical method rested upon premises implicitly subversive of orthodoxy. In purporting to discover the meaning of scripture by placing it in temporal context through the tools of philology, comparative religion, literary analysis, or historical research, the new learning generally diminished the role of the supernatural as an explanatory device. It also tacitly confessed that all things were historically conditioned. Thus the Bible often ceased to resemble a record of the unchanging faith once delivered to the saints and became instead a record of an ancient Near Eastern people's developing views of religion.[22]

Before 1880, the critical method exercised at best modest influence in the United States. Seminary faculties were aware of the new learning, and theological journals often apprised their readers of the latest European scholarship, though usually with the intent of exposing its deficiencies. A few professors such as Moses Stuart of Andover, Andrews Norton of Harvard, Edward Robinson of Union (New York), and Joseph A. Alexander of Princeton did contribute to the evolution of critical biblical scholarship, but their use of the new methods seldom took them far from traditional views. While often professing adherence to the idea that the Bible should be studied according to the same rules applied to other books, American scholars generally shielded themselves from the potentially radical implications of that principle. To the extent that they patterned themselves on the European critics, they generally chose conservative and unrepresentative figures. "With Keil and Delitzsch in his hand, or the successive volumes of Lange," Henry Preserved Smith remembered in 1912, "the American dogmatician could go to sleep comfortably in the conviction that the rationalists had been triumphantly routed, and the theology handed down by the fathers was in possession of the field."[23]

Around 1880, however, there were signs of a major stirring in American biblical studies. W. Robertson Smith, a minister in the Free Church of Scotland and a professor at Aberdeen, wrote the first of his controversial articles for the *Encyclopaedia Britannica* in 1875. Smith contended that the higher criticism was not inimical to evangelical faith, and he gave friendly notice to some of the more radical continental theories. Brought to ecclesiastical trial in proceedings lasting to 1881, Robertson Smith provided a cause célèbre of higher criticism, and the American religious press gave its readers extensive coverage of his case. In 1880, the Society for Biblical Literature and Exegesis was created, and the following year the society began publishing the *Journal of Biblical Literature*. Although among the first issues it dealt with was the relatively safe one of close textual criticism, the *Journal* was also soon broaching the larger critical issues raised by the new scholarship. The Revised Version of the Bible, a cooperative venture of British and American scholars, appeared in two stages in 1881 and 1885. The men responsible for the new translation generally adhered to conservative positions—the American Old Testament section, for example, was led by Princeton's William Henry Green who stoutly championed the Mosaic authorship of the Pentateuch against Wellhausen—but the very fact that the Authorized or King James version had been modified signaled to the masses that biblical learning was in ferment. Also, several young American scholars friendly to the higher criticism were entering their academic prime. In 1879 Crawford Toy resigned his professorship at Southern Seminary (Baptist) in Louisville because his openness to the views of Kuenen and Wellhausen was unacceptable to the trustees. A year later he began a long career at Harvard during which he wrote important works introducing Americans to critical theories. At Andover, George Foote Moore performed a similar service, and at Union Seminary Charles A. Briggs was launching the first salvos of his campaign to convert Americans to the higher criticism. The most energetic of these young scholars was William Rainey Harper. While still a professor at a small Baptist seminary near Chicago, he created a summer school for the study of Hebrew and founded a paper—*The Hebrew Student*

(1882)—to acquaint the multitudes with modern biblical scholarship. Subsequently, he accepted a position at Yale, and then returned to Illinois in 1892 to become the first president of the newly founded University of Chicago. The biblical studies that soon flourished there became synonymous with higher criticism.[24]

The new biblical scholarship generated its own momentum, but it received powerful additional impetus from the widespread acceptance by liberals of biological evolution. Although Darwin's *On the Origin of Species* had been debated sporadically in America since shortly after its publication in 1859, it was not until the late 1870s that prominent clergy began espousing evolution in significant numbers. The liberal Protestant recension of the theory, emphasizing God's immanence within biological change and the progressive and teleological character of the entire process, gave a distinctly non-Darwinian cast to the transmutation hypothesis. The departure from Darwin, however, made biological evolution more serviceable to the liberal theological agenda. Evolution became, in Jon H. Roberts's words, "paradigmatic of all divine activity" and "was equated with gradual, continuous, and progressive development." "God has but one way of doing things," Lyman Abbott declared in 1897. That way "may be described in one word as the way of growth, or development, or evolution." From this Abbott concluded, "that there are not occasional interventions in the order of life which bear witness to the presence of God, but that life itself is a perpetual witness to His presence." This interpretation portrayed change as the basic fact of the universe, explained it in terms of uniform principles of growth rather than through supernatural categories, and denied that events (whether biological or historical) had a timeless meaning in themselves. Meaning was always relative, conditioned by an event's place in the flux of time. These were the same principles that governed the new biblical scholarship, and therefore, observes Roberts, "Virtually all the outspoken advocates of higher criticism in the United States also endorsed the theory of organic evolution." Thus as evolution triumphed as a master metaphor for all of reality, it conferred added prestige and the aura of scientific invincibility to the new biblical scholarship.[25]

That scholarship forced a reappraisal of the nature of the Bible and its authority. Prior to the mid-nineteenth century, Protestants almost without exception assumed the Bible to be a reliable and authoritative revelation from God, but in many quarters, notions of infallibility or inerrancy had not yet been tightly defined. Thus the scriptures, wrote the *Bibliotheca Sacra* in 1858, "were preserved from such error as would interfere with the end which God, in giving this revelation to man, proposed." That end was "an absolute rule of doctrine and life." Or as a writer in the *American Presbyterian and Theo-*

logical Review put the case six years later: "Protestantism . . . stands on the infallibility of the scriptures as the rule of faith and life." Such statements, which linked infallibility to the spiritual purpose of the Bible, had left unanswered the question of whether or not the scriptures might err in incidental matters unrelated to their primary function. As the higher criticism with relativizing tendencies gained currency, some conservatives made stronger statements explicitly extending the domain of infallibility. For example, in 1881 Archibald A. Hodge and Benjamin B. Warfield contended in their famous article "Inspiration" that everything in the autographs—that is, the original manuscripts—of the Bible was inerrant. Thus "all the affirmations of scripture of all kinds, whether of spiritual doctrine or duty, or of physical or historical fact, or of psychological or philosophical principle, are without any error, when the *ipsissima verba* of the original autographs are ascertained and interpreted in their natural and intended sense." This Princeton theory of inspiration—so named because Hodge, soon to be followed by Warfield, taught at Princeton Theological Seminary—reflected the conservative conviction that hardier statements about the factual accuracy of the Bible were needed to combat the spread of the destructive aspects of higher criticism. Unless Christians firmly avowed the objective truth of the Bible, faith itself might dissolve into vague and subjective intuitions, subject to continuous change in the name of growth and development. Or as Warfield stated the matter in an article in 1893: "The authority [the Bible] which cannot assure of a hard fact is soon not trusted for a hard doctrine."[26]

Others of moderate to liberal conviction responded to the new scholarship by advocating more elastic notions of biblical authority. One sign of the change was a debate engendered within Baptist circles by the Reverend Norman Fox in an article appearing in the *Baptist Quarterly Review* in 1885. Fox set forth the thesis that the *"Apostles' writings were inspired just so far as their acts and oral utterances were inspired; no less, no more."* Since the apostles were not (by the Bible's own testimony) sinless and had sometimes erred in action, Fox concluded that their written pronouncements were not free from error. This attack on infallibility prompted a series of rejoinders in the *Review* the following spring. The diversity of responses is illuminating. While none of the seven respondents admitted the existence of errors in the Bible, and while three of the authors condemned Fox's argument harshly, the other writers were more noncommittal and in some instances engaged in a bit of scholarly hemming and hawing. Ezekiel Robinson of Brown University, for example, declared: "The most that we can safely say is that the Bible was written by men whom God inspired to write it; that the omniscient Holy Spirit so guided the minds of its writers that the divine will was perfectly accomplished in writing it. . . . The Bible is the Word of God, but communicated through finite and imperfect human understandings." Where that ambiguous declaration left the issue of infallibility was unclear.[27]

The most potentially radical response to Fox's thesis came from William Arnold Stevens, a New Testament scholar at Rochester Seminary. Without acknowledging that the biblical writers erred in any specific instance, Stevens denied in principle that human language—including the language of the holy scriptures—could ever permit "the perfect transmission of spiritual truth."

> The Bible, then, does not teach untruth. But it cannot without a perpetual miracle eliminate the ignorance, misconception, erroneous implication, and suggestion, the blended truth and untruth, that enter into the very fabric of human speech. All scientific interpretation starts from the postulate that language is but an inadequate and imperfect instrument for the communication of ideas. It not only does in fact, it must in the nature of the case "half reveal and half conceal."
> . . . Words are but figures; they speak figuratively; they are merely the rude signs of our facts and notions, not their exact equivalents. They stand for the blended truths and untruths that constitute our limited intellectual heritage. . . . In brief: the intelligent student of the Bible must bear in mind that it is a *record*—that it is revealed truth *in process of transmission,* not only after it left the hands of the sacred writers, but during its composition, and that the conditions of the case forbid us from the outset, if we use proper precision, to characterize it as composed of infallible or errorless documents, as being or expressing absolute truth.

Stevens's notion that religious language is symbolic and imprecise reflected the influence of Horace Bushnell, who had earlier made the same case. In any event, the Rochester professor's idea was worlds removed from Warfield's belief that the hard facts of the Bible yielded hard doctrines.[28]

Professor George Ladd of Yale was casting similar doubts upon the notion of infallibility. In his ponderous *The Doctrine of Sacred Scripture* (1883) and later in the popularized *What Is the Bible?* (1888), Ladd suggested that the question of inspiration had been improperly focused. They erred who treated inspiration as if it were primarily an attribute of biblical texts. "Inspiration," said Ladd, "in the primary and only strictly appropriate meaning of the word, applies to persons, and to persons only. It is in a secondary and somewhat loose meaning of the word that it can be applied to a writing. . . . Books and writings are, in themselves, mere paper and ink; they can no more be inspired than can sticks and stones." Inspiration consisted, then, not in the providing of errorless documents, but in the "illumining, purifying, and elevating of the thoughts and emotions" of persons so that they might perceive "the self-disclosure of God as the Redeemer of sinful man," a process that "culminated in Jesus Christ." In principle, the inspiration of the biblical writers did not differ from that enjoyed by subsequent generations of Christians, although the accounts left by those inspired men of former days did possess normative status. That status did not, however, imply that the scriptures were free of all error or that every passage had been written by people who enjoyed equal degrees of inspiration: as the record of a progressive revelation by God, the Bible forbade those suppositions. How, then, asked Ladd, could one know the Bible to have authority if its parts were of unequal value and subject to error? Its binding power comes, he replied, from its presentation of "the divinely commissioned and authoritative redeemer of mankind," and that presentation won the only vindication it needed in the collective moral experience of the Christian community.[29]

A blunter argument for inspiration on the basis of Christian experience was framed by a young professor at Middlebury College a year and a half after the Hodge-Warfield article. Frank Hugh Foster, Congregational minister and future author of a standard work on New England theology, eyed with suspicion arguments which tied the scriptures to theories of infallibility. Such linkage made Christian faith hostage to modern historical research. "So long as the facts of history constitute a part of the argument, the whole is likely to be shaken with every assault upon these facts. . . . If . . . [one] founds the doctrine of inspiration upon such premises as the genuineness of the fourth Gospel, every attack upon this Gospel seems like an attack upon the whole Christian faith." By contrast, Foster proposed that theologians argue for biblical inspiration "from the primary facts of Christian consciousness." The believers' awareness of sin, forgiveness, and subsequent moral improvement through Christ are for them facts which they can no more doubt than they can their own existence. Since the Bible confirms and mediates those realities, believers are compelled to acknowledge it as inspired of God. Or as Foster wrote of the Christian: "The Bible spoke unto him with God's voice, and it is to him, because of his own experience, the word of God." By establishing the scriptures on a foundation other than infallibility, the believer was thus free to "let the inspiration of the Gospels stand firm as witnessed by Christian experience" and could then await the settlement of historical critical problems "at leisure and without alarm."[30]

One could sketch numerous other assaults, some blunt and others subtle, against the notion of an infallible Bible. Some believed that the Bible provided an infallible rule for faith and practice—a rubric from the Westminster Confession—but denied that its observations about history, geography, science, and other secondary matters were invariably without error. Others drew the line between the major biblical teachings and the incidental ones or, alternately, distinguished the formal teachings of biblical writers from their private opinions, with only the former enjoying infallibility. Still others wished to make the moral insight contained in Jesus's words the touchstone of inspiration in other parts of scripture.[31]

One simplifies these complexities at peril, but when the revisions are viewed as a whole, the outlines of a new view of inspiration were becoming visible in the liberalizing quarters of Protestantism. Acutely aware of the intellectual challenges posed by biblical scholarship, liberal Protestants believed that the apologetic weapons employed by theologians like Warfield were now as useful as spears in an age of gunpowder. Or in the metaphor employed by Frank Hugh Foster, the older theologians were using arguments which "would sink . . . [Christian] faith deeper than the bottom of an Atlantic." (Briggs spoke even more caustically in describing these theories as "a ghost of modern evangelicalism to frighten children.") To deal with the Kuenens and Wellhausens, Christians needed new armaments. Liberals drew these chiefly from the romantic and idealistic tradition as represented by Kant, Schleiermacher, and Ritschl, as well as from home-grown figures such as Bushnell. From these sources they derived an interlocking set of ideas governing their understanding of inspiration: a suspicion of the power of language to state truth in timeless propositions, an emphasis upon the developmental or progressive nature of revelation, a desire to separate the transient from the permanent in Christian theology, and an ardent faith that religious consciousness—alternately depicted in terms of feeling or moral experience—was the source of theology and its sufficient justification. Viewed from the perspective of the older orthodoxy, the liberal approach represented a massive retreat from the commitment to establish Christianity by objective evidence. In order to secure Christianity from attack, the liberals had seemingly withdrawn from the world of hard facts and hard doctrines to the shadowy domain of subjective religious experience. Liberals, of course, saw the matter differently. By their espousal of hardheaded biblical scholarship, they saw themselves as firmly committed to the scientific endeavor. Moreover, they believed that their proofs of the faith from the moral and religious experience of Christianity were in their own way genuinely scientific, and by showing how widely generalized that experience was, they sought to establish it as a fact worthy of the same respect that flinty skeptics accorded physical data.[32]

There was in the new approach considerable ambiguity about the relationship of Christian faith to specific historical events, including those in the Bible. On one level, the detailed accuracy of the scriptures was a matter of indifference. If the Apostles occasionally erred and the prophets were sometimes mistaken, these lapses would not destroy the moral and spiritual experience mediated by the Bible, for that experience was self-authenticating. But on another level, the historicity of the biblical record as well as that of subsequent

Christianity was supremely important. Where else but in history—that is, in the collective experience of humanity—could one learn that this religious consciousness was more than the fancy of a few eccentrics? By a study of the past, beginning with the Bible, one discovered, in Foster's words, "the wide range of this experience through the centuries of the Christian faith; the fact that it has been confined to no one individual, to no one age of the world, but reaches back in its most primitive form to Abraham, that it has penetrated all classes of society, and been the common and homogeneous experience." Unless the Christian consciousness appeared throughout the ages, it would lose its certification as a universal faith. Likewise, only through the study of Christianity in its historically given forms could one learn the essence of the faith. Two decades later William Adams Brown, giving sympathetic expression to Adolf Harnack's views, wrote in a similar vein: "We must follow Christianity throughout all its changing historic forms, in order that in the great school of time we may learn what is the permanent principle in the midst of its variations, the abiding truth which outlives all change."[33]

In short, the historicity of the Bible remained important for Protestant liberals, but in a way very different from older views. Minute factual accuracy was insignificant—let the critics have their discovered errors, their documentary hypothesis, or their two Isaiahs—the evolving moral and religious experience related in the Bible was the thing of consequence. Moreover, liberals generally believed with Brown that they could disengage the essential features of this religious experience from its various temporary historical garbs, and thus supposedly outdated world views and erroneous statements were often tossed aside like clothes gone out of fashion.

The Repudiation of the "Millennial Mirage"

Among the antiquated clothes tossed aside were the views that had once sustained both pre- and postmillennial schemes. Liberal Protestants, with their modified views of inspiration and their openness to the new biblical scholarship, reevaluated the Hebrew prophetic tradition, explored the origins of apocalypticism, and raised troublesome questions about Jesus's views of the last things. To the extent that they did so, they began questioning the accuracy of biblical prediction—and with it the viability of millennial schemes. Such persons had begun to move outside the once common universe of Protestant eschatological discourse.

The study of Hebrew prophecy provides one useful gauge of the changing climate of opinion. In older schemes of interpretation, the prophetic writings served several purposes. Since the prophets had centuries before the time of Jesus predicted events minutely realized in the life of the Savior, their writings attested to the divine origins of the Bible and gave assurance that in due course other biblical predictions, as yet unfulfilled, would come to pass with similar precision. Although interpreters had been aware that some Hebrew prophecy was directed to then contemporary events, they often gave even these texts explicit Christological meaning by asserting that such predictions contained a divinely instituted typology whereby two events—one in the Old and another in the New Testament or in subsequent church history—were legitimate meanings of the text. Yet new studies of prophecy were placing its meaning more exclusively within the context of the writer's immediate situation, and were eschewing the double sense of Old Testament texts. The result was to lock the meaning of Old Testament scriptures, including the prophets, into their own immediate context and to foreclose efforts to find their meaning in more distant times. Moreover, the careful examination of the texts in their own historical milieu sometimes led to the disconcerting discovery that the prophets had misread the signs of the times and uttered erroneous predictions. In short, it was becoming increasingly difficult to sustain the traditional argument that prophecy was an errorless guide to times far removed from the prophet.

For those who accepted these findings even in part, it was necessary to form a new conception of prophetic fulfillment. Andover Seminary's William H. Ryder suggested in 1890 the form that reappraisal might take.

> The facts recorded in the Gospels are not the mere verification of predictions found in the prophets. The prophets' words are verified, to be sure. They predicted the fuller revelation of God's mercy and his judgments,—the triumph of virtue and faith, and the defeat of wickedness and the downfall of the wicked. But prediction is but one element of prophecy, and not its most significant or constant element. The fulfillment of a prophecy involves much more than the occurrence of an event which has been foretold. It sometimes involves the expansion of a prophet's conceptions, so that the prophet's words are fulfilled not by the occurrence of that which he thought was to happen, but by the growth of his idea, planted in a prophetic soil,—a growth which follows germinal lines, but which far surpasses what he had in mind.

This was a cautious statement, typical of Andover's faculty as they inched their way toward liberalism in the 1880s, but the direction of Ryder's proposal was clear. Without disavowing the predictive element in prophecy, he deemphasized it and limited it to a vision of good eventually triumphant. Fulfillment did not entail the minute occurrence of every prophetic word, only the coming to fruition of the inner substance or essence of the message. Thus the nineteenth-century Christian, searching for the meaning of Isaiah's famous prediction, as rendered in the King James Bible, that "a virgin shall conceive, and bear a son, and shall call his name Immanuel," could readily allow that the prophet expected an earthly king to be born in his own lifetime. It was ridiculous "to believe that the prophet supposed that seven hundred years would pass before the child of his prophecy should be born." Although Isaiah erred regarding the specifics of his forecast, he did discern the underlying redemptive purpose of God, and in this loose sense he could be said to have prophesied the birth and ministry of Jesus. Fulfillment, then, had little to do with specific predictions; these were "the garments—not the living body" of prophecy. Fulfillment consisted of the maturation of the "underlying ethical and spiritual meaning" of prophetic thought, and this process of growth was open-ended, for "the ever active Word of God spoken through the prophets, . . . [has an] ever expanding fulfillment in the life of Jesus Christ and in the history of his church."[34]

In his *Messianic Prophecy* (1886), Charles Briggs, who was seldom given to tactful utterance, condemned that "unwholesome apologetic that has been transmitted to us from the previous century, when there was a greedy grasping after anything and everything in the form of prediction that might in any way serve to exalt the supernatural character of the Bible." The emphasis upon minute accuracy rendered prophecy vulnerable to critics like Kuenen who replied "that Hebrew prediction has been proved false in so many particulars that the system cannot be regarded as true and divine." By claiming too much for biblical prediction, "self-constituted defenders of the faith" had made it an easy mark for scoffers, and Briggs saw his mission as the rescue of prophecy from these misguided souls. In order to secure prophecy from attack, Christians had to reduce their overextended lines to a more compact but defensible position. Or as Briggs explained: "We are not to find exact and literal fulfilments in detail or in general, but the fulfilment is limited, as the prediction is limited, to the essential ideal contents of the prophecy."[35]

A similar argument came from the pen of the Reverend J. W. Bashford, president of Ohio Wesleyan University. Writing in the *Methodist Review* in 1902, he argued that prophecy was chiefly a disclosure of the moral character of God and only in a secondary sense an augury of the future. To emphasize its predictive function unduly was to transform it into "a heathen book of fortune-telling." The forecasts it did contain would not admit a precise or "mechanical" fulfillment since human beings could, as free moral agents in cooperation with God, alter the predicted contours of the future. Moreover, the prophets were "imperfectly enlightened servants" at an early stage of "progressive revelation" and thus were liable to error in the details of their message. One could, Bashford quickly added, gather from their writings an accurate description, in very general outline, of the divine plan which was shown more fully in the New Testament. In short, Hebrew prophecy set forth, in terms appropriate to the writer's own time and under the limitations of his insight, specific instances of the principles by which God governed human affairs.[36]

Kemper Fullerton summarized the new view of Hebrew prophecy when he declared in 1919 that Jesus "fulfilled prophecy, *not because he is the fulfiller of prophetic predictions but because he is the fulfiller of prophetic ideals.* In the former case the emphasis is laid upon the adventitious and morally meaningless correspondencies between isolated prophecies and isolated events in Jesus' life. The prophecies are enigmas and the fulfilments are signs. . . . On the modern view of prophecy the emphasis is laid upon the great ethical and spiritual sequences running between the Old Testament and the New." There in a nutshell was the difference between the older and newer exegesis. To trace the fulfillment of prophecy, one should not treat that literature as if it were a code to be deciphered, each prediction referring with chronographic precision to a subsequent event. Rather one should examine the prophetic literature as a whole and then trace the organic growth of its moral ideals in subsequent history. In that development was the fulfillment of prophecy.[37]

The cloud darkening biblical prediction gathered with special fury over the apocalyptic scriptures. During the nineteenth and into the twentieth century, European scholars such as Frederich Lucke, Adolf Hilgenfeld, Wilhelm Boussett, Johannes Weiss, and preeminently R. H. Charles shattered older understandings of apocalypticism. As a result of this research, the books Daniel and Revelation, long the mainstays of millennial speculation, lost their uniqueness as critics analyzed them as mere instances of a larger genre of literature, much of it noncanonical. Moreover, scholars contrasted the apocalyptic mentality with that of Hebrew prophecy. They portrayed the latter as hopeful of redemption within history and characterized the former as despairing of the current age—apocalypticists entertaining the faulty expectation that the present order would shortly end in a supernatural upheaval. This contrast undercut traditional millennial speculation by suggesting that the Bible contained multiple views which could not be assembled into a single eschatology. Also, critics usually set prophecy against apocalypticism in order to derogate the latter. While prophecy allegedly represented the mainstream of biblical thought, the apocalyptic dream was an aberration, born perhaps of non-Jewish sources and representing the slightly unbalanced hopes of desperate men and women. The chief novelty of this critique was its overtness. Christians from Augustine to nineteenth-century postmillennialists had often found themselves uneasy with apocalypticism and had used various interpretive devices to mute it, but the canonical status of Daniel and Revelation had prevented direct onslaughts against that eschatology. Now, in light of newer scholarship and looser views of inspiration, the attack was more direct and self-conscious.

Apocalypticism was, in short, becoming an embarrassment to many Protestants. That view, said British exegete Arthur Peake in a widely read commentary, seems "remote and bizarre, its imagery pretentious or grotesque." "We are even compelled," added an American, "to explain away or make apology for, the presence of such teachings in the New Testament." According to one author, the Revelation was a "queer bird" hatched from "visions of the impossible"—visions which the Christian community had fortunately dropped for "saner and more spiritual conceptions." The liberal publication *Biblical World* asserted that modern scholarship had brought about the "passing of apocalypticism." The editor wrote: "A study of its origins inevitably brings its validity under suspicion for us." A product of a "highly imaginative Jewish thought," apocalypticism seduced the early Christian community for a time but was never consistent with the basic thrust of the church's message. Although books like Revelation "undoubtedly did a useful work" by steeling the nerve of the church during persecution, they were at best "the shell of a great truth," and the shell could now be sloughed off. While many liberals avoided such disparaging remarks about apocalypticism, they, too, were eager to dispose of its transient elements in order to discover the supposedly universal principles within it. Or as the Reverend A. B. Stormes of Des Moines said, one ought to treat the book of Revelation as "a parable of the moral meaning of history" and recognize that "the predictive element is confined largely to the statement of principles and moral issues which persist through all history."[38]

The distrust of apocalypticism was most evident in the effort to free Jesus from its taint. For precritical commentators, the apocalyptic elements in his teaching—for example, his discussion of "the Son of Man coming on the clouds of heaven" (Matthew 24:30)—had posed only minimal problems, for they assumed he was foretelling his Second Advent at the far distant end of the world. Hints that he expected this event in the near future were explained as reference to the imminent destruction of the Jerusalem temple (70 C.E.)—a cataclysm which Jesus was using as a type of the Last Judgment. To those imbued with the new learning, this interpretation was unconvincing. Modern research had demonstrated that apocalyptic writers generally expected an early overthrow of this age, and Jesus's use of such imagery thus raised an unavoidable question: did he, as Johannes Weiss and Albert Schweitzer had suggested, share the mistaken belief that the world was about to end? Anxious to avoid such a conclusion, most American proponents of biblical criticism either rejected the Weiss-Schweitzer hypothesis outright or accepted it in such qualified fashion as to negate its conclusions. Typical of this caution was the remark of Professor George Castor of Pacific Theological Seminary: "Jesus described the future in terms of Jewish apocalyptic speculation, and we probably ought to say that he thought in those terms, but his teaching was not determined by the eschatology of his time." By emphasizing the loving character of God and the possibility of experiencing his rule in the present age, said Castor, Jesus broke free of the prevailing outlook. Echoing these sentiments, Benjamin Wisner Bacon of Yale University admitted that Jesus shared current views and endorsed them, but Bacon insisted that the distinctive features of his thought—for example, the developmental and inward character of God's rule—did not derive from apocalypticism but worked to subvert it. Although Harris Franklin Rall of Garrett Seminary found considerable merit in the Weiss-Schweitzer position, he, too, insisted that the teachings of Jesus contained an "ageless message of truth" separable from their apocalyptic husk. That message was the announcement of ideal community—God and humanity in a filial relationship slowly evolving toward perfection.[39]

In place of the apocalyptic vision was a new understanding of the Kingdom of God. Along with Albrecht Ritschl (1822–1889), whose theology influenced many of them, liberal Protestants perceived this kingdom as a present ethical reality rather than as a dominion to be introduced in the future, and they believed that it advanced according to organic laws of growth, requiring no dramatic intrusions. According to these liberals, apocalypticism had suffered a double discredit: not only had critical studies exposed its fallacious predictions, but modern science, particularly evolutionary theories, rendered it irrational and repugnant. God did not work by coups de main. "Is anything in the whole universe of God, when rightly understood, supernatural?" asked retired Congregational minister W. B. Brown of Newark, New Jersey, in 1900. He replied in the negative. "Law and order are the agencies or instruments by means of which the creative and evolutionary processes of the universe are carried through." Throughout the cosmos, said Harris Rall, God's purpose was manifest in a seamless web of order. "As applied to the development of life upon the earth, the scientist calls it evolution; as applied to the story of mankind we call it history; as applied to God's supreme purpose we call it the development of the kingdom of God."[40]

In one sense, these assertions were scarcely new. Postmillennialists had argued a similar case throughout the nineteenth century. Against premillennialists, they had insisted that the Kingdom of God was already present, that it was spiritual and moral in character, that it was gradually improving the world, and that it required no supernatural display of power to achieve its ends. And yet postmillennialists had never abandoned the apocalyptic mentality entirely, for they still believed that the goal of history, however distant, was the literal return of Jesus to judge the quick and the dead.

The new biblical scholarship eroded even this attenuated apocalypticism. Many Protestants of liberal sentiment either ignored the notion of the Second Coming or denied it outright. For them, the idea had become, in the words of the Reverend Arthur Metcalf in 1907, a "thaumaturgical Advent"—a preposterous faith in a supernatural magic show—and he hoped that it would "fade from the vital interest of man." This conclusion represented a logical extension of views current among liberal Protestants. With predictive prophecy discredited and apocalypticism dismissed as an outmoded scheme, there was no longer a solid biblical foundation upon which to retain the traditional hope for the Second Coming.[41]

To be sure, not all Protestants who dismissed that hope were fully candid about what they were doing. Some found ways of scuttling this last vestige of the Apocalypse without acknowledging the radical import of their action. This was the course Israel Warren had followed in his *Parousia* in 1879. Instead of trying to recover some abiding spiritual significance hidden within that allegedly flawed eschatology, Warren boldly espoused it, but by his reading, apocalypticism was not what persons had taken it to be. Pictures of the heavens reeling, the earth in flames, and Christ returning on the clouds had never been intended by the biblical writers as literal descriptions of future supernatural events. The authors were drawing on lush oriental imagery to describe the spiritual and political changes attending the rise of the Christian movement. Thus when Jesus spoke of the Son of Man coming on the clouds of heaven, he referred to his return through the Spirit at Pentecost and to the destruction of the Jewish temple in the first century. No literal physical reappearance of Jesus and no cataclysmic end of the world had been predicted by the New Testament. For those who felt the force of modern critical theories and yet could not bring themselves to think that Jesus and his apostles had accepted an erroneous eschatology, this theory had immense appeal. Perhaps for this reason it enjoyed a minor vogue in the decades after Warren proposed it and won support, for example, from Daniel Curry, who edited the *Methodist Quarterly Review* for many years and supported the idea in the journal.[42]

And yet it was a bit disingenuous to pretend, as Warren and company did, that such a major change in Christian thought was really no change at all. These clever theories, charged Shirley Jackson Case of the Chicago Divinity School, "are evasive devices designed to bring these [apocalyptic] scriptures into harmony with present conditions while ignoring the vivid expectancy of the ancients." Perpetrators of such schemes were guilty of "retaining scriptural phrases while utterly perverting their original significance." Candor required an admission that apocalypticism pervaded much of the New Testament and that it meant what it said: the writers had believed that the present cosmos would soon be destroyed and replaced by another. Neither repristinating that eschatology (as the premillennialists wished) nor explaining it away (as the Warren school would do) represented intellectual honesty. Rather, the contemporary Christian must recognize the hope for what it was—a "millennial mirage"—and then search for elements of abiding spiritual worth hidden in the illusion. Beneath the "book's extravagant language" and "antiquated imagery," said Case, was "an inspiring example of loyalty in the hour of testing," a "contagious faith in the triumph of righteousness." These qualities made the Apocalypse a book for all seasons, in spite of much within it which no modern person could take seriously. But whether one sided with Case or with Warren, the result was the same: the last vestiges of apocalyptic eschatology disappeared.[43]

There were, of course, sectors of Protestantism where this generalization did not apply. Premillennialists, ensconced in the fortress of biblical infallibility, conceded little to the new biblical scholarship and reaffirmed that the Son of Man would soon return to claim his own. Nor did postmillennialism of the pre-1880 variety disappear suddenly from the face of the earth. But in the quarters where it had been most dominant—in leading pulpits and most major seminaries—it gradually ebbed into more liberal views of eschatology.

What, then, remained? With predictive prophecy in ruins and apocalypticism a bogey, could one affirm anything specific about the final destiny of the human race? William Newton Clarke, in his *Outline of Christian Theology*, an influential volume which went through many editions, provided a representative answer.

But his [Christ's] coming is not an event, it is a process that includes innumerable events, a perpetual advance of Christ in the activity of his kingdom. It has continued until now, and is still moving on. . . . No visible return of Christ to the earth is to be expected, but rather the long and steady advance of his spiritual kingdom . . . As to the length of future time on the earth, this doctrine leaves us in ignorance. According to this the Christian revelation does not show how long the present order of things is to continue. If science offers any light upon the question, we are free to receive it; and from this source we learn that God's processes are very long,—so long, in fact, that when once we have gained the point of view for the long perspective we wonder that we ever thought of a speedy ending for the great process of human existence. Life as we find it came out of the past, and is moving on to the future, and the end is out of sight. We find ourselves on the stream, but see neither the fount nor the ocean, nor can we tell how far away either is, except that both seem far remote. After all, what need have we of seeing either?[44]

With clear prophetic landmarks knocked down, there was no longer a definite eschatological goal toward which history moved. Humanity now floated on a stream in ignorance of both its origins and destination. What remained of postmillennialism was the genial hope that the tide was benign and moving toward better things. To change the metaphor, postmillennialism had become rather like Lewis Carroll's Cheshire Cat, faith in continuing moral and social improvement constituting the residual grin.

2

Millennial Dreams and Other Last Things

એ૭ⓒ૨૭

IN AN 1869 treatise on the meaning of death, the Reverend Peter Grant warned his readers that they should not be lulled into complacence by supposing that the Second Coming and Last Judgment were many years in the future.

> But how distant soever they may possibly be in themselves, yet to every one of us the day of eternal judgment is, in effect, very near, and even at the door. For aught that we can tell, another day, or even another hour, may behold us shut up in the prison of death. . . . Now, in whatever state we are when death lays his arrest upon us, the final judgment shall assuredly find us. . . . "Watch, therefore, and be ye ready, for in such an hour as ye think not, the Son of Man cometh."

This conflation of the moment of death with the Last Judgment and the return of Christ was a common hortatory device of the Protestant pulpit. It served as a reminder of the stark choice faced by every man and woman, a choice that destined each person to either the flames of hell or the bliss of heaven. According to this view, the life of each individual followed a course analogous to the apocalyptic pattern of history. In both cases, good confronted evil in sharply defined combat, punctuated by crisis and resulting in the final vindication of the righteous and the everlasting defeat of the wicked. Visions of individual destiny depicting the awesome finality of death and the irreconcilable contrast of heaven and hell made the Apocalypse for each believer his or her own story.[1]

In many sectors of Protestantism, the concept of individual destiny changed significantly during the last decades of the nineteenth century. Death ceased to be the great divide, heaven became an extension of this life, and hell's terrors diminished. With the passing of the older hope, the Book of Revelation—and the millennial schemes derived from it—seemed less a record of contemporary Christians' religious experience and more a relic of an antiquated world.

"What Has Become of Hell?"

An important part of evangelical piety had been the fearsome shadow cast by hell, but that specter gradually receded during the nineteenth century. One sign of its retreat was the success of sectarian movements rejecting traditional views of eternal punishment. Universalism, which (as its name implied) taught the eventual salvation of all people, emerged as a separate religious body in the post-Revolutionary period and grew to include nearly a thousand congregations by the late 1800s. The best-known American sectarian movement, the Latter-day Saints or Mormons, did not formally repudiate the idea of an eternal hell, but their stress upon an hierarchical heaven, in which the vast majority of human beings would reside, left hell relatively insignificant—and underpopulated. The remnants of the Millerite movement which coalesced to form Seventh-Day Adventism likewise altered the idea of perdition significantly. Rejecting the notion that some would suffer everlasting torment, they argued that the wicked would be annihilated instead. In the 1870s, a new religious movement influenced by Adventism—Charles T. Russell's followers (later to be known as the Jehovah's Witnesses)—taught a similar fate for the unrepentant. Christian Science, first publicly propounded by Mary Baker Eddy in the same decade that Russell launched his endeavor, also disposed of hell. Damnation, along with death and sin, was an illusion or error beclouding the human mind; it possessed no ultimate reality, said Eddy.[2]

In the orthodox denominations, there were few direct attacks on the idea of hell until the late 1870s, but even before that date the doctrine underwent a gradual metamorphosis. Postmillennialists entertained the hope that virtually all persons alive during the thousand years would be saved, and since the population of the earth would increase immensely during that happy era, the final ratio of the saved to the damned would be very favorable. While this theory left hell intact, it made it appear far less significant in the ultimate scheme of things. Thus William G. T. Shedd, professor of theology at Union Seminary in New York for many years and a strong defender of the notion of endless punishment of the wicked, wrote:

> It [hell] is only a spot in the universe of God. Compared with heaven, hell is narrow and limited. The kingdom of Satan is insignificant in contrast with the kingdom of Christ. In the immense range of God's dominion, good is the rule, and evil is the exception. Sin is a speck upon the infinite azure of eternity; a spot on the sun. Hell is only the corner of the universe.

While in some ages Jesus's words were accurate that the way to life was narrow and few would find it, the final demography of heaven and hell would yield happier results.[3]

The fate of those who died in infancy provided another clue that the orthodox were subtly changing their view of perdition. The Westminster Confession of Faith, the primary confessional document of Calvinist Protestants in America, had declared: "Elect infants, dying in infancy, are regenerated and saved by Christ through the Spirit, who worketh when, and where, and how he pleaseth." The implication of that ambiguous statement was that perhaps some who died in infancy were not elect and would therefore endure the pains of hell. Even to many staunch Calvinists that reading of the Confession became insupportable in the nineteenth century, and Charles Hodge, who regarded himself as a defender par excellence of that creed, interpreted it as including all dying infants in God's saving purpose. "All who die in infancy are saved," he declared. "The Scripture nowhere excludes any class of infants, baptized or unbaptized, born in Christian lands or in heathen lands, of believing or unbelieving parents, from the benefits of the redemption of Christ." For some individuals in the Presbyterian Church, these avowals were insufficient, and from the late 1880s to 1903, the denomination considered and finally enacted minor revisions to the Westminster Standards. The confession's ambiguity on the fate of those dying in infancy was one of the issues addressed by revision.[4]

These efforts to lessen the sting of hell derived in part from the fact that it was not readily compatible with the theological currents of the age. Since the late eighteenth century, under the influence of the Enlightenment and later Romanticism, Protestants had increasingly described God's character in terms of rational benevolence. As evangelist Charles Finney had written, God, like human beings, was obligated to promote the "highest well-being of the universe" and without this "good and sufficient reason" not even the Lord would have "a right to prescribe rules for" or determine the destiny of persons. Although this conception did not automatically transform its adherents into opponents of hell—Finney's sermons, for example, often reeked with brimstone—it did narrow the grounds on which perdition could be justified, and it placed a heavier burden on those who saw God condemning multitudes to everlasting punishment. Likewise, the waning of the doctrine of original sin made humans appear to be less deserving of such punishment, and young children seemed especially unlikely candidates for that fate. "If beauty and innocence are anywhere enthroned in this world," observed one writer in 1867 while professing his orthodoxy, "it is upon the brow of infancy and childhood."[5]

Gradual mitigation of the doctrine of eternal punishment broke forth into overt challenge in 1876 and 1877. In the former year, James Whiton, a Congregational minister and Principal of the Williston Academy in Easthampton, Massachusetts, published a book entitled *Is "Eternal" Punishment*

Endless? He replied that the Bible provided no definitive answer to this question. Although the Scripture taught "future punishment in terms sufficiently
explicit and severe for purposes of moral government, [it] does not positively
declare the duration of that punishment." After a careful survey of biblical
teaching, Whiton concluded that "a cloud of impenetrable mystery hides the
ultimate lot of the wicked." While the impenitent might suffer torment forever, it was equally conceivable that they might not. In November 1877, the
Rev. James C. Merriam expressed a similar agnosticism about the duration of
suffering in the future life. At a council of Congregational ministers called to
examine and then install him as pastor of a church at Springfield, Massachusetts, Merriam asserted that the Bible left "the question an open one" and
offered his personal opinion "that future punishment, if eternal in any sense,
is so in the sense that it is eternal death, or annihilation." The council deemed
that view (as well as the candidate's theory of the Atonement) unacceptable
and declined to install him.[6]

Soon the faculty of the Andover Theological Seminary cautiously advanced its own revision of traditional eschatology. With the inauguration of
the *Andover Review* in 1883, the faculty began proposing a modest liberaliza-
tion of orthodox Congregationalism, or as they put it, they were advocating
progressive orthodoxy. One plank in their program of tentative liberalism asserted that those who died without having heard the Gospel would most
likely receive, after death, an opportunity to respond to the message of Christ.
God was not "a Being who creates millions of men to whom He never offers
the means of salvation." The end of creation will not "be reached till all mankind, the least and the greatest, the wisest and the most ignorant, the purest
and the most depraved, have the knowledge of God's amazing love in Christ
Jesus"—whether in this life or the next. While this revision of the doctrine of
perdition applied only to the heathen and although it did not deny the reality
of an eternal hell, it nevertheless signified an important step away from inherited conceptions. Many Protestants were no longer comfortable with the notion of benighted multitudes stumbling to everlasting destruction, and they
had begun to suspect that death might not mark the boundary of God's love
or the possibility of redemption.[7]

This theory produced considerable controversy, especially in the American Board of Commissioners for Foreign Missions. The board refused en-
dorsement to missionaries suspected of sympathy toward the Andover view,
but by 1893, the board took the important step of accepting a candidate who
had openly avowed his hope for future probation. This action did not indicate
an acceptance of Andover's eschatology, but it did imply that tolerance for it
had grown immensely in the previous decade.[8]

A more direct attack against hell came in the form of conditional immortality or annihilationism. According to this theory, immortality was not an intrinsic property of the human soul. Only the righteous attained it, while the wicked passed out of existence after death. Although only sectarian and minor voices supported the notion initially, it began to win significant support in the 1870s and '80s. Lyman Abbott, Henry Ward Beecher's successor at the Plymouth Congregational Church in Brooklyn and influential editor of the *Christian Union,* explicitly avowed the doctrine. Those who resisted the love of God would eventually be "silent in an eternal grave, from which there is no resurrection." Abbott believed that the eventual nonexistence of the impenitent testified to the graciousness of God in a way that the traditional notion of hell did not. It guaranteed that "there will be no remote and far-off corner of the universe where, behind locked doors, the groans of an endless misery and the wrath of an endless sin shall prove that the devil has won a victory in some small corner of God's dominions." Likewise, the venerable Connecticut Congregationalist, Leonard Bacon, while somewhat inconclusive (and perhaps inconsistent) in his views on the subject, strongly tended toward the annihilationist view. "The faithless and ungodly have no lasting tenure upon life," he declared. Attempts to go beyond this simple fact to reassert traditional views of everlasting suffering for the wicked would, Bacon believed, serve only "to perplex this whole subject, and bewilder simple minds, and give occasion to adversaries to blaspheme." Conditional immortality possessed an additional advantage in an age increasingly enamored of evolutionary theory: it appeared a scientific solution to the problem of hell. It was merely the survival of the fittest exemplified in the religious realm. Or as Episcopal Bishop S. D. McConnell noted in a 1901 book aptly titled *The Evolution of Immortality,* conditionalism was an instance of "spiritual biology." Immortality was attained, said McConnell, "by an extension of the long path by which the soul has climbed up from the primordial slime." In the matter of immortality, as in all stages of evolution, only the fit could endure.[9]

Yet despite the support of notable divines, conditional immortality won only limited acceptance, for it created as many moral dilemmas as it resolved. In its own way, it posited an eternal loss nearly as terrifying as hell. Moreover, annihilation neatly divided humanity into the wicked and the righteous at a moment when many religious thinkers, sensing the possibility of good in virtually everybody, had begun to portray the moral life as a continuum with most people falling somewhere in the middle range. Many liberals preferred to resolve the problem of hell along other lines.

They suggested that death would not terminate the possibility of redemption and argued that other persons might enjoy the postmortem opportunity the Andover theologians promised to the heathen. According to Washington Gladden, it was illogical in any instance to make death the boundary beyond which salvation could not occur. That restriction "contradicts, absolutely, either the doctrine of the freedom of the will, or the doctrine of the righteousness of God, or both. To say that no man can repent after death is to say that no man after death is a moral being,—that death has wrought a revolution in his moral nature, and robbed him of the essential attribute of personality . . . If the doctrine that probation in all cases terminates at death does not imply the lack of power to repent, then it implies the refusal of God to grant his grace to a penitent sinner, and this implication is worse than the other. Let us not assert that the Father in heaven will ever, in any world, turn a deaf ear to the cry of any soul that seeks to escape from sin!" Echoing Gladden's argument, George A. Gordon insisted that it was utterly nonsensical to suppose that God loves sinners now but will, immediately after their decease, become an implacable foe. Since his gracious love is the fundamental law of the universe, that love operates in all places and times. To claim that it ceases operation at death, "is the same thing logically as to say that one can cut out a circle in space, within which the law of gravitation operates, and where the order and beauty that always follow may be beheld; but beyond which there is no gravitation, no law of space, and where nothing exists except chaos and utter contradiction."[10]

Would all men and women, then, be saved? Gordon did not hesitate to make that prediction. While the human being might "resist temporarily the Divine persuasions . . . in consequence of the irrationality that he has brought up with him from the animal world," Gordon could not believe that this lower inheritance could ultimately thwart God's saving purpose. Despite the animalistic residue, humans were fundamentally reasonable creatures to whom God "proposes a reasonable good." Therefore, at some point through countless eons, they must come to their senses and accept the love of God.[11]

Other liberals were less sure of universal salvation. If it was arbitrary to make death the end of probation, it was equally absurd, in Washington Gladden's words, to "teach that death regenerates men." Persons possessed, whether in this life or the next, the freedom to reject the love of God, and inveterate sinners might, by "the free action of the soul in rejecting the light" eventually bring themselves to a state of "moral paralysis" in which they no longer were capable of responding to God. Thus "the fact that death does not close the door of opportunity is no assurance of salvation after death." For those who did so harden themselves, punishment would be the inevitable result.[12]

But such punishment ought not to be understood as an act of God in any proper sense. "Retribution is," explained Gladden "part of the natural order and follows transgression as the effect follows the cause." Or in the words of W. B. Brown, a retired Congregational minister in Newark, New Jersey,

God is not to the wicked "their jailer to keep them in prison." The punishment of the wicked results from "the law of natural consequences," which is as constant in the moral as in the physical domain. God need not inflict suffering. From sinners' obdurate rebellion—and from it alone—flowed their pain. For his part, God remained unwearied in love for the wayward. "Does God hate such souls?" asked Brown. "Is he angry at them? Are they objects of His wrath? No. God is love. He pities them, and would do them infinite good if they would let Him, but they will not." And yet from the constancy of God, Brown derived tentative hope that at the last every soul would respond to God's offer. "But I hope tremblingly," he averred. In similar fashion, the future Episcopal bishop Charles Slattery declared in 1916: "Through eternity God's yearning Fatherhood will be seeking him. The desperate and wayward soul may go to the utmost bounds of the blackest night, but God will be there. And at some moment of eternity, we may hope (we cannot know) that the scarred and battered being will turn and recognize the Love that is seeking it everywhere, and will yield to the high use to which God created it, and will come out into the light of the morning." Thus while less certain than George Gordon about the ultimate salvation of all people, many liberals did entertain, in Brown's phrase, a trembling hope of universal redemption.[13]

Underlying these revisions of eschatology was a basic principle: future punishment must be consistent with nature. Thus Gladden asserted that a true theory of hell must be drawn from life, from the observed laws of humanity's moral and physical nature, or as David Swing expressed the issue: "It must be assumed . . . that in the realms called 'heaven' and 'hell' the occupants all live under the law of 'nature acting naturally.'" And nature as the liberals saw it was the realm of an immanent God who acted with invariable benevolence. One should, therefore, reject all views which sundered that seamless web of uniform love—for example, the idea that God arbitrarily decreed the punishment of sinners, or that during their earthly lives, he desired their salvation and then became an avenging judge as soon as they died. While punishment might come in the future, it derived naturally from the moral and physical laws already at work here. Life, both here and in the world to come, was a continuous natural process, and in that process liberals discerned hope for all people, for God was unchanging in his love.[14]

Liberal views drew, of course, rejoinders from defenders of eternal punishment. Some objected that alterations of the idea of hell undermined the fundamental truths of Christianity. The Gospel was an announcement of unmerited grace bestowed upon undeserving sinners through the merits of Christ's atonement. Any lessening of the horror of eternal punishment made sin less odious and diminished the role of Christ as Savior. As the pastor of the Calvary Baptist Church in New York City declared: "The preaching which fails to recognize the doctrine of eternal punishment, fails to give due honor to the holiness of God; it fails to emphasize aright the sinfulness of sin, and the greatness of Christ's atoning work. If man be not eternally lost, then the cross of Calvary is either a gigantic blunder or an unpardonable crime." Also, the liberal tendency to reduce God's character to love appeared dangerously one-sided, for the deity revealed himself in wrath as well as in grace. Moreover, many critics feared the mode of liberal argumentation. The modernists often appealed beyond the letter of Scripture to the evolving moral consciousness of humanity and found hell wanting by this standard. To conservatives, this approach was fraught with danger. It represented a "theological drift," said the president of Dartmouth College, which "unless arrested, will issue in a grave defection." As Professor E. D. Morris of Lane Theological Seminary in Cincinnati viewed the matter, the effort to judge any doctrine by the current religious consciousness risked abandoning the objective basis of Christian truth—the revealed Word of God—and of wandering into a morass of subjective opinions and "rationalistic fantasy."[15]

Some turned the liberals' appeal to nature against them. Did nature testify unambiguously to loving process? Was there not also a darker side to the natural world which constituted an analogy to hell? Dr. Joseph T. Smith, a former moderator of the Presbyterian General Assembly, observed:

> I wish earth were a paradise of innocence and bliss. . . . But it is idle for me to wonder or wish. God has not made the world after my ideals. His ways are not my ways; nor his thoughts, my thoughts. With the heroism of the true searcher after truth I must bid away these alluring visions, and school myself to the task of learning simply what is. . . . In point of fact, the worlds he has made are filled with all manner of physical disorders. They are rocked by earthquakes, torn by volcanoes, swept by tempests, deformed by deserts, frozen by arctic colds, and parched by equatorial heats. He has made crawling worms, and loathsome insects, and poisonous serpents, and cruel beasts of prey.

In other words, argued Smith, nature reveals that life is often broken and baffled; therefore, one could not reject the possibility of an ultimate frustration—namely, an eternal hell.[16]

Yet even the proponents of hell seemed eager to mitigate the doctrine they were defending. They reiterated arguments that the vast majority of humanity would be saved, emphasized that damnation derived from natural laws which did not require the direct intervention of a vindictive deity, reduced scriptural images of hell's physical torment to metaphor, and suggested that future punishment would be graded to the offense, some of the damned getting off with a relatively light sentence. One writer even suggested that God was being tender to the wicked by consigning them to perdition. "It is a kindness, therefore, in God to shut up in the blackness of darkness, men who hate him, and who would be a thousand-fold more wretched in his presence than they are in the prison-house of woe. . . . Transfer such men to heaven, and they would pray for the rocks and the mountains to fall upon them, to hide them from the face of Him that sitteth upon the throne."[17]

In short, while direct assaults upon the notion of hell were probably restricted to a minority of Protestants even after 1880, evidence abounds of a new attitude which, though hard to measure in quantitative terms, was probably more significant than overt challenges to the doctrine. Both friends and foes of the change noted it. Washington Gladden claimed those "most strenuous" in their defense of hell "now and then" deliver a perfunctory utterance on the subject and then "fling the sermon into the drawer when it is preached, with the thankful feeling that nothing more on that subject will be needed for some time to come." The Reverend H. O. Rowlands, a Baptist defender of the doctrine, lamented "that there is a drifting away from it" and that ministers usually observed silence on the subject. "In cold written controversy," the clergy might espouse the doctrine, but seldom did it intrude "in the living message of the pulpit, the Sabbath school teacher and Christian worker." Thus the popular evangelist Moody, while a believer in hell, seldom allowed it to shape his preaching about the love of God. The vivid pictures of hell with which Jonathan Edwards, Charles Finney, and others urged sinners to flee the wrath to come gave way in Moody to gentle images of a heaven beguiling the wayward to repentance. In 1916, the Methodist General Conference altered the church's funeral service to omit most references to the wrath of God or the possibility of future punishment. Here an entire denomination, "the symbolic center of nineteenth-century evangelicalism," as James Farrell properly calls it, was withdrawing into silence about hell. A little-noted ecclesiastical statistic underscores the nature of the transformation under way. The number of Universalist churches, having dramatically expanded during most of the nineteenth century, declined precipitously after 1890. With the harsh pictures of hell fading from the consciousness of the average Protestant, there was now little need for the once-distinctive message of that church. Much of the spirit, if not the formal doctrine, of Universalism had been absorbed into the major denominations. Liberals were only the most open and visible proponents of change which had occurred across much of the landscape of Protestantism.[18]

Writing of the state of theology at the dawn of the twentieth century, Dr. George W. Shinn, rector of the Grace Episcopal Church in Newton, Massachusetts, asked: "What has become of hell?" "There has been," he noted, "a remarkable change of late years in religious teaching with reference to future punishment. Whereas formerly in theological papers, in sermons and books of instruction, much was said about hell, now it is but rarely mentioned. . . . You do not hear of it in the pulpit, or see reference to it in the religious press, or in the modern theological book, nor is it often brought up in religious conversation. It is tabooed by the pulpit generally. When, under stress, the preacher has to refer to it, he may adopt the euphemistic method of one who spoke of 'the place which could not be named in the presence of cultured people.'" And if hell had become "the place which could not be named," what did this change mean? It meant that fewer Protestants now agreed with the assessment that Methodist minister S. M. Vernon delivered in 1886 when he said that the preacher must "plant the radiant cross over against the dark background of eternal night." With eternal night turned into twilight, Protestant hope was losing an element which once sustained the apocalyptic outlook.[19]

Heaven: "One Life Here and Hereafter"

At the same time that hell assumed a less awesome and terrifying appearance, the image of heaven also changed. Classic Protestant portrayals of the celestial state had emphasized pictures of release from earthly struggle, total abolition of sin, and unceasing adoration of God. The saints entered at death into everlasting rest, in the words of Richard Baxter's classic, and they were, as the Westminster Confession asserted, "then made perfect in righteousness." While these representations asserted the continuity of life beyond the grave, they also underscored the radical difference between the present and the heavenly state. Moreover, they emphasized that the chief business of heaven was not the fulfillment of earthly desires but rejoicing in the glory of God. As late as 1884, William G. T. Shedd, a man of pronounced sympathies with traditional orthodoxy, elaborated this theme:

> Here upon earth we see some faint streaks of the Divine glory, and we offer some faint and imperfect adoration. But when the full-orbed glory of God shall rise upon our clear and purged vision in another world, our anthems will be like those of the heavenly host. Here upon earth, our praise is to some degree an effort. We study, and we toil, to give unto God the glory due unto his name. . . . But when we shall "come and appear before God"; when we shall behold the Object of worship precisely as he is, it will cost us no effort to worship him. Our adoration will become spontaneous and irrepressible. For the Object itself prompts the service. We shall not need to urge our hearts up to the anthem. They will be drawn out by the magnetic attraction, the heavenly beauty of the Divine Nature.

Effortless praise of God, the end of earthly striving, and above all "the heavenly beauty of the Divine Nature"—these were the chief characteristics of the traditional Protestant vision of heaven, and they served to set heaven in sharp relief against the condition in which we now live. Yet Shedd also commented briefly that heaven would provide "a residence in which they [the redeemed] can unfold their powers in a well-defined and self-conscious manner." That passing phrase was a significant one, indicating a new direction in thought about heaven. For many, heaven was becoming continuous with the present life; it was a place where the best of this world would be writ large and where the realization of earthly dreams would be at least as important as the glory of God. Geoffrey Rowell succinctly describes the transformation: many mid-nineteenth-century Protestants came to look forward to "an immortality of self-realization, rather than an immortality of salvation." This eschatological revision, born among earlier visionaries and literary figures such as John Milton, Emmanuel Swedenborg, William Blake, and Jean-Jacques Rousseau, had begun to work its way into the thought of mainstream Protestant leaders.[20]

Consolatory literature manifested the hope of self-realization. William Branks, a British writer whose book *Heaven our Home* was widely read on both sides of the Atlantic, reflected the change. "I have often felt," he explained in the introduction to his work, "that the views which most divines have given of *heaven* are so utterly *negative*, in their *nature*, and so utterly unsocial in their *aspect*, that they are more calculated to *repel* the inquiries and longings and aspirations of the children of God after it, than to *allure* their thoughts upwards, and fix their desires upon the things that are above." Rather than depict heaven as Baxter's *The Saint's Everlasting Rest* or as a beatific vision of God, Branks wished to delineate it as "a *home, with a great and happy and loving family in it.*" Or as Adeline Bayard, writing in 1877 for the American Sunday School Union, suggested:

> Vague and floating ideas of Heaven weaken faith and render unsteady our religious life. . . . Heaven is described in this day as such a sublimated and ethereal state, so abstracted and removed from all the sympathies of the present life, that to many it seems profane to claim a present fellowship with it. Practically we are taught the heavenly life is so unlike this, to be entered by such violent transition, that, publican-like, we ought to stand afar off, hardly turning our eyes towards it. Instead of cold abstractions, we need a reviving of those father-land feelings which will enable us to approach our heavenly inheritance like children long absent going home.

This picture of heaven as home—a theme reiterated in numerous books emphasizing that recognition of our loved ones would be a major feature of heaven—reflected, of course, the triumph of the bourgeois cult of domesticity, but it also pointed to a larger theological shift. Heaven would not be so different from our current life, or in Adeline Bayard's words, the transition to heaven would not be "a revolutionary one."[21]

Popular fiction carried this theme to its logical extreme, and the works of Elizabeth Stuart Phelps are classic illustrations. A product of the Andover Seminary faculty in its orthodox days—she was the grandchild of Moses Stuart and the daughter of Austin Phelps—Elizabeth moved well beyond its cautiously progressive orthodoxy. In several works of fiction, she advanced the notion of heaven as an idealized New England projected into the skies. In her 1867 *The Gates Ajar*, Phelps's major character speculated about an afterlife so similar to this one that stolid farmers would cultivate their potatoes and artists write compositions to all eternity. In *Beyond the Gates* (1885), a forty-one-year-old woman named Mary, through what would now be called a near-death experience, briefly enters heaven to return with a detailed description of its precincts. The most striking feature of Mary's passage to the other world is its ease and naturalness. Even though the one who fetches her from her sickbed is her deceased father, her surprise at seeing him does not initially make her realize she has died. She walks from the house with him, as if death were as uneventful as a stroll from one place to another, and only gradually discerns that she has died. In heaven she encounters a world clearly analogous with the best of earth. There are, to be sure, differences. The rainbow possesses more colors, the spiritually adept can walk on water, and the saints can transport themselves through space by an act of will. Still, the essential contours of the afterlife are identifiably the same as here. Persons live in pleasant middle-class homes—graceful trees shade her father's cottage, and a friendly dog lies by the door. People continue the employments which they began on earth. Museums, universities, and concerts provide cultural improvement. Phelps even suggests that some marriages may persist for eternity. Mary's father, for example, has long since readied a room to receive his still-living wife. Just before Mary is snatched back to her earthly body, she hears the strains of the wedding march and encounters the boyfriend of her youth. Both, it would seem, are destined to find in heaven the consummation of love denied on earth. Never does God intrude in such a way as to mar the earth-like quality of heaven, and Jesus moves about unobtrusively, sometimes unrecognized by the inhabitants. Perhaps the character of Phelps's heaven is best explained by Mary's father when he tells her: "Each comes to his own by his own. . . . The nature is never forced. Here we unfold like a leaf, a flower. He [God] expects nothing of us but to be natural."[22]

Phelps's novels drew fire from some critics. She later noted wryly that "religious papers waged war across that girl's notions of the life to come, as if she had been an evil spirit let loose upon accepted theology for the destruction of the world." An Episcopal professor of divinity, for example, regarded these efforts "to furnish heaven with toys and playthings . . . , and pianos and Jew's harps" as a "wretched and degrading travesty of the heavenly state." Yet despite hostile reviews, Phelps's works enunciated hopes which many eagerly received. *The Gates Ajar* and *Beyond the Gates* had combined sales of over 100,000 copies in America alone, and advertisers, sensing a powerful marketing device, hawked *Gates Ajar* capes, collars, pieces of music, and even cigars.[23]

Phelps offered a simple analysis of her success. Her works appealed to a natural instinct that "if there be another world . . . , it will be no theologic drama, but a sensible wholesome scene." In short, it will be a world much like this one, and the same laws of natural growth and progress which operate here will operate there. Even writers who eschewed Phelps's immodestly specific speculations about the future life seldom took issue with those central principles. When the New York Presbyterian minister David Gregg described heaven, he depicted it as a state in which the vigor of youth would combine with the "wisdom of age" in a career of ceaseless activity and improvement in which the unique talents of each person would be fully utilized. "To me," he explained, "heaven means only myself with larger opportunity. It means this earth-life grown into perfection." The popular religious writer Lucy Larcom offered a similar message. Earth and heaven did not exist as two separate states, for even now heaven permeated life here below.

> Surprises doubtless await us all, across the boundaries of this earthly existence. But none, perhaps, will be more surprised than those humble, faithful, self-sacrificing souls who have often almost dreaded the strange splendors that might open upon them beyond the gates of pearl, when they find that it is the same familiar sunshine in which they have been walking all their days, only clearer and serener. They will wonder that they have no new language to learn, no new habits to form, almost no new acquaintances to make. They will at last discover what their humility hid from them here, that while on earth, without knowing it, they had already been living in heaven.

Or as George A. Gordon explained, eternal life was a present possession, and when the saints crossed the bar, they would discover that "death is no more than an impressive incident in the life of such a soul. It is but a bend in the river around the spur of a mountain."[24]

Writers were turning away from older, static images of heaven. To be sure, symbols of rest lingered and found expression in gospel hymns suffused with languor and promising release "in the sweet by and by." Analyzed in context, however, this rhetoric gave a new meaning to the saint's everlasting rest. The rest heaven promised was no longer primarily the fulfillment of being through the worship of God; it was often—as Phelps, Branks, Bayard, and others contended—the serenity of an earthly home projected into the skies. Although heaven would end certain aggressive forms of striving, it would not terminate the gentler pursuits of a busy family. The high visibility of the domestic heaven in popular piety must not, however, be overemphasized to the exclusion of countervailing images also present in nineteenth-century religious thought. Even the proponents of a home-centered heaven often allowed room for extradomestic pursuits along ever-expanding lines. Phelps's redeemed, for example, continued to work at trades and engage in other public activities. By the 1880s and 1890s, when Americans were in search of the strenuous life and muscular Christianity had come into vogue with its dreams of evangelizing the world in this generation, this energetic conception of heaven assumed even greater prominence. Few would then have agreed with—or even understood—Richard Baxter's classic description of heaven: "Rest is the end and perfection of motion." Certainly such a state would not be heaven to Teddy Roosevelt, noted one writer, adding that even the sometime Rough Rider would find new worlds to conquer in the hereafter—a suggestion which raises images of the afterlife as something akin to an eternal reenactment of TR's charge at the Battle of San Juan in the Spanish-American War.[25]

In virtually all of these depictions of heaven, continued growth and activity were crucial components. The Rev. Walter Ulyat, a sometime Baptist pastor who spent part of his career working in the library at Princeton's Presbyterian seminary, suggested that the redeemed would not all be on the same level. After death, they would be ranked according to their moral attainments and from that position would press forward in an eternal quest to advance. "There will still be something more to learn. God will keep in advance of his creatures. . . . Our course will still be onward, bearing a banner inscribed, 'Excelsior.' In the heavens beyond, there will be fresh work to be done, and fresh summits to reach." C. C. Hall of Union Seminary, New York, assured his readers that heaven would not be a "bald monotony of perfected existence," for "the meaning of Christ's coming into the world was to open to us the vision and experience of life fulfilling itself on ever broadening lines." Even S. D. Gordon, a Protestant writer who ordinarily wrote in defense of moderately conservative theological positions, could not resist the pull of the new activistic vision of heaven. Reflecting on a hymn he had learned as a boy—two lines of which described a heaven "Where congregations ne'er break up, And Sabbaths have no end"—Gordon concluded that this conception of the afterlife would no longer suffice. It "hymned away out of touch with true human feelings." It conjured images of eternal worship services in which people forever sat "on plain hard wooden benches with straight stiff backs." Surely heaven, though it would be a place of adoration, was more than these "unnatural restraints." The afterlife had to be a place where a person enjoyed "the zest of seeing things grow under one's touch. For that belongs to true life. Each one up yonder has his task and round of occupation, and a rare joy in doing it. It's a busy purposeful active life, up there, but without any strain or worry, crowding or drudgery."[26]

Perhaps William Adams Brown best summarized the new thought about heaven. He complained,

> Too often in the past, the contrast between the present and the future has been unduly exaggerated. The life after death has been isolated from all relation to the present, and defined purely by contrast. The result is a certain hollowness and unreality which all the glowing imagery of the Apocalypse . . . has been powerless to warm into the semblance of a true life. How empty and shallow the heaven to which we have often been asked to look forward, a heaven of untroubled bliss, with nothing to achieve and nothing to anticipate, a heaven freed from suffering indeed, but free also from the struggle of which suffering is born, a heaven in which there is nothing to do but to enjoy, year after year, and aeon after aeon, through a monotonous eternity.

But heaven would not be monotonous. It was an eternal progressive purposeful activity already begun here. "Our hope for the life to come is not different from our hope for the life here. There is but one life here and hereafter, and the change we call death is but opening the door from one room to another in the Father's house." Heaven, in short, had been annexed to this life, and the result would be an eternal movement through purposeful activity, similar to that of this life, with no clear terminus in view. John Haynes Holmes, the Unitarian pastor of the Church of the Messiah, summed up the direction in which even mainstream Protestants had moved: "Heaven, in other words, is simply the next step in the evolution of the spiritual life. We shall begin there just where we left off here—our growth will be resumed at just the point, high or low, where it was suspended by the dissolution of the body. . . . The morning after death will be exactly like the morning after sleep, so far at least as the inner life is concerned. Where we stopped yesterday, we shall begin again today, as though nothing at all had happened."[27]

The Resurrection of the Body?

Holmes's notion that one could dismiss death "as though nothing at all had happened" would have struck many earlier generations of Protestants as odd. They had assumed that death, while it released the soul to be with Christ, was nevertheless a tragic event whose horrors they described with realism. Writing in the mid-1700s, Jonathan Edwards described the "pale, horrid, ghastly appearance of the corps [sic], its being laid in the dark and silent grave, there putrifying and rotting and becoming exceeding loathsome and being eaten with worms." The gravestone of a man who died in Rockingham, Vermont, in 1794 similarly recognized the loss of death: "Here in this place, the human face will in oblivion lie till Christ on high shalt rend the sky and bid the dead arise." Another inscription from 1808 in the same cemetery declared: "Death, thou hast conquer'd me and by thy dart I'm slain. But Christ has conquered thee and I shall rise again." While these lines affirmed the ultimate victory of Christ over death in the final resurrection, they recognized that death had at least temporarily visited an awful destruction upon the deceased. Even as late as 1864, Davis W. Clark, a Methodist bishop, could write in a similar fashion of the gruesomeness of death:

> Its dread attendants make it terrible—the cold death-sweat, the quivering, failing pulse, the darkened vision, the dying agony, and the utter stillness, helpless, and rapid decay of the body from which life has departed, never fail to inspire dread. Death is appalling when viewed only as the separation of the soul from the body. This mysterious blending of our physical and spiritual natures, this union of matter and mind, seems here to constitute our very being. . . . The separation of these elements, the bursting asunder of this bond of our being, leaving the body a lifeless wreck, a despoiled and wasted ruin, while the spirit departs to regions and to scenes unknown, cannot be realized without a pang. . . .

While Davis avowed that the body would eventually be raised and that the spirit even now enjoyed communion with Christ, he reminded his readers that their bodies—an important part of their selves—would be, at least until the sound of Gabriel's trumpet, "lonely tenants of the grave."[28]

The question of the grave's "lonely tenants" raised one of the thorniest difficulties in traditional Christian eschatology: the fate of the individual during the intermediate state, that is during the period between death and the resurrection. The problem derived from the fact that the New Testament itself contains two divergent eschatologies—one centered upon the future raising of the dead, the other upon immortality of the soul. According to the first, redemption awaits the intervention of God when Christ returns in glory at the Last Judgment, and according to the second, each person goes at death either to reward or punishment. For example, the Pauline epistles speak alternately of the resurrection as the moment of redemption, and of death as a departure to be with Christ. Similarly, the synoptic Gospels emphasize the resurrection of Christ and his future return in glory, but they also contain passages—for example, the story of the rich man and Lazarus and Jesus's words from the cross to the penitent thief—which imply that individuals enter into either bliss or suffering at the time of death. How then are these two conceptions to be synthesized? While some theologians argued that the person slumbered in unconsciousness between death and resurrection, the characteristic compromise was to assert that the souls of the redeemed had already entered into joy but awaited reunion with their bodies which moldered in the grave until the last trumpet.[29]

And when the trumpet sounded, what would be raised? Would Christ resuscitate decayed corpses and gather together again bodily elements long dispersed by putrefaction? To some of literal mentality, resurrection meant precisely this. For example, the eighteenth-century English poet and royal chaplain, Edward Young, had written in *The Last Day* (1714):

> Now monuments prove faithful to their trust
> And render back their long committed dust;
> Now charnels rattle; scatter'd limbs and all
> The various bones, obsequious to the call,
> Self-mov'd advance; the neck perhaps to meet
> The distant head; the distant head the feet.
> Dreadful to view, see, thro' the dusky sky
> Fragments of bodies in confusion fly,
> To distant regions journeying, there to claim
> Deserted members, and complete the frame.

While Young's works were widely republished and read well into the 1800s, it is doubtful that many sophisticated Protestants in the nineteenth century would have endorsed the macabre details of his vision of the Last Day, and few—if any—theologians would have taught the eventual reassembly of every particle comprising the body at death. Yet most continued, despite the admitted logical difficulties, to insist on the identity of the body laid in the grave with the one which would be raised. (Perhaps here was part of the lingering appeal of Young's poetry.) As late as 1893, Lewis F. Stearns, a Congregational theologian espousing a moderate liberalism, noted: "We lay away our dead in the grave, and our hearts are full of pain that the precious body should be treated thus. . . . Is this all? Is the body thrown away like a cast-off garment? Must it be forever hidden from our sight? Christ answers, No, a thousand times, No! This dust is precious. Nothing of what we prized will be lost. Every power, every capability, every possibility will be preserved. The body, in spite of the appearance which shakes our faith, is not dead but sleeps, sleeps in Jesus. The grave is its quiet bed, where it awaits the last trump."[30]

But a number of other Protestants had begun to think that the idea of an intermediate state was untenable and that the very notion of the resurrection needed rethinking. One of the first Americans to state that position systematically was the Rev. T. A. Goodwin, a Methodist minister and editor in the Midwest. In *The Mode of Man's Immortality*, Goodwin argued that a resurrection of the physical body was a revolting absurdity which could only drive intelligent people away from the church. As a sample of this nonsense, he quoted some of the more lurid passages from Edward Young and asked: "Is it any wonder that many thinking men have been repelled by such sense-less jargon, and have been led to doubt human immortality altogether . . . ?" Rather than imagining the resurrection as a future reanimation of the body laid in the grave, Christians should think of it as "the rising of a spirit form from the earthly house at the moment of death." According to Goodwin, this conception performed a useful pastoral service. It eliminated the intermediate state—a "doctrine which separates man into parts"—and provided the reas-suring word that all of that which constituted the person passed immedi-ately into glory. "Not the least of the commendations which the first edition [of *The Mode of Man's Immortality*] elicited," Goodwin boasted in the reprint, "have been numerous testimonials from those in various walks of life who had been led to look upon death and the grave with horror. The more cheerful, hopeful, trustful, Scriptural views herein taught have mitigated the grief they have endured in the loss of loved ones and removed from their anticipations all dread of the cheerless charnel house." Cheer was indeed appropriate, for Goodwin's theory reduced death to a virtual nonentity. With the totality of the person passing instantaneously into a higher life at death, the former king of terrors could not claim even the provisional victory which he had enjoyed under older theories of the intermediate state. Death was reduced, in Goodwin's words, to "that point of time . . . [when] the vital forces cease to retain in organized form, the earthly matter which composes the body. This definition sounds as curiously bloodless as Ivan Illich's characterization of twentieth-century medical technicians who regard death as "that point at which the human organism refuses any further input of treatment."[31]

Although Goodwin did not specifically address the issue of the Second Coming, that question was implicitly raised by his discussion of the resurrec-tion. Any theory about the time of the one is, by implication, a statement about the time of the other, because the Bible and subsequent tradition have linked the two events. Hence persons such as Israel Warren, who contended that the so-called "Second Coming" was not a future event but rather a con-tinuing dispensation begun near the outset of the Christian era, likewise en-dorsed a theory of resurrection similar to Goodwin's. At death, each person receives a spiritual body; there is no waiting for the trump of Gabriel. In this hope, Warren found profound comfort, alleviating the terror of death. When Jesus said, "He that liveth and believeth in me shall never die," he did "not mean that the body would not be put off in the ordinary course of nature, but that this would no longer be *death*." That is, the dead "shall pass directly into his presence, without going through that intermediate place." Thus, said

Warren quoting Longfellow, "There is no death; what seems so is transition."
William Urmy, who wrote in defense of Warren's thesis in 1900, drew a similarly consoling conclusion from the theory.

> This, then, is the comfort with which we are "able to comfort them that are
> in any affliction, through the comfort wherewith we ourselves are comforted of
> God" (2 Cor. i,4). We are allowed to tell them that as soon as their bodily eyes
> close on earthly scenes they will open the eyes of their spiritual bodies upon the
> realities and glories of the mansions of the Father's house. Yes, better; they open
> those eyes upon the glory which the Father bestows upon his beloved Son. All
> the resplendent scenes of the glorified state burst upon the enraptured vision; all
> the enchanting harmonies of angelic choirs and the symphonies of the redeemed
> greet the ears of the glorified saint.

For Urmy, as for Warren, the doctrine of resurrection at the moment of expi-
ration was a confirmation of Longfellow's line "There is no death!" Urmy concluded with lines from Allen Walker:

> He is not dead
> Whose good life's labor liveth evermore;
> He is but sped
> To join the noble spirits gone before.
> He is not dead.

The new theory of resurrection and the elimination of the intermediate state
were means of denying that death won any victories, however provisional,
over humanity.[32]

That view also commended itself because it appeared to accommodate
the scientific mentality. To William B. Brown the theory exemplified the principle of natural continuity. "The normal operations of nature," he observed,
"are not spectacular or catastrophic, but quiet, silent, uniform, and without
observation." The traditional notion of a visible return of Christ to revive
dead bodies broke the seamless web of natural law, but the new eschatology
exemplified it. According to the new view, Christ perpetually comes in secret to the hearts of men and women through all generations, and as they die,
they move on to the next stage of life. Resurrection is simply a spiritual body
"rising out of the death of the [physical] body to a higher form of life." It is,
in short, a continuation of the same organic laws of nature visible to the scientist.[33]

The most systematic effort to restate views of death, immortality, and
resurrection in light of modern science came from the prolific pen of
Newman Smyth. The longtime New Haven pastor believed that the Darwin-
ian revolution made this reappraisal especially necessary, and he avowed: "The

next reconstruction of Christian theology will be a vital one; it will result from a deeper knowledge and a truer interpretation of the sacred Scripture of Life, which the hand of God has written in nature. The coming theologian, there-fore,—the next successful defender of the faith once given to the saints,—will be a trained and accomplished biologist." Although he recognized that bio-logical science had much to learn before it could be used as a basis for a definitive apologetic, Smyth thought that a tentative beginning could be made, and on the basis of his own reading in the field and his puttering in the biology labs at Yale, he offered a modest contribution in his 1897 book *The Place of Death in Evolution.*[34]

Looking at the development of life as a whole, Smyth derived a central principle about the place of death in evolution. "Death, with its attendant evils, does not spring up in the path of life as a sudden foe, to turn life back, to frustrate its purpose of good, to mangle the form, to wound the spirit, or to break the heart of nature." Rather death is ever the servant of life, "burying the useless waste, removing the outworn garment, and providing ever-needed nutriment, as life struggles and marches on to its height and joy." Indeed death as we know it probably did not exist among the original single-celled creatures. Death appeared along with the emergence of more complex forms of life, and then its function was to improve the species and to prepare the way for more advanced forms of life. Without death to clear a path, the prog-ess of life would have been balked.[35]

Death was only comprehensible when one remembered the grand pur-pose of evolution. Unlike some (including Darwin himself) who doubted whether evolutionary theory implied teleology, Smyth insisted that it did, and the telos was humanity. "Darwinism, which seemed at first to degrade man, has in reality replaced him upon the throne of creation." Rightly understood, the evolutionary theory resulted in the "exaltation of man as the goal toward which the whole dramatic movement of evolution has tended." Or in the words Smyth borrowed from John Fiske: the human being is "the terminal fact in that stupendous process of evolution whereby things have come to be what they are," and this "fact" possessed immense significance for the ques-tion of death's role in human existence.

> Has not the evolution of life . . . reached in our spiritual being and possibility that kind of existence, that point of perfection, intended from the beginning, in which it has become capable of surviving the death of a body no longer fitted to its use, and of persisting afterwards in some other form and relationship, in which it shall no longer need death or regeneration to help it further on? Or, to put in other phrasing the same thought of death: Has not life in our spiritual nature gone already so far as to have no more need of dying in order that in others beyond us the fulness of life may be attained?

Smyth did not mean, of course, that the physical body would not die or that death was an illusion. But for humans, death was merely the "disentangling" of the spiritual from the physical, since the latter was no longer needed. With the evolution of humanity, death ceased its ministry on behalf of life and received its final discharge. Thus comes to pass the great truth contained in the "Biblical doctrine of the resurrection." Death "shall be swallowed up of life. It will disappear in the abounding life. Death, we are told, shall be no more. Then, at last, when life in its spiritual renewal and power shall have gained the heights of immortality, the ladder may be cast aside up which it has climbed. . . . " The other truth contained in the notion of the resurrection was that "the spirit was made for some embodiment" and "that in some manner, beyond present experience and hence impossible for us now to visualize, our human life is to be continued in its wholeness." But, Smyth emphasized, that did not mean a future revivifying of the physical body. Such a "crude" belief "is as impossible for us now to accept . . . as it would be for us to receive the old Ptolemaic astronomy."[36]

Smyth was well aware that the Bible presented an alternate vision in which death was a curse for sin rather than a natural event. These two views represented different levels of analysis—one scientific and the other moral—but they did not ultimately contradict one another. While sin gave death the added meaning of punishment, "the course of redemption tends gradually to divest death of this moral consequence which it receives from man's fear of it, and to drop it back once more to its primitive place and original function in the benign process of ascending life. In the Christian hope of endless life death loses its acquired character as a curse, and becomes to faith a natural and often happy transition to another and better life. . . . Death to the Christian conscience, becoming natural again, loses fear." Thus in the end, an optimistic version of evolution and the Christian faith yielded similar conclusions: death was but a servant in the ascent of life, and resurrection merely a natural transition to a higher form of spiritual embodiment. Death won no victories in Smyth's cosmos, or as he summed up: "Life, therefore, to the children of the Highest, can have no broken lines. . . . There is nothing really sad, for there is no eternal sorrow in the heart of God."[37]

A publication by the faculty of the Episcopal Theological Seminary, Cambridge, in 1925 summarized the liberal reevaluation of the resurrection: "There is no resurrection of the flesh." The authors regretted that the Christian church had ever allowed itself to espouse "an outworn materialism that demanded flesh and bones." Yet the notion contained a kernel of truth which could not be abandoned in favor of the immortality of the soul. If it were to be a real life, postmortem existence had to have form. An unembodied life was inconceivable. The task of theology was to disengage the doctrine of resurrection from crass materialism and to return to St. Paul's notion of the spiritual body. Such a body was probably "on the borderline of matter and spirit, not exactly matter as we know it through the senses, yet akin to matter and capable of being the alert and efficient instrument of the spirit." In all likelihood, these ethereal bodies even now "interpenetrate" our earthly forms and merely await death to begin their independent career. Happily, modern science had lent credibility to that notion. In its examination of apparitions and other paranormal phenomena, psychic research had demonstrated (at least to the authors' satisfaction) the plausibility of another dimension of reality beyond the material. For these writers, the loss of materialistic ideas about the raising of the dead was really a gain, for now theologians could affirm unambiguously "the spiritual truth which ancient Christians tried to express in a crude fashion": namely, "the survival after death of all that is essential to human personality." On this happy note, they concluded their essay.

> When we recite the words, "I believe in the resurrection of the body," we do not affirm that the flesh we commit to the grave will ever see the light of day again, but we do affirm that the spirit which thus casts aside "the muddy vesture of decay" will survive in the fulness of its powers, clad in a new garment, a suitable medium for self-expression and manifold activity. We proclaim the victory of life over death. And when the harsh and repellent facts of physical experience, the external phenomenon of death, overshadow us with doubt and seem to reduce our loved dead to bodiless abstractions, we cry with the poet:
>
> > Nay—but as when one layeth
> >   His worn-out robes away
> > And taking new ones—sayeth,
> >   "These will I wear to-day,"
> > So putteth by the Spirit
> >   Lightly its garb of flesh,
> > And passeth to inherit
> >   A fairer garb afresh.

In such lines, the traditional sense that a portion of the self was held captive by death—one thinks of Davis Clark's "lonely tenants of the grave"—had vanished entirely.[38]

"The Dying of Death"

These changes were part of a larger cultural phenomenon which James Farrell, borrowing a phrase from a late-nineteenth-century author, calls "the dying of death." By that expression, Farrell means "not the banishment of biological death, but the cultural circumvention of the dread of death." Many influences, in addition to Protestant liberalism, inadvertently conspired to bring about this result. Funeral customs changed. Beginning in the 1830s, the rural cemetery movement sought to make the necropolis a beautiful park to which the living would repair for edification and recreation. In its environs vanished the negative associations of the old graveyard—the place where, in Jonathan Edwards's vivid language, the "ghastly" corpse lay "putrifying and rotting and becoming exceeding loathsome." Funerary art often depicted the dead in lifelike settings, and the topography of the rural cemetery evoked the sense of the sublime, not of the morbid. As one proponent of the new places of interment noted:

> The cemeteries of the present day are places of loveliness. Such they should be. Take Nature's choicest spots; let the fountains murmur and the rivulets sparkle; let the green valley and the shaded hill-top mingle in the scene; bring all along the borders around the quiet home of the dead, for it makes us think of the "green pastures," the "crystal stream," and the fadeless flowers of which we have been told as belong to paradise—that place where the happy dead have gone.

After the Civil War, the lawn cemetery, characterized by inconspicuous markers and open spaces, continued the revolution in burial practice. While the rural cemetery had sentimentalized the home of the dead, the lawn cemetery went a step further and removed the most blatant reminders that the dead were present, but both institutions agreed in making the cemetery a pleasant site, devoid of negative associations. The increasing use of undertakers and funeral parlors served the same end. The unpleasant business of preparing the deceased for burial—formerly a task of the family—could be remanded to the professionals, and the now more common practice of embalming guaranteed that the corpse would appear lifelike rather than "ghastly" when presented for burial. Cremation, though remaining the choice of only a tiny minority of the bereaved, did win greater popularity after the Civil War, and it, too, served to eliminate the reminders of mortality. By a swift sanitary stroke, the body was gone, spared the gruesomeness of decomposition. Cremation was a ritual enactment of John Holmes's dictum that at death it was "as though nothing at all had happened."[39]

In addition to liberal Protestantism, many other religious movements testified to the cultural shift in attitudes toward death. Mormonism, for example, centered its entire theology about the eternal progression of humans toward the status of gods—a process in which death constituted only one of many forward steps. The insignificance of death was further underscored by the fact that marriages and other familial ties would continue unaltered in the afterlife, and thus "we must," wrote Mormon Parley Pratt, "leave death entirely out of the consideration, and look at men and families just as we would look at them if there was no death." A rising tide of spiritualism, usually dated from the spirit rappings of the Fox sisters in the late 1840s, brought similarly reas-suring tidings. Through strange noises, articulate messages, and sometimes materializations, the dead testified that they were indeed close at hand, living in a world similar to the one they had left behind. Mary Baker Eddy, who began the Christian Science movement in the 1870s, took the inconsequentiality of death to its logical extreme: death did not exist and was merely an error of perception. In a somewhat different fashion, Charles T. Russell's followers suggested that death would be a matter of little moment. Expecting the imminent establishment of God's kingdom, the movement believed that saints then living would never taste death, or as Russell's successor, Joseph Rutherford, put it in a memorable aphorism, "Millions now living will never die." They, along with persons raised from the insensibility of death, would live forever on an earth transformed into paradise. The ultimate goal of the redeemed was not, in "Pastor" Russell's words, a heaven radically dissimilar to this world, but a "perfect earthly life in a perfect earthly home." In Russell's scheme, the faithful would either escape death entirely or would experience it as a hiatus in consciousness after which their lives would resume in a familiar (though improved) setting.[40]

Even premillennialists, who in many respects adhered to views preserving the darker contours of eschatology, found ways of softening the importance of death. A prime example was the notion of the rapture, a concept associated with the dispensational brand of premillennialism and which gained wide popularity in conservative Protestant sectors during the late nineteenth century. According to the most common form of that doctrine, the true believers would, before the tribulations near the end of the age, be caught up in the air to meet with Jesus. Transformed instantly into the likeness of his resurrected body, they would never know the terrors of physical dissolution. Since many dispensationalists believed the rapture would probably occur soon, they entertained the hope that death would be for them a nonevent. The Rev. Adoniram J. Gordon of the Clarendon St. Baptist Church, Boston, expressed this dream poignantly:

> Caught up to meet the Lord
> With sweep of angel wing,
> No winding sheet for me, or house of sod!
> O death, where is thy sting?[41]

Given the diverse cultural and religious expressions of "the dying of death," one cannot attribute that trend solely—or even primarily—to Protestant modernism, but liberals did set forth a rationale for the change with a consistency and influence unmatched by other groups. Although Mormons and Christian Scientists may have surpassed the modernists in the thoroughness with which they diminished death, most Americans dismissed the former as marginal people or eccentrics, and their influence was minimal. Spiritualism labored under the same difficulty. It did, to be sure, win the support of numerous prominent Americans and perhaps of hundreds of thousands of the unknown, but it never completely escaped a popular prejudice that it was composed of crackpots and charlatans. In any event, its heyday had already passed by 1875. The effort of the American Society for Psychical Research, founded in 1885, to subject spiritualist claims to careful scrutiny and perhaps to arrive at scientific evidence for the afterlife came ultimately to very little. Despite the interest of men such as William James, the organization never won credentials from the scientific community at large. Premillennialism, dominating a large subculture of conservative Protestantism, came to enjoy a greater influence than the sectarian movements or spiritualism, but unlike some of them, it could never endorse the "dying of death" wholeheartedly. A moderate premillennialist of the stamp of Dwight Moody might take much of the sting out of death by virtually ignoring hell in his preaching and by sometimes depicting heaven as if it were little more than a Victorian home in the skies. Those of more militant dispensational persuasion might dream of a Rapture whose imminence would spare them the pains of death. Yet these persons could never completely affirm the uneventfulness of death. Committed to an infallible Bible, including scriptural warnings that death is the penalty of sin and that hellfire awaits the wicked, they could never forget entirely the darker significance of mortality. Thus it was left to liberalism, from its platform in influential pulpits and seminaries, to enunciate a more consistent theology of "the dying of death." Liberals had thrown off the constraints of biblical inerrancy and had made divine benevolence, evolutionary process, and the moral consciousness of humanity the touchstones of religious truth. Using those tools, they discovered a new way of fulfilling the ancient text: "Death is swallowed up in victory."[42]

The Religion of a Mature Mind

These changes converged in a new understanding of the religious life itself. With hell diminished to insignificance and heaven transformed into a mere enlargement of this life, with eternal life depicted as an arena for the ever deepening realization of the self's longings and death reduced to a minor incident in this progression, it no longer made sense to portray the Christian life as a stark confrontation between terror and joy or time and eternity. An earlier generation of Protestants had believed that the essence of Christian piety consisted in living "as if we were acting our own death-scene, which in reality we are doing." True religion had entailed acting "as if the flaming eye of our divine Judge were now turned full upon us, . . . as if the thunders of eternal retribution were already rolling over our heads." In large sectors of Protestantism, such descriptions of Christian experience sounded increasingly quaint or anachronistic, for in the new vision of human destiny there were neither flaming eyes nor the thunders of eternal retribution. Humanity instead engaged in a life-affirming quest for never-ending self-improvement and for the renovation of this world.[43]

In *The Religion of a Mature Mind* (1902), George Albert Coe, a young professor at Northwestern University and the intellectual mentor of the soon-to-be formed Religious Education Association, gave voice to this outlook.

> [T]his life and the future life are one life. . . . God lives in us, and we live in God; the eternal abides in the temporal, and the temporal in the eternal. . . . When God gives us himself, time, with its modification called death, ceases to be significant. The eternal is already ours, and heaven belongs to us. The heaven that is to be is identical with the kingdom that now is, a community of finite souls progressively realizing their union with one another and with the eternal life of God.

Given that fact, Coe saw "Christian consciousness" moving toward the time when "the supreme question of life will be not, 'Am I saved?' but 'What am I good for?' Not, 'Does God pardon and accept me?' but "How can I contribute most to the progress of the kingdom of God?'. . . . 'What can I learn from this day that will make me more efficient to-morrow?'"[44]

Thus Coe argued that the "old-fashioned revival, . . . such as took place under the preaching of Wesley, Whitefield, Edwards, and Finney" was waning. "How many persons not yet beyond middle life," he asked, "have ever heard sinners groaning with a sense of their undone condition? How many of us have ever known a whole congregation to be seized with terror as the preacher has thundered about sin and its consequences?" The contemporary religious life was "less signalized by emotion. The tragic intensity, the high lights, and the deep shadows of other days are little more than memories cherished by a few of the older members of the churches."[45]

The religious life was to be understood not as the product of a crisis supernaturally wrought but as a process natural to humankind. Throughout the late nineteenth and early twentieth centuries, assertions of the naturalness of the Christian life echoed in liberal Protestant pulpits. In a series of lectures to young men, Theodore Munger argued that "Christianity, in its broadest definition, is simply *the reality of things*. It is a setting forth of the true order of humanity. When a man grasps this secret, he must accept Christianity. He does violence to himself, if he refuses." Washington Gladden said the same thing: "[T]he real gospel truth is, that Christ comes to put us in possession of ourselves,—to help us to drive out the usurping powers of darkness, and to take the rights and dignities that belong to us as men." To suggest that "the Christian life is an unnatural life" or that "in conversion we take on a new and foreign selfhood" was to caricature Christianity. Or as Coe wrote, the claim of the gospel upon each man and woman "is what we are, demanding to express itself, to be fed, to grow. It is as natural and inevitable as our instincts, and what we call submission to it is nothing but self-expression in one of its highest forms."[46]

Notions of the naturalness of the Christian life represented an outworking of ideas first advanced by Horace Bushnell. Written in 1847 and enlarged in 1861, his classic *Christian Nurture* criticized the notion that spiritual regeneration had to occur at an identifiable moment when one renounced his or her sinful past. In Christian homes, parents could instead rear children so that renewal began with the first stirrings of consciousness. A child so nurtured would grow up never remembering a time when he or she was not a Christian. Although Bushnell's view drew on venerable Puritan and Reformed traditions asserting that God included children in the covenant of grace, the theory was novel in its explicit avowal that the regenerate need have no consciousness of ever having been at enmity with God. The development of faith could be a gentle unfolding unmarked by sharp breaks or agonizing stress. There need be no dark shadows prior to light, only gradually increasing luminescence.[47]

Bushnell's approach to Christian nurture reflected his view of the way in which the natural and the supernatural were contempered. In an 1858 work, he argued that human beings lived simultaneously in two orders, theoretically different but in practice intertwined. As denizens of nature, men and women were part of an inflexible chain of causes and effects, but as free moral agents, they—and God—simultaneously inhabited another, more indeterminate domain and had the power to initiate actions reordering the causal sequences of nature in new combinations. This realm of freedom was the supernatural. Despite Bushnell's desire to distinguish the two realms, the impact of his theory was to blur nature and supernature, the divine and the human. To paraphrase the classical Lutheran formula explaining Christ's presence in the Lord's Supper, the supernatural operated in, with, and under nature. The supernatural, in short, indwelt the natural, and this principle of immanence informed Bushnell's understanding of Christian nurture. The spirit of God did not produce Christians by sudden direct influences but by using the laws of normal psychological and social formation. "What higher ground of supernaturalism can be taken," he asked, "than that which supposes a capacity in the Incarnate Word, and Sanctifying Spirit, to penetrate our fallen nature . . . and be a grace of life, traveling outward from the earliest, most latent germ of our human development." Thus the ethos of the home, proper physical care, and sufficient recreation could become means of grace for the maturing child.[48]

By the time Protestant liberalism was at full tide around the turn of the century, Bushnellian notions of nurture and religious development were central features of the movement. William Adams Brown of New York's Union Seminary spoke for a generation of Protestant liberals when he declared in 1906 that "the Christian life, being natural to man, may and normally should begin with the beginnings of conscious experience," and it should continue to grow throughout life. "It is not," he explained, "that conversion has no place in the Christian life, but that its place is too important to be exhausted in a single choice. The true life is a continual turning from the lower to the higher, from sin to God." Liberals, of course, recognized that some people would face dramatic moments of decision, and they were not averse to seeing value in these crises. They tended, however, to explain the moments of storm and stress in terms of natural processes in the life cycle. Research in the psychology of religion by G. Stanley Hall, Edwin D. Starbuck, James H. Leuba, and George A. Coe—all indebted indirectly to Bushnell—related dramatic conversions to natural phenomena such as the onset of puberty. Most liberals hoped that, as the laws of human development were understood and applied, these traumatic instances would recede in importance and in fact had already begun to do so. In their place was a more natural Christian growth, stressing sunnier themes and practical service rather than morbid introspection.[49]

Numerous signs testified that this approach was gaining ground. Sunday School reformers, among them George Coe and the Religious Education Association, lobbied for graded curricula that would nurture children in a fashion appropriate to their ages. The YMCA, without formally abandoning its commitment to the older evangelical piety, increasingly placed heavier emphasis upon libraries and athletics as instruments of Christian growth. In 1905, Elwood Worcester and Samuel McComb inaugurated at the Emmanuel Episcopal Church in Boston what became known as the Emmanuel Movement, spawning imitators in many other cities across the country. The movement attempted to unite medical doctors and ministers in a program of joint therapy stressing upbeat religious counseling. Like liberalism in general, the Emmanuel movement accentuated the natural, gradual growth of Christian faith in the souls of men and women. McComb exemplified one of the deeper propulsions of liberalism when he noted that the goal of Emmanuel's therapy was "to substitute for false or inadequate ideas of God and of His relations to men a conception of His real character as Christ reveals it, until the sufferer feels as if God were a new being, the very embodiment and guarantee of all his better aspirations and ideal longings."[50]

To know the naturalness of faith and its development was to be open to deeper sources of energy or power. As E. Brooks Holifield has observed, Protestant leaders toward the turn of the century "spoke more often about the vitality of human nature—either the force or the will or the dynamism of subconscious impulse. They talked about power and energy, effort and mastery, force of character and boldness of decision, and 'the natural processes of human life.' Indeed, they wrote repeatedly of the 'natural,' and they began to reconceive their idea of nature. . . . Nature was a 'play of forces,' and men and women were 'powers' within that natural dynamism." Thus Samuel McComb wrote of a vast "sleeping psychic energy" which, once tapped, would lift men and women "to new and permanent levels of life and power." Washington Gladden predicted that as Christians understood the naturalness of faith "the kingdom of heaven will come with increasing power." In the same series of lectures in which he extolled Christianity as "simply *the reality of things*," Munger fairly gloried in "muscular Christianity." Drawing upon literary depictions of vitality, he offered images of heroes with blood flowing in their cheeks, hair streaming behind them as they stretched out arms and shouted "in simple exultation of life." To embrace Christianity was to put oneself in tune with powerful life-enhancing forces.[51]

This outlook resonated with the new eschatological ideas of Protestant liberalism. Life, whether here or in the age to come, was a continual becoming, a limitless process of attaining ever greater self-realization, fulfillment, and power. To this conclusion, the new views of prophecy, the Kingdom of God, heaven, hell, death, and the religious life itself all tended.

3

"A Summary Court in Perpetual Session"

✧◈✧

NEAR THE END OF *An Outline of Christian Theology,* William Newton Clarke
contrasted the older Protestant eschatology with the new views of liberal theology. Under the former conception, said Clarke, people might anticipate a
finite period of "moral strain." Once death or the return of Christ concluded
their probation, they would then enjoy "endless release from pressure and responsibility," but according to the emerging liberal conception, the future
promised an eternity "as real, active, intense, responsible, and full of solemn
meaning as the present." The last things, in short, were not so much the definitive end of time as a never-ending process. Clarke preached this message
as a liberating one, bringing reassurance that human possibilities for mastery
of the future and for self-fulfillment were unbounded. How could it be otherwise, since God had decreed that time would follow benevolent, rational principles that humans could learn and use? Clarke voiced the assumptions of
people who believed time was on their side. Indeed time to them appeared to
be without end, and therefore they had an infinite measure of it within which
to work their will.[1]

Yet one might read other less sanguine meanings in Clarke's lines. An
endless time "as real, active, intense, responsible, and full of solemn meaning
as the present" might be, as Franz Kafka put it, "in reality . . . a summary
court in perpetual session." With the tribunal continuously sitting, there
could be no single moment of reckoning, no point at which the trial would
be declared over and the defendant finally vindicated or condemned. If this
view gave people endless chances to reverse a negative verdict, it also afforded
infinite possibilities to forfeit a favorable one. Unlimited time posed unlimited
burdens as well as unlimited possibilities.[2]

Psychologically as well as theoretically, the new eschatology also prevented
closure. The older pictures of hell or a terrible day of wrath and the frank
acknowledgment of death's hideousness, having been banished, no longer provided the images whereby the problem of radical evil could be symbolized and

resolved. How could these perennial problems be handled by a theology that only dimly acknowledged them? What Karen Halttunen has written of the macabre horror stories and the sensationalist treatments of violent crime that have flourished in the modern world offers a suggestive parallel:

> The modern cult of horror thus does not explain evil so much as it captures the raw experience of evil in a liberal humanitarian culture which offers no consistent and intellectually satisfying explanation of it.
>
> This is why, in the modern cult of horror, evil tends first to hide and to leap out at us: it is by nature the bogey under the bed, the dismembered corpse beneath the floorboards in Poe's "The Tell-Tale Heart," the mummy of Norman Bates's mother stowed in the fruit cellar in Alfred Hitchcock's *Psycho*.

Evil comes as the "monstrous moral alien" which cannot be incorporated into the prevailing culture; and because it cannot be assimilated, "horror returns, it moves in an endless loop, it fails to satisfy intellectually, because liberal humanitarianism offers no way of articulating or transcending major acts of human transgression."[3]

Similarly, in the late nineteenth century, the blood, the chaos, and the terror of the Apocalypse—all of those elements that had been suppressed in the new eschatology—leapt out like the bogey from under the bed. Moderate and liberal theologies might not provide a satisfactory outlet for such fears and longings, but popular literature with its dystopic and utopian visions certainly did. So also did premillennialism, which enjoyed a powerful resurgence in conservative sectors of Protestantism after 1875. It was as if ideas of a cataclysmic End, denied adequate symbolization in the emerging theology of liberal Protestantism, migrated elsewhere from whence they periodically erupted.

These developments left liberal eschatology caught in the endless loop. With no way of explaining or encompassing the evil their eschatology had banished to the corner of the universe, they had to work at a more frenetic pace to demonstrate that the terrors of time could be rationally controlled and managed. To make this observation is not to suggest that the optimism of the new eschatology was unreal. It was quite genuine, but it was also driven by nagging anxieties and fears which, since they could not be fully acknowledged or explained by liberal humanitarianism, tinged that hope with a nervous activism and urgency. Owen Chadwick's assessment of the spiritual crisis of Victorian England applies equally to the condition of liberal Protestants in America. "Within this earnestness was the haste of beleaguered men. Though Christians felt assured of their safety, they could hear wolves prowling in the undergrowth and built their protective hedges a little higher."[4]

This drama was not, of course, played out in an historical vacuum. It occurred in the midst of massive social, political, and economic transformations fundamentally altering the character of American life. To examine these changes is to understand the cultural meaning of the new eschatology and to probe sources of the often frenzied activism of Protestantism.

The Divided Mind of the Gilded Age

Not the least of the revolutions in American life were the extraordinary triumphs of technology and industry. The national economy, fueled by technological innovations and the mobilization of capital via newly formed corporations, grew dramatically and provided an increased prosperity for a significant portion of the American people. Almost every statistical measure attested dynamic growth. The rail system, including 30,000 miles of track in 1860, grew to 193,000 miles in 1900; the production of steel doubled between 1889 and 1900; and the gross national product increased nearly eight-fold from the mid-1880s to 1919. One of the best symbols of the age was the Corliss engine at the centennial exhibition at Philadelphia in 1876. This "beneficent Titan," as one observer called it, had two massive cylinders which powered 8,000 other machines and thus bespoke the restless energy of American enterprise. Writing in the *Atlantic Monthly* of his encounter with the Corliss Engine, William Dean Howells was moved by the "vast and almost silent grandeur" of the machine. He pictured the engineer sitting in the midst of "this ineffably strong mechanism" and "reading his newspaper, as in a peaceful bower." Although Howells expressed fleeting concern that this technological behemoth could "crush . . . [the engineer] past all semblance of humanity with his slightest touch," his primary emotion was patriotic enthusiasm for "the glorious triumphs of skill and invention." "Wherever else," he added, "the national bird is mute in one's breast, here he cannot fail to utter his pride and content."[5]

Another symbol of the age, a symbol that also traded on promised contentment, was the department store. Merchant princes such as John Wanamaker, Marshall Field, and Edward Filene recognized that the extraordinary productivity of the American economy counted for nothing unless men and women could be enticed to purchase the goods that industry had produced. Through magnificent displays of color, light, and glass showcasing their wares, these merchants created a vision of an alluring fantasy world. It was appropriate that L. Frank Baum, author of *The Wonderful Wizard of Oz* and that tale's glittering Emerald City, was an authority on department store displays, for merchants and advertisers were selling dreams of perfect contentment. As William Leach has written, "American corporate business," of which he sees the department store as a prime instrument, had begun "the transformation of American society into a society preoccupied with consumption, with comfort and bodily well-being, with luxury, spending, and acquisition, with more goods this year than last, more next year that this." In so doing, the department store symbolized the creation of "a future-oriented culture of desire"—a culture, in short, in quest of the Emerald City.[6]

In their foreign relations, Americans found similar reasons for confidence. After its fratricidal war, a reunited nation suppressed the last Native American uprisings and, still protected by the broad expanse of two oceans, enjoyed thirty-three years of unbroken peace with nations beyond its borders. When the United States did take up arms against Spain in 1898 in what Secretary of State Hay called "a splendid little war," it won an astonishingly swift victory, spilled relatively little blood, wrested control of the Philippines and Puerto Rico, and thus established itself as a world power with far-flung domains.[7]

Yet American culture after the Civil War exhibited numerous signs of fear as well as of complacent optimism. One of the tokens was the apparent prevalence of a newly named ailment, neurasthenia. Literally "nerve weakness," neurasthenia was popularized as a peculiarly American disease in *American Nervousness: Its Causes and Consequences* (1881) by neurologist George M. Beard. The symptoms of the illness might include indigestion, sleeplessness, morbid thoughts, sexual dysfunction, lassitude, excessive irritability, or diffuse pains. It could manifest itself as a fear of open spaces or of closed ones, as hay fever or in spastic muscle movements, as hysteria or nearsightedness. This grab bag of symptoms derived, said Beard, from a lack of adequate "nerve-force." He assumed that the nervous system contained a limited supply of energy, and whenever overtaxed, like an electrical circuit whose lights grew dim when too many bulbs were plugged in, the weakened nerve system could not support its various activities.[8]

Neurasthenia was important not only because so many important figures suffered from it—William James and Theodore Roosevelt come to mind—but also because people believed that modern American culture was especially conducive to the disease. Beard contended that only the most civilized and modernized societies suffered from it. It derived from assaults on the nervous system such as overspecialization of work, the necessity of punctuality imposed by omnipresent clocks and watches, the noise of the railroads, the angst created by political liberty, and the excitement of Protestant revivalism and propensity for religious schism. In a word, neurasthenia derived from the same sources as America's greatness. It was simultaneously a badge of national honor or exceptionalism and a fearful warning of the precariousness of that grandeur. "All our civilization," warned Beard, "hangs by a thread."[9]

Part of this anxiety derived from the unease many Americans felt with the new shape of their economy. As the percentage of wage earners increased, the older work ethic, predicated upon the attainment of self-employment as the path to independence and mobility, seemed less credible. Likewise that ethic's stress on productive labor and its fear of leisure as a threat to character slipped out of sync with the realities of an economy requiring consumption as much as work. The regimen imposed by modern corporate culture, with its office duties for the white-collar employees and its dreary factories for the blue collar, appeared stifling. Along with William James, many feared that life was being desiccated or, in the words of a recent scholar, that it was becoming "weightless," unreal, and cut off from sources of vitality. Henry Adams supplied another, now classic, metaphor. The dynamo symbolized the age, and the machine ran humanity, not humanity the machine. America's mechanized civilization, its energies dissipating, exemplified the second law of thermodynamics—the principle of entropy.[10]

Fears of national decay also reflected the social and economic turmoil within the United States. Despite rising economic productivity during the Gilded Age as a whole, wealth was very unequally distributed. In 1890, 1 percent of families owned slightly over half the property of the nation, while the more than 44 percent at the bottom of the economic ladder claimed only 1.2 percent of the wealth. Even those comprising the broad middle classes, themselves about 44 percent of all families, could claim only 12 to 13 percent of the national wealth. Moreover, periods of recession, of which there were several severe and prolonged instances in the thirty-five years following the Civil War, made the position of the working classes and even of some in the middle classes precarious. Workers in the 1870s and 1880s began unionizing in greater numbers to demand eight-hour work days and better pay—and in some instances, simply to resist the reduction of wages. Hundreds of strikes took place throughout the era, and certain years were marked by especial unrest. In 1877, a nationwide rail strike paralyzed transportation and provoked federal intervention. In the spring of 1886, a labor strike in Chicago turned bloody. After the police harassed strikers and killed several, protesters gathered in Haymarket Square on the evening of May 4. When the police ordered the crowd to disperse, someone threw a bomb, killing seven officers. The police opened fire on the crowd, and four more persons died. Within several weeks eight anarchists were arrested on flimsy evidence, and by August a jury had convicted all eight defendants. In 1892, management broke a steel strike at Andrew Carnegie's plant in Homestead, Pennsylvania, by bringing in "scab" laborers and by summoning a private police force of Pinkerton agents to suppress the strikers. Then in 1894, George Pullman, the mogul of the railroad sleeper-car industry, faced rebellion among his workers in Chicago, and President Cleveland sent in troops to restore order. Farmers, especially in the west and south, were also restive. Heavy indebtedness to banks, overcharging by railroad companies, and falling crop prices prompted agrarian revolt. First through Granges and later through cooperative farmers' alliances, agrarians sought to alter a system that they believed kept them in economic bondage.[11]

These frustrations entered the political arena through a series of third parties. The Greenback Party and later the People's Party (commonly called the Populist Party), along with several minor labor parties, assaulted the tight money policies that they viewed as the instrument by which the moneyed classes, personified by Wall Street, oppressed them. Although many of the proposed reforms—for example, the popular election of U.S. senators—later became law, most middle- and upper-class Americans viewed these groups as dangerous fanatics threatening the very existence of the nation itself.[12]

The immigrant origins of many workers added a nativist twist to the fears of radicalism. With immigration patterns shifting toward eastern and southern Europe and with many of these newcomers joining the industrial proletariat, many in the middle classes feared that the nation's lower orders were being infiltrated with people whose alien ways made them unsympathetic to American institutions. Even when the newest Americans escaped identification as political incendiaries, they were often disdained as pawns of the political machines despised by the genteel. Yet perhaps more significant than the fears that the foreign born were the agents of radicals or of hack politicians was the simple fact that the immigrants were here and that there were so many of them—nearly nine million came between 1880 and 1900. By numbers alone, they threatened to overthrow the cultural hegemony of the old-line Protestant middle classes. Newcomers were not the only objects of fear. As federal troops withdrew from the South, the Reconstruction state governments fell to white "Redeemers," and blacks descended into new forms of bondage. Stripped of voting rights, subject to newly created systems of segregation, they were terrorized by the burning crosses, epidemic lynching, and mutilation practiced by the Ku Klux Klan and similar groups. In this environment, Anglo-Saxonism or Teutonism became an intellectually fashionable ideology. Scholars stressed the superiority of the people and institutions of Germanic and British origins, associated the strength of America with that heritage, and buttressed the argument with appeals to pseudo-Darwinian racialist theories of the survival of the fittest. At first glance a smug assertion of the supremacy of old-line Protestant Americans, the new racialism was in fact the desperate cry of people who feared that they were about to lose control of their country and were determined to preserve "race purity" at all costs. It signified a massive loss of confidence in the ability of the nation to assimilate the foreign born and prefigured the immigration restriction legislation that the U.S. Congress later passed in 1924.[13]

Political upheaval on the farms notwithstanding, these anxieties converged with especial force on the cities. In the sprawling and rapidly growing urban areas, the new immigrants congregated in large numbers, labor unrest was most visible, and political machines flourished. These, along with the cities' saloons, red-light districts, and rowdy neighborhoods, symbolized a massive assault on moral order as understood by the middle classes. "There is no denying," wrote the British observer Lord Bryce, "that the government of the cities is the one conspicuous failure of the United States." The judgment was one shared by many Americans themselves. For years, Paul Boyer notes, Protestant moralists had engaged in "formulaic cluck-clucking over the city as a menace to personal virtue," but in the Gilded Age that concern expanded into an "intense and growing fear over the threat urbanization posed to society itself."[14]

Uncertainty regarding gender roles also provoked uneasiness. In the early nineteenth century, ideal images of men and women had been codified into an ideology of separate spheres. Males, supposedly more suited to conflict and more given to rationality, were to compete in the rough and tumble of the economic realm to win a living for their families. Women, who had an innate inclination to more refined and spiritual matters, found their callings as mothers and wives. Theirs was the task of creating a private haven in the midst of the world's hurly-burly, to reproduce something of the Garden of Eden in a fallen world, and thereby to provide a redemptive moral balance against the harsher realities of the public or male-dominated realm. The actual lives of women, of course, never fully embodied the ideal. Its translation into experience was often problematic among women in the working class, for African American or immigrant women, and for those who labored on farms or the frontier. Even among the urban middle classes, where the ideology had its greatest strength, women often subverted it. In the name of pious benevolence (a cause deemed eminently suitable for women), they ran charitable agencies, lobbied politicians, and sometimes claimed their role as moral housekeepers of the nation as a warrant for demanding major changes in the social order. Yet despite inconsistencies and evasions, the theory of separate spheres provided a measure of stable identity to women and men. Events in the post–Civil War era put this security at risk.[15]

Although far from achieving anything close to parity with men, many women moved beyond home in more visible ways. Between 1890 and 1910, the number of women enrolled in college doubled. The number of employed females increased nearly twofold in the twenty years after 1880, and by 1910 nearly a quarter of all American women had a place in the job force—a figure 10 percent higher than in 1880. The character of the employment also changed. In the 1870s service as domestic help constituted the chief occupation for working women, but during the following half century, women in increasing numbers became clerks, secretaries, salespersons, nurses, and teachers. Moreover, women moved into the public sphere through groups such as the Women's Christian Temperance Union (WCTU), founded in 1873. Using the rubric "home protection," the group's second president, France Willard, tied the WCTU to traditional notions of women's proper role even as she maneuvered the organization into advocacy of women's suffrage as well as temperance. Women's clubs, boasting at least a million members by 1915, provided an opportunity for cultural improvement and, for some, afforded a staging ground for forays into civic reform. Beyond these subtle subversions of the feminine role were the more overt challenges offered by radical suffragists such as Elizabeth Cady Stanton. Underscoring the apparent threat posed by these developments were hard statistics. Divorce increased eightfold between 1860 and 1900, the birth rate among old-line Anglo-Saxon Protestants was falling, and college-educated women were demonstrably less likely to marry than were their noncollegiate sisters. All of this occurred as immigrant peoples, mostly non-Protestant, poured into America at a dramatic pace. With the old-stock Protestant homes in apparent disarray and producing fewer children, disordered gender roles appeared to be the path to the loss of Protestant hegemony in America.[16]

The uneasiness of middle-class men about their own roles exacerbated the dilemma. In a "corporatized and bureaucratized world," asks Peter Filene, "what could a man measure as his own achievement . . . ? As a corporate employee, even at the lower executive level, he lost touch with the product of his work. He put his hands only on the typewriter, the account books, the documents—on the process that created somewhere else, a corporate product." Perhaps in search of a lost sense of masculine autonomy, men entered lodges and secret fraternal organizations by the hundreds of thousands, thus making the last third of the nineteenth century the golden age of these societies. Around 1900, over five million men were enrolled in groups such as the Masons, the Odd Fellows, the Improved Order of Red Men, the Scottish Rite, or (for Union veterans) the Grand Army of the Republic. The growth of these bodies is especially noteworthy in view of the hefty sums members had to pay for initiation, continuing membership, and costumes used in the societies' elaborate rituals. Those rituals said much about the appeal of the secret lodge movement. Amid images of angry fathers, sin, blood, vengeance, darkness, and wastelands, the initiate was often ceremonially "killed"—or at least threatened with death—as part of a rebirth to a new identity. Despite the obvious components of sheer playfulness in these rites, they freighted important symbolic meanings. As men gathered in lodges—away from women, their jobs, and perhaps also away from a liberalizing Protestantism that had increasingly less use for images of sin, blood, and vengeance—they reconnected with more elemental (and patriarchal) understandings of masculinity.[17]

The desire to reclaim a more vital and aggressive understanding of masculinity also appeared in the cult of the strenuous life. By the 1890s, American culture increasingly glorified muscular exertion or frenetic activism. Camping trips in the wild, a mania for sports, and praise of conflict and military virtues were all in vogue. Perhaps the best symbol of the age was an eastern "dude" and former neurasthenic who turned cowboy, then Rough Rider, and who as President Theodore Roosevelt transformed the White House into a dynamo of energy. In an address to the Hamilton Club of Chicago on April 10, 1899, shortly after he had become a war hero, then Governor Roosevelt disclosed the inner logic of the call to the strenuous life.

> In the last analysis a healthy state can exist only when the men and women who make it up lead clean, vigorous, healthy lives. . . . The man must be glad to do a man's work, to dare and endure and to labor; to keep himself, and to keep those dependent upon him. The woman must be the housewife, the helpmeet of the homemaker, the wise and fearless mother of many healthy children. . . . When men fear work or fear righteous war, when women fear motherhood, they tremble on the brink of doom; and well it is that they should vanish from the earth, where they are fit subjects for the scorn of all men and women. . . .

In short, the strenuous life and the reaffirmation of women's "traditional" roles were also confessions of fear that America might be too enervated, too neurasthenic to maintain its glory. Failure to rise to the challenge would prove that the "nation is rotten to the heart's core," and "then the bolder and stronger peoples will pass us by, and win for themselves the domination of the world." Roosevelt's linkage of images of virile men and dependent women with forebodings of unspecified "bolder and stronger peoples" suggests the complexity of the anxieties felt by many Americans in the late nineteenth century. Overlapping and reinforcing one another, fears about gender, class, race, and cultural hegemony coalesced in a determination that Protestant civilization be protected—and extended—at all costs.[18]

Visions of the End

In this setting, prophetic voices spoke alternately and often extravagantly of both hope and doom. In 1879, the journalist Henry George published *Progress and Poverty*, which sold over two million copies by the end of the century. As its title suggested, the book probed the scandal of persistent poverty in a society of increasing wealth. George attributed the anomaly to a fundamental economic injustice: the owners of land were not taxed according to the value of their property. The enactment of a "single tax" on land would promote equity and prosperity for all classes. The appeal of *Progress and Poverty* lay partly in the simplicity of its economic analysis, but also in its fervent moralism and its evocation of apocalyptic images of destruction and rebirth. Christian civilization stood at a moment of truth. "Christianity is not simply clearing itself of superstitions," George warned, "but in the popular mind it is dying at the root, as the old paganisms were dying when Christianity entered the world. And nothing arises to take its place. . . . The civilized world is trembling on the verge of a great movement. Either it must leap upward, which will open the way to advances yet undreamed of, or it must be a plunge downward, which will carry us back toward barbarism." The single tax offered to avert the abyss and bring to pass "the Golden Age of which poets have sung." Such a time would fulfill "the glorious vision which has always haunted man with gleams of fitful splendor. It is what he saw whose eyes at Patmos were closed in a trance. It is the culmination of Christianity—the City of God on earth, with its walls of jasper and its gates of pearl! It is the reign of the Prince of Peace!"[19]

Images of cataclysm and golden age recurred frequently in literature. In 1889, Mark Twain's *A Connecticut Yankee in King Arthur's Court* provided a classic, if oblique and sometimes contradictory, commentary on the age. Transported back to the middle ages, the novel's protagonist—a foreman in a gun factory—sets about introducing medieval folk to the glories of nineteenth-century technology. In Arthurian England, Hank Morgan creates schools, telephones, newspapers, and factories. But to defend progress against reactionary forces, the Connecticut Yankee also constructs Gatling guns, slaughters opponents, and at the end of the tale is trapped in his own fortress behind a wall of corpses. Unlike Twain, Ignatius Donnelly placed fictional characters in the future rather than the past and portrayed destruction on an even grander scale. *Caesar's Column* (1891), set in the late twentieth century, described an America where technological wonders wrung from the misery of the masses confer opulence on a few. After the "Brotherhood of Destruction" brings the system to a bloody end, a handful of survivors found utopia in Africa. Other futuristic fiction was often far cheerier. Edward Bellamy's immensely popular *Looking Backward* (1888) told of Julian West, a young Bostonian, who, falling into a hypnotic trance in 1887, awakes in the year 2000 to discover a society from which discords have vanished. All citizens spend a term of service in an industrial army providing abundant goods for everyone, leisure and consumption are the chief pursuits of life, and efficient technocrats keep the system running smoothly. To West, that order seems "the new heavens and the new earth wherein dwelleth righteousness." Yet even in *Looking Backward,* the hope of a coming golden age derives its power from its implicit contrast to the darkness of the late nineteenth century—a time when, in the words of Julian West, "humanity [was] hanging on the cross."[20]

Political movements sometimes echoed this rhetoric. The revolt of western and southern farmers against economic peonage in the 1880s and '90s became something more than a list of grievances or an agenda for political reform. It offered redemption to an America rapidly sliding toward disaster. When the People's Party composed its first national platform in 1892, the preamble, written by Ignatius Donnelly, opened with a description of unprecedented crisis: "We meet in the midst of a nation brought to the verge of moral, political, and material ruin." A year later a populist newspaper in Atlanta, Georgia, described the Populist Party in light of the final cosmic upheaval—the Battle of Armageddon—when "unrighteous mammon" would perish and the poor be vindicated. Nineteen years later another leader of a third party movement invoked the same biblical image. Bolting the Republicans to lead the Progressive Party in 1912, former President Theodore Roosevelt declared: "We stand at Armageddon, and we battle for the Lord."[21]

Among explicitly religious movements, none invoked the sense of cosmic End and rebirth more consistently than premillennialism. From the early 1870s until his death in 1916, Charles Taze Russell and his adherents built a following around that theme. Flailing the inequities of society with as much fervor as a Marxist, Russell indicted all existing institutions—business, labor, government, and churches. No earthly agency could arrest certain destruction, but soon Christ would return to create paradise on earth. Although Protestant leaders could dismiss Russellites as an heretical fringe group, the premillennial message was not limited to sectarians. After the mid-1870s, that eschatology gained new prominence within major denominations, initially through Bible and prophecy conferences and later through a growing network of Bible institutes and publications. Like Russell, these premillennialists insisted that the present age was growing worse and that nothing save the supernatural Advent of Jesus could inaugurate a better world. To be sure, they did not always press this view consistently and on occasion sounded more hopeful of earthly progress than their theology seemed to warrant, but whenever they spoke the millenarian vocabulary, images of doom were seldom absent.[22]

Premillennialists claimed to expect disasters because of their interpretation of the Bible, but they were not unaffected by contemporary portents of decline and catastrophe. Several months after the disaster in Haymarket Square, the International Prophetic Conference convened in Chicago. Voicing pervasive and nearly hysteric fear of radicalism, Baptist millenarian A. J. Frost from California asked: "What mean these seething, surging, rioting masses of the dangerous classes of the ground tier? What mean these armies marching and countermarching with banners on which are emblazoned dynamite, anarchism, nihilism? What means this ominous tramp of gathering legions? What mean these lowering clouds, dark and tempestuous, all around the horizon?" To Frost the meaning was self-evident in the "sure word of prophecy." The world's last night had come.[23]

Premillennialism's power came in part from its ability to make sense of a discordant age. For those who adhered to the scheme, it brought profound comfort. They knew that history, far from being a series of haphazard or adventitious events, was God's plan moving toward God's predetermined goal. Discerning their place in that plan, they knew their lives to be related to an End that human machinations could not foil. Thus William L. Pettingill of the Philadelphia School of the Bible declared in 1919:

> It is a great thing to know that everything is going according to God's schedule. It is a great thing to know that the purpose of God is not thwarted, is not set aside. Is it not a fine thing that He tells us beforehand all about it? We are not surprised at the present collapse of civilization; the Word of God told us all about it. We are not surprised that everything in this old world is in a state of flux today; that nothing is fixed; that the whole world is in unrest. . . . We are not looking for progress where God told us we should see collapse. We are not surprised at things as we see them; we are on the train and we are moving along the tracks, and we are on time, and we know where we get off![24]

Premillennialists knew where they were getting off the train of history, but they also had a goal for the meantime: to live holy lives free from the burden of sin and anxiety. In stressing holiness, millenarians adopted an ideal already widely suffused through evangelical piety and hymnody in the post–Civil War era, but they did so in the new vocabulary coined by the Keswick Movement. That movement grew out of a series of meetings organized in England by Americans William Boardman and Hannah Whittall Smith and her husband Robert Pearsall Smith in 1873. Designed to promote holiness, the meetings drew an enthusiastic response, prompting the holding after 1875 of a regular conference at Keswick in England's Lake District. Under the influence of Anglican clergyman H. W. Webb-Peploe, Keswick teaching evolved into a distinctly non-Wesleyan form of perfectionism. Webb-Peploe stressed that Christians might triumph over all known sins, but he rejected what he believed to be the teaching of many Methodist interpreters: namely, that the innate sinfulness of human nature could be eradicated in this life. Men and women, said the Keswick teachers, remained liable to sin all their days, but if they yielded themselves to Christ, his grace would counteract their sinful nature, give them victory over sin, and empower them for greater Christian service—as long as they maintained the posture of surrender.

Keswick ideas spread to the United States in the 1890s through speakers at Dwight L. Moody's summer conferences at Northfield, Massachusetts. Some premillennial participants at Northfield had initial reservations about Keswick, for most came from Reformed backgrounds where perfectionism was a highly suspect doctrine. But soon the vast majority of millenarians accepted Keswick—or some variation of it—and leading watchers for the Second Coming such as C. I. Scofield, Reuben Torrey, A. B. Simpson, A. T. Pierson, and A. J. Gordon made holiness a central part of their teaching. In fact premillennialism and Keswick ideals became virtually coextensive in most quarters. Charles Trumbull, who edited *The Sunday School Times* and had experienced the victory over sin during a youth conference at Westminister College (Pa.) in 1910, used the pages of his journal to propagate the ideas of the Keswick Movement and in 1913 organized the Victorious Life Testimony. After holding meetings for a number of years in various cities, Trumbull's movement selected a permanent home, appropriately named Keswick Grove, New Jersey. Trumbull summed up the Victorious Life message succinctly: "It is the privilege of every Christian to live every day of his life without breaking the laws of God in known sin either in thought, word, or deed."[25]

At first glance, millenarianism and the victorious life may appear to have been a theological odd couple. The former taught that the world, fatally corrupted, hurtled downward toward unavoidable cataclysm; the latter professed that Christians might, by the power of the Holy Spirit, experience an immediate and total victory over sin. Perfectionist ideals would appear more consonant with the kingdom-building optimism of postmillennialism. In fact, in the antebellum period the two ideas had surged forward together. Yet the marriage of Keswick and premillennialism was not so strange as it might seem. From the beginning, millenarians affirmed a high doctrine of the Holy Spirit and recognized that the Bible frequently connected the outpouring of the Spirit with the latter days. Was it not therefore to be expected that in these latter days, the Spirit would empower women and men to live more thoroughly consecrated, holy lives? Moreover, both premillennialism and the victorious life envisioned victory—whether the triumph of the individual over sin or Christ's triumph in history—in similar terms. In neither case did victory come from the natural development of capacities inherent in humanity or from some force resident in history. Success came from outside of mundane time by the supernatural power of God. Charles Trumbull made the connection explicit: "If we cannot, by muscular power, help Christ to catch us up to meet him at his coming, neither can we while we await his coming help him to set us free or keep us free from the power of sin. It is *all* his work, and exclusively his." That work was the work of one who intruded from eternity into time in order to redeem it, or as Trumbull explained:

How then can Christ really lift us out of our past and enable us to live as though there had been no past sin in our life? Here is the answer: Christ makes himself our life, literally our life. Christ's life is from everlasting to everlasting; it has no beginning and it has no ending. He has no past nor future, he lives in a timeless eternity. Then when you let the Lord Jesus Christ make himself wholly your life, so that it is no longer you that live but Christ liveth in you, he is as completely your past as he is your present and future; he is from everlasting to everlasting, and you have the life that is not a matter of mere eternal duration, but an absolutely new *kind* of life, filling your whole being.

In short, both premillennialism and the victorious life theology assumed that time was bounded by the purpose of a God who gave it a definitive End beyond itself and who could now, for the saint individually, and in the future, for the saints collectively, interpose his power to bring the consummation.[26]

Premillennialism and the victorious life addressed the cultural dilemmas of Protestants in the late nineteenth century. For a people uncertain of their vitality, the perfectionist message was "power-giving." Christ himself would take fragile selves, make them literally his own, and thus enable the anxiety- or guilt-ridden to transcend burdens effortlessly. "All I had to do," testified a business executive at a Victorious Life conference, "was to use the common sense which he [God] gave me, and then stand back and marvel at what he was going to do, and is doing. God has given me great responsibilities, but I would be almost ashamed to tell the stockholders and directors of our company how little I have thought of the place since I came here." Although the Victorious Life rested on different theological assumptions than Christian Science or Mind Cure, it addressed the same fears and perhaps much of the same constituency. To troubled souls, it offered a similar assurance: those who opened themselves to the divine would be empowered to live triumphantly or successfully despite their myriad temptations and responsibilities. What perfectionism promised individually, premillennialism offered collectively. God would soon subject a disordered world to his own supernaturally imposed order. By identifying themselves with that order, premillennialists might vicariously attain control. Their eschatology, Douglas W. Frank has written, gave millenarians, "a line on the future, and that line allowed them to place under their own intellectual or spiritual control every event that might transpire in the last days."[27]

The Kingdom and "the Methods Demanded by Modern Civilization"

But what of those who had abandoned the hope of supernatural intervention or who had collapsed it into theories of God's immanence? How might they who awaited the kingdom but not the literal return of Christ assert control over a discordant age? The writings of Josiah Strong provide a clue to the path they took. At the age of thirty-eight, this Congregationalist minister achieved renown in Protestant circles for his book, *Our Country: Its Possible Future and Its Present Crisis* (1885). By the time a slightly revised version appeared in 1891, 130,000 copies of the original edition were already in circulation, and prominent newspapers had serialized major portions of it. Strong wrote the book on behalf of the American Home Missionary Society, and the work resonated with themes long familiar to readers of the society's literature. America needed a Christian citizenry, Strong insisted, in order to sustain democracy, but major obstacles—for example, the traditional bugbears of Mormonism, Catholicism, and intemperance—imperiled the nation's Christian character. The stakes were, however, broader than the fate of a single nation, for God had destined America to become "God's right arm in his battle with the world's ignorance and oppression and sin." Therefore, said Strong, "our plea is not America for America's sake; but America for the world's sake." *Our Country* employed an often-used Protestant strategy. Linking piety and patriotism, it limned a potentially glorious American destiny, played on fears that this future was at risk, and then channeled anxiety into renewed moral dedication.[28]

Yet *Our Country* was more than a set piece rehashing antebellum themes. Strong was acutely aware that Protestantism confronted *new* as well as old problems: the growth of the cities and industries, the disparities between rich and poor, the monotony of mechanicalized labor, the inability of wage earners to rise into the ranks of entrepreneurs. Strong also analyzed problems in a fashion different from the older literature. While he sometimes used dramatic anecdotal illustrations common in older appeals, the bulk of his argument was carried by statistical information drawn from the census and from expert researchers. In his closing chapter, "Money and the Kingdom," he suggested that cultivation of sacrificial and *systematic* giving by Protestants held the key to bringing in the kingdom. Strong was intimating, though he did not say so explicitly, that a new social order required a new strategy to bring in the kingdom.[29]

In his next book, *The New Era* (1893), Strong expanded those hints. Undergirding his argument was the new theology of the kingdom emphasizing the realities of this world. The kingdom, said Strong, "does not mean the abode of the blessed dead, but a kingdom of righteousness which he [Christ] came to establish on earth." Abandoning the false distinction between secular and sacred, the church would discover that it must use secular instrumentalities as well as religious ones to achieve its ends. Once the church "employs the methods demanded by modern civilization, she will mightily hasten the millennium." Or as he explained in another passage, "Science, which is a revelation of God's laws and methods, enables us to fall into his [God's] plans intentionally and to co-operate with him intelligently for the perfecting of mankind, thus hastening forward the coming of the Kingdom." In particular, Strong urged that Christians make use of the advances in statistical science and called upon the churches, now "shattered into scores of fragments," to learn ways of cooperating more effectively. As moral passion, wedded to efficient religious structures and professional expertise, "rules the organized life of men, social wrongs will disappear, the strife of classes and of races will cease, and wars will be no more."[30]

One is tempted to call Strong's program an instrument of secularization, and the assessment is correct, though only partially so. He indeed redirected greater attention to the things of this world than did many of his Protestant predecessors, but his intent was to sacralize the secular, to take its manifold complexities and to infuse them with religious significance. Strong manifested what Richard Wightman Fox has recently called one of liberal Protestantism's most salient traits: its ability "to convey a pervasive aura of spiritual and cultural unity, while laying down a broad welcome mat to an array of secular and religious forces." To such liberals, Fox adds, "the merger of religion and secularism was not so much the joining of two distinct institutional or intellectual forces but a deepening of 'immanentization'—for want of a better word to describe the embrace of the world as the prime location of salvation."[31]

In its restless search for new institutions and professional skills to embody the ideals of the kingdom, Strong's own career exhibited the "embrace of the world as the prime location of salvation." He served as General Secretary of the Evangelical Alliance after 1886, but finding its vision too limited, he left in 1898 to establish the League for Social Service. While acting in the latter capacity, he was asked to prepare a report for the Paris Exhibition of 1900. Published as *Religious Movements for Social Betterment* (1900), the work illustrated the direction in which his thought was moving. Strong praised the proliferation of innovative religious organizations—orders of deaconesses, institutional churches, and settlement houses—and suggested that such experiments held the key to church growth. In the same year, he participated in the creation of the New York State Conference of Religion, which aimed at promoting a unified religious approach to the problems of modern society and included Jews and Unitarians within its membership. After 1908, he chaired the Research Committee of the Commission on the Church and Social Service, an arm of the newly formed Federal Council of Churches.[32]

We must not distort the meaning of these endeavors by viewing them through the perspective of the late twentieth century. Today a standard criticism—leveled in both academic and popular discourse—holds that the

growth of specialized professions, the explosion of knowledge, and the proliferation of organizations have fragmented society and overlaid the common
life with bureaucracies resistant to popular control. Stereotypes of bloodless
technicians, bean-counting bureaucrats, and faceless organization men testify
to that bias. Strong himself anticipated these concerns in his last book.

> In our exceedingly complex civilization, with its multiform and often conflicting
> claims; with our field of observation widened by the press until our knowledge
> of most of the subjects which interest us is necessarily superficial; with a speciali-
> zation of occupation, and a division of labour which inevitably narrows the scope
> of our activity, we are in great danger of losing our sense of proportion and our
> perspective. We stand in profound need of a generalization wide enough to em-
> brace all human life.[33]

No contemporary critic could frame the issue more sharply, but unlike
many of today's commentators, Strong retained his faith that a single passionate religious-moral vision could inform diverse organizations and new forms
of professional expertise. "Now *the Kingdom of God . . . ,*" he insisted, "affords
precisely the needed generalization. . . . Thus the full acceptance of the teaching of the kingdom . . . makes not only conceivable, but distinctly possible, a
life as seamless as the unrent garment of our Lord, and knit of a single thread
of unbroken purpose." A Kingdom of God to be realized in the mundane
realm legitimated the use of scientific knowledge and the creation of a welter
of new organizations and professions. But it also promised to maintain a culture and society united by a single religious vision. For Strong, this was the
basis for a new order in America, indeed for a new order in the world.[34]

In *The Times and Young Men* (1901), Strong juxtaposed the themes of
ardor and order in an especially revealing fashion. He echoed the charge of
Carlyle and Ruskin "that the present age is commonplace and sordid, and
that commercialism has robbed life of its imagination and poetry." Similarly, he warned that the "effeminate" religion prevalent in "the typical church
life of to-day" had "not enough of effort, of struggle . . . to win young men."
Yet Strong averred that men—the gender-specific designation is appropriate
here—need not and would not remain effeminate. They would tap into an
elemental vitality, "a deep and resistless current" at the heart of nature itself.
"Another Age of Chivalry" was aborning, he asserted, an age that would "inspire imagination and poetry anew, and lead forth nobler crusades against
every wrong." Once aroused, however, this "noble passion" would not surge
blindly, for intelligent men would sluice the current into proper channels and
thus imitate nature itself which is "ever law-abiding."[35]

Strong's desire to evoke elemental manly passions and simultaneously to control them illustrated many of the deeper longings and anxieties of his age, but it also pointed to the outworking of an even older ambivalence within Protestant thought. Thanks to Max Weber's famous work on the Protestant Ethic, it is a commonplace that Protestantism, especially in the Calvinist-Puritan tradition, prompted its adherents to subject both their interior and exterior worlds to rational order. But what Colin Campbell has called "the Other Protestant Ethic" coexisted alongside the better-known phenomenon described by Weber. By its emphasis upon religious introspection and subjectivity, this ethic nourished an inner life rich in fears and dreams. Once this imaginative faculty was released from its shell of doctrine by eighteenth-century Romanticism and sentimentalism, it easily became the vehicle of grandiose longings and fantasies that could never be fully satiated nor easily controlled. The desire of Josiah Strong's generation to connect with elemental vitality and power and its equally intense desire to control that impulse illustrates the dilemma produced by the two Protestant ethics.[36]

That quandary was most obviously manifest in the new consumer culture which Campbell believes was the product of "the Other Protestant Ethic." America was becoming what another writer has called "a land of desire." The emerging corporate economy required that men and women consume more goods and thus rejected the idea of stasis. Merchants and advertisers sold dreams of perfect contentment—visions of an Emerald City. Yet because they vended fantasies, their actual products could never fully satisfy the longings they had aroused. In fact, the logic of the market demanded that want remain partly unslaked, for if this year's goods indeed delivered paradise, no one would purchase next year's supply. The Emerald City gleaming in the distance always receded with the horizon, and the pleasures of consumption aroused the desire for more. Unquenchable desire, as William Leach observes, "fostered anxiety and restlessness"—an anxiety made worse, one might add, by the residual conviction that desire was to be controlled and mastered.[37]

It was to this dual task—legitimating and mastering elemental desires—that Josiah Strong and many in his generation committed themselves. Warning of "the perils of luxuriousness," Strong insisted that "safety demands the preservation of a balance between our material power and our moral and intellectual power. . . . Increasing wealth will only prove the means of destruction, unless it is accompanied by an increasing power of control, a stronger sense of justice, and a more intelligent comprehension of its obligations." Yet Strong objected to the misuse of consumerism and abundance, not to their existence. He gloried in the fact that "the process of civilizing" was in essence "*the creating of more and higher wants*" and boasted that "Christian civilization performs the miracle of the loaves and fishes, and feeds its thousands in a desert." "An exhaustless treasure-house of wealth" was now blessedly open to all. The key to the kingdom was to manage or direct the "creating of more and higher wants."[38]

Strong's diverse commitments came together in his theology of the kingdom, that ideal which would make modern life "as seamless as the unrent garment of our Lord." The kingdom was not a final goal for Strong so much as it was the ongoing process by which men and women constantly strove for the fulfillment of God's purposes without ever quite reaching the goal. In Strong's words, the kingdom brought an end to "dreams of 'immortal idleness'" and launched men and women [into] "here and now the work which will always be ours, namely, cooperating with God in helping to perfect existence in this world or some other." "Man was made to grow," he said quoting Robert Browning, "not stop." Here was the religious energy that drove Strong from committee to committee, from job to job. In Strong as in so many other moderate to liberal Protestants of the late nineteenth century, one sees the fruits of an eschatology which held that the future offered "an ever expanding fulfillment," that "the meaning of Christ's coming into the world was to open to us the vision and experience of life fulfilling itself on ever broadening lines," that humans were sailing "on the stream [of time], but see neither the fount nor the ocean, nor can we tell how far away either is, except that both seem far remote." The new eschatology was, in short, the last things with finality removed. It was a prescription for ceaseless striving and perpetual crisis. Austin Phelps, a retired Andover Seminary professor and father of the novelist Elizabeth Stuart Phelps, spoke perhaps more perceptively than he realized when, in the introduction to *Our Country,* he drew this moral from Strong's book: "Every day has been a day of crisis. Every hour has been an hour of splendid destiny. Every minute has been 'the nick of time.'"[39]

Strong's eschatological quest was bedeviled by a fundamental incongruity. Behind the desire for mastery lay considerable moral passion and anxiety. Strong brought a nearly apocalyptic vision to his discussions of the evils of the cities, the neurasthenic character of American civilization, the threat of the new immigrants, and the inequitable distribution of wealth. Yet when he turned to the ways Christians should address these perils, he fell into the language of rational direction, statistics, and programs. His notion of the kingdom—using "[s]cience . . . to fall into his [God's] plans intentionally and to co-operate with him intelligently"—seemed mismatched to the atavistic fears and grandiose dreams that impelled him. His theology was one which, in George Coe's words, removed the "tragic intensity, the high lights, and the deep shadows." Unable to incorporate the deep shadows—and there were many of these specters in the Gilded Age—Strong's eschatology could only return again and again with renewed energy to try to subject the terrors of time to rational control. Although he undoubtedly did not fully realize the fact, his views of the last things were a prescription for living in Halttunen's endless loop or standing before the bar of judgment in Kafka's "summary court in perpetual session."[40]

To view the issue from a slightly different angle, Strong's eschatology illumined one of the central cultural problems of late-nineteenth-century Protestantism—the loss of a sense of stable selfhood. Buffeted by seemingly impersonal forces of technology and bureaucracy, uncertain of hegemony in a world of new immigrants and shifting gender roles, the Protestant (male) self had become indeterminate, its reality less a matter of fixed character than of its capacity to generate energy and motion. The new eschatology with its emphasis upon open-ended development tried to alleviate anxiety by suggesting that the propulsive self moved onward and upward. Yet the solution was also part of the problem: a self defined by kinesis was but a fluid, shifting constellation of will and energy. For it to cease moving, organizing, and controlling would be to die. Thus movement *had* to continue.

In a classic description of the rationalization of modern society, Max Weber offered the *bon mot* that "the idea of duty in one's calling, prowls about in our lives like the ghost of dead religious beliefs." There was much indeed that was haunting in the kingdom-building zeal of late-nineteenth-century liberal Protestantism. Without the prospect of closure, activism became compulsive and steadily lost a transcendent frame of reference. While the growth of corporations, consumer culture, and bureaucracies promoted this transformation within Protestantism, the change was not simply one imposed on the churches from without. In large measure, liberal Protestants' theology and practice abetted the process. How they did so is the subject of the remaining pages.[41]

4

A Kingdom "as Wide as the Earth Itself"

eʌⓄⓄ〜ꝶ

WHEN Lewis French Stearns, a professor in the Bangor Theological Seminary in Maine, wrote a survey of religious thought published in 1893, he declared that the "greatest achievement of recent theology" was the rediscovery of the Kingdom of God. Although that kingdom would find its fulfillment beyond this world, its focus was upon the present age, and it was not limited to the church. "The kingdom is to come *here*. This earth is to be redeemed." From this fact, Stearns drew a practical conclusion:

> We must, therefore, beware of too narrow a view of the kingdom. We must not confine it to the things of the church. We must recognize the fact that our Lord is King in the secular sphere as truly as in the religious, and that in this view nothing is common or unclean . . . Viewing the subject thus, we shall see that the kingdom comes not only in the addition of converts to the church and the building up of Christians in holy living, but in the establishment of better principles of business, in the equitable settlement of the relation between capital and labor, in the moral reforms by which deep-seated social vices or abuses are overcome, in the elevation of politics, in the advance of civilization, in the cessation of war, in improved sanitary arrangements in our cities, even in the prevention of cruelty to animals and the increasing sense of obligation to avoid waste and needless destruction in the use of the products of material nature. The Christian who grasps the conception of the kingdom cannot be narrow-minded. His interests are as wide as the earth itself.

No less than the church, all other human institutions—the family, the state, "labor, commerce, the trades and professions, science, art, and literature"— fell under the broad shadow of the kingdom. It followed, then, that "true Christianity is not that which separates itself from the world and selfishly wraps itself in the mantle of its own salvation, but that which goes out into the world in the spirit of the Master, to win it and all that is in it to him."[1]

Stearns had sketched a theological rationale for what Sydney Ahlstrom has called the age of "crusading Protestantism." The determination to subdue the world to Christ, to build a kingdom "as wide as the earth itself," became the goal of a growing segment of American Protestantism after 1880. That ideal, despite the presence of alternate rationales, gave impetus to the crusade for foreign missions. It shaped the struggle of the rising Social Gospel movement to create a more just economic order and undergirded efforts to promote cooperation and federation among various churches. Protestants sang the hope militantly in new hymns:

> Rise up, O Men of God!
> His Kingdom tarries long;
> Bring in the day of brotherhood
> And end the night of wrong.[2]

In their effort to bring in a tarrying kingdom, many Protestants looked to the extraordinary proliferation of organizations, bureaucracies, and new forms of professional expertise. In the years after 1880, America was groping toward a new sense of order. Business led the way. First among railroads and then in other economic areas, what Alfred Chandler has called "a managerial revolution" took place. Subdivisions of corporations, which theoretically might have existed as separate entities, were organized under a hierarchical chain of control. Various phases of production, distribution, and advertising were placed in specialized departments and subjected to coordination by managers. Other aspects of American society exhibited a similar consolidation. With the new research universities in the lead, higher education segmented itself into discrete departments, regularized procedures for academic appointments and responsibilities, and sought means to assess the efficiency of their faculties. Out of the new academe came a host of professionals, armed with statistical surveys and eager to use their expertise to reshape America along more rational or efficient lines.[3]

The churches were not immune to these blandishments. To build a kingdom "as wide as the world itself," religious commitment enlisted worldly instruments: scientific planning, businesslike management, rational organization, and professional expertise. Thus, despite some misgivings, many focused their attention upon the mundane mechanics and processes of the kingdom as much as upon its goal, and the sense of an End receded still further from view.[4]

"The Evangelization of the World in This Generation"

Of the various dreams for a new world, none stirred the churches more profoundly than the hope of converting heathen lands to Christ. Protestant missions abroad had formally begun with the formation of the American Board of Commissioners for Foreign Missions (ABCFM; 1810) and the first dispatch of missionaries two years later. Originally an interdenominational venture, the ABCFM had become an exclusively Congregational enterprise by the early 1870s. During the antebellum era, individual denominations had begun creating their own agencies and commissioning their own foreign workers. In these years, the foreign missionary movement constituted a significant but still relatively modest part of Protestant life. Major expansion occurred in the decades after the Civil War. The organization of a Woman's Board of Missions (Congregational) in 1868 soon found eager imitators among women in other denominations. By 1915, more than three million women held membership in forty denominational women's missionary societies. At a time when women controlled relatively little money, they raised impressive sums, recruited candidates for the foreign field, and helped arouse greater interest in the cause among male church members. By 1888, a series of earlier YMCA-sponsored conferences at the Massachusetts home of renowned evangelist Dwight L. Moody produced the Student Volunteer Movement (SVM). Through its traveling agents, the movement preached the imperative of missions on campuses around the country. In the next half century, the SVM persuaded thousands of young men and women to pledge themselves to work abroad, converted even more to ardent support, and raised to prominence dynamic young leaders—men such as John R. Mott and Robert E. Speer—who exercised decisive influence on the shape of American Protestantism for decades to come. Other interdenominational organizations such as the Laymen's Missionary Movement (1906) sought to carry the enthusiasm to adult males, especially business and professional men. The success of these enterprises is partly visible in raw numbers. American missionaries abroad numbered 934 in 1880, ten years later the figure climbed to almost 5,000, and by 1915 it exceeded 9,000. Yet statistics alone cannot capture the hope and enthusiasm of a movement whose adherents sang with fervor the 1894 lines of Laura S. Copenhaver:

> Heralds of Christ, who bear the King's commands,
> Immortal tidings in your mortal hands,
> Pass and carry swift the news ye bring:
> Make straight, make straight the highway of the King.[5]

Just as secular leaders touted camping trips and sports as a remedy for the banality of ordinary life, advocates of missions often presented their cause as an antidote to the flaccidity and spiritual mediocrity of American religion. As one Methodist writer observed in 1889:

On its religious life rests all the good there is in the nation. To successfully maintain it among ourselves we must labor to diffuse it to others. . . . As righteousness alone exalts a nation, our people should recognize that their true glory is to be found established in this, and their highest mission to diffuse its blessings to the ends of the earth. . . . It is only as we aid in molding for good the destiny of humanity, as we exert our mighty energies in ameliorating the condition of mankind, in redeeming the world from ignorance and sin and renewing it in knowledge and in holiness, that we can conceive or realize a mission worthy of the great American Republic.[6]

In 1906, at the centennial observance commemorating the Haystack Prayer Meeting which led to the formation of the ABCFM, a number of the addresses stressed the theme. Dartmouth's President William Jewett Tucker declared, "we need the balance and corrective of foreign missions to match the overwhelming appeal of the material world to the imagination." Baptist Edward Judson of New York City concurred: "The only faith that is adequate to the task of conquering our own country is the faith that is robust enough to achieve the conquest of the world." As for the "spiritual declension in our own land," "the cure of it all is the foreign missionary spirit." More dramatic were the words of Newell Dwight Hillis, pastor of the Plymouth Congregational Church in Brooklyn. After decrying the "mammonism" of contemporary society, he dared hope that the heroic age was not dying. "The history of foreign missions will make a new chapter for Carlyle's 'Hero Worship.'"[7]

Six years earlier, Protestant missionaries who perished during the Boxer Rebellion in China had furnished such heroes. The description of one of the dead exemplified the merger of the heroic cult of strenuosity with the missionary ideal. Sherwood Eddy recalled the days of training he and his friend, the martyred Horace Pitkin, shared at Union Seminary in New York. "I remember as we went down for exercise in the old gym after grinding Hebrew and Greek all day, how the missionary purpose gave zeal even to our exercise and as we did our mile together or had a round or two of boxing, the thought often was 'We must put on muscle for China. We must train for something better than the football game. This will carry the Gospel many a mile.'" The symbolism of Eddy's passage was significant. The banality of ordinary life—in this instance, grinding Greek and Hebrew—was redeemed from insignificance by the strenuous and heroic endeavor upon which the young men were about to enter.[8]

William T. Ellis, a secular journalist and frequent speaker at missionary conferences, provided one of the most graphic evocations of the heroic theme in *Men and Missions* (1909). "Beneath the overlay of commercialism, sordidness, self-centredness, and artificial civilization," he argued, "beats a passion for life and conquest—for some larger, manlier, diviner expression of one's own personality." Fortunately, the present generation of Americans had the opportunity to fulfill the longing. Because their nation embodied dreams to which people everywhere aspired, its citizens had an unprecedented "opportunity to impress . . . [their] ideals and values" on the world. Neither Alexander the Great nor Napoleon had enjoyed the prospect of power or influence on so grand a scale, and the cause of foreign missions preeminently exemplified Americans' task "to impart the genius of their land, which is the gospel of Christ, to the last man whom their consecrated skill and power will enable them to reach." Modern man glorying in his power to span continents with railways or to tunnel under the Hudson River would find in the foreign missions movement "an enterprise harder than the building of a great railroad, the laying of the Atlantic cable or the mastery of aerial flight"—a task, in other words, capable of enlisting the highest energies of "a full-orbed manhood."[9]

Such discourse did not, of course, represent the totality of missionary rhetoric. Appeals for the enterprise often stressed other themes: the necessity of fulfilling Christ's Great Commission to go unto all nations and make disciples of them, the need to save perishing souls from eternal damnation, or the importance of providing humanitarian assistance. Overtly masculine, crusading language can also mislead by obscuring the fact that a significant majority—probably in the vicinity of 60 percent—of all missionaries were women. Moreover, women in the United States remained the most consistently loyal supporters of the cause. By stressing the "essential masculinity" of the missionary movement, Ellis and others were not describing reality as much as they were trying to change it by drumming up greater male support. Nor should one assume that images of valor and great deeds had appeal only to men, for as one female missionary to China observed in exulting over a success: "It's great to be a hero." Likewise language associating missions with nationalism and with notions of western superiority sometimes can hide the many instances when missionaries criticized the pretensions of their own culture. Yet, having made these allowances, the rhetoric of the movement testified to a restless, anxious energy seeking release in a momentous, world-shaping cause.[10]

The urgency of foreign missions was captured in the watchword of the Student Volunteer Movement: "the evangelization of the world in this generation." Coined by premillennialist Arthur T. Pierson, it carried for him and others of his persuasion a message derived from Matthew 24·14: "And this gospel of the kingdom shall be preached in all the world for a witness unto all nations; and then shall the end come." Premillennialists did not assert that missions would Christianize the nations nor even that preaching would produce large numbers of converts. Evangelizing the world within a generation meant taking the gospel to all peoples so that prophecy might be fulfilled and Christ return on clouds of glory. Thus believers might hasten the day of the Lord through their vigorous exertions. By contrast, the liberal Baptist William Newton Clarke offered a very different vision of missions, one which he called "inconsistent with the ordinary second-advent doctrine." "We seek," he said, "the conversion of individuals to Christ. . . . [W]e build up the institutions of Christianity, and we seek to leaven the entire life of the community with Christian influence and quality. In a word, we labor with the purpose that the people and their life shall become and remain thoroughly Christian, and the human race at length be Christianized." In the interest of promoting united support, many leaders sought to interpret the missionary imperative in terms transcending these polarities, and none excelled in that task more than John R. Mott. He repeatedly insisted that the watchword did not imply the conversion of the world (an idea anathema to premillennialists) nor did it suggest "hasty or superficial preaching" (the logical consequence, said opponents of millenarianism, of the latter's view.) The watchword offered no prophecy regarding the results of missions. It meant, no more and no less, than the obligation of each generation of Christians to confront the world with the claims of Jesus Christ.[11]

Yet, however carefully missionary leaders and propagandists tried to balance their statements, they often implicitly espoused an eschatological vision. That vision usually contained more images of Christians building a Kingdom of God on earth than pictures of believers awaiting one to come down from heaven.

Many of Mott's own statements, at least before the Great War, implied that Christians could accomplish almost limitless things. In an address at the Ecumenical Missionary Conference in 1900, after the usual disclaimer against assuming that the world could be converted in a generation, he produced argument after argument that suggested otherwise. Surveying the multitudes of missionaries already at work, the vast wealth at the disposal of western Christians, and the ease of modern communication and travel, he asked: "Why has God made the whole world known and accessible to our generation? Why has he provided us with such wonderful agencies? . . . Every one of these wonderful facilities has been intended primarily to serve as a handmaid to the sublime enterprise of extending and building up the kingdom of Jesus Christ in the world. The hand of God, in opening door after door among the nations, and in bringing to light invention after invention, is beckoning the Church of our day to larger achievements." Those achievements might be grand indeed. Mott closed by citing other conference speakers who had expressed the conviction that ten million people might be converted to the faith in the next decade and that by the end of the twentieth century, possibly within the lifetime of some assembled there, Christianity would win predominance in both India and China. Perhaps the watchword really did imply the conversion of the world—or at least huge chunks of it—within this generation.[12]

Optimism also appeared in glowing claims that missions were improving civilization and that this progress represented the advance of the Kingdom of God. "Is the Kingdom of God growing?" asked Sidney Gulick, an American Board missionary to Japan, in 1898. Emphatically yes, he replied, "and never so fast as in the last decades of the nineteenth century." Evidence of that growth could be read not only in increasing church rolls but in the moral and social results Christianity produced throughout society: improved opportunities for education, heightened sensitivity to injustice, and the proliferation of charitable organizations. "The seed Christ planted has sprouted, the leaven has spread slowly, Christian civilization has developed. It is still far from perfect. Nevertheless, it is here, doing its work, bestowing its blessings; those nations who accept it heartily, and adopt its inmost principles, are ever to prosper, materially, mentally, morally, and spiritually." Although Gulick focused his book chiefly on Christian lands, the implication for missionary work was clear. Just as the flourishing of Christianity brought advance in western lands, it would do so among the heathen. James S. Dennis, who served for a time in the Presbyterian Mission in Syria, argued that Christianity had already performed this service. In three ponderous volumes bearing the title *Christian Missions and Social Progress* (1887–1906), he offered an apparently exhaustive—and exhausting—catalogue of the beneficial social results of the missionary movement in nonwestern lands. Wherever Christianity had taken hold, it promoted industrious habits, restrained gambling, elevated the status of women and children, abolished cannibalism, introduced modern medicine, brought relief from famine, established orphan asylums, promoted sanitation, developed industrial training, produced better government, wrought technological advance, and produced a more prosperous standard of living. Dennis's list went on almost ad infinitum. He hoped that his demonstration of the "tendency in missionary activities to work for human betterment" would induce Christians to yet more vigorous labors "for the expansion of Christ's kingdom."[13]

Both Dennis and Gulick insisted that the improvement of society was not the chief aim of missions, but they and others like them had decisively shifted the balance in an old debate concerning missionary policy. Should workers concentrate solely on the preaching of the gospel or should they also engage in "civilizing" activities? Powerful mid-nineteenth-century leaders— men such as Rufus Anderson of the American Board and Francis Wayland of the Baptist Board of Foreign Missions—had answered unequivocally. "The Son of God," Wayland insisted in 1853, "has left us no directions for civilizing the heathen, and then Christianizing them. We are not commanded to teach schools in order to undermine paganism, and then, on its ruins, to build up Christianity." To be sure, those whose cry was "Christ, not civilization" sometimes allowed policies at odds with the dictum, and they never really doubted that the new churches would promote social progress. Nevertheless, in theory they maintained the absolute priority of evangelization. By the age of Gulick and Dennis, evangelization itself was becoming a more amorphous term inclusive of a broad range of activities promoting secular progress as well as Christianity.[14]

Many influences contributed to this shift. As workers flowed more numerously into the mission stations in the late nineteenth century, not all could be put to work as preachers of the Gospel. This was especially true of women, who were denied ordination by most denominations. Many of these persons, men as well as women, found their place in an expanding array of new institutions—schools, hospitals, and medical facilities, for example. The ethos of imperialism also left its mark. Although many supporters of missions wanted no truck with U.S. expansionism, foreign missions often became, in William Hutchison's expression, "a moral equivalent of imperialism." To the extent that both movements rested on assumptions of Anglo-Saxon superiority and destiny to uplift the world, that ethos subtly moved missionary advocacy from narrowly religious to more broadly cultural and social concerns. The new theology also played a role. Its lessening concern with conversion and its emphasis upon an immanent Kingdom of God coming to fruition in all areas of life promoted a more inclusive vision of the missionary enterprise. Lewis Stearns had observed of the kingdom: "We must not confine it to the things of the church. We must recognize the fact that our Lord is King in the secular sphere as truly as in the religious, and that in this view nothing is common or unclean." The increasingly variegated face of the missions movement and its growing zeal to promote progress in all forms was, in part, a manifestation of that expansive view.[15]

A small home staff could not administer this far-flung empire, nor could haphazard appeals for money finance it. The day of the missionary endeavor as a kind of "mom and pop" operation had, by the turn of the century, started giving way to the era of missions as a series of highly structured corporations. The most obvious change was the sheer proliferation of agencies: the Student Volunteer Movement, the Laymen's Missionary Movement, the Missionary Education Movement, and the Foreign Missions Conference of North America, to name only a few. According to the computation of Robert E. Speer in 1928, organizations promoting or sponsoring missions had numbered only two dozen in the 1880s but had risen to 122 at the time he wrote. Yet far more significant than increasing numbers of organizations were the changes which took place within them. For example, the Board of Missions of the Methodist Church had twelve staff members in 1890, twenty-six by 1908, and sixty-three in 1919. Before 1893, the three executives functioned as ministers without portfolio, dabbling in various phases of administration and dividing up duties in an informal manner. Gradually the board demarcated lines of authority and placed executives over discrete administrative units. By 1919, the board consisted of a central executive staff and three subordinate divisions: Foreign, Home, and Treasury. Each of the divisions in turn had five to seven separate departments. Similarly, the Presbyterian Board of Foreign Missions divided itself into two major departments, one for the supervision of the missionary enterprise itself and the other to maintain support among the home churches. For promotional purposes, the board also created regional field representatives in the United States and for a time employed a fund-raiser whose task was to cultivate wealthy donors. Similarly, the women who led the female missionary societies increasingly structured their work in accordance with the canons of professionalism, science, and businesslike organization. Raising money became a major preoccupation of all missionary groups. They increasingly favored central agencies to coordinate budgets, and to raise moneys they inundated the local churches with promotional literature extolling the virtue of stewardship, defined as proportionate giving. By encouraging the every-member canvass, they hoped to rescue finances from the uncertainties of the old haphazard system which relied on special offerings. Systematic finance was the watchword of the hour.[16]

A new kind of leader flourished in this environment. An earlier generation had thrilled to the adventures of missionaries like Adoniram Judson and his wife Ann Haseltine as they braved the dangers of Burma. Although the romance of missions did not die out, and the heroism of a Horace Pitkin still inspired supporters at home, the missionaries themselves were generally less prominent by 1900. The commanding presence was the missionary executive. Often a layman and more a man of affairs than a theoretician, the administrator was a hero because he set himself to great organizational tasks and accomplished them. John R. Mott provides an example par excellence. Often described as a missionary and ecumenical statesman, Mott held up to the churches a global vision of Christian work and cooperation. In service to that goal, he traveled the planet, spoke at conferences, and inspired countless men and women with his dream. Yet it was as an organizer that Mott left his greatest mark. He played a leading role in creating the Student Volunteer Movement, the World's Student Christian Federation, the Foreign Work Department of the International YMCAs, and the Continuation Committee of the Edinburgh Missionary Conference. With consummate skill and mastery of the smallest details, he sat through or presided over countless meetings, composed differences, set new organizations in motion, and kept existing ones functioning. What has been said of his friend Robert E. Speer, an executive of the Presbyterian Board of Foreign Missions for forty-six years and an ecumenical statesman in his own right, could be applied with equal justice to Mott himself: He "had a way of making bureaucratic transformation seem filled with high moral and spiritual purpose."[17]

Missionary leaders were themselves aware of the change and spoke in new accents. "The Lord's work as well as man's," said Arthur Judson Brown of the Presbyterian Board of Foreign Missions, "calls for business methods." He boasted that mission boards often included "bank presidents, successful merchants, railroad directors, great lawyers, managers of large corporations," who applied their common sense skills to "the extension of the kingdom of God." According to Brown, even "the typical missionary is more like a high-grade Christian business man of the homeland than a professional cleric." Baptist William Newton Clarke insisted that "the romantic period" of missions, with its dramatic accounts of exploits abroad, was of necessity giving way to a more prosaic era. Successful foreign work demanded "sound business methods, and skill in administration, and versatility in operation" as much as piety. Clarke also wrapped board executives in the arcane mantle of professionalism. Possessing the full command of the facts and issues, they deserved the benefit of doubt from outsiders, few of whom were "thoroughly qualified to criticize" any policy or decision. Samuel B. Capen likewise vaunted organizational prowess in his centennial address to the American Board in 1910. "In harmony," he declared, "with the highest business methods of our time, mission work is being consolidated in order to prevent waste and insure economy and efficiency." Turning missions into a species of religious corporation promised extraordinary things. "It is the age of great plans and of great enterprises in the business world; our Christian merchants and capitalists should be equally generous in their plans and gifts for missions. . . . If they will[,] our rich men can plant Christian institutions everywhere in the East and rule it for Christ." With this grand vision set forth to his hearers, Capen recited familiar lines evoking the hope of the coming kingdom:

> He has sounded forth the trumpet that shall never call retreat;
> He is sifting out the hearts of men before His judgment seat;
> Oh, be swift my soul to answer Him! be jubilant my feet!
> Our God is marching on.

The kingdom was coming, but it was coming through big budgets and large organizations self-consciously patterned after corporations. Kingdom building now required a great deal of organization tending.[18]

"Where Cross the Crowded Ways"

The kingdom imposed near as well as distant tasks. By the 1880s, numerous Protestants viewed with alarm the disorder of American cities, the unrest of the laboring classes, the conspicuous wealth of the very rich, the growing power of giant corporations, and the apparent inability of conventional politics, often tainted with corruption, to address these problems. Some turned alarm into a summons for reform. At first their voices were few, but during the first fifteen years of the twentieth century they swelled into a major chorus in American Protestantism. This rising sentiment was often called social Christianity and later acquired the name by which subsequent generations have known it—the Social Gospel.[19]

On May 9, 1894, the Reverend Washington Gladden of Columbus, Ohio, in a sermon to the State Association of Congregational Churches delineated the theological heart of the Social Gospel. The address unfolded two basic themes. First, the Kingdom of God was already present and growing stronger, but it was far from complete. "Every department of human life,—the families, the schools, amusements, art, business, politics, national policies, international relations,—will be governed by the Christian law and Christian influences. When we are bidden to seek first the Kingdom of God, we are bidden to set our heart on this great consummation." From this inclusive vision, Gladden drew his second theme: the church, while a part of the kingdom, was not the totality of it. The church should be to the rest of society what the brain is to the body—the center from which emanates governing impulses. "Exactly in the same way," he explained, "is the church related to all other parts of human society. Its life is their life; it cannot live apart from them; it lives by what it gives to them; it has neither meaning nor justification except in what it does to vitalize and spiritualize business and politics and amusement and art and literature and education, and every other interest of society."[20]

Nine years later, Frank Mason North, the leader of the Methodist Church Extension and Missionary Society of New York City, put Gladden's hope in a verse which soon became a well-known hymn:

Where cross the crowded ways of life,
Where sound the cries of race and clan,
Above the noise of selfish strife,
We hear Thy voice, O Son of Man.

O Master, from the mountainside,
Make haste to heal these hearts of pain;

Among these restless throngs abide,
O tread the city's streets again.

Till sons of men shall learn Thy love,
And follow where Thy feet have trod;
Till glorious from Thy heaven above
Shall come the City of our God.[21]

Both Gladden and North called upon Christians to move beyond narrowly ecclesiastical concerns, to enter the crowded ways of common life, and thus to redeem the secular. This was the charter bestowed by the Kingdom of God and the central motif of what became known as the Social Gospel.

Although the Social Gospel had significant roots in the reform-minded, postmillennial evangelicalism of the pre–Civil War period, it also represented a break with that tradition. Social Gospelers generally rejected what they perceived as the individualism, the otherworldliness, and harshness of the old faith. For them, the message of Christianity was that a loving God wished to save this world in all its parts. "The kingdom of God," said Walter Rauschenbusch, who was the most systematic expositor of the movement, "is . . . a collective conception, involving the whole social life of man. It is not a matter of saving human atoms, but of saving the social organism. It is not a matter of getting individuals to heaven, but of transforming the life on earth into the harmony of heaven." According to that understanding, persons one by one still needed to confront the claims of Christ, and they might look forward to an afterlife, but neither an individualistic conversion nor salvation beyond the grave constituted the proper focus of the religious life. The overriding task of the believer was to realize his or her solidarity with all humanity in struggling for the kingdom here and now.[22]

Such language recurred again and again among advocates of social Christianity. The economist and lay theologian Richard Ely wrote popular essays in the 1880s to rouse Christians to the task of changing current economic conditions and invoked the Lord's prayer as his warrant: "Thy kingdom come, Thy will be done on earth." "Christianity," he explained, "is primarily concerned with this world, and it is the mission of Christianity to bring to pass here a kingdom of righteousness and to rescue from the evil one and redeem all our social relations." When Walter Rauschenbusch and his fellow Baptists Leighton Williams and Nathaniel Schmidt formally organized in 1893 a group to promote a vision of social transformation, they called themselves the Brotherhood of the Kingdom. The preamble to their constitution stated: "The Spirit of God is moving men in our generation to a better understanding of the idea of the Kingdom of God on earth. Obeying the thought of our Master, . . . we form ourselves into a Brotherhood of the Kingdom, in order to reestablish this idea in the thought of the church, and to assist in its practical realization in the life of the world." Through yearly conferences and scholarly as well as popular writings, the group sought to reach the laboring classes and to propagate the kingdom ideal within the churches.[23]

Social Gospelers did not always agree about the specific contours of the coming kingdom. Their prescriptions for society ranged from outright socialism to more modest, piecemeal reforms. Yet despite manifest differences and ambiguities, the major voices of the Social Gospel clearly affirmed common themes. They rejected laissez-faire economics, wished to soften economic competition by greater cooperation, and generally adopted a pragmatic approach to questions of reform. Their pragmatism fit into a larger pattern of social democracy and progressivism which emerged in both Europe and America after 1870. James T. Kloppenberg has aptly described this outlook as one stressing "knowledge as an unending experiment whose results can be validated only in activity rather than reflection, and whose conclusions are at best provisional and subject always to further testing in practice." Thus one could not in advance of events specify particular ethical or political programs as *the* answers to the quest for a just society, and answers, once found, would have to yield to yet other solutions as history rolled onward. Time defied definitive resolutions. Or in the explicitly religious language employed by Walter Rauschenbusch in *A Theology for the Social Gospel,*

> An eschatology which is expressed in terms of historic development has no final consummation. Its consummations are always the basis for further development. The Kingdom of God is always coming, but we can never say "Lo here." Theologians often assert that this would be unsatisfactory. . . . Apparently we have to postulate a static condition in order to give our minds a rest; an endless perspective of development is too taxing. Fortunately God is not tired as easily as we. If he called humanity to a halt in a "kingdom of glory," he would have on his hands some millions of eager spirits whom he has himself trained to ceaseless aspiration and achievement, and they would be dying of ennui. . . . [But] we are on the march toward the Kingdom of God, and getting our reward by every fractional realization of it which makes us hungry for more. A stationary humanity would be a dead humanity. The life of the race is in its growth.

Rauschenbusch's lines echoed the sentiments of his friend William Newton Clarke: Christ's "coming is not an event, it is a process that includes innumerable events, a perpetual advance of Christ in the activity of his kingdom." The key word is process, for the growth of the kingdom was the goal of the kingdom.[24]

Believing that God's coming reign entailed an open-ended quest to subject all of life to the imperatives of the gospel, advocates of social Christianity reflected that enlarged view in the profusion of activities they undertook.

Washington Gladden, longtime pastor of the First Congregational Church in Columbus, Ohio, and one of the earliest leaders in the Social Gospel, served a term on the city council, acted as a mediator in labor disputes, helped create an agency that coordinated the work of religious and charitable organizations in Columbus, and lobbied Congress for the creation of a federal commission on industrial relations. During his pastorate in New York City, Walter Rauschenbusch actively supported the mayoral candidacy of the radical Henry George. After assuming a professorship at Rochester Theological Seminary, Rauschenbusch interjected himself into a public dispute over the rates charged by the local gas and electric utility, organized efforts to make the city's streetcar line more responsive to the needs of the poor and middle class, gave a nominating speech for another unsuccessful mayoral candidate, and chaired a committee investigating the public school system. Probably no individual better illustrated the Social Gospel's expansion of the ministerial role than Graham Taylor. A pastorate in downtown Hartford, Connecticut, acquainted him with the forces shaping the lives of the poor, aroused his interest in sociology, and redirected his career. In 1892, he became the head of the newly formed Department of Christian Sociology at the Chicago Theological Seminary. Two years later he founded the Chicago Commons, a settlement house where he and his wife, along with their four children, took up residence. The Commons ran a day nursery, a kindergarten, and open forums where persons of all persuasions (political and religious) could vent their ideas. Moreover, Taylor and his colleagues were heavily involved in efforts to elect reform-minded candidates to office in Chicago. In conjunction with the University of Chicago, he founded and directed what ultimately became the Chicago School of Civics and Philanthropy.[25]

Why did Social Gospelers engage in such a dizzying round of activities? Taylor pointed to the Book of Revelation, whose picture "of Christianity triumphant was not in another world, but in this one; not of a Church, but of a 'Holy City'; not a mere multitude of saved souls, but of the 'nations of them which are saved,' organised into a saved human society, in which 'the tabernacle of God is with men and he will dwell with them and they shall be his people and God himself shall be with them and be their God.'" Washington Gladden gave a similar answer: "Christianity is not merely for Sundays and prayer-meetings, for closet and death-bed; it is for shop and office, for counting-room and factory, for kitchen and drawing-room, for forum and council-chamber." This was the essence, he said, of the "Gospel of the Kingdom"—the message "that God is organizing on earth a divine society; that the New Jerusalem, whose walls are salvation and whose gates are praise, is rising here upon sure foundations."[26]

Searching for effective ways to build the New Jerusalem, Social Gospelers turned to science, especially to the social sciences, which were then emerging as distinct disciplines within the hierarchy of schools and departments that made up America's new universities. The move was eminently logical. Although the flagship institutions of higher education had begun to weaken or abandon ecclesiastical ties, and although they increasingly emphasized specialized teaching and research, they had not become "secular" in the late-twentieth-century sense of the term. To be sure, their métier was empirical study or the inculcation of liberal culture, which sometimes allowed questions of ultimate meaning to be bracketed out. Nevertheless, a sense of religious vocation continued to inspire many academicians. G. Stanley Hall, the president of Clark University, declared: "Where the spirit of research breaks out, there is life; the Holy Ghost speaks in modern accents." The young John Dewey, while a professor at the University of Michigan, told the Student Christian Association that prayer for moderns was identical to the attitude of scientific inquiry and that science could aid mightily in "the building of the Kingdom of God on earth." William Rainey Harper of the University of Chicago saw Christianity and the modern university as fully consonant means by which America would achieve its millennial mission to renovate the world. The task of the university, he once said, was to inculcate a sense of obligation to serve society and to form individuals who, with their special knowledge, would build up the common life and like elder brothers guide the human family.[27]

In the nascent social sciences, the connection to Christianity was particularly intimate. The career of Richard T. Ely illustrates the affinity. After 1877 he pursued postgraduate study in Germany and took his Ph.D. in economics at Heidelberg under Karl Knies. Knies repudiated classical laissez-faire liberalism and stressed the discipline's active role in helping the state control and direct economic policies. For Knies and his American disciple, the task of the economist was not merely to describe immutable laws of the marketplace but to prescribe ways by which ethical values could direct the market. After returning to the United States, Ely secured an appointment at Johns Hopkins University in 1881 and eleven years later moved to the University of Wisconsin. From his academic positions, Ely sought to advance that vision on a popular and a professional front simultaneously. In the 1880s and early 1890s, he wrote for middle- and upper-middle-class church people as well as for fellow economists and political theorists. His works championed the cause of labor, attempted to give socialism a sympathetic hearing, and sought to mobilize the Protestant conscience on behalf of reform. He lectured at Chautauqua, the best-known forum for adult education in the late nineteenth century, and he helped organize the Christian Social Union in the Episcopal Church in 1891. He intended the American Economic Association, founded partly at his instigation in 1885, to include the general educated public as well as professional scholars.[28]

Behind these endeavors lay a conviction Ely expressed in 1889:

> We cannot love our fellows effectively unless we give them our mind. We must devote ourselves long and carefully to the study of the science of human happiness, social science. . . . What is wanted is not dilettanteism [*sic*] with respect to those duties which we owe our fellows, but hard study, pursued with devotion for years. . . . Philanthropy must be grounded in profound sociological studies. Otherwise, so complex is modern society that in our efforts to help man we may only injure him. Not all are capable of research in sociology, but the Church should call to her service in this field the greatest intellects of the age. The seminaries which train ministers of religion should be great leaders of thought in economic and social studies. It is the office of philanthropists gifted with insight and blessed with means, to encourage such studies by the foundation of prizes, professorships, and publication funds.

Rather like Harper's elder brothers, trained social scientists would provide the church "with the greatest intellects of the age" and enable it to fulfill its world-redeeming mission without succumbing to ""dilletanteism." Ely wished to position himself and the social sciences midway between academic professionalism and popular advocacy, with a religious vision uniting the two.[29]

Social Gospelers also promoted the kingdom through new organizations, some within and others without the church. After 1880, a number of urban congregations moved beyond traditional forms of outreach to provide community services. Graham Taylor's work at the Fourth Congregational Church in Hartford prefigured this style of ministry. Congregations in other cities expanded their work even further to include the running of libraries, gymnasiums, nonalcoholic "saloons," medical clinics, employment bureaus, kindergartens, and workingmen's clubs. Styled institutional churches, these bodies aimed at what Charles L. Thompson, pastor of one such Presbyterian congregation in New York City, called "salvation for the whole man for the regeneration of society." In 1894, Thompson became first president of the Open and Institutional Church League, created to encourage the formation of additional institutional churches, and by the end of the century a very conservative estimate placed the number of these at 173. Elias Sanford, secretary of the league, explained its goals very simply: "We are helpers, servants, co-workers in a movement that has in it the spirit, methods and fulfillment of the Kingdom of God." In 1901, the ideal of social service played a major role in the formation of the National Federation of Churches and Christian Workers and seven years later gave impetus to the creation of the Federal Council of Churches.[30]

Closely allied to these ventures were the settlement houses. Inspired by the example of the Christian socialists who had gone to live in the slums of East London at Toynbee House (1884), a number of young Americans created similar houses in their homeland. In 1886, Stanton Coit founded the first of these—the Neighborhood Guild—in New York City. By 1891, six settlement houses existed in the United States, and by 1910 that number had risen to over four hundred. Among the better known of these were Hull House led by Jane Addams and Ellen Gates Starr in Chicago, Robert Woods's Andover House in Boston, Graham Taylor's Chicago Commons, and the College Settlement in New York City. Not every person who founded or worked in a settlement did so from avowedly Christian motivation. For example, Coit espoused Ethical Culture, and Lillian Wald, one of the prominent settlement leaders in New York, was Jewish. Yet on the whole the movement had distinctly Protestant roots. A 1905 survey of nearly four hundred settlement workers indicated that almost 90 per cent were active church members, about half were Protestant, and almost all were deeply influenced by religious faith in some form. Many founders had a theological education. Impelled by an organic understanding of society and by liberal theology's emphasis upon the brotherhood of man, the leaders viewed with alarm the economic divisions of the nation's industrial cities. They wanted to bear witness to a higher religious and social unity transcending economic differences. Or as Graham Taylor said, in words which could have been equally descriptive of most other settlements:

> So we called our household and its homestead Chicago Commons, in hope that it might be a common center where representatives of the masses and the classes could meet and mingle as fellow-men, to exchange their social values in something like a clearing house for the commonwealth. Here we hoped friendship, neighborship, and fellow-citizenship might form the personal bonds for that social unification which alone can save our American democracy from being cloven under any economic stress and strain. We dreamed that here the brotherhood of which we talk and sing might be more practically lived out and inwrought, as it must be if Christianity continues to be a living faith and its churches the people's fellowship.[31]

The tendency of the Social Gospel to expend energy in a variety of civic, charitable, and political organizations found clear expression in the ministry of Worth Tippy. A cofounder of the Methodist Federation for Social Service and after 1917 the executive of the Federal Council's Commission on the Church and Social Service, Tippy made a reputation as a dynamic Social Gospel pastor at the Epworth Methodist Church in Cleveland, Ohio. In an account of his work at Epworth, Tippy described his objective in these terms:

> Early in my pastorate I began systematically to push out workers from the church
> into the social movement of Cleveland. . . . I have not hesitated to urge persons
> who were manifestly fitted for special forms of community work to give to it
> practically all their free time. . . . I have deemed it important to recognize this
> community service as if it were a part of the work of the local church, and to
> consider these workers as, in a sense, loaned to the community.

Epworth sought to work in a cooperative manner with all philanthropic and
civil agencies. It had a charities council that stayed in touch with the juvenile
court, the legal aid society, and others. Tippy himself served on housing and
recreation committees of the Chamber of Commerce, as chairman of the
Child Protection Committee of the Humane Society, as an organizer and
president of the city's federation of churches, and on at least two official city
committees.[32]

The Social Gospel, in short, encouraged men and women to look to
nonecclesiastical activities and institutions to fulfill religious ideals. For many,
an activist state was the foremost of these. In 1909, Baptist Samuel Zane
Batten provided one of the most systematic statements of that conviction in
his *The Christian State: The State, Democracy and Christianity* (1909). Batten
argued that the state, as a divinely appointed domain "in which the life of the
kingdom seeks expression and realization," offered one of the chief means
whereby people achieved a true Christian identity. "The individual," declared
Batten, "comes to self-realization as he sacrifices himself for the common life.
He that findeth his life for himself shall lose it; but he that loseth his life in
the State, shall find it." Batten believed "that there must be a wide extension
of State activity into man's social and industrial life" if God's kingdom were
to come. To realize that mission, the state would require the expertise of "the
scientific and sociological spirit," even though every program drawn up by the
professional social scientists would be "more or less provisional." In essence,
Batten made technical experts and specialists, tentatively probing their empirical data, the high priests of a government promoting the kingdom of God
on earth. In its faith that the state might employ technical expertise in an
experimental, open-ended quest for a more rational and just society, Batten's
work provided a religious counterpart to the writings of secular theorists of
progressivism such as Herbert Croly and Walter Lippmann.[33]

Social Gospelers were in search of new ways, in Robert Crunden's phrase,
of "preaching without pulpits." The irony was that many of these enterprises
gradually became less explicitly religious in character. The history of the settlement houses provides a case in point. As institutions aimed at the reconstruction of entire communities, they often found that too close an identification with Protestant religious bodies impeded that purpose, especially among
the immigrant population. Thus in 1895 Robert Woods changed Andover

House—named for the liberal seminary where he had studied—to South End House "in order to release the settlement from certain restraints which the old name placed upon its natural progress." Even where churchly ties persisted, as at Chicago Commons, which maintained a link to a nearby chapel, mundane work overshadowed explicitly religious activity. The interest of the settlers in gathering information through surveys also impelled them toward the social sciences and eventually, after initial misgivings on both sides, toward alliances with the charity organization movement, which was seeking to rationalize and systematize work with the poor. The result was a gradual turn toward what Mina Carson has called "the partial professionalization of settlement work." Moreover, despite their initial interest in reconstructing society through face-to-face encounters among individuals of different classes, the settlers discovered that the problems they faced required political solutions. They were drawn into the role of lobbyists on behalf of playground construction, new housing codes, better street lighting, and child-labor laws. Initially they exercised this role at the local level, but particularly with the political rise of Theodore Roosevelt, many turned to national political advocacy.[34]

In similar fashion, the Christian impulse so prominent in the creation of the social sciences quickly attenuated into a more narrowly conceived professionalism. Richard Ely's desire to wed Social Gospel reform to scientific expertise, for example, foundered. Accused of teaching socialism, he was subjected to investigation by the Board of Regents of the University of Wisconsin in 1894. He secured exoneration in part by denying the charge and thereafter adopted a cautious stance. Concentrating on scholarly more than popular work, he made his subsequent public contributions chiefly through highly technical analyses on behalf of the state legislature, private foundations, and business corporations. Similarly, Albion Small, a former ministerial student who shortly before becoming the first head of the Sociology Department at the University of Chicago spoke of his discipline's "tendency . . . toward an approximation of the ideal of social life contained in the Gospels," soon eschewed explicitly Christian rhetoric and diminished his connections with reformers. He and his Chicago colleagues attained renown for their highly specialized studies of urban conditions and the production of demographic maps. Yet the irony ran deeper than the standard litany of religiously inspired organizations turned secular. The ethos of professionalism and science pervaded Social Gospel institutions *within* the churches as well as without. Concern for social redemption prompted the creation of new agencies. Initially these were voluntary societies—for example, among Episcopalians, the Church Association for the Advancement of the Interests of Labor (1887), the Society of Christian Socialists (1889), and the Christian Social Union (1891), and among Baptists, the Brotherhood of the Kingdom. But after 1900, the Social

Gospel carved out a niche within official denominational structures. In 1903, the Presbyterian Church in the United States of America created a Workingman's Department within its Board of Home Missions and called as its head Charles Stelzle, an ordained minister and himself a son of the immigrant working class. In 1907 the National Council of Congregational Churches made its industrial committee a standing body, and the same year the Methodist Federation for Social Service came into existence. Although formally a voluntary society, the federation often functioned as something more. It successfully lobbied behind the scenes at the General Conference of 1908 for a statement strongly endorsing Social Gospel principles. (The document became known popularly as the Social Creed of Methodism and served as the basis for the Social Creed of the Churches adopted at the founding meeting of the Federal Council.) In 1912, Methodists recognized the federation, despite its ostensibly unofficial character, as the administrative agency of the church in matters of social service, and the organization acquired sufficient funds to employ Harry Ward as a full-time executive. The American Baptist Convention formed a Commission on Social Service in 1908 under the leadership of veteran Social Gospeler Samuel Zane Batten, who four years later received a paid appointment as head of the newly created Department of Social Service and Brotherhood within the Publication Society. In 1910, the Congregationalists employed Henry Atkinson as secretary of labor and social service, and by 1912 Episcopalians had a Joint Commission on Social Service with Frank M. Couch as full-time field secretary. From his position as secretary of the Federal Council's Commission on the Church and Social Service, Charles Macfarland abetted this process. Encouraging the member churches to hire full-time executives to run their various social agencies, he then arranged to have these people appointed to his commission and thereby made it a central clearinghouse for the social ministries of major denominations. The matrix of specialization and social science was now ensconced within growing denominational bureaucracies themselves.[35]

The career of Warren H. Wilson, a Presbyterian denominational official, illustrates the mentality that often accompanied this institutional change. After graduating in 1893 from Union Seminary in New York City, Wilson took an upstate parish in the small village of Quaker Hill. He loved the community but was appalled by the economic and religious divisions within it. To combat this fragmentation, he created a nondenominational congregation, including his own Presbyterians as well as members of four other religious bodies. He wished to revivify the notion of the congregation as a parish with the church as the community center. After six years, Wilson left Quaker Hill to pursue a Ph.D. in sociology because he had become convinced that rural churches needed a scientific Social Gospel. In 1908, he took a position in the

Presbyterian Department of Church and Labor under the prominent Social Gospeler, Charles Stelzle. There Wilson conducted programs on the rural church. Playing on rising public interest in the problems of the country, he persuaded the church to create a separate Department of Church and Country Life in 1910. With that organizational base, Wilson and his staff conducted surveys of rural areas, sponsored educational programs for rural ministers, and created "demonstration parishes" in the countryside.[36]

In a 1915 address at his undergraduate alma mater in Oberlin, Ohio, Wilson reflected on the meaning of his vocation. He had come of age intellectually in the late 1880s during the heyday of what he called "the first missionary adventure." In that era of the Northfield Conferences and the Student Volunteer Movement, young people looked "into the naked sun of soaring purpose" and aspired to "cosmic" achievement. Summoned to spiritual exploits comparable to the conquests of Julius Caesar and Alexander the Great, they expected to move the world. Yet even while thrilling to these visions, said Wilson, his generation had moved toward a "second missionary adventure" very different in spirit from the first. His own journey had begun in his junior year at Oberlin when his professor of botany assigned him the task of performing a minute study of the algae in a particular pond. It continued at Columbia when he took courses forcing him to concentrate on criminology, statistics, and taxation. The shift culminated when his mentor Franklin Giddings "ordered me to make a study of the social population resident upon a rural hilltop in New York state, where I had begun my ministry. I begged him to give me something more important, but he declined, insisting . . . that I learn the living population of a certain limited habitat. . . . " In short, Wilson had learned to find the cosmic in narrowly defined fields of labor pursued with scientific rigor. Or as he put it: "Specialization in service may perhaps be called the spirit of this new religious experience."[37]

Wilson had not lost the old vision, for he could still speak of Christian activity hastening the time "when the world shall have all been redeemed, . . . when the Kingdom of God shall have indeed come." But that kingdom would advance only as Christians allied themselves with academic expertise. Churches had to serve as the "channels by which the knowledge that the universities have in store can come to the use of the people." In so doing, the churches would make "little mention of regeneration of the individual, at least . . . [they would have] little to say about anything miraculous or magical or incapable of measurement." Statistics and scientific research would be their tools. True to the scientific spirit, the second missionary adventure was provisional as well as specialized. "The open mind," said Wilson, "takes nothing for granted and regards no conviction as a finality. . . . [Christians] do not engage in their adventure by reason of knowing it is a true way of service, but by reason of not knowing. They are investigating by means of action." Wilson's Kingdom of God entailed the reign of professional specialists discovering and perpetually refining truth through scientific inquiry. Wilson's Kingdom of God—pragmatic, tentative, empirical, and specialized according to the canons of modern professionalism—had as much to do with mundane processes as with transcendant goals for history.[38]

It was, of course, far from the intent of Social Gospelers to supplant Christianity with merely secular purposes and activities. Thus Graham Taylor argued that the new preeminence of secular organizations and methods did not imply the waning of Christianity, but its growth. He maintained "that religion was never more irrepressible than now," precisely because "it cannot contain itself, or be contained, within church walls." Taylor acknowledged possible difficulty, for specialized institutions stood in danger of losing their sense of participation in the whole. The remedy lay in ever more vigorous proclamation of the all-encompassing message of the Kingdom of God. The church's task was to maintain that ideal through its public worship, which "is the flag of the kingdom. The Church which maintains it is the color-guard of the community." Yet Taylor remained acutely aware that in an age of scientific expertise something more than preaching or worship was required to keep the flag aloft. Unless the church drew deeply on sociological wisdom and collected facts with "judicial impartiality," it could not assert its preeminence in the modern world. "It is the mastery of authoritative facts," Taylor averred, "patiently, practically, intelligently applied to concrete situations that wins religion's way."[39]

"To Manifest the Essential Oneness of the Christian Churches of America"

Advocates of both foreign missions and the Social Gospel knew that their hope of building the kingdom confronted major obstacles. In the face of the social dislocations wrought by urbanization and industrialization and in light of the swelling tide of Catholic and Jewish immigration, one had to ask if Protestants were up to the task. "It surely does surpass the courage and faith, the influence and resources of the divided churches," Graham Taylor admitted, but he insisted that united Protestant forces still had the power "to meet and master the situation in almost every community." The task was to get Protestants to understand the necessity.[40]

The notion that Protestants needed to act in concert was not by itself novel. They had already worked together in the early nineteenth century through numerous voluntary societies. They had formed organizations to support domestic or foreign missions, to establish evangelical colleges, to promote temperance, to enforce Sabbath observance, and to further sundry other causes. Yet these early efforts at united action did not, strictly speaking, represent cooperation among churches. The societies brought together like-minded individuals—not denominations—to work on behalf of common causes. After the Civil War, voluntary societies continued to enjoy notable successes in such movements as the YMCA, the Women's Christian Temperance Union, and the Student Volunteer Movement.[41]

After the war, a new approach to cooperation gradually evolved from the voluntary societies. The Evangelical Alliance provides a case in point. Originally formed in London in 1846 by unofficial representatives of various Protestant bodies, the alliance quickly lost its American adherents because of the antislavery stand it had taken. Once the Civil War removed that issue from contention, a group of Protestant leaders revived the American branch of the alliance in 1866. The revitalized body remained a voluntary society—it was an association of individuals, not churches—but during Josiah Strong's tenure as General Secretary (1886–1898), the alliance moved toward innovative modes of cooperation. Deeply committed to the Social Gospel and convinced that a Protestantism "shattered into scores of fragments" could neither Christianize America nor hasten the kingdom, Strong sought new paths to unified action. He called upon churches in every area to coordinate their work with each other and with philanthropic and civic associations. His goal, in short, was federation of churches at the local level.[42]

Despite the alliance's ultimate rejection of Strong's policies, other Protestants also groped toward fresh strategies for unified Christian action. In 1890, five denominations in Maine created an Interdenominational Commission. During the next decade church federations emerged in Connecticut, Massachusetts, New York, Ohio, and Rhode Island. Churches in some urban areas also federated. Growing out of the Open Church League, the National Federation of Churches and Christian Workers (1901) sought to promote church federation at the national as well as the regional level. In 1902, it issued invitations asking Protestant denominations to send official delegates to a conference which would draft a plan for a national federation of Protestant churches. In December 1908, the appeal came to fruition with the first official meeting of the Federal Council of Churches, composed of thirty-three denominations. The aim of the council's founders was succinctly stated in the preamble to its constitution: "to manifest the essential oneness of the Christian Churches of America."[43]

The search for new institutions to embody their "essential oneness" simultaneously reflected Protestants' optimism and anxiety regarding their prospects in the United States. Protestants hoped, for they assumed with Graham Taylor that "united religious forces are still adequate to meet and master the situation in almost every community." Presbyterian Stephen W.

Dana at the first meeting of the Federal Council pictured Protestantism advancing "as one solid phalanx against every enemy of truth and righteousness." Yet fear also marked Protestant efforts, for church leaders knew that they had to march in step because their enemies were strong and beyond the capacity of any single group to combat. Acting in piecemeal fashion, Protestants could never hope to mold the ethos of America. From the gatherings of the Evangelical Alliance through the meetings of the Federal Council, countless addresses and sessions enumerated those problems: unchurched masses, a new immigrant population alien in religion and mores to old-line Protestants, intemperance, industrial unrest, creeping secularism. Thus Josiah Strong could write of the Evangelical Alliance: "This movement sprung from a recognition of the perils which threaten our Christian and American civilization." His words found echo among other proponents of ecumenism. At a meeting of the National Federation of Churches and Christian Workers, Methodist Levi Gilbert emphasized that the "necessity of combining to meet the solidarity of vice" was "compelling the various brigades in Christ's army to move in concert." John R. Mott declared to the conference drafting the plan for the Federal Council: "In the presence of an unbelieving world, whose unbelief is more extensive and more intensive than can be realized in any other way save by facing a great work like this, we have come to see that anything short of union in spirit and practical effort is destined to be futile." In 1908, the Congregational minister Newman Smyth framed the charge more sharply still. Faced with the loss of control over vast areas of modern life, Protestantism "has frayed out into so many separate strands. No single thread of it is strong enough to move the whole social mechanism; it is like so many ravellings; at most one strand may move a few wheels."[44]

Unity would find its basis in common tasks, not in common theology. The Federal Council, for example, was forbidden by its constitution to draw up a creed for its constituents. Its task was "to bring the Christian bodies of America into united service." Preaching at the 1912 meeting of the Federal Council, Shailer Mathews graphically summarized his philosophy of the council:

> The world does not care whether we are closed or open communion. It does not know what we mean when we talk about different shades of belief. All those things may be vastly important but when it comes to the real issue, what is more significant than all such matters is this great question: is honesty, is purity, is social service an expression of the need of society? The fundamental issue that we face is the world with its selfishness, its commercialism, its harshness, its industrial injustice, its cheapening of young men's manhood—a terrible, often a hideous enemy. The Federal Council of the Churches of Christ in America embraces thirty different denominations seeking unity. The Council of Nicaea also sought

unity. It, too, tried to bring peace into its society and the State and sought it in theological definition. This representation of 17,000,000 of Protestant Christians comes to discuss how they can best carry on co-operative work for the good of mankind. If the Council of Nicaea, instead of wasting weeks over the discussion of a word had organized a mission society to go up into Germany, what a different story history would have told.[45]

Because of their preference for action over theory, the new cooperative movements were able to encompass persons of divergent persuasions. Historians have rightly noted the role of important Social Gospel figures—men such as Frank Mason North, Josiah Strong, and Charles Stelzle—in the burgeoning of ecumenism. But individuals of rather traditional evangelical faith and with no ties to the Social Gospel also played an important role. For example, William Henry Roberts, the veteran stated clerk (1884–1920) of the Presbyterian Church in the United States of America and a conservative of the first water, chaired the executive committee of the Inter-Church Conference on Federation (1905) which prepared the way for the formation of the Federal Council.[46]

Theological diversity, however, was not unlimited. The Federal Council restricted membership to Trinitarian churches, and the organization was animated by its hopes for God's kingdom on earth. At the 1908 meeting of the council, Frank Mason North summarized the body's goal succinctly: "Primarily we are engaged in establishing his kingdom in these United States." Before adjourning, the council sent to the constituent denominations a letter, pledging itself to "wiser and larger service for America and for the Kingdom of God." At the next quadrennial session, the council heard Francis J. McConnell declare: "Every representative here tonight will say that he is trying to bring in the kingdom of God and make men like Christ." Even conservatives like Roberts used similarly expansive rhetoric. In his opening remarks to the first meeting of the council, he reminded his audience of its duty "to hasten the coming of the day when the true King of Men shall everywhere be crowned as Lord of all. This Council stands for the hope of organized work for speedy Christian advance toward world conquest." The next day Roberts welcomed the Council's first president and played upon the fact that the group was meeting in a city with a biblical name. "There was a church in the days of old before which an open door was set," he said to President E. R. Hendrix, "and it bore the name of Philadelphia [Revelation 3:7–8], and we here in this city of Philadelphia, set before you as the leader of the Council an open door for co-operation in Christian work in this great Republic which should be the beginning of the thorough Christianization of the whole land."[47]

To be sure, the leaders of the council sometimes spoke in differing accents. Roberts stressed traditional evangelism, while McConnell and North had much more to say about rebuilding the social order. Yet all employed a common language to describe a similar hope: United Protestant efforts would turn aside threats to the nation and would bring in the kingdom. Perhaps the ecumenists best embodied their aspiration in worship. At one of the conferences preparing the way for the Federal Council, the assembly sang "I Love Thy Kingdom, Lord" and "My Country 'Tis of Thee."[48]

Despite giddy visions of Christianizing the whole land, the Federal Council remained a shoestring operation in its early years. By the end of its first quadrennium, its central headquarters consisted of a single room, twelve feet by thirty, on an upper floor of a New York City warehouse. To reach the office, a visitor ascended in a freight elevator and walked "down a hall lined with big wooden packing boxes." The expenses of the council in 1912 totaled $36,500. Even that tiny sum could not be fully raised from the constituent denominations, many of whom praised the council but proved indifferent when the time came to ante up the expenses. Sympathetic individuals provided slightly more than one half of the budget that year. Limited in resources, the council increasingly recognized that it could not yet function as a coordinator of the churches' total work. "For a time," remembered Charles Macfarland, "the council was evidently to be mainly a state of mind." He concluded that the council ought to take a more limited purview and concentrate "on areas of service on which the churches needed creative leadership." Through the Church and Social Service Commission headed by Macfarland, the council sponsored a study of labor conditions in parts of the steel industry in Pennsylvania, and soon the Committee on Church and Country Life, after a field study conducted by Charles Gill, published *The Country Church: The Decline of Its Influence and the Remedy.*[49]

Although the Federal Council may have been more "a state of mind" than a truly effective federation of churches, it nevertheless represented a significant state of mind. Along with the Social Gospel and the foreign missions movement, the council disclosed a Protestant leadership increasingly inclined toward new forms of professionalized service, faith in the power of scientific expertise, reliance on businesslike organization, and confidence in rational management. In following this path, Protestants hoped, as Charles Macfarland wrote, to "transform a chaotic democracy into an ordered Kingdom of Heaven." The new theology of the kingdom was not the sole source of these developments, but it did provide a major rationale for them. To create a "kingdom as wide as the earth itself," Protestant leaders expended furious energy, born out of elemental anxieties and hopes, and sought to shape that force into a new basis of social harmony. The results were churches where, in John R. Mott's phrase, each pastor became a "director general" raising money and recruiting supporters, where missionary leaders styled themselves business executives, and where social prophets became specialized professionals or full-time ecclesiastical bureaucrats. None of these things were done, of course, to displace religion, but rather to extend its influence. Nevertheless, the outcome was an institutional life in which routinized earthly processes occupied as much attention as transcendent ends. But perhaps one should not expect otherwise from those who adhered to the radically immanent, open-ended eschatology that Walter Rauschenbusch had summarized: "An eschatology which is expressed in terms of historic development has no final consummation. Its consummations are always the basis for further development. . . . The life of the race is in its growth."[50]

5

The Kingdom of God and
the Efficiency Engineer

❧❧❧

IN THE LETTER announcing its formation, the Federal Council of Churches in December 1908 called upon the denominations to combine and concentrate their "scattered forces." "The production of power," the council predicted, "will surely follow the reduction of waste." The happy results would be "increased efficiency in Christian service," "the maintenance of social righteousness," "the abatement of civic and national evils," and the promotion of "the broad interests of the Kingdom of God." The rhetorical linkages were significant: efficiency, power, righteousness, and the Kingdom of God standing on one side; waste and national evils on the other. These suggestive associations were soon to be spelled out.[1]

About 1910, Americans entered upon what Samuel Haber has called "an efficiency craze—a secular Great Awakening, an outpouring of ideas and emotions in which a gospel of efficiency was preached without embarrassment to businessmen, workers, doctors, housewives, and teachers, and yes, preached even to preachers. . . . Efficient and good came closer to meaning the same thing in these years than in any other period of American history." Two pivotal events in 1910–11 epitomized the new mentality. In a celebrated case before the Interstate Commerce Commission in 1910, Louis Brandeis argued against a rate increase for major eastern railroads on the grounds that scientific management of the companies would save a million dollars a day. Then Frederick W. Taylor, long noted for his time efficiency studies at Bethlehem Steel and other workplaces, published in 1911 *The Principles of Scientific Management*. Soon books, conferences, and articles swelled a chorus extolling efficiency as a panacea for the ills of the nation.[2]

The mania for efficiency appeared during the peak of the Progressive Era in American politics. The connection was not accidental, for the idea of efficiency pulled together the diverse features of that complex movement. Progressivism called for greater popular control of government through such reforms as primary elections, the referendum and initiative, the direct election of U.S. senators, and (in some instances) the enfranchisement of women. Yet Progressives also championed an expanded role for the expert and administrator—witness their desire for professional city managers, their fondness for expert fact-finding commissions to draft legislation, and the various governmental regulatory agencies they created. Under the rubric of efficiency, these disparate tendencies could unite. The people would willingly accept the guidance of the experts, for the latter possessed power not by superior wealth or birth but by mastery of objective facts which, once disclosed, would command the assent of the citizenry. Efficiency also had a seductive appeal because it resonated with many other traditional commitments of the American people. It invoked the prestige of engineering and the faith in technology, it legitimated the search for profit, and it promised a social harmony, transcending the clash of labor and capital, if only its scientific, class-neutral principles were obeyed. But above all, efficiency had a moral appeal. As Haber has observed, it "promised a moral clean-up. The high wages and low costs provided by the efficiency systems would check the greed of the employer and the laziness of the employee." Efficiency was the Protestant work ethic reborn in modern guise, and it offered a seemingly painless, rational solution to the agonizing conflicts and debates Americans had undergone since the Gilded Age. As John M. Jordan has observed, the "substantial sum of Christian moral capital" invested in efficiency was apparent in the religious terms used by Taylorites to describe their movement: "'Converts,' 'pilgrims,' 'orthodoxy,' and 'heresy' describe various aspects of the effort to teach American industry the One True Faith, which had been 'born' at Bethlehem Steel."[3]

Protestant leaders likewise found in efficiency a congenial theme. In part, institutional exigencies pushed them in this direction. The growth of agencies within the churches and of organizations they spun off had occurred in an often haphazard manner. Efficiency promised the consolidation of these enterprises in a coherent pattern. It also condensed under one rubric the various ideals many Protestants had been extolling for at least two decades: scientific planning, businesslike management, rational organization, and professional expertise. It offered a way of building the Kingdom of God in America by means of ecclesiastical technocracy. A Methodist writer summed up the matter with admirable brevity in a 1914 article: "Ah! the city which John saw! . . . It will take considerable engineering as well as preaching to get the whole world there. Hail, Engineer, coagent of the millennium."[4]

The Men and Religion Forward Movement

The Men and Religion Forward Movement provided one of the first large-scale attempts to promote efficiency among Protestants. It did so almost inadvertently as a means of attaining its primary goal: winning men for the churches. The idea for the movement originated in YMCA circles, and Fred Burton Smith, with over twenty years of service to the "Y," became its head. Other key leaders included Charles Stelzle, the executive of the Department of Church and Labor of the Presbyterian Church in the U.S.A., and Raymond Robbins, a staff member of Graham Taylor's Chicago Commons. Taylor himself, along with fellow Social Gospelers Frank Mason North, Walter Rauschenbusch, and Washington Gladden also participated in the movement. A sense of impending crisis and chaos impelled the movement. One report declared: "Face to face with life as we know it—the sordid life of the crowd, the selfish life of the privileged, the worsted life of the sinful—we have learned that unless there is a power that is not man's power our American democracy, under the fearful strain of class competitions at home and international antagonisms abroad, must end in disruption and despair." Of particular concern to the organizers of the movement was the relative absence of men in the churches, and they spoke mournfully of three million men missing from America's pews. Although females had far outnumbered males in many religious groups for more than two centuries, that fact had produced little alarm prior to the 1880s. In fact, during much of the nineteenth century, Protestants derived comfort from the allegedly greater piety of women. Religious women, tending their homes and making them into replicas of Eden before the Fall, supposedly provided a balance wheel to the aggressive striving of their husbands in the marketplace of laissez-faire capitalism and thus created social equilibrium. By the '80s that symmetry was vanishing. Women were moving into the public domain in greater numbers, and the old entrepreneurial ethos was giving way to the consumer-oriented mentality of corporate America. The threat of social unrest and the new immigration further unhinged social balance. Thus many men asserted the need to establish a new form of social control, one of whose hallmarks would be a more prominent religious role for males. Their endeavor appeared in assertions of a more muscular or masculine version of Christianity. and the slogan of the Men and Religion Movement stated their credo succinctly: "More Men for Religion, More Religion for Men."[5]

To achieve that goal, the movement spoke in accents of efficiency derived largely from the male-dominated corporate world. "There was a manifest stirring to self-examination of existing organizations," said a concluding assessment of the movement, "and a questioning as to their real efficiency." Significantly, the first major account of the Men and Religion Forward Movement bore the title *Making Religion Efficient.* Efficiency was a program as well as a slogan. Fred Smith, a salesman before he went to the "Y" and later a representative of the Johns Manville Company, set about organizing the Men and Religion Forward Movement as a well-integrated, streamlined business operation. Under the direction of an executive committee, teams of experts in evangelism, Bible study, boys' work, missions, and social service fanned out to study conditions in ninety major cities. Meeting in Silver Bay, New York, in July 1911, the teams discussed their findings with 300 church representatives. They plotted a standardized campaign, beginning in September, for each of the major cities. Teams of experts in the five areas—not charismatic generalists—would conduct meetings in seventy-six metropolitan areas. The local sponsors would agree to adopt standardized committee structures, comparable to the divisions of the national organization, and would in turn visit adjacent areas to hold meetings. At the close of the campaign, a national Conservation Conference—as well as local ones—would be held to summarize what had been learned and to lay plans for putting it into effect.[6]

To entice men to the meetings of the movement, the leaders drew upon the promotional expertise of advertisement experts. Catchy ads were placed in the sports sections of newspapers with such messages as: "Christianity Is for All Men and for All of a Man; Go to Church Next Sunday and Find Out." "Not to Allay but to Help Statisfy Social Unrest Is One Aim of Present Day Christianity. Think Things Through and You Will Go to Church." In New York, sponsors illuminated Broadway with electric signs written so that they who ran might read.[7]

When the campaign ended in April 1912, the reports of the various committees at the final Conservation Conference hammered home again the necessity of efficiency. The Social Service Commission argued the importance of "some central organization in all the larger cities corresponding to the office of the associated charities already established in many places." Such an office could "maintain a staff of experts," keep records of applications for relief, serve as a clearing house avoiding duplications of effort, and secure correlation of effort. This office would probably need "to employ a social service expert as executive secretary, to supervise the work of the committees and keep the wheels moving." The Commission on Christian Unity averred: "We simply must get together in a nation-wide Christ [*sic*] propaganda. With the universal channels of knowledge and commingling our nation is coming to possess a sort of common soul and nothing but the titanic can move it. Our haphazard and distributed touch on our population will never give the result for which we all fondly pray." Reporting for the Evangelism Commission, Presbyterian John Timothy Stone cautioned against viewing new organizations as a panacea and summoned Christians to make existing agencies more productive: "If you and I are to do effective work we must discriminate as to the valuable expenditure of time. . . . I do not mean we do not need organization, but what the world wants is to see the raw material turned into a finer product. . . . What we want is not more organization, but to use what we have, and begin by using it in a concentrated and intensive way. . . . " Although the reports sometimes disagreed as to whether new organizations or retooled old ones were the chief desiderata, they dovetailed in asserting the necessity of eliminating waste and coordinating effort. "The day of the amateur," said one report of the Commission on Social Service, "is over in all the more serious lines of effort and the demand for trained efficiency has the floor."[8]

The report of the Publicity Committee, composed chiefly of journalists and publishers, was especially provocative in spelling out the implications of efficient work. The Men and Religion Movement had in large measure succeeded, they insisted, because the papers deemed it worthy of report. "It was 'something doing,' the kingdom of heaven busy upon this earth, and in the newspaper's own city. The masculine note in it all, the bigness of the Movement's sweep, its emphasis upon social problems and its frank recognition of news values, all appealed to the editorial instinct." This favorable coverage did not simply "happen"; the movement's "publicity experts" planned it systematically. The committee urged churches in every community to build on this example by encouraging newspapers to create departments of religious news. Once created, these agencies ought to be fed information by the churches' own publicity committees, which would, of course, include "men who understand the science of advertising." At the national level, the Federal Council of Churches should establish "a *central Publicity Bureau* . . . to which news agencies and newspapers may apply, by day or by night, for [the] latest information upon news affecting any of the American religious organizations." To achieve these goals, however, the churches needed to change their attitudes. They needed to surrender the "delicacy of feeling" that shrank from the use of billboards or "flaring announcements of religious notices in amusement columns or on sporting pages." They needed to stress the element of human interest in religion and to accent the sensational to attract coverage. They summed up their message in an epigram: "Publicity is personality in seven league boots; religion, the guiding star of human life. The work of publicity is not done until the personality-transmitted message of the star is carried to every man."[9]

The committee provided examples of paid copy that churches might display in the newspapers. Although the sample ads acknowledged that the chief purpose of religion was "to express our belief in God, and to do Him reverence," they generally tried to lure prospective members with the mundane benefits of church attendance: friendship, social stability, the sense of being part of a large enterprise, and help in times of personal crisis. The faith advertised was Christianity in general, "of which the local congregations, under various denominational names, are the branches."[10]

The Men and Religion Forward Movement recast Christianity in the image of the corporation. The movement's hierarchical control of standardized operations, reliance on specialized experts, and its use of promotional techniques mirrored the characteristics of the business corporation in a consumer economy. This correspondence was anything but accidental. It was a deliberate attempt by Protestant leaders to address the lament voiced by one report to the Conservation Conference: namely, "that in spite of the development in our age of a general efficiency in all matters of trade and commerce, the church has in no wise kept pace. Her efficiency and resourcefulness are in unfavorable comparison with the achievements and impressive activities everywhere else." Thus the Men and Religion Forward Movement was a self-conscious effort on "behalf of the modernization of organized Christianity"— an effort premised on the assumption that "forces that are employed in other realms of human activity may properly be utilized by the church." Here "the children of light [were learning to] be as wise in their generation as the children of this world."[11]

Although the immediate statistical results of the Men and Religion Forward Movement were negligible, the movement may have been part of a longer trend toward the increase of church membership among males. By the 1920s the proportion of men in several major Protestant denominations had increased by 10 to 20 percent. (Of course, these fluctuations did not alter the fact that women continued to hold numerical superiority in church membership, as they had throughout much of America's religious history.) Moreover, the movement had sketched the outlines of a gospel of efficiency to large gatherings of men in over a thousand communities. It did so in the conviction that "the dream of the prophet will come true. We shall see a new earth wherein dwelleth righteousness." About the time the movement ended, others sketched in the details of that outline for creating "a new earth."[12]

Scientific Management in the Churches

Long before the efficiency craze, many Protestants believed that the work of the Lord required orderly planning. In his *Lectures on Revivals of Religion* (1835), for example, Charles G. Finney argued that proper understanding of spiritual laws would enable ministers to promote awakenings "with the same expectation [of success] as the farmer has of a crop when he sows his grain," and the *Lectures* provided step-by-step guidance in the use of those principles. Despite the controversial nature of his theology and of his revivalistic practices, Finney typified a major thrust of nineteenth-century evangelical Protestantism: confidence that rational planning and organization could achieve mastery of events.[13]

By the late 1880s, however, concern for technique was becoming more self-conscious and deliberate. In 1888, for example, Dr. Charles Thwing, who had pastored two Congregationalist churches and later would become president of Case Western Reserve University, described his ideal of *The Working Church*. The book, which went through several printings, argued that the pastor was the "chief executive officer" as well as spiritual leader of his flock and set forth guidelines for effective ministry, including instructions on the promotion of systematic giving and ways to work with particular groups in the congregation. In *Modern Methods in Church Work* (1896), George W. Mead of the Institutional Church movement provided detailed instructions for efficient use of ushers, choirs, young people's societies, women, Sunday schools, and even church architecture. Two years later Washington Gladden, in *The Christian Pastor and the Working Church*, offered advice on many of the same topics and averred that the "largest . . . part of his [the pastor's] work to-day consists in enlisting and directing the activities of his people." Behind this effort to systematize the work of pastors and their churches lay both confusion and hope. "Many ministers to-day," said Brown University President W. H. P. Faunce in 1908, "have a dim and baffled feeling that their work is not fully correlated with the life of the modern world. They stand like David when he had rejected Saul's armor and had not yet found his own—bravely facing the gigantic form, but uncertain as to the method of attack." The problem arose from the fact that a multitude of specialized professions and organizations had arisen both within and without the church, and the answer lay in pastors whose synoptic vision would bring all the pieces of modern life into a unity. "An age of specialism can be coordinated and unified," said Faunce, "only by the perception of a kingdom of ends, which is the Kingdom of God. It is the prerogative of the minister to bring back into a generation distraught by its own knowledge, and bewildered by its own disintegrations, the sense of the unity of true life. . . . " Mead, too, believed that the multifarious activities of modern religion found their coordinating center in a "new movement that looks to nothing less than the realization of the Kingdom of God."[14]

Since Frederick Winslow Taylor, more than any other individual, provided the catalyst which enabled Americans to fuse these concerns into a gospel of efficiency, a few words on his life and thought are in order. Born into a well-to-do family of Philadelphia Quakers in 1856, he was greatly influenced by a mother whose strong personality exhibited itself in ardent loyalty to the causes of antislavery and woman's suffrage and in her decision to leave the Friends for Unitarianism. By contrast, his lawyer father was a less decisive figure whom he recalled as possessing "a gentleness which was almost that of a woman." Perhaps the parental reversal of stereotypical roles produced problems of gender identity for the young man, for he performed skits of female impersonation at a cricket club and alternately affected a macho stance. He deliberately taught himself to curse, threw himself into sports, abandoned his father's wish that he study law, and worked for a time as laborer in a steel factory. He displayed other symptoms of psychological turmoil: recurrent nightmares, insomnia, and indigestion. He blanched at the mention of death or sickness. Samuel Haber shrewdly observes that his "program for systematizing the factory," which he came up with later, "should be seen in terms of his attempt to systematize most things, including himself."[15]

After receiving a degree in mechanical engineering, Taylor devoted himself to studies of factory work, especially the problem of malingering. He analyzed each task scientifically, broke it into component parts, and then determined by the stopwatch how long each segment should take. After Taylor made these assessments, managers would standardize all operations, and every employee would "become one of a train of gear wheels." To enforce the system, monetary incentives were given—or withheld—to the extent that the worker executed the task properly. Although many labor leaders as well as subsequent critics accused Taylor's system of overworking employees and reducing them to machines, he insisted that it protected their individuality and shielded them from exploitation. The system encouraged industriousness and self-discipline, each woman or man receiving exactly what she or he deserved. Moreover, the scientific determination of optimal performance prevented managers from making arbitrary demands upon their subordinates. The Taylor system promised to harmonize the interests of labor and capital by awarding higher wages to the former and cheaply produced goods to the latter. Indeed, Taylor believed his plans offered a moral renovation of the workplace, and in his more exuberant moments dreamt of remaking "every conceivable human activity" in accord with the beneficent principles of scientific management. An agnostic in his later life, he nevertheless retained the religious and reformist zeal of his mother, and after his death in 1915, he was eulogized as one who not only longed for "an industrial social millennium" but "told in detail exactly how this long-hoped for condition might be actually accomplished at once."[16]

Taylor did not stand alone in advocating scientific management. In addition to disciples who developed facets of his thought, other persons with positions less doctrinaire than his advanced the crusade. Harrington Emerson, for example, won wide popularity as a proponent of an efficiency loosely defined as a compound of common sense, morality, and proper management techniques. After the Eastern rate case, the cause of efficiency was taken up by the conservation movement and by supporters of home economics. It became a watchword of those who wished to Americanize immigrants through standard courses of education or indoctrination. It also lived on in the thought of major political theorists of Progressivism—men like Herbert

Croly and Walter Lippmann—who called for a more activist state led by expert technocrats. In 1911, enthusiasts with aspirations to remake America formed the Efficiency Society [of New York], and Charles Stelzle chaired its subsidiary, the Church Efficiency Committee. In short, efficiency transcended the system of Taylor and became a widespread rallying cry. Yet he remained the best-known and most fitting symbol of the movement.[17]

He was so because his own search for order corresponded to that of many others. To be sure, his alternations between female impersonation and masculine swagger or his efforts to move simultaneously in the world of the genteel and the laboring classes were, in their particulars, unique to him, but they clearly mirrored larger concerns. Taylor's anxieties paralleled those of middle-class folk who felt the need for strenuous exertion in a "weightless" corporate culture, who feared labor unrest yet sympathized with the worker's plight, who recoiled from the vulgarity of the newer immigrants but were attracted to their vitality, and who adhered uncertainly to traditional gender roles. At Taylor's grave, the Reverend Langdon Stewardson said of the deceased what could have been said of many Americans: "His effort was, by readjustment in the chaos of life's jumbled parts, to set things right." It is little wonder that the would-be systematizer and tamer of so many demons attained the status of guru among his contemporaries.[18]

Shailer Mathews of the Divinity School at the University of Chicago was one of the first church leaders to offer a systematic application of the efficiency ideal to religious life. He was the perfect person to do so. A scholar activist whose frenetic energy rivaled that of William Rainey Harper, who brought him to Chicago in 1894, Mathews initially held a post in New Testament history but subsequently transferred to the field of theology. At the time of his retirement in 1931, he was simultaneously Dean of the Divinity School, Chair of the Department of Christian Theology and Ethics, and Professor of Historical Theology. Heavy teaching and administrative responsibilities notwithstanding, Mathews was an active churchman, serving as one of the chief movers in the organization of the Northern (later American) Baptist Convention and as president of both that body and of the Federal Council of Churches. He also published prodigiously. His works emphasized what he called "pragmatic Christianity." By this term, he denoted a religion that was a way of life rather than a set of fixed tenets, and as an historian, he called attention to the numerous changes in doctrine that had occurred over the centuries. There was, however, a continuity beneath the sands of shifting belief: Christians exhibited loyalty to Jesus and to his values and sought to embody the latter within their societies. The dogmas Christians affirmed were the tools, shaped in accord with particular cultures or world views, to promote these larger ends. In the modern age, Mathews believed, Christians were attaining a more thorough awareness of the instrumental character of doctrine, and he predicted "a de-theologizing of the Christian movement." Henceforth, Christians would no longer look for "common theology" but to a "solidarity of undertaking . . . in the activities of the Christian group," and this unity would find expression in "a more intelligent attempt to put the attitudes and spirit of Jesus into the hearts of men and the operation of institutions." This functionalist understanding of Christianity found its logical expression in the philosophy of efficiency. In businesslike management, the churches discovered the device they needed to make their faith socially efficacious in an age of corporations.[19]

A few years prior to his reflections on scientific management, Mathews published a book disclosing some of the deeper concerns moving him toward efficiency. *The Church and the Changing Order* (1907) betrayed major anxieties about American society and Protestants' place in it. Society heaved with potential revolution while would-be healers of its distress offered two equally unacceptable cures: either the "unmodified individualism" of traditional religion and economics or the "atheistic materialism [of socialism] which would seek to exploit the discontent of the masses in the interest of class hatred." A "general breakdown among Christian people of conventional morality," "a search for wealth and creature comforts," and "animalism in the theatre" pointed to a culture in crisis. While acknowledging that "a democracy of the sexes" must arise in the future, Mathews viewed the emergence of the new woman with misgivings. Women income earners had to be freed from materialism in order "that they may continue to leaven a commercial age with non-economic interests," that sexuality not be cheapened, and that homes be "idealistic centres of religious influence." "What sort of society would that be," he asked, "with childless homes and business-centred male and female bachelors at the top, and prolific immigrants at the bottom?" Yet in the midst of these crises, many Protestants were preoccupied with resisting new intellectual currents, defending ancient orthodoxies, and ferreting out heresies.[20]

To Mathews, all of this was "desperate foolishness."

Theology, indispensable as it is, always has been and is always likely to be a disintegrating force in Protestantism. . . . With all the stern realities of uncoordinated social life pressing in upon Christian people, it is suicidal to waste time discussing the calculus of religion. With the sanctity of the home threatened by reckless divorces and even more reckless marriages, with a generation polluted by a mania for gambling, with saloons and brothels at its door, why should the church pause to manicure its theology? Facing a world in the darkness of heathenism, a submerged tenth rotting in our cities, an industrialism that is more murderous than war, why should the church stop to make a belief in the historicity of the great fish of Jonah a test of fitness for cooperation in aggressive evangelization? If it would make toward fraternity, the appeal of the church must be to life; and so far as social significance is concerned, the church that does not make this appeal is dead while it lives.

Yet despite the shrillness of his jeremiad, Mathews remained hopeful. A new religious revival was underway—one that would address the "uncoordinated social life."[21]

Mathews delineated the central lines of the revival in *Scientific Management in the Churches,* delivered at the Sagamore Beach Sociological Conference in the summer of 1911 and published the following year. The book assumed that the preeminent task of Christians was "to serve God and bring in his Kingdom" and that to this end "the Christian spirit must be institutionalized if it is to prevail in an age of institutions." Using principles derived from Frederick Taylor and Harrington Emerson, Mathews argued that efficiency required "the centering of attention on operation." By this bureaucratic phrase, he meant that churches needed to know what they were trying to accomplish. Too often content with affirmations of general purpose, congregations should frame highly specific goals on the basis of a careful annual survey of their respective communities. Efficiency also mandated standardized operations and the division of labor. Mathews advocated the formation of a "committee of management" to educate church members regarding their tasks, to assign them to appropriate work, to avoid duplication of effort, and to coordinate all activities. "Theoretically," he observed, "the church should be regarded as a body of workmen ready to perform definite tasks as these tasks are outlined for them by its committee of management." To be efficient, churches needed proper equipment such as kitchens, clubrooms, libraries, classrooms, and gymnasiums. Much record keeping was also necessary. In addition to a roster of its members, a church should provide "application blanks for membership which cover pledges to render service, cards for the assignment of particular tasks to the various members, [and] blanks on which they shall report." Ideally the pastor should have a paid clerical assistant to handle these matters. "If this seems to make the church something of a business establishment," he admitted, "it is precisely what should be the case." To mobilize "the most devoted church members" for efficient service, an appeal to build the kingdom might suffice, but to arouse the rank and file, the pastor would need to play on other motives: pride in the congregation's activities, loyalty to the denomination, and a sense of esprit de corps. This work demanded a new type of minister. He must be "a man who institutionalizes a belief and an attitude toward life rather than a man who simply proclaims a truth." People of this sort would be "trained to be chairmen of committees of management with the capacity to study situations and adjust churches to situations, rather than merely to preach good sermons." Or as Mathews summarized in an article four years after *Scientific Management,* a minister might "set churches into operation by spiritual preaching," but would fall short of ultimate success without the "grace of committees."[22]

Mathews did recognize the limits of scientific management and opposed what he regarded as illegitimate uses of it. "The Spirit of God," he insisted, "is not to be replaced by staffs of management or church members trained to definite tasks. A prayerless church will be impotent as a church, no matter how well organized or well instructed." He also scoffed at those who, in a rage for efficiency, attempted to calculate the average cost of converting souls to Christianity or regarded the size of a church as a gauge of its effectiveness. The "ultimate efficiency of a church" was "difficult to standardize," for in its highest aims "church activity cannot be reduced to concrete tasks with definitely measurable products." How could one quantify the work of inspiring men and women to service or of infusing Christian ideals into society? "A standardized cost of conversion," he snorted, "is as fatuous as a standardized cost of parenthood." But he maintained with equal vigor that the "secondary and more immediate tasks" of the church could readily yield to the calculus of efficiency, and it was these penultimate, mundane tasks that preoccupied him. In light of his functionalist understanding of Christianity and his desire for the "de-theologizing of the Christian movement," he had few resources upon which to draw in order to explore the implications of his own reservations. Thus, despite the disclaimers, Shailer Mathews did much to recast the church in the mold of an efficiency-minded business corporation.[23]

Paul Moore Strayer, a Presbyterian pastor in Rochester, New York, echoed Mathews. Like the Baptist dean, Strayer heard the rumbling of a social revolution to which Protestants were responding inadequately. In *The Reconstruction of the Church* (1915), he intoned a standard litany of problems: the cry of the workers for justice, their alienation from Protestantism, the movement of churches to the suburbs, the relative absence of men in the pews. The church stood at the fulness of time.

> Evolution has been at work for centuries, and the Kingdom of God is ever among us, but evolution at some point becomes revolutionary when the Kingdom is mightily set forward or back. The moment of birth is such a time, and to-day we are at the birth of a new social order. Far-reaching social movements are nearing their peak, and whether they be toward destruction or fulfillment is the question of most vital importance. The social revolution is on! It cannot be stopped. It may be guided.[24]

To guide that great movement, the churches needed to transform themselves into more efficient entities. An effective church had first to understand its purpose—an admonition suggestive of Mathews's "centering of attention on operation." The church, Strayer explained, was a body existing "as the modern school exists, for training in manhood and womanhood; not to fit men and women for a distant heaven, but to fit them to live here on earth, not to train them in the service of some absentee God, but in the service of those whom God has given us to love and to serve." With this criterion in mind, congregations should analyze their current activities with a view toward abolishing "any meeting or organization in the church which requires more energy to keep it going than it contributes life and power to the church." To make these determinations, Strayer suggested that churches hold periodic efficiency exhibits with "charts, diagrams and maps showing the character of the parish" and thus illuminating how well "present activities are meeting the needs of the community." Then an efficiency commission would propose changes to bring program in line with community need.[25]

In a manner similar to Mathews's, Strayer recognized the difficulty of assessing the efficiency of the church. "The unit of efficiency in a church," he warned, "is not so easy to discover as in a factory. . . . The results that the Bible is concerned for—the tests of efficiency which the gospel itself presents—are summarized in a very interesting list as 'love, joy, peace, long-suffering, kindness, goodness, faithfulness, meekness, self-control.'" Yet, having issued his caveat, Strayer urged a major retooling of ecclesiastical life. The first requisite was a larger vision of justice and mercy that would attract the "virile leadership" then lacking in the churches. "What is needed to change defeat into victory is a real battle in the name of Christ. "It is," he suggested, "the militant church which attracts red-blooded men and makes leaders." To that end the church must lay out a systematic "plan of battle." With a "new program" of social service laid out, pastors would discover that "men are as loyal to Christ as they ever were, but they cannot be rallied to the church without a plan of battle that gives promise of victory." Pastors needed to restructure services of worship, and Strayer recommended that the standard service consist of three parts: "a half hour of worship, with the aid of ritual and other adjuncts that appeal to the imagination," a half hour of moral instruction, and "then a half-hour of earnest conference and discussion with regard to our common Christian duty." Moreover, the modern church needed to advertise aggressively, placing its message before people "as the politician does his theories of government and the merchant his wares." With the aid of a card file, churches might target persons to receive periodic announcements. Publicity agents or committees might place ads in the newspapers or set up billboards. "The church needs boosting," Strayer concluded. "Every friend of the church should go into the advertising business."[26]

Despite minor variations in emphasis, Strayer and Mathews outlined common characteristics for the efficient church. It adjusted itself to the needs of its community and rigorously assessed all of its programs in light of this grand aim. With a pragmatic and functional vision of the kingdom, the efficient church valued theology to the extent that it promoted social harmony and justice. In an aside, Strayer quoted with approval the German theologian who had allegedly declared that "Christ would be more interested in our political developments than in our so-called church movements" and "that the discovery of the steam engine was of more value to His Kingdom than the Councils of Nicaea and Chalcedon." Thus while Strayer and Mathews acknowledged elements of Christianity that could not (and should not) be reduced to a narrow utilitarian calculus, they stressed the kingdom's mundane techniques—its committees of management, efficiency commissions, clerical assistants, and advertising gimmicks—which could be subjected to precise computation and control. Although both men had interests and identities too complex to permit stereotyping them as mere ecclesiastical managers, they did embody many of the traits of the prototypical organization man.[27]

According to Edwin L. Earp, professor of Christian sociology at Drew Seminary in New Jersey, the organization man was precisely what America and its churches needed. Or as he phrased the issue in 1911, "we must develop a new type of minister or religious worker, a religious social engineer." A specialist in some aspect of ministry, the religious engineer would be a person "who can help . . . establish a desired working force in any field of need, and keep it in sympathetic cooperation with all other forces working for the establishment of the Kingdom of God on earth." He would supervise those "at work with the machinery" of the church and assure that no "social friction" jarred the gears. With the help of these engineers, the churches could achieve their ultimate goal: an "administrative efficiency that will result in permanent social control." Every problem Protestant America faced—for example, the saloon, the assimilation of immigrant groups, the alienation of the laboring classes—would yield to this benign authority. Like machines, American society and its churches needed only the expert technocrat to make them hum synchronously.[28]

One major task for the expert was the community survey. According to Charles Carroll, who wrote a guide on the subject for church workers in 1915, the survey was essential to the achievement of efficiency. By ascertaining scientifically the needs of their communities, the churches would learn how better "to bring religion from the stars to the streets" and to achieve "the Kingdom of God in this world." Ministerial education should henceforth include training in the science of the survey, and every candidate for ordination should actually conduct one "before he is turned loose to practice upon a parish." This policy "would not be so very unlike, in educational principle, to the dissecting of a cadaver in a medical school." A successful survey required not only workers trained in scientific research but also considerable structure. Carroll offered an "organization tree" including an executive committee, a superintendent, and members for advisory, district, canvassing, finance, and publicity committees. Although this heavy investment in committees consumed time and energy, it amply rewarded the churches, for they knew scientifically whether a given field "is a losing or paying proposition from the standpoint of the Kingdom, by showing the numerical trend of the church work."[29]

Yet committees and surveys worked only if pastors could persuade men and women to staff them. Hence many argued that good publicity was the key to efficiency. Christian F. Reisner was one of the foremost proponents of this view. As pastor of a large Methodist congregation in Denver shortly after 1900, he won success as a moderate Social Gospeler and as one who deliberately sought to catch the public eye. Later, in New York City, he discovered that capturing public attention required more aggressive measures than it had in Colorado. He helped lay plans in the mid-1920s for the Broadway Temple, a skyscraper church topped with a 30-foot lighted cross and situated in Washington Heights. From Denver to Manhattan, Reisner emphasized the importance of systematic advertising, and he achieved renown as its advocate in several books.[30]

Reisner believed the essence of the minister's work to be persuasion. "Surely we can afford to spend and be spent as personal persuaders," he declared in 1910, "if by it we may win disciples, and so speed the coming of the Kingdom," and persuasion in the modern world meant advertising. The willingness to advertise, he explained three years later in *Church Publicity*, resembled Jesus's decision to surrender the sheltered life and become a public person. Resistance to advertising merited Jesus's condemnation in Matthew 10:37, as paraphrased by Reisner: "And if a man is not willing to forsake father and mother, ease and home itself for him, then he had better turn back." Through advertising, the church fulfilled its obligation to "be recognized as the heart of the community" as an organization that "ought and must make itself felt all through the week" as well as on Sundays. In language suggestive of Earp's desire for "permanent social control," Reisner called publicity "the modern way to compel them to come in."[31]

Reisner advocated control via enticement. People, he insisted, would come to church if lured with the expectation of lively or pleasant experiences. "The people must have entertainment," he declared. "In the stress of this day it is more necessary than ever." Through advertising, the church could compete with lower forms of entertainment and people could "be shown that they get a better kind as real and as invigorating from a vital religious service." Reisner's *Church Publicity* offered a veritable catalogue of clever sermon titles, pictures, newspaper inserts, and signs to attract outsiders. One sketch showed a friendly hand beckoning the wayfarer with the admonition: "Come In: No

Rented Pews. The best seat in the house is yours, if you reach it first." Another depicted two men greeting each other heartily and bore the inscription: "The Church That Gives You the Glad Hand." Another advertisement read: "You're Alive; We're Alive. Be thankful. Come to a church that is alive—The First Methodist." Humorous cartoons promoted church functions and, by implication, the rollicking good time people could enjoy there. The smiling faces of Sunday School students exuded sociability and happiness. The cumulative effect of the sample ads was to link Christianity with never-ending pleasure, power, vitality, and companionship. The New Year's letter he sent to his own congregation in 1908 epitomized the promise of ceaseless self-fulfillment and growth:

> God's good year of 1907 is gone. A better is before us. Each day brings growth to Christ's disciples. . . . Complaint crushes cheerfulness. Glowing growth gives God glory. Frowns form frozen furrows. Smiles stimulate sunniness. Christ continues to conquer. Heathen nations are gladly bending the knee. Golden sheaves lie near every disciple. Men were never so eager to meet Jesus. Church membership is increasingly a mark of honor. Excuses pale before God's offers. Optimism is on the throne. Victory is in the air. Let us "go up" and possess the land. "Behold now."[32]

Reisner used his own personality as an instrument of publicity. Creating a ministerial persona embodying happy vitality, he systematically projected it. During his vacations, he regularly sent his parishioners postcards, often with pictures of himself. For example, one year in Colorado, he had a photograph of himself, his son, and wife made into a card. The picture showed the smiling Reisners standing beside their little boy, who was seated on a burro. The caption read: "We have started for home." On the other side, Reisner assured his people how glad he would be to see them again, promised them "beautiful stereoptican pictures" of the trip, and signed the note as "your pastor-friend." With obvious pride, Reisner reported that "a keen business man sent word that it [the card] was the finest piece of advertising he had ever seen."[33]

The work of Reisner and other church publicity advocates may at first glance appear to have little to do with efficiency, for the promise of self-fulfillment seemingly grates against the demands of scientific management. In fact, Reisner viewed the lure of pleasure as a way of mobilizing men and women for efficient service. The membership card issued by his first New York congregation illustrated the connection. The card bore the title "A Homelike Church"—a logo deliberately chosen because it conveyed "tender and winsome thoughts"—but the card concluded with the member's pledge to accept the "responsibilities . . . of working to advance this branch of the

Kingdom." A "decision card" Reisner recommended for signature by converts at revival meetings made his goal even more explicit: the new disciple pledged to join a church "as a means of publicly confessing Christ and of employing my gifts efficiently to bring His kingdom on earth."[34]

Reisner sensed intuitively what others argued more explicitly. In an age of abundance, consumption—whether of material goods, entertainment, or religion—might be a means of efficient social control. Simon Nelson Patten, professor at the Wharton School of Finance and Commerce (University of Pennsylvania), was one of the foremost theorists of this proposition. Civilization, he contended in 1907, had formerly rested on the assumption of economic scarcity and the concomitant necessity of self-discipline. But with an expanding economic order offering plenty to all, control could be "attractive" rather than "restrictive." Lured by the gratifications that income might purchase, persons would willingly submit to the constraints of civilization. Satisfaction of wants would in turn stimulate still greater desires and increase the willingness of people to labor for their fulfillment. The great engine of social and economic progress would move forward with pleasure and work "united in just proportions"—and all "without the cost of pain." Fueling that engine would be "desires . . . intensified and multiplied."[35]

Although it is unlikely that Reisner read Patten, he and other advertisers—whether religious or secular—operated on the premises of the Wharton professor. By associating Christianity with pleasure and self-fulfillment, Reisner sought to create a disciplined body of church workers. However bright the smiles in his photos of young Sunday School–goers, control—not pleasure—was the ultimate goal. John F. Kasson's perceptive description of Coney Island at the beginning of the twentieth century is equally applicable to the advertising methods of Christian Reisner.

> Coney Island was necessarily an imperfect Feast of Fools, an institutionalized bacchanal. It represented a festival that did not express joy *about* something, but offered "fun" in a managed celebration of commercial ends. Dispensing standardized amusement, it demanded standardized responses. Beneath the air of liberation, its pressures were profoundly conformist, its means fundamentally manipulative. While encouraging the revelry of the crowd, Coney Island's managers aimed always to shape and control it. Not only did they have to winnow out undesirables; they also needed to engineer the environment to keep customers in the role of active consumers.[36]

By no stretch of the imagination would Christian Reisner's church have prompted a comparison to a feast of fools or a bacchanal, even an imperfect or institutionalized one, but it did promise fun. That fun was carefully managed. Rather like Muzak, the pleasures promised in his ads played only in the bland middle range of the emotional scale. Reisner's blurbs reduced the joys and sorrows of friendship to a hearty handshake and the sense of vitality to a church social. He plumbed neither the heights nor the depths of human emotion, for these were less amenable to manipulation. The pleasures he offered were self-referential. He evoked feelings of sociability, good times, and vitality but failed to ground them—despite perfunctory religious language—in a reality or context higher than themselves. Dislodged from a place in a transcendent universe of meaning, these experiences promised no ultimate fulfillment. They required repetition again and again, for a ceaseless round of new pleasures was all that remained of an End. The "customers," in Kasson's apt words, were kept perpetually "in the role of active consumers." Or as Reisner would have phrased it, there is always a better day before us. "Each day brings growth to Christ's disciples." The structure of *Church Publicity* reinforced the message. Despite the book's organization into sections on discrete subjects, it provided little sense of linear argument. It moved toward no particular denouement. It presented a succession of catchy phrases, gimmicks, and images that could have continued indefinitely beyond the author's 408 pages. Activity without closure and the promise of an unceasing progression of new experiences—these were the messages of the advertiser.[37]

Many propounded efficiency as a sideline to their primary professions. For example, Reisner served as a pastor emphasizing church publicity, Mathews as an historian-theologian and divinity school administrator, Strayer as a pastor, Earp as a sociologist studying the rural church. A few, however, strove to identify themselves chiefly as specialists in the scientific management of churches. Among this group, Albert F. McGarrah lectured on church efficiency at McCormick Seminary in Chicago and at several other theological schools during the second decade of the twentieth century. In *A Modern Church Program: A Study in Efficiency* (1915), *Modern Church Finance: Its Principles and Practice* (1916), and *Modern Church Management: A Study in Efficiency* (1917), he sought to turn church efficiency into a detailed program touching every area of ecclesiastical life. Although others had sketched in outline most of his proposals, his unique contribution was to gather up the pieces and hints they had provided and to fuse them into a comprehensive vision of an efficiently managed church.[38]

McGarrah viewed scientific management as a means of building the Kingdom of God and of affirming America's world mission.

American churches are entrusted with most unusual duties and responsibilities in connection with His [God's] world program for the perfecting of His Kingdom on earth. As goes America so goes the world. As goes American Christianity, so will America and the rest of the world go. . . . As God has given American Christians the clearest present understanding of the political, social, moral, and spiritual ideals which He expects them to develop and perfect and impart to the rest of the world, so He has entrusted to American churches the clearest understanding of the intellectual and educational and evangelistic and social methods which are to be used by the churches of the future that we may perfect these as contributions to the ultimate efficiency of all Christendom.

Yet despite his grand dream, McGarrah also betrayed the usual anxieties that the churches were proving inadequate to the moment. Secular organizations were "taking thousand-league steps" while churches lagged behind. Less than 10 percent of the population worshipped every week, according to his estimate, and the "average weekly attendance at theatres and movies is, in many cities, five times the church attendance." Only 40 percent of Sunday School students joined the church, while as many as half of the people who joined dropped from the rolls within a few years. Not more than two or three churches in a hundred had the money they really needed—and this at a time when their mission demanded that they "have unprecedented funds at their command" and "an almost unlimited increase in their incomes."[39]

Efficiency required that leaders dream big dreams and lay big plans. Many churches, McGarrah said, labored under notions of false economy. Before enlarging their programs, they insisted on having more money in hand. "To secure large results," he advised, "ask large things." By spending more, a congregation could improve its attractiveness and thus secure greater funds. He suggested that churches ask more money for benevolent causes, for religious education, for newspaper ads puffing the church, for social activities such as picnics and church suppers, for gyms and nurseries and kitchens, for raising the pastor's salary, and for improving the physical appearance of the sanctuary. "Church members of to-day," McGarrah declared, "want service and quality and results just as truly as do the patrons and stockholders of department stores and railroads, and they can be induced to pay the price when they receive the service which they want, or see the results which they desire."[40]

Proposing large expenditures was not, of course, the same thing as paying the bills. A visionary budget needed the assistance of systematic fund-raising. In an efficient church, the governing body formulated a unified and detailed budget in order to make a single annual appeal for funds rather than a series of haphazard requests. The minister prepared the way by preaching sermons on stewardship (defined as proportionate giving), articulate lay people drummed up support through public speeches, and printed leaflets promoted the campaign. In the best circumstances, all the congregations in a particular area—regardless of denominational affiliation—made their appeal at the same season. Working in tandem, the churches saturated the local newspapers with ads emphasizing the economic and social value of Christianity. The jointly timed appeal also encouraged an esprit de corps and a sense of participating in a great cause that would inspire enthusiasm. On a duly appointed date, teams of visitors fanned out to every member of their respective congregations. The day of visitation—ordinarily a Sunday afternoon when no one had business obligations—required careful selection so that it would not fall at a time when people were likely to be on weekend holiday. During the visit, the teams sought to secure a written pledge to donate a specific amount during *each* week of the coming fiscal year. McGarrah stressed the importance of the weekly pledge, for he believed that people gave more if they were committing themselves to fifty-two relatively small increments rather than to a single lump sum for the entire year. The visitation teams were not sent out as sheep among wolves. Training sessions gave them a message to convey: a vision of worldwide redemption, a patriotic appeal to America's need, and the linkage of both to loyal financial support of local and denominational programs. The visitors received advice regarding the proper approach to particular constituencies within the church. Possible objections to pledging were anticipated and answers supplied. The teams went armed with information cards telling how much each person was currently giving and targeting an increase for which they should aim. Once the campaign ended, the church followed up methodically by providing numbered and dated envelopes for the weekly offering. Two treasurers—one for local expenses, the other for benevolent giving—kept up-to-date records of donations and gently prodded those in arrears.[41]

McGarrah regarded the systematic financial campaign as a paradigm for the entire life of the church. Each congregation was to have a single board of governance. It in turn appointed various committees to specific tasks and took care that their activities did not overlap. The committees regularly submitted written reports to the governing board, preferably on standardized forms and in duplicate. Irrational or redundant organizations demanded streamlining. For example, the multiple women's groups in many churches needed consolidation into a single body. Women's activities needed to be more integrally related to the general work of the church with female representation on the governing board and on key committees. Moreover, councils of churches in local communities should seek to maintain proper coordination among the various congregations. Efficient structure also required up-to-date implements "from departmental classrooms to duplex envelopes, from religious motion pictures to addressographs and complete modern office equipment, from kitchen and social rooms to a 'pastor's auto' to save his time when visiting." Just as generals had modernized warfare and merchants sales techniques, so, too, the church must modernize. "We are often told that churches are now over-organized," McGarrah observed. "Rather, they are trying to work antiquated and outgrown organizations."[42]

The essence of McGarrah's efficiency program was centralized control by experts. According to his summary the purpose of church organization was

> to give all competent specialists and leaders those definite responsibilities where their powers will count for the most; to give to every member adequate oversight in his development, and co-operation in his Christian services; . . . to provide for the co-ordination of the work and the co-operation of all the workers under a single directing head. . . .

While insisting that the church must function democratically, McGarrah sketched an administrative style that suggested otherwise. Responsibilities lay with "competent specialists"; the receiving of oversight and coordination was the portion of members. "Practical men everywhere now admit," said McGarrah, "that every corporation and institution from a vast army to a country club . . . must have a single directing head." The church was no different. Although the governing board of the church might fulfill much of this function, it, too, needed a head. No one other than the pastor could fulfill that role. "He alone devotes his entire life to the interests involved and his entire time to the problems to be solved. No one else comes into complete and constant touch with the policies and needs and attitudes of all the organizations and individuals concerned. No one else has opportunity . . . to see the entire work of the congregation." Yet centralized leadership did not mean rule by dictate. A good pastor worked cautiously by educating the people slowly, by knowing when to send controversial ideas into committee for further study, or by privately winning key members of the governing board before a program was formally introduced. In short, the minister-executive was a consensus builder, the quintessential organization man.[43]

Had these ideas been the fancies of a few writers only or merely dreams of the tiny Federal Council staff ensconced in their warehouse office by the freight elevator, they would not be historically important. But efficiency received embodiment in restructuring taking place within the major denominations themselves. Although the several churches followed slightly different paths, owing to their distinctive polities and theologies, the general contours of the transformation in the years after 1875 were similar. Initially the numbers of people engaged in various home and foreign missions grew; new agencies, often created willy-nilly, supported the ventures; and the numbers of workers for these boards increased dramatically. Similar to the jerry-built expansion of many businesses in the early Gilded Age, Protestant operations after the 1870s enlarged and proliferated, often with little thought as to how these activities fit into a coherent pattern. Denominational agencies often acted as independent fiefdoms competing with one another for the dollars of the folks in the pews. Pastors resented a chaotic situation which forced them to spend many Sundays a year dunning their congregations on behalf of various agencies and causes. Then came efforts to streamline and coordinate these sprawling enterprises by merging boards, demarcating responsibilities, strengthening central administrative control, and promoting systematic budget-planning and fund-raising enterprises. Thus the Northern Baptists organized in 1908 what later became known as the American Baptist Convention to give order to their various enterprises. The Disciples of Christ tried to coordinate a number of their activities in a United Christian Missionary Society in 1919, and the Northern Presbyterians in 1923 condensed the work of more than a dozen independent boards and committees to four agencies supervised by a General Council meeting in the interim between the church's annual general assemblies. Methodists, having theoretically placed their various agencies under the legislative control of the quadrennial General Conference as early as 1872, established in 1912 a Commission on Finance which had power to apportion funds to the various agencies. Eight years later, that committee was replaced by the Council of Boards of Benevolence, empowered to set the budgets and goals of individual boards.[44]

In this transformation, organizational matters often became an imperative defining the identity of the churches themselves. A committee charged with studying the restructuring of the American Baptist Convention concluded in 1925 that the size of its task "required a concentration of attention more on the means of accomplishment than on the ends—more on machinery than on the goal. The Committee could not assess the spiritual values . . . or give adequate recognition in this report to these imponderable objectives." Similarly, when Will Hays, a prominent Republican politician and lay leader of his denomination, reported to the 1927 Presbyterian General Assembly on the successful completion of a drive to create a ministerial pension plan, he boasted: "If there were no other evidence of the essential unity of our great denomination than this . . . , this fact alone—that practically every self-supporting church voluntarily cooperated in a united effort for a common cause is overwhelming proof of our desire and ability to work together in the interests of the Kingdom." Hays did allude to "many other" (unspecified) evidences of unity, but, significantly, he accented the importance of the "common cause"—in this instance, a successful fund-raising drive. Efficient programs to promote the kingdom were becoming a chief defining mark of ecclesiastical identity. "Spiritual values" or "imponderable objectives" were, of course, never disavowed as the preeminent ones, but they did not receive prime attention precisely because they were "imponderable" and thus incapable of submitting to the exact measures of the efficiency experts.[45]

Maintaining the efficiency of the organization was a perpetual chore, not once performed and then forgotten. "Eternal vigilance is the price of organized efficiency," according to Albert McGarrah's recension of an old dictum in 1916. "Church organization is not a mechanical process to be perfected once and forever but an organic process which should constantly advance toward perfection." Thus he suggested that each church create an efficiency committee to subject all programs to continuous scrutiny and change. Efficiency, like the Kingdom of God in whose name it was invoked, apparently had no End, and within several years of McGarrah's observation, the Protestant churches would in fact be making plans for still larger projects on behalf of the kingdom and efficiency.[46]

6

Efficiency and the Kingdom
in a World at War

ल७⑥Ⴆ

On April 2, 1917, the Congress of the United States convened in special session at the summons of President Woodrow Wilson. At 8:30 P.M., the president appeared before the senators and representatives. Explaining that America could no longer honorably maintain a policy of neutrality toward the European conflict, he requested a declaration of war against the Imperial German Government. Wilson spoke primarily of the lofty principles at stake. America sought "no selfish ends." It desired "no conquest, no dominion." It battled "for the rights of nations great and small and the privilege of men every where to choose their way of life. . . . The world must be made safe for democracy." Yet success demanded more than idealism. "It will involve," the president predicted, "the organization and mobilization of all the material resources of the country."[1]

Wilson's prophecy proved accurate. Under the leadership of financier Bernard Baruch, the War Industries Board fixed prices of industrial goods, maintained oversight of the economy, and directed resources into the production of war matériel. The Treasury Department temporarily took over the railroads. Herbert Hoover's Food Administration engaged in public jawboning to persuade families to observe "meatless Tuesdays," to plant "victory" gardens, and to utilize every scrap of garbage. The old nineteenth-century military system—regiments raised locally and then pieced into a national force—gave way to a system resembling scientific management. Under a chief of staff heading a bureaucracy analogous to that of a business corporation, planners controlled the logistics of arming, transporting, and feeding more than four million men in uniform. Congress impressed time itself into service, ordering that clocks be moved ahead one hour at 2:00 A.M. on May 31, 1918, and thus saving daylight for productive labor. The Committee on Public Information mobilized popular opinion on behalf of the war, or as the director, George

Creel, phrased the matter, the committee "advertised America." Aware that in the years just before the nation's entry into war "the land had been torn by a thousand divisive prejudices," the committee engaged in a "fight for the *minds* of men, for the 'conquest of their opinions.'" "What we had to have was no mere surface unity," Creel later wrote, "but a passionate belief in the justice of America's cause that should weld the people of the United States into one white-hot mass instinct with fraternity, devotion, courage, and deathless determination." To that end, the committee enlisted over 75,000 "Four Minute Men" who gave brief speeches plumping America's righteous cause in communities across the land. It prepared patriotic exhibits and festivals, assembled artists to produce war posters, and distributed photographs as well as slides. Making its most creative venture in the new area of motion pictures, the committee distributed films such as *Pershing's Crusaders* and *America's Answer* to whip up enthusiasm for the struggle. If mobilization by persuasion failed, sterner sanctions remained close at hand. President Wilson sent troops to enforce order among rebellious western workers in 1917, and the head of the Selective Service threatened to draft strikers into the armed forces. Behind these official actions was a firestorm of popular patriotic fervor readily turned against anything or anyone manifesting less than "one hundred per cent Americanism." As Alan Dawley has written: "Total war involved a devastating combination of rationality and irrationality, modern efficiency and atavistic hatreds, the machine gun and war hysteria."[2]

The harsh conformity demanded by war may have sounded the death knell for the more humane elements of Progressivism, but 1917 also promised to realize some of the movement's hopes. The Progressive zeal for efficient, coordinated management found fulfillment in the war machine. Thus Walter Lippmann rejoiced, believing that a supervised economy during war would set the precedent for peacetime blueprints of a better society. Similarly, Robert Woods of the settlement house movement exulted that mobilization prepared the way for a properly managed nation that would promote justice and prosperity for all citizens. "In no previous . . . generation," he noted, "would it have been possible that every nook and corner of our cities, would have been under the close, responsible, friendly surveillance of men and women representing much that is best in our national life—that in this way the dangers to a nation at war coming from nests of dissipation, of contagious disease, of crime, of disloyalty, of espionage, of actual resistance to the government, could be everywhere effectively minimized." America was achieving the efficiency engineer's dream, one that Woods condensed in an Orwellian phrase— "the regimentation of the free."[3]

Amid the crosscurrents of savage passion and soaring idealism, Protestant leaders saw an unprecedented opportunity to reshape the nation and the world. Success or failure in that endeavor hinged upon the denominations' ability to speak with one voice and to work together. Several years after the armistice, Union Seminary's William Adams Brown observed that the war "revealed to American Protestantism its essential unity." Yet in face of the task to be done, Brown added, the war also showed the churches "that they lacked agencies through which that unity could express itself effectively in action." Much Protestant activity during the conflict was an effort to create and coordinate such agencies. For the churches as well as the nation, the war gave a new and more urgent outlet for an efficiency crusade to bring in the kingdom of God.[4]

"For a New America in a New World"

When the guns of August 1914 shattered the European peace, President Wilson initially proclaimed neutrality above the sordid *Realpolitik* of the Central Powers and the Allies. America's mission was to embody the ideal of a just international order—an order in which peace without victory might be achieved. In time, he hoped, the warring parties would repair to this platform. Despite the fact that some clamored for American intervention, most church leaders appeared to embrace their president's goals. Shortly before the nation abandoned neutrality, the *Homiletic Review* canvassed the opinions of a number of leading clergymen and educators. They, too, looked for a universal vantage point above the conflict. William H. P. Faunce, the Baptist president of Brown University, called upon American churches to drive out racial hatred, to cultivate an international mind-set, and to work for a world organization which would promote peace. A New York minister urged the American church to "demand arbitration instead of force . . . Then alone will she rise to her duty, and command the world's respect and love." E. Y. Mullins, the moderately conservative Southern Baptist leader, called for lifting "the whole question of diplomacy to a higher level. . . . If the nations of the world will adopt Christian principles in dealing with one another, it goes without saying that another war such as that which is at present raging in Europe will be impossible." Newman Smyth, the liberal patriarch of New England Congregationalism, demanded an attack upon all parochial allegiances, including ecclesiastical ones, as a means of addressing the causes of the war. He envisioned a new John the Baptist, proclaiming that "even now the ax is being laid at the root of . . . denominational trees . . . Now is the time for each church to repent of its part in the common sin of continuance in a state of schism. Confessing our sin we are to take up all together the work of preparing the way of the Lord."[5]

Yet once Congress declared war against Germany, Protestant leaders generally offered their ardent support. The chief exceptions were the historic peace churches and some German-American churches that still felt tugs of sympathy to the Fatherland. Not a few presented the struggle as an unvarnished holy war. A naturalized American pastor born in Syria declared: "The present war is not a *mere* war. It is a moral earthquake which calls for the supreme choice by individuals and nations between right and wrong, liberty and bondage. This conflict seems to me to uncover the hidden secrets of the universe itself and to reveal to the human vision the primordial and everlasting struggle between good and evil." After visiting a training camp for American soldiers, one Methodist minister composed a lexicon of shame to describe the enemy America fought: the United States struggled against "hideous savagery," the "devils of the Potsdam gang," "murderous banditry," "a fiendish Kaiserism," "unspeakable slaughter, and rape, and arson, and frightfulness"— all of which would soon be consigned to the "lowest hell." Newell Dwight Hillis, pastor of the Plymouth Congregational Church in Brooklyn, collected stories of atrocities allegedly committed by Germany and advocated the sterilization of its soldiers at the close of the war. Popular evangelist "Billy" Sunday, invited to offer prayer in the House of Representatives on January 10, 1918, declared to the Almighty: "Thou knowest, O Lord, that we are in a life-and-death struggle with one of the most infamous, vile, greedy, avaricious, bloodthirsty, sensual, and vicious nations that has ever disgraced the pages of history. . . . We pray Thee that Thou will make bare Thy mighty arm and beat back that great pack of hungry, wolfish Huns, whose fangs drip with blood and gore."[6]

Despite sanguinary rhetoric aplenty, many leaders saw the war as the lesser of evils. Harry Emerson Fosdick, a young Baptist minister already becoming one of America's best-known preachers, endorsed America's effort to restrain wickedness in *The Challenge of the Present Crisis* (1917). But war, he insisted, must never be deemed glorious or ennobling. A travesty of the ideal will of God, war degraded humanity and prostituted its highest ideals "to destructive ends." The best case to be made for the war held that "We must help to meet the crisis, with all its wretched necessities, as sharers in a mutual responsibility which no one rightly may evade. . . . For, however heartily we may hate the emergencies that the evil of the world presents, we must stay within the problem of international entanglements, as we stay within the economic system, to play our part as best we can in the redemption of both."[7]

Robert E. Speer of the Presbyterian Board of Foreign Missions, in an address to the Intercollegiate YMCA at Columbia University in February 1918, insisted that the war aims of the United States needed to rise above "pure national individualism" to embrace "universal ideals and the universal spirit."

America needed to address the underlying causes of the war if it were to advance the cause of true peace. These included, said Speer, the imperfect development of democracy, the pretension of nationalism to transcend morality, and the persistence of racial prejudices. He indicated that America, not only Germany, partook of these failings. When critics accused him of "weakening patriotism" and of displaying "Teutonic susceptibilities," Speer replied that one must not in the name of loyalty "deny facts or tolerate in America what he is warring against elsewhere."[8]

The Federal Council of Churches, in whose leadership he played a prominent role, paralleled Speer's attempt to balance patriotic loyalty with larger, more inclusive moral imperatives. At a specially called meeting in May 1917, representatives of the constituent churches as well as some invited delegates from other bodies adopted a report written by William Adams Brown. Professing a dual loyalty to both Christ and country, the statement gave thanks that the two allegiances did not in this instance conflict. The goals America sought—liberty and righteousness—were thoroughly consistent with Christian principles, especially since the nation was pursuing them "without haste or passion, not for private or national gain, with no hatred or bitterness against those with whom we contend." The council promised to work to ensure "that this war shall end in nothing less than such a constructive peace as shall be the beginning of a world democracy." It pledged "to rebuild on this war-ridden and desolated earth the commonwealth of mankind, and to make of the kingdoms of the world the kingdom of the Christ."[9]

The Rev. William Barton of Oak Park, Illinois, summed up in a few pungent lines what Fosdick, Speer, the Federal Council, and many other leaders wished to affirm. "The Church is the bride of Christ, and not the concubine of the State. If the Church gives of its membership and its prayers to the winning of this war, the Church must be able to give a reason for its faith and for its fighting, and that reason must be something else than the word of Stephen Decatur, 'My country right or wrong.' It must be something other than an appeal to hatred and brute passion." That something was an invocation of cosmopolitan ideals. "God is on the side, not of America against Germany," Barton explained, "but on the side of humanity against inhumanity, on the side of justice against injustice. We shall win . . . because we have allied ourselves with the cause of humanity, which is God's own cause." Barton's "cause of humanity" echoed Speer's call for a "universal spirit" and the Federal Council's prediction of "a world democracy."[10]

Indeed, an international vision was a major component of Protestant thought during the war. "The republic can never again," declared Methodist Bishop W. F. McDowell, "be isolated and insular, neutral, or self-complacent. . . . We are citizens, henceforth, not strangers or sojourners in the whole kingdom of Jesus on earth and in heaven." W. H. P. Faunce asserted: "The true patriot, like the true Christian, is a citizen of the world. He cannot rest in the thought of a world made up of eternally hostile units." Faunce looked forward to a "league of all civilized states" that "shall foreshadow, if it does not establish, the Kingdom of God." Harry Emerson Fosdick was more emphatic still: "*We must have a federation of the world. No other solution is great enough to deal with our critical need....* A Christianity that is not international has never known its Master." These and many other Protestant leaders stood in full accord with President Wilson, whose diplomacy helped produce the classic embodiment of a new internationalism: a proposed League of Nations. In presenting to the Senate the treaty containing provision for the league, Wilson explained that it would "establish a new order which would rest upon the free choice of peoples." As the president understood the matter, American entrance into the league did not repudiate the nation's special mission, but fulfilled it. "The stage is set," he declared, "the destiny disclosed. It has come about by no plan of our conceiving, but by the hand of God who led us into this way. We cannot turn back. We can only go forward, with lifted eyes and freshened spirit, to follow the vision. It was of this that we dreamed at our birth. America shall in truth show the way. The light streams upon the path ahead, and nowhere else."[11]

Wilsonian rhetoric about America's role as a light to the nations—an echo perhaps of the prophecy of Isaiah 60:3 that "nations shall come to your light"—serves as a reminder that his internationalism left plenty of room for American pride, even tub-thumping patriotism. In this respect, too, the president spoke for many Protestants. Charles R. Brown, dean of the School of Religion at Yale University, contended that the universal values for which America struggled made the United States a unique player on the stage of world history. "May we not believe," he asked, "that this country, strong and brave, generous and hopeful, is called of God to be in its own way a Messianic nation in whose mighty unfolding life all the nations of the earth may be blessed?" Precisely because the United States embodied ideals transcending the parochial, loyal support of the war became a sacred duty which none could honorably escape. "The very conscience of the country has put on khaki," declared Brown. Even Fosdick, despite his insistence that Christians avoid love of war, concluded *The Challenge of the Present Crisis* by quoting, with approval, the letter of a French mother to her son in Canada. Informing him of the death of his two brothers in the army, she advised: "while I am not going to suggest that you return to fight for France, if you do not come at once, *never* come." Fosdick applied the lesson to his American readers. "Multitudes are living in that spirit today. He must have a callous soul who can pass through times like these and not hear a voice, whose call a man must answer, or else lose his soul. Your country needs *you*. The Kingdom of God on earth needs *you*. The Cause of Christ is hard bestead and righteousness is having a heavy battle in the earth—they need *you*." Worth Tippy, believing that America had "entered upon a great adventure for humanity," likewise fused the cause of the kingdom and the cause of America. He called upon the church to become "an inseparable part of the life of the people, strengthening them, comforting them, speaking their highest vision and morality." The church must "strengthen the morale of the nation in every conceivable way. It is to do everything within its power . . . to hasten the victory. . . . The watchwords of the church to the people are faith, courage, greatness of endeavour; not hesitancy, reservations, moral perplexities, conscientious objections."[12]

Such leaders generally sought to allay doubts and to promote the integration of the churches into the war effort. They did so without the crude excesses of a "Billy" Sunday declaring that hell was made in Germany or of a Newell Hillis recommending the sterilization of German soldiers. Nor did they endorse the widespread hysteria against the foreign-born or join the crusade to give everything with a Teutonic ring, from German shepherds to sauerkraut, more patriotic names such as Alsatian shepherds and liberty cabbage. Sober, responsible people, they aspired to a global moral renovation, not a narrow chauvinism. In the words of Oberlin College president Henry Churchill King, they worked "for a new America in a new world." Yet at the end of the day, the call of the kingdom and the summons of the nation were, at least for the moment, one and the same. Despite their humane intentions, Protestant leaders contributed to the climate of opinion in which tribal passions could masquerade in the guise of universal morality and thus remain relatively immune to criticism.[13]

Protestants recognized that the war had tapped elemental impulses, but they believed that these promised spiritual regeneration. Samuel McCrea Cavert, soon to begin a distinguished career with the Federal Council of Churches, argued that war was "the training school of a more vigorous and more heroic type of life." It was saving Americans from their "old flabbiness" and developing "spiritual muscle and brawn." "The great cause to which we are now committed," Cavert added, "is making the same appeal to the heroic in men that Jesus constantly used." The doughboys would become major instruments of this spiritual revival. According to Episcopal Dean H. P. Almon Abbott of Cleveland, Ohio, the "tommies" were "playing the Twentieth Century *Christos*—laying down their lives that we may live." Through their sacrifice they were learning that religion consisted of deeds, not of the fine points of doctrine. To keep abreast of such men, the churches, too, would need to stress truths equally fundamental: "manliness—honesty—consistency of life—reality, and simplicity." A Brooklyn minister suggested that soldiers would return with "a new creed, simpler, plainer than the creed of the church-men." Having discovered that denominational affiliation "counts for nothing when the Hun is just ahead," veterans would espouse a streamlined credo: belief in God, homage to Christ, service to one's fellows and one's country.[14]

Henry Tweedy, a professor of practical theology at Yale, rejoiced that many clergy served with the men in France and likewise participated in the "directness and sternness in camp and military life which is singularly invigo-rating and even Christ-like." Life in the trenches would render these men "more virile" and purge them "of all softness and sentimentalism." As persons "who have been under fire," these ministers in years ahead "will increasingly merit and possess the respect of laymen and of soldiers." Former soldiers would remember them as "jolly good fellows in camp" and as loyal comrades in No Man's Land. Thus when the minister knocked at their doors in the fu-ture, the veterans would "not be so apt to call, 'Mother, the dominie has come to see you!' It will be no longer the pastor who wishes to meet and to know the male parishioner; the male parishioner will be equally eager to meet and to know the pastor." Tweedy predicted that "All this will come to the minister as a reward for having realized the picture as painted by an English chaplain. 'I like to think of the parish priest as fulfilling the Shakespearean stage direc-tion—"Scene: a public place. Enter First Citizen";—for his ministry should mostly be spent neither in church nor in the homes of the faithful, but in public places; and he should be the First Citizen of his parish.'" Having gained the confidence of his male congregants and having won his place in the public square, the former chaplain would never again be content with small aims or with the cloistered life of the traditional parish minister. He "would not suffer his people to travel in the old ruts or . . . countenance out-worn and inefficient methods." "Nothing less than the ambition to take the world and its kingdoms for Christ" would satisfy him and his former com-rades in arms.[15]

Clearly, the war had stirred up what Tweedy's Yale colleague, Luther Weigle, called a "deep, elemental common religion of America." For Weigle, the chief question was what form this impulse would take and whether or not it would "recognize its fundamentally Christian character." The answer lay in the response of the churches. If they concerned themselves "more directly with life, and . . . put less emphasis upon dogma," if they gave priority to action over correct belief, they might direct wartime faith into Christian chan-nels. That stress on life and action meant that denominational loyalties must be effectively "incorporated into a higher loyalty to the inclusive fellowship of Christ's church."[16]

That theme was repeated almost incessantly. According to H. P. Almon Abbott, the war had taught "that *Christianity counts for much, and that Denomi-*

nationalism in Christianity counts for less than nothing. . . . It is essential, then—before this War is over and the men return from the Front—that there should be a most real *rapprochement* between all the organized religious forces in the United States of America." Fosdick offered a similar observation. By his count, 165 separate religious bodies existed in America. "In the presence of a gigantic task, calling for a federated Church, we stand a split, dissevered flock of churches." Even within each of those separate bodies, "bickering over details of polity" and "endless splits twixt Tweedledee and Tweedledum" frayed unity. "Are these times that seem to call for such minute finesse?" he asked. "As one thinks of the world today, shaken in an earthquake that brings clattering down about our ears the dearest dreams our hearts have cherished, it does seem that religion should grow great . . . [and] ought to speak great words about God and the Kingdom, lest men's hearts turn to water in them and their strength be gone."[17]

Methodist church historian Daniel Dorchester put the issue in broader perspective. The world, he explained, was "travailing in pain" for "spiritual guidance and control" in large measure because the churches had failed to provide them. He traced the failure to earlier centuries when the Christian community forgot its "ideal of a Divine Kingdom transcending Church and State, and immanent in both," and "in its lust for temporal power . . . antagonized every State it could not rule and denied the divine mission of the State." In reaction, the state "became degraded into a secular institution which recognized no higher law than its own necessity and no power other than military force." Thus moral and spiritual concerns were effectively segregated from political policies. Unfortunately the church, riven into fragments, had little power to alter this situation. It "has no unified command, no proper subordination of sectarian and secondary interests to an overmastering purpose to carry forward the Kingdom of God." He ardently prayed that the church would acquire "the power to speak in righteousness with one voice."[18]

There were signs of hope. Just as the nations, said Worth Tippy, had seen the necessity of "stupendous organization . . . for the conduct of the war," many Protestants now understood the necessity for a similar arrangement among themselves. Tippy called for "centralized leadership." Events had demonstrated the unreadiness of the churches for war and indicated "the need of some method by which the church may anticipate events, and analyze social movements so as to be ready when they come." Informal cooperation would not meet the demand. The churches must either create "a new official organization to correlate the Protestant communions" or "expand and perfect the Federal Council and allied interchurch organizations." From his own vantage point as an executive of the Council, Tippy preferred the latter course.[19]

The war recapitulated in condensed and urgent form the dynamics that had played themselves out so often in Protestant life during the previous several decades: fear of chaotic forces displacing Protestantism from a controlling place in American life, a desire that churches and ministers repossess that role ("Scene: a public place. Enter First Citizen"), the effort to build new organizations to effect the reclamation, and finally the need to streamline and coordinate those bodies according to the principles of efficiency. What began in elemental impulse ended in agencies and in committee rooms.

To tap and tame elemental hopes and fears during the war, Protestants did more than theorize about the need to form and correlate organizations. They created them by the scores. The YMCA played a leading role in the process. For two decades prior to the war, it had already busily expanded its programs. Sporting activities, boys' work, ministry to African Americans and to Indians, work with industrial groups (especially skilled railroad employees), service to rural communities—all had found departmental niches within the structure of the "Y" and had produced a cadre of specialized YMCA professionals. The "proliferation of program" occurred in a fashion analogous to the growth of large businesses, and the imposing edifices built by many YMCAs during this era reinforced the symbolic linkage. As C. Howard Hopkins has observed, "Stately entrances, marble staircases, and lobbies rivaling public buildings were calculated to class the new Association facilities with the communities' major downtown headquarters of business or government." The war brought an exponential increase in program. The day Congress declared war, John R. Mott, the general secretary of the International YMCA, wired President Wilson to pledge the association's full support to the government and six days later convened a special meeting of the movement's leaders. That group organized a National War Work Council to supervise what soon became a far-flung empire of ministries. By the time the war was over, the council had sent out nearly twenty-six thousand workers. The council's various agencies constructed more than nine hundred buildings in the United States alone, served as the major director of recreational activities in the military training camps, operated 4,000 canteens for American soldiers in Europe, sent forth more than a thousand athletic directors to administer physical education programs for the men in arms, served as impresario recruiting nearly fifteen hundred entertainers, conducted religious services, and worked with prisoners of the war.[20]

Although uttered prior to the conflict, the address of George Coe to the graduates of the YMCA's Springfield College in 1910 encapsulated the rationale for the organizing process that reached its culmination in the war: "the kingdom of God will surely come, yet it will not come down upon us (as in primitive Christian belief) but up through us. . . . Analysis of conditions in the spirit of science, organization of forces in the spirit of business, definiteness and comprehensiveness of attack like that of an experienced strategist—these have of right the same place in the religion of Jesus as in concerns that are called secular."[21]

The Federal Council provided the other major instrument for cooperative Protestantism. Five months after the United States entered the conflict, the council created the General War-Time Commission of the Churches whose purpose was "to coordinate existing and proposed activities . . . so as to avoid all waste and friction and to promote efficiency." Composed of 100 members drawn from denominational agencies and from the ranks of prominent pastors and laypeople, the commission included persons of various persuasions, but those of a socially and theologically liberal outlook predominated. The commission ran its programs through an executive committee, meeting twice a month, and through various subcommittees. By the time the commission completed its work in April 1919, it had created twenty-eight of these. The committees brought together officials sharing similar responsibilities in their respective denominations and thus helped to make interchurch cooperation more than a shibboleth.[22]

Especially in the early days of the commission's work, the growth of structure outpaced performance. As John Piper observes, "New committees were numerous, plans abounded, and new faces in the Council offices exercised new authority; but actual programs were still few and financial support remained uncertain." Nevertheless, the General War-Time Commission achieved important goals. Even before the start of the conflict, the council had used its newly created Washington office to lobby for a change in the laws governing the appointment of naval chaplains. An act passed in 1914 increased the numbers of chaplains and eliminated the patronage system whereby they secured appointment. In 1917, the council created a General Committee on Army and Navy Chaplains through which the government received nominations of Protestant chaplains—a task that assumed considerable importance once mobilization swelled the numbers of soldiers and chaplains alike. Other agencies of the War-Time Commission collected information on military cantonments, investigated munition-producing communities to ensure that the needs of workers were being addressed, launched a successful fund-raising campaign sponsored by fourteen denominations, and prepared a manual showing how local churches might fully integrate their work with the war effort.[23]

Worth Tippy, who helped prepare the manual, rejoiced that the churches were offering the government and allied agencies an efficient means of promoting food conservation, Red Cross drives, and the sale of government bonds. The loyal church, Tippy declared, recognized that "requests of the Government are in a class by themselves. They constitute a privilege and an opportunity for service which cannot be denied." During a war of the sort the United States was waging—a war which was "a great adventure for humanity"—the task of the church was to "to express the spirit which moves the nation" and "to strengthen the morale of the nation in every conceivable way." While Christians needed always to keep in mind the larger spiritual dimensions of the conflict, the present moment was not the time to express "moral perplexities" about warfare, or to ponder whether Americans bore some "remote share in the guilt of the war." Through the Allied Expeditionary Force, "the Kingdom of God has rough work to do in the world, work like that of surgeons in hospitals, and men who hesitate at conflict, or draw back lest they miss the right in some particulars, cannot do that work."[24]

Tippy had inadvertently identified the reason that the call for efficient, united religious service received an overwhelmingly positive response from so many Protestants. War had fused the vision of the kingdom with the appeal to crusading patriotism. Or as another minister said with simplistic brevity: "the building of America for Americans and the bringing in of the kingdom of God become one and the same. . . . Patriotism and religion have found their common ground." For those who had eyes to see, there were already signs that this "common ground" might prove insufficient. Denominations, while often willing to submerge their differences during the war, jealously guarded their prerogatives. Some churches, fearing overcentralization and the loss of autonomy, stayed out of the commission's fund-raising drive, and they bickered occasionally over denominational quotas for the military chaplaincy. Moreover, the reformist, international vision of many Protestants coexisted uneasily with the fervent 100-percent Americanism the war had inspired, and behind the facade of unity rumbled the sounds of what would become the fundamentalist-modernist controversy. Yet as the guns fell silent, most leaders remained confident that the experience of wartime mobilization could be repeated in peace. Henry Churchill King, writing to doughboys soon to be sent home, held out the hope of "a new America in a new world"—a United States whose churches and politics alike would henceforth be rationally ordered to promote conservation of natural resources, the management of public utilities, the establishment of a national education policy, economic justice, and the maintenance of an international vision. Having learned to subsume their differences in the trenches, they must now respond to "a Divine call to a great new Oath of Allegiance, to such a solemn rededication of the living, to the unfulfilled tasks of democracy and of the Kingdom, as Lincoln called for on the field of Gettysburg."[25]

"A Combination in Restraint of Waste"

On December 17, 1918, a month after the armistice was signed, representatives of thirty-five Protestant agencies gathered in New York City. They came, William Adams Brown later recalled, because "they had seen a vision—the vision of a united church in a divided world, and under the spell of what they saw all things seemed possible. Difficulties were waved aside, doubters were silenced. In face of an opportunity so unparalleled, there seemed but one thing to do, and that was to go forward." Going forward meant a new experiment in cooperative Protestant work. After additional meetings in early 1919, the venture acquired a name—the Interchurch World Movement (IWM)—and a large agenda: "a scientific survey of the world's needs from the standpoint . . . of evangelical Christianity," the development of "a cooperative community and world program" to meet those needs, and the mobilization of "resources of life, money, and prayer" to make the program a reality. The leaders of the movement described its goal with audacious simplicity. "The program of the Interchurch World Movement calls for an unprecedented degree of cooperation among the churches of North America in their entire missionary program at home and abroad. Its two-fold responsibility is first to find the facts and second to face the facts. Once the facts are discovered and confronted, the titanic task of the cooperating Christian churches will be to make the kingdoms of this world the kingdoms of our Lord and of his Christ." To achieve these large aims, thirty denominations agreed to conduct a campaign to raise more than $336 million, over half of which was to be collected in 1920.[26]

The movement drew upon the enthusiasms and successes of the war years. Just as separate nations had pooled their resources to defeat the Central Powers and just as Americans had bought Liberty Bonds, subscribed to Red Cross drives, and observed "meatless Tuesdays," the Protestant churches would now unite in sacrificial service "to make the kingdoms of this world the kingdoms of our Lord." Yet the Interchurch World Movement was more than a last spasm of wartime fervor. It represented the culmination of trends that had been underway long before the United States had sent its young men to battle the Kaiser: emphasis upon centralized and standardized administration, sophisticated publicity, systematic fund-raising, and scientific expertise. Although the leaders of the movement denied that they wished to infringe on the prerogatives of denominations, many aspired to create a religious analogue to a well-integrated, efficient business corporation. In an ironic twist to the language of the Sherman Anti-Trust Act (1890) that forbade combina-

tions in restraint of trade, the IWM boldly styled itself a good corporate mo-
nopoly—"a combination in restraint of waste."[27]

Movement literature spoke of establishing a "joint headquarters" for
Protestantism in New York City. Here would find a home "the seventy-five or
more international, national, metropolitan and civic religious agencies now
inadequately located in almost as many different offices in widely scattered
buildings." The IWM foresaw a building including assembly and conference
rooms, a hospital, a restaurant, a recreational center for employees, a reference
library, central shipping and purchasing divisions, and departments providing
maps, charts, and slides. The joint headquarters would have "every practical
facility for promoting efficiency and economy in the great advance program
of the Protestant churches of the entire country." Initially, some proposed
the construction of a forty-story interchurch building at Madison Square
Garden, but the projected twenty-five million dollar price tag was prohibitive.
In the end, the IWM settled for smaller but still commodious quarters on
West Eighteenth Street. More than half of the Movement's 2,612 employees
worked in the five-story building, and the unused office space, it was hoped,
would in time attract various denominational agencies.[28]

Both the structure and the management of the IWM bore a striking re-
semblance to those of a business corporation. Under the supervision of an
executive committee chaired by John R. Mott and administered by his fellow
Methodist S. Earl Taylor were two major groups—survey and education—
each run by an executive. These in turn were broken down into numerous
departments, and the latter were subdivided into divisions. The departments
touched virtually every area of ecclesiastical life: women's work and men's
work, the rural church and the city church, home and foreign missions, stewardship and publicity, missionary education and industrial relations. To assure
the smooth functioning of the movement, an Organization and Methods Unit
kept tabs on the entire operation. The management of the IWM resembled
that of corporate America in another respect. "Like many big businesses after
World War I," Eldon Ernst has written, "the Interchurch World Movement
organized its large staff of employees into a cohesive social unit, assuming the
functions of a variety of social organizations." The personnel department organized sporting activities, offered cultural opportunities, and maintained a
nursing staff to care for employees who fell ill.[29]

John D. Rockefeller, Jr. reinforced the image of the IWM as the headquarters for a corporate Protestantism. A devout Baptist who sat on the executive committee and donated large sums to the movement, Rockefeller
wrote and spoke on its behalf. "The Interchurch World Movement," he declared, "gives the best hope that has appeared yet that the wasteful era of
ecclesiastical competition is over and that one of ecclesiastical efficiency and

co-operation has begun." The old haphazard method of "determining how the work of the Kingdom should be done" was giving way to a scientific, businesslike approach. The IWM started its work "in the same way that every business man developing a new field would commence—by carefully looking over the ground and discovering all the facts in the situation." Having looked over the ground through its surveys, the IWM made it possible "for the first time in the history of Christianity . . . [that the churches might] visualize the whole task that awaits them." Now with the facts in hand and with plans synchronized, Protestants could make a united appeal to win the loyalty of a multitude "of good, earnest Christians, who for one reason or another are not definitely affiliated with any particular church." The IWM augured an immense "gain in power—power in numbers, in leadership, and in spirituality." Rockefeller saw in the movement a herald of national and spiritual re-birth. The IWM was "the greatest force for righteousness that the world has ever known." It would raise up as leaders "the ablest, the broadest, the best-educated men and women, who will recall the early days of the republic." It would "generate such an outpouring of the power of the spirit as the world has never seen since the days of the Apostles." Rockefeller was attempting to do for ecclesiastical life what he and his family had done for the oil industry and higher education: to rationalize and integrate its operations. Yet, as his extravagant rhetoric testified, the quest for "efficiency in the Lord's business" was far from the spirit of the stereotypical bloodless bureaucrat. Although Rockefeller was indeed promoting the bureaucratization of American Protestantism, he did so with passion, believing that the restructuring of religious institutions meant nothing less than the salvation of the world. As he wrote for the *Saturday Evening Post* in February 1918, "I see the church moulding the thought of the world as it has never done before, leading in all great movements as it should, I see it literally establishing the Kingdom of God on earth."[30]

Rockefeller asserted that "discovering all the facts" was the first step to efficiency, and the IWM collected data assiduously. It offered its preliminary findings in two volumes entitled *World Survey,* one being devoted to the United States and the other to the rest of the world. Attractively presented, *World Survey* was more than a compilation of facts. The use of graphs, pictures, clever ads, and a lean narrative emphasizing dramatic findings constituted artful publicity. These devices aimed to move men and women to action and thus to fulfill the IWM's motto. "Know—then do."[31]

In presenting both the home and foreign fields, *World Survey* followed a three-part strategy. The authors sketched a series of perils faced by American Christianity, indicated the available resources already possessed by Christian institutions, and then offered general suggestions regarding the proper deployment of those resources. Underlying this approach was the assumption that the facts would speak for themselves. To present them through graphs and dramatic incidents or to highlight them in sidebars with snappy quotations would be sufficient to arouse churchgoers to their duty. "To have this knowledge," Rockefeller wrote, "if not half the battle, is at any rate a good start in winning it." Also, *World Survey* never doubted the ability of American Christianity—the authors meant chiefly Protestantism—to master the United States, indeed the world itself. If Protestants raised enough money, integrated their activities, standardized their operations, relied on professional expertise, and engaged in centralized planning, the future would be theirs.[32]

Virtually every section of the two volumes illustrated the IWM's strategy and assumptions. For example, the authors painted a picture of urban life distressing to native Protestants: the foreign born and their children had achieved a numerical majority in many cities, Protestant churches had retreated to the suburbs, tenantry outpaced home ownership, the divorce rate climbed dramatically, and children played under conditions both morally and physically unsafe. Yet signs of hope existed: city mission societies, federations of churches, YMCA and YWCA programs, and social service commissions. Once Protestants "evolved a science of procedure" to systematize and augment these movements, the struggle for urban America could be won. "Given a combination of all these forces," said the report, "a cooperating group of trained workers under competent leadership, wise strategy and an adequate budget," then "almost any problem in the city may be solved by the church of Jesus Christ."[33]

Similarly, small towns and the countryside groaned under the burden of poorly allocated resources. Some areas had far too many weak churches wastefully duplicating each other's efforts, while adjacent regions often remained unchurched. Virtually all rural or small-town churches lacked adequate facilities to provide religious education, opportunities to the young for recreation, or specialized ministries to particular groups. The rural church, its energies fragmented and dispersed, had failed "to become a community center of real practical service." Yet as in the city, hopeful movements had emerged as seminaries established chairs of rural sociology and as "agricultural colleges, government agencies, welfare organizations and the churches" collaborated with increasing frequency. The task of the churches was to promote still greater expertise and encourage even more cooperative planning. Warren H. Wilson, the veteran Presbyterian leader of the rural church movement, saw the IWM as a means whereby "the assembling of all American resources might occur" and moneys might be directed to needy rural areas. The IWM represented "the nationalizing of the responsibility for the local community," the "Americanization" of the pastor's work. Thus when the IWM survey team approached a pastor for information, he would do well to respond. "The kingdom of God has come near him in the visit of the County Survey Committee."[34]

Kingdom building required a similar consolidation in the field of education. Meager attendance at Sunday Schools and low financial support for them—only two cents out of every dollar spent by the average church—were "imperilling the safety of the nation, threatening the future of the church, and seriously impeding the Christianizing of the world." Churches needed to increase funding dramatically but also to restructure the agencies responsible for religious education. The IWM proposed greater administrative centralization, for local churches should not be left to their own haphazard devices. "Religious education," said *World Survey,* "must be organized by cities, counties, and states as well as separately by each denomination." Centralization in turn demanded larger staffs. Every statewide organization needed "a standard official force, including a general secretary; a superintendent of religious education; divisional specialists for work with children, youth, adults and general officers; an office secretary and additional specialists and assistants as each field may need." In the IWM's discussion of denominational agencies, the bureaucratizing thrust of its proposals stood out in even sharper relief. The report counted twenty-three categories of professionals and office workers needed to staff Christian education boards.[35]

The analysis of financial compensation for the clergy followed the familiar pattern. A survey team painted a dreary picture of churches underpaying their ministers and providing poorly (if at all) for their retirement. As a result, debt harried pastors and distracted them from their work, well-qualified young people looked to other careers, and the efficiency of the church suffered. Again, an exertion of centralized leadership provided the remedy. Denominations should set minimum salaries for ministers and establish national funds to supplement the compensation paid by poorer churches. To assure that aged clergy not go begging, denominations needed to set up or strengthen pension plans. The IWM called upon these groups to emulate the methods of "secular corporations [which] are in advance of the churches in plans for providing old age and disability pensions."[36]

In one notable instance, however, a survey by the IWM prompted it to utter a sharp criticism of a business corporation. On September 22, 1919, a quarter of a million workers—about half of those employed in the industry—walked off their jobs in the steel plants. Thirteen days later the Industrial Relations Department of the IWM appointed a special Commission of Inquiry to investigate the strike. Chaired by Methodist Bishop Francis J. McConnell, the commission conducted an extensive probe of the causes and issues of the walkout. The commission secured technical assistance from the Bureau of

Industrial Research, New York, held open hearings in Pittsburgh where the strike was centered, and interviewed Judge Elbert Gary, whose U.S. Steel Company was the flagship of the industry. Although the strike ended in a rout of labor on January 8, 1920, the commission pressed ahead with the compilation of its findings. Endorsed by the executive committee of the IWM, the report of the commission appeared in two volumes—*Report on the Steel Strike of 1919* (1920) and *Public Opinion and the Steel Strike* (1921).

The two books, while venturing some mild criticism of labor, were on balance a stinging indictment of the U.S. Steel Company. Portraying Judge Gary as a mossback out of sync with enlightened opinion in business, the reports thoroughly documented—and condemned—the prevalence of the twelve-hour work day, inadequate wages, and resistance to collective bargaining at U.S. Steel. The commission also charged that the company had employed the "undemocratic and un-American" practice of spying on its employees and that it had mobilized public opinion against the strikers by spreading false charges of Bolshevism and radicalism. The IWM investigation found no credible evidence that "Reds" played any significant role in the walkout, but it did uncover abundant proof that the press had uncritically disseminated this view and had not given the true facts to the public. The commission also exposed the denial of civil liberties to strikers in a number of communities in western Pennsylvania. On the basis of their findings, the investigators recommended that the steel industry adopt the eight-hour shift (with no more than ten hours per day to be allowed), that a "minimum comfort wage" be paid to all, and that the right to unionize be recognized. McConnell's group, which sent a copy of its report to President Wilson, also called upon the government to establish commissions on minimum wages and a commission to investigate the violation of civil liberties. The report closed with a stirring summons. "We recommend to the press that it free itself of all the too well founded charge of bias . . . and redeem its power as a promoter of truth. . . . We plead with the pulpit that it be diligent to discharge its legitimate prophetic role as an advocate of justice, righteousness and humanity in all such conflicts of human interest. . . . We condemn unsparingly those authorities who suspended the right of free speech and peaceful assemblage, before during and after the steel strike." The report also called upon the industrial relations department of the IWM to conduct further "studies of general conditions in industry" as a way of "enlightening public opinion, begetting impartial judgment, and promoting industrial justice and peace."[37]

The report on the steel strike was a powerful piece, one of the most impressive analyses of a social problem ever produced by an American religious body, and it helped to shift public opinion to a more favorable assessment of the steelworkers' plight. Yet one must not read the recommendations of the Commission of Inquiry as an attack upon corporate business per se. Despite its unsparing criticism of one company and its president, the report did not propose to scrap the current economic order. Bishop McConnell and Daniel A. Poling, the vice chairman of the commission, emphasized this point in the foreword to the second volume of their study. "To all of those who have thought of the Interchurch Report as radical," they wrote, "we would like to say that every condition in the steel industry which the Report criticized is remediable—and remediable without the inauguration of anything even resembling social revolution. There is no improvement which we suggest which the leaders of the steel industry cannot themselves put into effect." For the commission, the choice did not lie between corporate business and some form of socialism or syndicalism—though conservative critics of the report acted as if these were the alternatives. The decision was between two competing visions of the corporation: the one view, represented by Elbert Gary, operated on outdated principles of industrial autocracy; the other, symbolized by IWM backer John D. Rockefeller, Jr., invited labor to form shop committees, heard its grievances, and worked with it to create a more democratic corporate America. Alva Taylor, one of the commission's members and social service secretary of the Disciples of Christ, made the point succinctly in an article entitled, "Mr. Rockefeller versus Judge Gary." The task of the hour was not to abolish corporations but to make them more humane and cooperative.[38]

In fact, the Commission of Inquiry presumed that the churches themselves needed to function rather like a unified corporation if they were to perform their ministry to society. Bishop McConnell hinted at this conclusion in his analysis of the role of the Pittsburgh pulpit and of Pittsburgh's Council of Churches during the steel strike. He commended the council for attempting to get at the facts and praised those ministers who dared challenge the policies of U.S. Steel. "To have raised any question about the strike in Pittsburgh," he observed, "showed more social spirit and courage than more radical action at the distance of San Francisco or Boston." Yet in the end, events in western Pennsylvania demonstrated "that little can be accomplished by a local organization in dealing with a widespread strike." The Pittsburgh churches lacked the resources to investigate "the entire field of the steel industry," and they were hobbled by the campaign of misinformation perpetrated by U.S. Steel and large segments of the press. Only "an organization which in some sense represents the united forces of all the churches of the nation" would be powerful enough to overcome these obstacles and to have "an influence on the general course of public opinion." "To be concrete," he concluded, "the final responsibility here comes back to organizations like the

Interchurch Movement and the Federal Council of the Churches of Christ in America." Only such bodies could mobilize the resources to conduct the continuing surveys recommended by the commission, and only they could galvanize public opinion. They alone could effectively lobby the federal government—a task that McConnell himself tried to perform on behalf of the commission's report. To shape America in an era of giant corporations and big government, the churches needed to act like a corporation.[39]

Among its various operations, the interchurch publicity and fund-raising campaigns most fully illustrated the movement's commitment to the corporate ethos and the ideal of efficiency. The volumes of *World Survey,* originally presented as reports to an IWM conference at Atlantic City, New Jersey, in January 1920, were themselves a form of publicity designed to win financial support. The movement was not content, however, with these two slick volumes. Determined not to be a "piker" in the field of publicity, the movement announced soon after its formation that "plans are now in preparation for the biggest campaign of paid advertising of the Gospel and the church of Jesus Christ that has ever been attempted." The IWM engaged two New York ad agencies—the Joseph Richards Company and Barton, Durstine and Osborn, Inc.—to manage the fund-raising campaign. A weekly newspaper and several magazines (one in Spanish) touted the cause. A national training conference prepared about a hundred denominational leaders in November 1919 and sent them out to speak on behalf of the movement and to recruit still more speakers. The IWM, as Eldon Ernst has observed, also advertised through "lapel buttons, window flags, posters, street car cards, window display material, windshield posters, stamps, trade and technical and other class papers, fraternal order papers, mail-order magazines, business men's magazines, foreign language press, and bill boards."[40]

The IWM coordinated its work with a variety of denominational campaigns. The Methodists inaugurated the Centenary drive (named for the centennial of Methodist missions), the Disciples of Christ had already launched a Men and Millions crusade, and the Northern Presbyterians embarked on a New Era campaign. The very names suggested the world-shaking tasks these denominations understood themselves to be undertaking. Presbyterians spoke of their venture as a way of putting their money "behind all of their great agencies in one unified presentation" and of placing "upon the nation and the world the impact of a united Protestantism, which alone can meet the incoming tide of social and economic unrest, as well as religious and moral unbelief and depression." To the leaders of local Presbyterian youth groups, the denomination sent out a letter addressed to "the Captain-President of the Young People's Society." The letter asserted: "You are hereby notified that all of the forces of the Presbyterian army are federated in allied strategy under the name of 'The New Era Movement.'" An accompanying pamphlet concluded with the stirring summons:

> The great Comrade in White [Jesus] is seeking recruits for an invincible and conquering company of Comrades of the forward-look, Comrades of His holy cross, Comrades of His coming Kingdom.
>
> > The Son of God goes forth to war,
> >   A kingly crown to gain,
> > His blood red banner streams afar,
> >   Who follows in His train.

In less militaristic and more prosaic language, S. Earl Taylor, who headed the Methodist Centenary before becoming general secretary of the IWM, saw his denomination's campaign as a way of lifting "the program of the Kingdom into new terms greater and more expansive than those of all other organizations."[41]

At the heart of "the program of the Kingdom" was money. The leaders of the interchurch and allied campaigns knew that they required large sums to fund ambitious enterprises, and they had little doubt that Protestants had the means to supply these needs. The problem was to motivate church members and sympathetic citizens to do so. Having demonstrated through surveys what the facts demanded, leaders sought a religious rationale to encourage giving. They found it in stewardship, the biblical notion that everything a person is or possesses is held in trust for God. Theoretically much broader than the issue of money, the idea of stewardship became in the hands of the promoters virtually synonymous with systematic financial contribution. In I Corinthians 16:2, they discovered their favorite scriptural text: "Upon the first day of the week let each one of you lay by him in store, as he may prosper." Regular, proportionate giving, they insisted, was the biblical standard for Christians. In a series of graphic ads, the IWM demonstrated the wonders this principle would work if larger numbers of Christians adopted it. If only 10 percent of Protestants earning $1,000 a year tithed their incomes, the revenues would pay the total of existing church budgets. "If one out of 11 members has an income equal to the average wage of the hod carrier, $3.27 per day, and tithes it, the tithe would pay the total church budget as per 1918 with a margin of $21,897,196." The message was clear. Should even a significant minority of Protestants adopt biblical standards for giving, vast new wealth would flow into church coffers and make the great enterprises of the IWM a reality. Shortly before the war, Albert McGarrah had asserted that the churches needed "an almost unlimited increase in their incomes." Many church leaders in 1919–20 believed that goal to be within their grasp.

A little book written by David McConaughy on behalf of the New Era movement illustrates the mentality of the fund-raising drives. Although McConaughy acknowledged that money constituted but one part of stewardship, the subject of finance dominates the book. (Indeed his title—*Money: The Acid Test*—makes an almost total equation between the donor and the steward.) Numerous pages laid down the principles one should use in determining the amount to give to God's work. Money spent for oneself must be geared to *legitimate* needs; contributions must be proportionate, the proportion increasing with one's means. Case studies of sample family budgets made the principles explicit. Beneath these admonitions lay the essence of modern sales technique. Alan Trachtenberg, for example, has written that modern advertising serves "not only to instill desires for goods but also to disguise the character of consumption, to make it seem an act different from a merely functional, life-enhancing use of an object." Products are identified "with something else, with ideas, feelings, status." McConaughy's "product" was in a sense money itself, and in dealing with the subject, he mystified it, associating it with the achievement of Christian discipleship and God's purposes. Money became more than a neutral medium of exchange. According to the author, money measured a person's time, skill, and talent. Money had a "magic power" to shape character, for in its proper use (especially in its disposal through charitable giving) one attained a greater nobility of character. Properly used, money had the power to bring in the kingdom. McConaughy cited lines from Horace Bushnell: "What we are waiting for is the consecration of the vast money power of the world to the work and cause and kingdom of Jesus Christ; for that day when it comes will be the morning, so to speak, of the new creation. That tide [*sic*] wave in the money power can as little be resisted, when God brings it, as the tides of the sea; and, like these, also, it will flow across the world in a day." Appending his own gloss to Bushnell, McConaughy added: "According as Christians fulfil or fail to fulfil this function they become stepping-stones to higher things or stumbling blocks in the way of those who are waiting to enter into the kingdom of God."[42]

In 1919, as plans for the IWM were being laid, John Marshall Barker, professor of sociology at the Boston University School of Theology, summarized what many Protestants were attempting to achieve through elaborate surveys, the creation of more agencies, and gargantuan financial drives. "The Church has come to a time," Barker avowed, "when it is to be tested by its social efficiency and utility." Even worship, he added, "is not an end in itself" but must subserve that larger purpose. Guiding this utilitarianism was the conviction that "the faith and interest which Christian people once felt in the realities of another world, should more and more be transferred to the realities of this world." To make its commitment to the world efficacious, the church at all levels needed to integrate and coordinate its activities—nationally through cooperative movements such as the IWM and in each congregation through an interlocking system of committees. At the head of this advance were "statesmen of the Kingdom" with "a broad, comprehensive vision and forward-looking policies." In the local church, a new kind of minister—"the social engineer"—stood ready to play his part.[43]

Was there an overarching purpose to this preoccupation with "the realities of this world"? Barker replied with an emphatic affirmation that could have stood equally well as the answer of those who created the IWM or labored for New Era or for the Men and Millions campaign: contemporary Protestants, in building a more efficient church organization, were "coworkers with God to actualize the Kingdom in community life." And yet on occasion the search for an efficient Christianity appeared to be largely self-referential and little more than a call to ceaseless motion. Thus one piece of interchurch literature argued for "a continuous survey," "a continuous adaptation . . . in plans," "a continuous campaign of education and publicity." It was as if surveys or organizations were becoming goals unto themselves and the process of efficiency its own aim.[44]

And there was yet another question: could this relentless drive to rationalize the religious life, this determination to subject passion to bureaucratic mastery, succeed in taming and using all the elemental fears and hopes that the war had unleashed? The answer would not be long in coming.

7

The Fundamentalist
Controversy and Beyond

❧❧❧❧

Despite all of the publicity and organization, the Interchurch World Movement (IWM) swiftly collapsed. The related denominational fund-raising drives did reasonably well, but moneys to underwrite the IWM itself fell woefully short. The most thorough student of the movement attributes its demise to several causes: interchurch goals were too grandly and vaguely stated; the nation, weary of crusades, preferred to return to what presidential candidate Warren Harding called "normalcy"; the report on the steel strike alienated conservative interests. Perhaps most significantly, promoters assumed that Protestantism was so thoroughly the religion of the average American that they could appeal to "friendly citizens"—those unaffiliated with any church— to raise a large portion of the funds needed by the IWM. That judgment was a fatal error, for friendly citizens proved to be either nonexistent or tightfisted. Also, many Protestants simply wanted no part of the organization's efficiency-minded, kingdom-building program.[1]

Isaac M. Haldeman, pastor of the First Baptist Church of New York City and a pugnacious defender of premillennialism, was one such dissenter. In a pamphlet marked by his usual thrust and slash, Haldeman called the IWM an abomination. Zealous to remake the world, the movement was attempting to build "a colossal machine," "to multiply wheels within wheels, to extend the system of internal and humanly created organizations" until the church succumbed to "ecclesiastical sovietism" and a "concentrated dictatorship." The interchurch campaign ignored the true mandate of the church—to preach Christ to perishing sinners—and it had "no time to speak of Heaven and appears to have forgotten there is a Hell." At the root of this apostate effort lay a false eschatology. "The Interchurch Movement," charged Haldeman, "is the combined, aggressive effort" of would-be kingdom builders "to render meaningless the last promise of an ascended Lord: 'Surely I come quickly.'"[2]

Haldeman's polemic was one of the shots in the fundamentalist-modernist controversy that embroiled churches (chiefly the Northern Baptists and Presbyterians) in the 1920s and spilled over into a broader cultural battle concerning the teaching of evolution in the public schools. A multilayered phenomenon involving struggle over the Bible, the nature of doctrine, and the relationship of science and religion, the fundamentalist controversy was much bigger than the issue of premillennialism. In fact, not all fundamentalists were premillenarians. For example, J. Gresham Machen, the Princeton Seminary professor whose *Christianity and Liberalism* (1923) made him the leading theorist of ultraconservatism, rejected premillennialism. William Jennings Bryan, identified in the popular mind as the foremost crusader against evolution, was in most respects a reform-minded progressive standing far closer to the evangelical postmillennialism of the mid-nineteenth century than to the dispensationalism of Isaac Haldeman. But although premillennialists constituted only one portion of the fundamentalist coalition that emerged after World War I, they were the most visible and probably the most numerous segment of the movement, and it was against them that the advocates of kingdom building directed their most withering fire. In a series of articles, books, and pamphlets beginning during World War I and stretching well into the 1920s, moderate and liberal Protestants savagely attacked the premillennial view. In part, these polemics turned on the nature and meaning of time. The issue was this: was time bounded by the purpose of a God who gave it a definitive End beyond itself and beyond human control? Or was time a virtually limitless process which humans could master and whose only goal lay in its own indefinite improvement? The kingdom builders who spun out a plethora of new organizations, professional specializations, and bureaucratic procedures opted decisively for the latter opinion. By contrast, the rising premillennial party led by men such as Isaac Haldeman assessed the possibilities of time very differently. They regarded the current age as hopelessly corrupt and incapable of redemption until the supernatural advent of Christ inaugurated a new heaven and a new earth.[3]

The battle over this and allied questions was fought out amidst deep cultural anxieties. At the outset of World War I, fear of the "Hun" (the German) verged on paranoia. After the armistice and in the wake of the Bolshevik Revolution, fear was displaced onto supposed subversives of foreign birth. Nativist anxieties found voice in a resurgent Ku Klux Klan, refounded in 1915 and transformed into a national organization by the 1920s, and the uneasiness attained legal recognition in the immigration-restriction legislation of 1924. The enactment of Prohibition with the passage of the eighteenth amendment in 1919 carried a similar meaning. Although Protestant zeal for temperance had often been linked to a progressive or reformist political agenda (and still was in quarters such as the Federal Council of Churches), Prohibition is the 1920s often assumed nativist overtones. It became a means of reasserting the hegemony of old-line Protestant mores in face of serious challenges from other groups. Behind these lurches toward reaction was the nagging question French observer André Siegfried posed in 1927: "Will America remain Protestant and Anglo-Saxon?" Even within its own precincts, old-line Protestantism seemed insecure. Divorces mounted in number, the birthrates fell among Anglo-Saxon Americans, women continued to enter the workforce in greater numbers. The so-called new woman, recently enfranchised by the nineteenth amendment and perhaps most graphically symbolized by the flapper of the 1920s, asserted her independence of both home and traditional mores. Although some of these trends had been the object of concern for several decades, they appeared especially dangerous in the surcharged atmosphere after the war. On the outcome of these matters, many felt, hinged the fate of Christian civilization in America, and that concern added fury and fear to the fundamentalist-modernist wars.[4]

"The Premillennial Menace"

The nineteenth century had already produced a stylized catalogue of objections to premillennialism: it was defeatist, paralyzing the motivation for evangelism and for improving this world; it was morally offensive because it pictured God winning his way through force rather than persuasion; it was irrational, for it represented God ringing down the curtain of history before the play was done; it was unscriptural, resting upon fallacious principles of biblical interpretation.[5]

Yet despite very real differences and often heated exchanges between premillenarians and their critics, there had been no irrevocable parting of the ways in the nineteenth century. Pre- and postmillennialists generally operated out of a common cultural assumption that America was—or at least ought to be—under the control of Protestant values. Their writings betrayed anxiety about similar threats to Protestant hegemony: the alienation of the masses from the churches, the new immigration, intemperance, and challenges to the Victorian ideal of the family. Before about 1910, the two groups could engage in parallel forms of ministry to meet those challenges. While liberal Protestants founded institutional churches and settlement houses, some premillennialists opened city missions that offered comparable services, albeit with a less specifically reformist agenda. And of course there was the grand cause of foreign missions to which all alike pledged allegiance, although again with differing rationales.[6]

Moreover, until postmillennialism had eroded into the more open-ended eschatology of the kingdom, antimillenarians and their critics possessed certain common assumptions about the Bible that made possible a genuine discourse. Today in libraries, gathering dust, are countless old volumes testifying to this fact: Millerite and anti-Millerite tracts, pre- and postmillennial polemics, all attempting to grapple with each others' arguments within at least a partially shared frame of reference. Even as the new eschatology gradually grew within the shell of the older postmillennialism, controversy was often muted by irenic figures such as the evangelist Dwight L. Moody, who managed to bring both liberals and dispensationalists to the lecture platform of his summer conferences in Northfield, Massachusetts. "And though we may not now see alike," one Baptist postmillennialist had declared of his millenarian counterparts in 1880, "we can walk and work together, and then it may be pleasant some millions of years hence to talk over our present differences. Possibly we may then laugh each at the other, and every one at himself, as we note how short of the mark and how wide of the mark were the confident judgments of both sides and all sides alike."[7]

By the years around World War I, there was no longer much walking and working together and no prospect of laughter. Confident that events were confirming their reading of prophecy, millenarians grew more aggressive. At the Philadelphia Prophetic Conference in May 1918, one speaker declared: "When the war came, the intelligent world thought that it was going ahead in a constant improvement which would bring in its own millennium, a word which most people used without the slightest idea of where it came from or what it meant. Under the leadership of men of science and philosophy, and, in most cases, of men in Germany, somehow or other, by a process of education, of evolution, we were to have a constantly improving world in which presently peace would reign. . . . Now all of that has been shattered." The only hope for a better world, concluded the speaker, lay in "the blessed hope of the glorious appearing of our Lord." C. I. Scofield, one of the grand old men of the movement, who was too ill to attend the conference, wrote a letter avowing his belief that the final apostasy had come and "that we are in the awful end of the Times of the Gentiles." Some at the conference were tantalized by dramatic events relative to the Near East. In November 1917, the United Kingdom had issued the Balfour Declaration declaring that "His Majesty's Government views with favour the establishment in Palestine of a national home for the Jewish people." One month later the forces of British General Edmund Allenby captured Jerusalem from the Turks. A. E. Thompson, pastor of the American [Protestant] Church in Jerusalem until the outbreak of the war, told the prophetic conference that Allenby's victory was "that which was spoken by the prophets." That triumph prepared the way for the restoration of the Jews and suggested that the clock of biblical prediction had begun to tick off the final moments of the current age. About the same time, Reuben A. Torrey published *What the War Teaches or the Greatest Lessons of 1917,* which concurred with the conclusions of the Philadelphia conference. The Bible had predicted a multiplying of wars near the end of the Gospel dispensation; it foretold the restoration of the Jews, and it avowed the "utter failure of man without God." All of these things were coming true before the eyes of those who had lived through 1917. What could these things mean but that "the coming of our Lord Jesus draweth nigh"?[8]

Millenarian pronouncements were taking on a more militant edge, and there was no little gloating that events had falsified the hopes of those who wished to build the Kingdom of God on earth. "There are preachers," said Isaac Haldeman to the World Conference on Christian Fundamentals in 1919, "who tell us the sudden coming of the Lord would derange the affairs of the world and put an end to all human progress." Haldeman scoffed at the objection. "If the Lord should come His coming would put an end to the progress of sin and unrighteousness." The speaker following Haldeman argued even more bluntly: "Nervous prostration is the necessary corollary of postmillennialism, and, when pressed to its logical sequence, will lodge men either in the grave or the insane asylum. It is not that postmillennialists are hypocrites; it is only that, not knowing the truth, they are deceived, and are looking for that which is not in the program." Renovating the earth prior to the Second Coming was not in the program.[9]

Those who believed otherwise heard the rumblings from the millenarian camp and responded with a torrent of books and articles. These works exhibited, if not "nervous prostration," at least considerable anxiety and anger at a movement threatening the writers' deepest commitments. Millenarianism, said Shirley Jackson Case in a widely noted article published in 1918, should be styled "The Premillennial Menace." "Under ordinary circumstances," noted the University of Chicago professor, "one might excusably pass over premillennialism as a wild and relatively harmless fancy." But his article made clear that the times were not ordinary, and millenarianism was no longer harmless. It was a threat to the democratic way of life, lent itself to use by socialist radicals (the International Workers of the World or "Wobblies") desiring the overthrow of American institutions, and threatened to paralyze the nation in time of war. To extirpate this "menace," Case and many others spilled gallons of printer's ink.[10]

Incensed by attacks on their patriotism, millenarians protested that it was their enemies—men like Case—who promoted Germanic ideals fatal to Christianity and America alike. At the 1918 Prophetic Conference in Philadelphia, Dr. Cortland Myers of the Tremont Baptist Temple in Boston identified the "ripe, rank, rotten, new theology made in Germany" as the "abomination of abominations in the modern religious world." "Permeating and poisoning our theological seminaries" (including especially the University of Chicago Divinity School), this modernism prepared the way for both apostasy and the war. "If the churches of Great Britain, America, and France, fifty years ago," said Myers, "had fought this iniquity, this infamous thing, there never would have been any war in the world now. Go back to the fountainhead and you will find that your crimson stream has its source in the rank German theology that has been forcing its way into the veins and arteries of all our religious life. We ought to fight it to the finish." Another speaker at the conference was equally dismissive of the German-tainted higher criticism which denied the "blessed hope" of the Second Coming. "Mr. Higher Critic," said Harris H. Gregg, "the Lord Jesus Christ says the Scriptures cannot be broken. If you say that they can, we have no time to debate with you. We will just sit down and watch the debate through with you in your casket and that Man of the Cross; and, Mr. Higher Critic, the debate will be finished at the judgement of the great white throne."[11]

The vitriol and name calling resulted in part from the fact that millenarianians and liberals were spelling out more sharply the logic of their differences. Unlike the new theologians who viewed the Scriptures as historically conditioned documents composed under the influence of God's progressive revelation, millenarians insisted that the texts came directly from God. Thus the Bible, which had predicted with minute accuracy the details of Jesus's first coming, could be trusted to foretell with similar precision the events surrounding his second. For modernists, predictive prophecy was an absurdity exploded by the results of modern biblical criticism and patently at odds with ordinary laws of human development. And this was the nub of the larger issue. While modernists wished a God acting in consonance with ordinary developmental principles, millenarians rejected any cosmology "that would limit God in His own universe." Millenarianism was also becoming for devotees a kind of litmus test. Or as Mark Matthews suggested, it was a "stabilizing doctrine" indicating that its adherents held sound opinions on a number of other issues in which the same basic principle was at stake: the virgin birth, the vicarious atonement, the bodily resurrection of Jesus. Millenarian views, in short, symbolized what Timothy Weber has called an "overt supernaturalism" and stood as a breakwater against any supposedly naturalistic effort to force God to act in accord with the ordinary laws of time and space.[12]

The conflict also reflected the fact that millenarians and their liberal opponents were living in increasingly different social spaces, from which they sallied forth periodically to struggle against one another over contested terrain. Modernists had triumphed in the prestigious centers of American culture. They dominated most of the leading seminaries and divinity schools, and they allied themselves with the forces creating and reshaping the modern university. A moderate liberalism controlled important sectors of the Federal Council of Churches as well as the various agencies of social witness of the denominations. Many leading periodicals and eminent pulpits trumpeted the liberal gospel. The millenarians, however, were not without their own bases of support. Forty or so Bible institutes taught millenarian views to hundreds of graduates annually, popular magazines such as *The King's Business* and *The Sunday School Times* did likewise, and after 1909 the *Scofield Reference Bible* (named for its editor Cyrus I. Scofield) disseminated the eschatology in the first of its numerous printings. By themselves, separate institutional entrenchments might have led to an uneasy armed truce, but neither group was prepared—at least initially—to tolerate an ecclesiastical *Sitzkrieg*. Each claimed the right to set policy and define doctrine for their respective denominations and to set the moral tone for America at large. This disputed social space became the religious "no man's land" in which the fundamentalist wars were fought.[13]

Although millenarians viewed liberal triumphs in the centers of cultural prestige as evidence of the apostasy of the last days, they nevertheless resented being relegated to the periphery. William Bell Riley, for example, complained that any modernist minister could readily obtain an invitation to speak in a university chapel but that a "radical conservative" had "about as much chance to be heard in a Turkish harem as to be invited to speak within the precincts of a modern State University." He also grumbled that an inferior "little two by four preacher" (again, presumably a modernist) who could scarcely fill a sanctuary acquired, once "called to a professorship in a great University," an aura of invincible authority on all subjects.[14]

For their part, modernists harped on the marginality of their opponents. The millenarians were theological Neanderthals. They approached biblical prophecy, said George Ricker Berry, like "paleolithic man with his stone axes trying to build a twentieth-century skyscraper." Herbert Willett of *The Christian Century* suggested that one could account for millenarians only by supposing them knaves or fools, and opted for the latter alternative. They suffered from "intellectual inability to understand the basic elements of biblical literature and history." James Snowden of Western Theological Seminary in Pittsburgh reported that he had surveyed theological faculties in twenty-eight seminaries. Among 236 professors, he could find only 7 premillennialists. "This fact may be allowed to speak for itself," he said. With "authoritative works" of scholarship against it, millenarianism "is going, if it has not already gone, the way of other obsolete theories that cannot stand our modern light. . . . It is a fish out of water and it is gasping for breath."[15]

Yet these dismissive comments notwithstanding, modernists were deeply worried, for they knew that the paleolithic men were numerous. One met them on trains, as Herbert Willett did when he encountered an energetic man who explained that Kaiser Wilhelm was the beast described in the thirteenth chapter of Revelation and that Jesus would appear within months to "rapture" the saints. Willett did not doubt that "tens of thousands of people" adhered to this nonsense, and he was equally certain "whence this wretched kind of biblical teaching originates": from Bible schools such as those in Los Angeles and Chicago and from widely read publications of the ilk of Charles Trumbull's *Sunday School Times.* Or one might, while visiting a strange city, wander by chance into a Bible class, as the Reverend Arthur Metcalf did in a midwestern town, and hear the arcana of dispensationalism explained to a credulous multitude. Premillennialism was, by modernist accounts, an anachronistic movement that ought to be extinct or dying. Yet it was thriving, and its success threatened the modernist view of an orderly world in which men and women were the masters of time. "Were it possible," Metcalf said wistfully, "to close Bible institutes of a certain type, simple New Testament religion might have a better chance." Since it was not, he recommended a vigorous and widespread campaign of Sunday School education and expository preaching to combat "the oddities and crudities" he had heard in the midwestern Bible class. Willett concurred. Christian ministers and educators had "no higher duty than to free the church from these puerilities of magic and superstition." Modernist assertions that millenarianism stood at the periphery of American life were as much an attempt to create marginality as they were a description of it.[16]

In these struggles over the direction of history and the meaning of time, millenarians and their critics were contending for high stakes. Each group assumed that sound belief, the future of Christianity, and the survival of Christian civilization hung in the balance. Amid the cultural dislocations of the war and its aftermath, each saw in the other the chief example of disorder. At the head of one of their numerous antimillenarian articles, the editors of the *Biblical World* added a note affirming that they engaged in no ordinary religious controversy. "We . . . are endeavoring," they proclaimed, "to save the faith of thousands of men and women in Christianity." That one sentiment at least they held in common with the millenarians.[17]

"There is no end in sight."

Certain telling images recurred frequently in the barrage of antimillenarian literature. Shailer Mathews spoke of premillennialism as a "liberally financed and widely organized movement" that had "honeycombed" the churches to the extent that "the spiritual and moral nature of Christianity" was at risk. Methodist minister Levi Gilbert of Cincinnati styled millenarianism a "contagion" which no vaccine was "potent enough to stay," and George P. Mains, a coreligionist from Harrisburg, Pennsylvania, called it a "cancerous virus." Herbert Willett in one of a series of articles run by *The Christian Century* in 1918 associated growing interest in the eschatology with the discord of the hour. "[I]n days when war has torn great gashes in the quivering flesh of humanity, when all things have assumed monstrous and distorted form, and portent seems the expected and normal method of disclosing the meanings of the great drama, the mind is swept away from its accustomed anchorage of fact, and is in danger of submergence in the welter of troubled and chaotic ideas that are rushed everywhither [sic] in the flood."[18]

The metaphors used by the premillennialists' opponents were highly suggestive. Millenarianism connoted a movement pitting the church with rotten cavities, an illness subverting health, wounds slashed into human flesh, and an uncontrolled flood inundating the ordinary landmarks of life. Premillennialism was, in short, a symbol of chaos and disintegration—a sign made more fearsome because it fit into the larger picture of disorder so evident after the start of the war. Millenarian eschatology stood as a painful reminder that faith in the human capacity to master time and to build the Kingdom of God on earth rested on a crumbling foundation. The hope was not even secure within the Protestant household, as the growing popularity of millenarianism attested. Therefore, the would-be kingdom builders struck—and struck hard—at an idea calling into question their most cherished assumptions about the order and rationality of the universe.

Shailer Mathews fired one of the first salvos in the assault against premillennialism. In a pamphlet entitled *Will Christ Come Again?* (1917), he acknowledged that the earliest Christians "believed that Jesus would return during the lifetime of their generation." Since he had not, "simple honesty" required an admission "that they were mistaken." But premillennialists, repudiating common sense, tried to repristinate that hope and fell into absurdities making them a people "cut loose from the modern world." At odds with the best contemporary biblical scholarship, they also disavowed what science had revealed to be the fundamental law of both history and nature: evolution. "Facts make it evident that we are in a constant process; that change leads to change" according to uniform laws of development. The moral effect of premillennialism likewise offended modern sensibilities. For a God "capable of bringing about His victory by spiritual means," the watchers for the Second Coming substituted a deity who had "to revert to physical brutality" and who worked his will by "miraculous militarism," and, awaiting a new world order to descend from heaven, they gave up the struggle to reform the institutions of this one. By contrast, those who correctly understood biblical prophecy knew that it was not an infallible set of "highly ingenious puzzles to be worked out" but rather a progressive "discovery of God and his laws in social evolution"—a process of development fully congruent with "the growing knowledge of the universe and society given by science." The Christian hope, in a word, was "sufficiently reasonable to be worthy of acceptance by men and women who are in hearty sympathy with our modern world." Knowing these reasonable laws, people could then cooperate with them—and with the God whose active presence indwelt them—to build an ever brightening future.[19]

The association of the Christian hope with methodical progress according to uniform laws amenable to human control was a consistent theme of the critiques of millenarianism. Harris Franklin Rall of Garrett Theological Seminary argued that God everywhere worked according to law, for he was a God of regularity and order. "As applied to the development of life upon the earth the scientist calls it [God's uniform law] evolution; as applied to the story of mankind we call it history; as applied to God's supreme purpose we call it the development of the kingdom of God." God worked with unvarying consistency because only "a world of reason and order" would enable humans to be responsible co-workers with the divine to "bring the kingdom of God on earth."[20]

Similarly, George Mains faulted premillennialism because of its contempt for scientific as well as practical rationality. It was illogical to posit an imminent, cataclysmic end to history. Given the vast amount of time during which evolution had gradually fitted the earth for humanity, God could not be expected to terminate "by a stroke of catastrophe" that for which he had so long prepared and which had only recently arrived upon the planet. Moreover, the triumphs already wrought by science—diseases cured, superstitions exorcised, waste places turned into gardens, and commerce and communication "binding the whole world together into a community of instant superintelligence and common interests"—augured an even grander future. Science and revelation concurred in prophesying a time "when, under man's trained and culturing hand, the very earth itself . . . shall be transformed into a human paradise." Humankind, by continuing to discover and harness the fundamental laws built into the scheme of things, had "infinite possibilities of development." The premillennial doctrine to the contrary was an anomaly to the modern mentality. "The scientific mind," Mains predicted, "will stand in perpetual revolt against such teaching. A sane philosophy of thought will condemn it as irrational. The hard practical sense of the business world will repudiate it. The very stars in their silent march will fight against and finally destroy its absurdities." For those who objected to his vision of a technologically engineered Kingdom of God, Mains had a ready rejoinder: "Not all the piety in the world, in the absence of knowledge, could substitute for the beneficence of science. Sacrifices do not stop the ravages of plague, incantations do not ward off contagions, and even prayer does not furnish a general cure for tuberculosis."[21]

In his critique of millenarianism, George Eckman, too, argued that the Kingdom of God came not with supernatural portent but through the systematic use of humanly contrived instruments. He made the point by way of analogy:

> When Joshua and his hosts came to the Jordan River, which separated them from the land of Canaan, they were dependent upon a miracle for their safe crossing of the overflowing stream. . . . But when the English army came to the Jordan during the recent war no miracle was required for their transit. They threw a steel bridge across the stream and marched their troops over it in due order and redeemed Palestine by the skill of their military engineers. That is a fair type of the business of Christ's church in these days. Christians are to do the work of the Lord by the best means which the inventive genius of man has placed at their disposal. The interests of Christ's kingdom must be set forward as wisely and expeditiously as the commercial or political enterprises of the world at large. Indeed, if the church is alert and sees its actual responsibility, it will quickly excel secular institutions in the shrewdness, business sagacity, and materials with which it does its work.[22]

As Eckman's comments hinted, opponents of premillennialism had an extremely pragmatic objection to it. They were generally supporters of the new ecclesiastical machinery, the federative efforts, and the fund-raising drives that had become such a common feature of the Protestant quest to build the Kingdom of God. Millenarianism, they believed, called this activism and organization-building into question. Referring to the Methodist Centenary Movement, Harris Rall noted: "The church is moving forward to-day with a great program and upon that program it is basing a great appeal." The appeal for money to support expanded enterprises assumed that the Kingdom of God was in part "already here," that it would yet "come in fullness," and that it would do so as God "works with men and through men." "Over against this faith," he concluded sadly, "stands modern premillennialism." To our "high hopes," it declares that "true Christians" should "expect as little as possible from churches under the present dispensation." But the kingdom builders were not prepared to expect little or to renounce their faith in human capacity to build a better future. "It is truer to the facts," said Congregational minister William E. Hammond of Harvey, Illinois, "to believe that the date of the millennium rests with man, himself, to decide. . . . The millennium is ours the minute we are ready for it."[23]

This objection recalled nineteenth-century criticisms that millenarianism, promoting despair over the present age, paralyzed the will to labor for God's kingdom. Other attacks also recapitulated the stock charges of a previous generation. Premillennialism rested on a false principle of biblical interpretation, displacing New Testament visions of a spiritual kingdom with a Jewish hope for a carnal domain. It was unethical because it longed for a millennium established by force rather than persuasion. It called into question the rational order of the universe by predicting a premature termination of history. It made the Gospel into a failure by impeaching its power to win all nations. But despite the obvious continuities with an older antimillenarian tradition, the polemics of 1917 and afterward did not simply repeat former arguments. The war against the "premillennial menace" used many new weapons and took place on a very different intellectual terrain.

As heirs of liberal theology and modern biblical scholarship, the critics attacked premillennial views of the Bible far more thoroughly than mid-nineteenth-century postmillennialism had ever done. They asserted that millenarians erred, not because watchers for the Second Coming lapsed into faulty exegesis of a few verses in Daniel and Revelation or because they occasionally adopted a defective principle of interpretation. The premillennialists' error was far deeper and more fundamental. They mistook the very nature of the Bible and of the God who gave it. God did not reveal himself, Harris Rall explained, through infallible writings. Revelation was not "intellectual but vital." God disclosed himself gradually and progressively through the moral and spiritual lives of men and women. Instead of providing a compendium of error-free truths, the Bible told the story of fallible people in a deepening encounter with the divine. To understand that narrative, one had to study the Scriptures historically with a proper respect for the context of its ideas. One needed also to distinguish the experience of the divine from the historical forms it had assumed and thus to discriminate between its transient expressions and its abiding truths. By this understanding of the Bible, premillennialism was woefully deficient. It was guilty of teaching a "mechanical" view of the Scriptures and of making God's revelation into "an external force that overrides and compels the human spirit." Moreover, it fell into an "intellectualism" that assumed "religion is primarily a matter of correct ideas, that Christianity is a sum of truths to be accepted, that revelation is a set of ideas and the Bible a textbook of theology."[24]

These fallacies led to a gross misreading of the Bible's apocalyptic literature. Although premillennialists rightly discerned that books like Daniel and Revelation fairly resonated with the expectation of an early supernatural overturning of the current age, they drew a preposterous conclusion from their discovery: they proposed to make the hope of late antiquity a scenario for the twentieth century. This attempt flew in the face of the documents themselves, which made clear that the writers had predicted a cataclysm in their own time and thus had been wrong. It also contradicted the fact that the Bible contained multiple eschatologies which could not be harmonized into a consistent system. Intellectual honesty required an admission of these diversities and an acknowledgment that the apocalypticists had erred in the specifics of their predictions. The task of a sound interpreter was to find beneath their mistakes and extravagances—which no intelligent modern could take seriously—something of abiding spiritual worth. That something was a powerful faith that God's purpose in the end would be triumphant, though the means of that victory would be far different than the ancients had supposed.

This liberalized eschatology was almost as uncongenial to traditional postmillennialism as it was to premillennialism. Those who believed that the Bible contained discrepant and frequently mistaken eschatologies had no basis for drawing any *specific* predictions from it. Thus Professor George Cross of Rochester Theological Seminary argued that premillennialism was a deluded but "consistent attempt to resuscitate ancient millenarianism with its primitive world view," and postmillennialism represented "an inconsistent attempt to unite modern spirituality with the primitive view." Neither offered a viable option to the contemporary church, which needed to move beyond millennialism of any sort. Herbert Willett reached the same conclusion. He credited postmillennialism with having wrought the "release of the term 'Millennium' from the hard and fast literalism which makes the entire idea impossible to such a large proportion of the Christian world." Also, postmillennialists had rightly discerned that God's plan was for "the gradual realization" of his purposes in accordance with developmental principles. Yet even the postmillennialists had not gone far enough, for biblical scholarship and natural science "have made less and less convincing any theory of millennialism whatever."[25]

In part, the problem was the millennial view of time. Time had a definitive End, albeit one long deferred in the case of postmillennialism, but Willett and many others had difficulty conceiving a final denouement. To be sure, they affirmed that history moved toward the Kingdom of God, but it was eternal movement toward the kingdom rather than its realization that concerned them, and they also knew that eventually—millions, perhaps billions, of years hence—the earth would no longer be habitable, but that event lay so far beyond ken as to be nugatory. Time was a process of seemingly limitless improvement to which no specific End was discernible. The author of the Book of Revelation, said Herbert Willett, "did not expect the world order to last more than a few years. . . . Onward through the years, past the date which he set for the coming of the Lord and the overthrow of Rome, went the undisturbed course of affairs, with the gospel gradually winning its way among the nations. Onward even past the date he set for the close of the millennium and the blessed consummation of all things has the stream of human experience run. And the end is not yet. In fact, there is no end in sight." People now understood, Willett argued, that the earth was not nearing an "end at any period within calculable time," that the "world is very young," and that building the Kingdom of God "is an enterprise so overwhelming and sublime that centuries and millenniums to come will not see it completed." "Man's intellectual nature," said George Mains in a similar temper, "carries in itself the prophecy of infinite possibilities of development. No goal is in sight beyond which the race may not make unmeasured increase in knowledge and wisdom."[26]

With no end in sight, the Second Coming itself had to be reconceptualized. It was no longer sufficient merely to postpone it to the far side of the millennium. "Will Jesus come again?" Shailer Mathews asked in the pamphlet by that name. "We answer in all reverence, not in the sense in which the early Christians . . . expected. . . . Never in the sense that the premillenarians of to-day assert." Jesus would "come again in the true sense of a spiritual presence, leading us through the Holy Spirit into all truth, regenerating men and institutions." Herbert Willett concurred: The Second Coming "is not an event either of the past or of the future. It is a continuous process by which the spirit and ideals of the Lord become increasingly the motives of his people." "He came," said Levi Gilbert. "He is evermore and continuously 'coming.' The future will see him, in spiritual manifestation, 'coming' even more gloriously." According to William Hammond, he was "coming in cleaner politics, better industrial conditions, purer recreations, a fairer distribution of wealth, a more wholesome social life, in greater kindliness and kindly consideration for each other, in the abolition of vice, in a permanent and richer peace, and best of all in a deeper, richer, growing religious consciousness."[27]

In 1919, the Methodist Book Concern published a work designed to put at rest forever erroneous notions about eschatology. In *The Second Coming of Christ*, James M. Campbell noted that "the portentous events" of the war and looming social upheavals had caused many to expect the early return of Jesus. Campbell bluntly avowed that Christians had no warrant to expect such an advent, either now or in the aeons to come. The early Christians had made a "mistake" in expecting a literal return of Jesus, and twentieth-century Christians should not repeat their error. The only advent Christians need expect was "a progressive coming of Christ" through the processes of history. "Startling things, staggering to faith, will happen in the future, as they are happening to-day; but with every crisis a new upward process will begin. Through every revolution will come a new evolution." And so the process would continue indefinitely. Although publication by the Book Concern did not confer an imprimatur, it did suggest considerable denominational tolerance for this revision in eschatology, and it testifies to the eagerness of many Protestants to be rid of the last shred of apocalyptic eschatology.[28]

With "no end in sight" and the Second Coming a "continuous process" rather than "an event either of the past or future," humanity moved toward the kingdom of God through unbounded time. By the use of scientific knowledge, professional skill, and efficient organization, that march would be an eternal progression. "Disease is to be cured or prevented," said Shirley Jackson Case, "by the physician's skill, society's ills are to be remedied by education and legislation, and international disasters are to be averted by establishing new standards and new methods for dealing with the problems involved." The kingdom builders insisted, of course, that without God these things by themselves could not advance humanity. God was the indwelling presence inspiring and empowering the forward movement. In Harris Rall's phrase, he was "our Comrade and Fellow Worker," one who "fights in the ranks" with us for a better world. Yet God worked only in and through the orderly process of moral and natural law. He never suspended the rules or worked by fiat.[29]

One must again remember that the battle over the nature of time and its end was only one front in the complex fundamentalist-modernist wars. The combatants spent at least as much—and probably more—energy slugging it out over such matters as biblical criticism and inerrancy, the nature of doctrine, and evolution. Nevertheless, questions about time and final destiny disclosed a deep and widening fault line within Protestantism, and often that same divide appeared in contexts other than the fight over millenarianism. For example, in the undelivered summation he wrote for Scopes's jury in 1925, Bryan charged that evolution "obscures all beginnings in the mists of endless ages." It was a "cold and heartless process . . . disputing the miracle, and ignoring the spiritual in life." Evolution, as Michael O'Malley has interpreted Bryan, "severed the link between time and God. . . . Like a machine, evolution, operated on imperatives of efficiency, according to an arbitrary framework of time."[30]

To view the issue from a slightly different angle, the new eschatology of liberal Protestantism exemplified a central theme: the principle of natural continuity. The arbitrary or disconnected event was everywhere anathema. That perspective informed the dismissal of traditional "artificial" readings of prophecy. It motivated the rejection of apocalypticism and of the sharp dichotomies between the lost and the saved, heaven and hell, time and eternity. It lay behind faith in a Kingdom of God advancing by rational planning. In a word, the triumph of the new eschatology signaled the waning of supernaturalism. Arguments over that trend were at the heart of virtually all the questions in dispute during the fundamentalist-modernist controversy. In 1924, Edgar Y.

Mullins—president of Southern Theological Seminary (Baptist) in Louisville, Kentucky, and a nonmillenarian of moderately conservative stripe—recognized this fact when he criticized the direction of modernist theology. Having reduced Christianity to "the lowest possible minimum of the supernatural," liberal theologians believed "in such a God as never opens his mouth save in natural forms and manifestations." Although many who counted themselves liberals or made common cause with them could have fairly objected that Mullins had created a caricature of their position, the description nevertheless accurately conveyed the central thrust of modernist theology.[31]

Legacies

The battle with fundamentalism resulted in a qualified victory for modernists. In the denominations wracked by the controversy—the northern Baptists and Presbyterians—modernists rallied sufficient support among moderates and irenic conservatives to stave off being dislodged from pulpits, seminaries, or church boards. The fundamentalists failed to capture the machinery of existing denominations. They were forced to establish enclaves within those churches or to withdraw and set up their own ecclesiastical organizations. In the struggle over evolution in the public schools, the fundamentalists won a battle but lost a war. At the so-called "monkey trial," the fundamentalists achieved a legal victory—John Scopes was convicted of violating the law by teaching evolution—but the verdict was later set aside on appeal. What is more important, the Scopes trial stereotyped fundamentalists as the rubes or hicks whom H. L. Mencken and others were portraying.[32]

Yet even as fundamentalists moved or were shoved into subcultures, they were far from beaten. Having already built a significant network of institutions, they strengthened these during the 1930s and beyond, though this success went largely unnoted by outside observers. In some respects, these institutions were shadow organizations mirroring even as they combated mainstream structures such as the Federal Council of Churches and the IWM. Occasionally one could hear in conservative quarters language reminiscent of mainline church bodies when, for example, the largely premillenarian World Conference on Christian Fundamentals in May 1919 sought means to coordinate and standardize the curricula of the Bible schools, spoke of the importance of "economy and efficiency," and called for a more unified witness to the truth. In fact, Virginia Brereton has characterized the Bible schools as "religious empires that demanded energy and organizing abilities worthy of a Rockefeller or a Carnegie," and Martin Marty has described the activities of conservative evangelists as being "as bureaucratized and rationalized as anything Max Weber was portraying in business and government." Yet fundamentalists could not take to organization with unalloyed enthusiasm.

The premillenarian belief that apostasy would claim organized Christianity in the latter days made institutions somewhat suspect, and the revivalist and holiness roots of fundamentalism rendered structural questions incidental to soul-winning. Reuben A. Torrey spoke for many in the movement when he declared: "Our [ecclesiastical] machinery is wonderful, it is just perfect; but alas it is machinery without power; and when things do not go right, instead of going to the real source of the failure, our neglect to depend upon God and to look to God for power, we look around to see if there is not some new organization we can set up, some new wheel that we can add to our machinery. We have all together [sic] too many wheels already." Moreover, the organizations created by fundamentalists tended to be more decentralized and often more dependent upon the personalities of magnetic leaders than were the mainline institutions. Rather than weakening the movement, these traits gave fundamentalism resilience and power in mobilizing popular support.[33]

More impressive still was the astonishingly rapid growth of various Pentecostal bodies during the 1920s and 1930s. A relatively new family of churches, most of which traced themselves, directly or indirectly, to the so-called Azusa Street revival of 1906 in Los Angeles, they had grown out of the nineteenth-century holiness tradition and made their distinctive doctrinal contribution through the claim that God had restored the primitive gifts or charismata (healing and speaking in tongues) enjoyed by the earliest Christian church. Otherwise, Pentecostals were theologically close to the fundamentalists in their views of dispensationalism, the Bible, and holiness. Yet they generally moved in a world of their own, rejected by other conservatives and ignored or dismissed as "holy rollers" by mainline church leaders. Neither indifference nor hostility, however, diminished their successes. In 1930 the rate of increase for Pentecostal and holiness groups peaked at approximately 300 percent, this at a time when the old-line churches comparatively limped along, with gains in the vicinity of 10 percent. While the pace of Pentecostal growth slowed significantly in the 1930s, it still far outstripped that of mainstream religious bodies.[34]

Such trends were symptomatic of the qualified victory won by liberals. Though unquestionably secure within their denominations, they now discovered that these very organizations exercised influence over a more limited domain. The fundamentalist-modernist battles had, as Martin Marty notes, "split up what was left of a Protestant establishment, leaving it ever less prepared to hold its place of dominance in the decades to come." Moreover, many of the crusades that kingdom-building Protestants had espoused waned in the 1920s. In the mainstream churches, both the foreign missionary movement and the Social Gospel began to lose momentum, and in the decades ahead the balance of power in foreign missions, at least insofar as numbers count, shifted toward more conservative bodies. The Federal Council of Churches presented a more ambiguous case. Partly because it proved itself a useful official representative for dealings with the federal government, Catholicism, and Judaism during World War I, the council attained greater recognition. In the years after the armistice and especially after 1930, the Federal Council began to provide many valuable resources to the individual denominations. In view of these services, critics were willing to overlook the Social Gospel activism still ensconced (though often in diluted form) in some of the Council's agencies. The Council was succeeding, but in a fashion very different from the way its founders had hoped it would. At the 1908 meeting, the council's first president declared: "It is the voice of many millions that speaks here to-day like the voice of many waters." The council's subsequent career indicated that it was nothing of the sort. Only on selected issues and occasions—for example, when it threw its support behind prohibition— could the council fairly claim to articulate a relatively united Protestant opinion. Otherwise the organization functioned as a provider of services and as a holding company for various specialized ministries, some of which had little support within the constituent denominations.[35]

Waning enthusiasms and internal divisions, harmful as they were, formed only part of the churches' problem. By the 1920s, it was clear that Protestant prestige and influence had diminished in important sectors of American life. Among men and women of letters, the genteel tradition of literature, which had generally affirmed the values associated with middle-class Protestantism, was giving way to Sinclair Lewis's portrayals of religious hypocrisy on Main Street, to H. L. Mencken's savage lampoons of intellectual mediocrity among America's (largely Protestant) "booboisie," to F. Scott Fitzgerald's depictions of an amoral "lost generation," to Joseph Wood Krutch's skeptical vision of a meaningless world in which "living is merely a physiological process," and to Ernest Hemingway's debunking of the idealism with which the nation and its churches had fought "the war to end all wars." The nation's universities had by the 1920s pulled farther away from their religious origins—a fact made clear by the sharp drop in the number of minister-presidents and in the percentage of trustees drawn from the clergy and in the gradual reduction or elimination of compulsory chapel at most institutions of higher learning. In ensuing decades the churches experimented with new ways of making their presence felt in colleges and universities by promoting independent campus ministries and the academic study of religion, but these efforts tacitly confessed that Protestant faith was no longer central to higher education. Existing "on the margin," it had to find some way to break back into the institutions it had once shaped. Also by the 1920s, as R. Laurence Moore has noted, "a neutral model of behaviorist interpretation gained a strong hold on the

American social science imagination" and thus made irrelevant the religious commitments of those scientists who had been the erstwhile allies of the kingdom builders. At the level of popular culture, a similar displacement of religion appeared to be underway. Many observers argued that—as a result of the freedom afforded by the automobile, the diversions offered by movies, radio, and sports, and the alternate forms of sociability provided by clubs such as Rotary and Kiwanis—the churches were losing their central role in the lives of adherents. In *Middletown,* their pioneering examination of the institutions and mores of Muncie, Indiana, Robert and Helen Lynd noted trends "forcing upon religion a narrowing place and time specialization: as religious rites tend to concentrate in church and allied building rather than pervade home, club, and civic and social groups, so, too, there is a tendency to center them more exclusively in the one day in seven that traditionally "belongs to the Lord."[36]

Yet one must not infer that religion was becoming insignificant. Despite its diminished role in the life of the denizens of Middletown, the Lynds had no doubt that religion continued to provide needed solace and meaning. "In church," they noted in an often quoted line, "question marks straighten out into exclamation points, the baffling day-by-day complexity of things becomes simple, the stubborn world falls into step with man and his aspirations, his individual efforts become significant as part of a larger plan." In the universities, voluntary or extracurricular religious organizations often maintained a vitality belying images of the uniform secularization of higher education. Moreover, the links between social scientists and kingdom-building Protestants had not been completely severed. For example, the Institute of Social and Religious Research, itself a spin-off of the abortive IWM and a recipient of Rockefeller largesse, sponsored about fifty studies, including *Middletown.* Director Harlan Paul Douglass was a Congregational clergyman who, in the spirit of Josiah Strong, Warren Wilson, and other earlier pioneers, sought to use social surveys as a means of facilitating intelligent planning and coordination by religious bodies.[37]

Nor had calls ceased to reorganize churches in accord with the canons of businesslike efficiency. If anything, that rhetoric increased during the 1920s, a decade in which business leaders were lionized as heroes and in which Warren G. Harding could begin an address in 1923, saying: "Our government is the biggest business in the world. . . . I am rejoiced to speak to you as your President reporting on the state of affairs of the stockholders of your Republic." A new periodical, *Church Management,* appearing in 1923, devoted itself entirely to articles on the running of various aspects of church life. *Church Management* was part of a growing genre that was blatantly utilitarian, even manipulative in character. William H. Leach, for example, in explaining *How to Make the Church Go* (1922), described the minister as an executive—he should have an office, not a study—and provided advice on the "forces which move men," among which were the need for recognition, self-interest, the competitive spirit and "the desire to be of some service in the world." Significantly, the desire to serve was the last motive enumerated. Worthwhile worship services should be constructed so as to leave the congregants with a "pleasant after feeling." Roger W. Babson, president of a statistical organization and a Congregationalist layman, warned of the thousands of "inefficient little churches" that were "a disgrace to religion" and created an impediment to "the entire religious industry." Bruce Barton—advertising executive, a liberal Protestant son of the manse, and after 1937 Republican representative to Congress from Manhattan's "silk stocking" district—in his best-selling *The Man Nobody Knows* (1924) depicted Jesus as the quintessential advertiser and executive, the embodiment of manly hardiness and sociability, the founder of modern business. The blatancy of such portrayals demonstrated the awe in which many Americans held business leaders in the era of Harding and Coolidge. The stridency, even crassness, of the rhetoric perhaps also suggested mainstream Protestants' uneasiness about their position in American culture and their need to grasp at every means to shore it up.[38]

Among the clergy, William Adams Brown provided one of the most sophisticated analyses of the religious situation. A noted Presbyterian theologian and a leader in numerous ecumenical ventures, Brown came as close as any single person could to summing up in his own person the aspirations of the liberal elements of the Protestant mainstream. His book *The Church in America: A Study of the Present Condition and Future Prospects of American Protestantism* (1922) thus provides an appropriate closing (or at least penultimate) word to this study. Brown believed that Protestant denominations had reached a moment of truth. "We are trying an experiment," he noted, "which will have a far-reaching effect upon the future of democracy, an experiment which will show whether it is possible to supply the unifying spiritual influence needed in a democracy by means of a strong, coherent, free Church, and so make possible under the conditions of our modern life the coming of the new social order called by our Maker the Kingdom of God."[39]

Brown acknowledged that Protestants faced serious difficulties in bringing this "experiment" to a successful conclusion. Strife between labor and capital, the grievances of African Americans, the divisions within denominations, and the failure of most churches to admit women into positions of leadership were among the moral issues by which the denominations were being judged and found wanting. The fundamental dilemma, however, lay deeper, in the "provincialism and individualism" of Protestants. Unable to think beyond their own congregations or denominations, they were also limited in their conception of Christianity itself. To document his charges, Brown drew upon a study of the views of young men in uniform during World War I. While religious, the soldiers exhibited an "exceedingly vague and undeveloped" faith. "There was indeed but a meagre understanding of the Church's teaching." Particularly troublesome was the "self-centered and negative" character of a piety "having to do primarily with one's own personal welfare here and hereafter." The doughboys had little awareness of "the Kingdom of God, as a better social order for which to work." All of this added up to a dismal "failure of the churches to furnish the young men who had been under their instruction with an intelligent understanding of Christian beliefs, Christian ideals, and Christian history."[40]

Brown's analysis was colored by his deep disappointment at the failure of the IWM, whose collapse he attributed to the revival of the denominational spirit and to the poor timing of the ecumenical appeal. After two years of war-imposed "self-denial and renunciation," people were not prepared for additional sacrifice and more crusading. Yet Brown tried to put the best face on the situation. The recrudescence of denominationalism might prove a blessing if the individual communions used the occasion to improve their own internal programs. "It was not the presence of highly efficient denominational organizations," he observed, "which proved the greatest obstacle to our successful co-operation in the war, but their absence. . . . A chain is only as strong as its weakest link, and if the churches are to co-operate effectively with one another, they must first learn to co-operate effectively within themselves." In other words, the breakdown of the IWM might prove to be only a momentary setback during which the denominations retooled, made their work more efficient, and then surged forward better prepared for ecumenical cooperation. Despite gloomy signs, Brown dared to hope. "The older individualism is breaking down," he commented, "and a new spirit is abroad in the churches." That spirit needed only "the proper machinery for its expression."[41]

Brown had clear ideas about the "proper machinery." In each denomination, there needed to be "a central executive body" with power to act between conferences, conventions, or general assemblies. Failure to take this action was to leave the denominations without practical unity and direction. "It is as though Congress tried to run the government without any executive and then decided to meet only once in two or three years, and never for more than a week or ten days." He envisioned that the denominations, more centrally organized, would organically merge with those in the same theological tradition, and that all major denominations would participate in a strengthened Federal Council of Churches. Similar structures of ecumenical unity would emerge worldwide. Under the canopy of this centralized and federated ecclesiastical organization, specialized ministries would flourish, social surveys proceed, and inefficient churches be closed.[42]

In view of the "provincialism and individualism" that he acknowledged to be endemic to American Protestantism, Brown's prescription seemed to run against the tide of his own analysis. His solution was a massive program of education to remake the consciousness of American Protestantism. At all levels of instruction, beginning with better-equipped Sunday Schools and continuing through the universities, men and women needed to be taught more thoroughly the origins and growth of the Christian tradition. The national leaders of the churches also had a responsibility to take part in this endeavor, for they "are not simply agents to carry out the will of the churches; they are in a very real sense teachers of the Church as to what ought to be done. Much of their energy is spent in preparing informational literature and in bringing home to the consciences of their constituency facts regarding the needs of their field." And what was it they were to teach? Preeminently, church leaders had to instill a vision of the kingdom, a sense of the Second Coming of Christ "as a spiritual process in which little by little the institutions of society as well as the lives of the men and women who live under them are to be conformed to the mind of Christ."[43]

Brown's analysis ended where it began—with the Kingdom of God. For Brown, that kingdom was a worldwide humane order for which Christians were to strive here and now. As a cosmopolitan ideal, it demanded the submergence of every parochial and irrational loyalty within a larger Christian community that would increasingly standardize and coordinate all religious activities. Faced with evidence that most rank-and-file Protestants did not share his vision, Brown refused to retreat. He called upon mainline Protestant leaders to redouble their educational efforts to bring their people out of "provincialism and individualism." With its defiant determination to press ahead with the building of the kingdom, *The Church in America* was in many ways the rallying cry of a theological position whose day had begun to pass. Perhaps Brown might more aptly have chosen the title that a soon-to-be colleague at Union Seminary bestowed upon one of his works: *Reflections on the End of an Era.*[44]

Indeed, Brown's view of the kingdom would soon be in disrepute as liberalism found itself embattled on a wide front against a new theological enemy. That foe, usually called neo-orthodoxy (but sometimes termed dialectical theology, the theology of crisis, neo-Reformation theology, or Christian realism), exerted a powerful influence upon American seminaries in the 1930s. More a mood and a common perception of crisis than a single intellectual system, neo-orthodoxy turned with renewed appreciation to Christian themes neglected by nineteenth-century liberalism: the centrality of biblical revelation, the transcendence of God, and the sinfulness of humanity. What this new theological perspective meant for eschatology was succinctly expressed by Drew Seminary's Edwin Lewis in 1941: Notions "about 'bringing in the Kingdom' . . . [are] exceedingly remote from the complete Gospel." "There is," said Lewis, "a growing conviction that the New Testament idea of the Kingdom of God cannot be fitted into any naturalistic evolutionary scheme; or into any philosophy of history which operates exclusively with the category of divine immanence." Talk about "building the kingdom" became increasingly passé.[45]

Of course, the organizational revolution that such slogans had helped to legitimate has remained very much a part of American religious life, but the present is not an altogether propitious movement to make a balanced appraisal of this enduring legacy. Today it is fashionable to criticize mainline Protestantism for its preoccupation with matters of structure and polity, and that censure fits into a larger cultural pattern of resentment against allegedly distant, unresponsive bureaucracies, whether secular or religious. We are not disposed to assess favorably a generation which, in the name of bringing in the kingdom, built up organizations. It is important to recall that despite their inevitable shortcomings, those who dreamed of a kingdom "as wide as the earth itself" promoted many laudable goals: a greater sensitivity to issues of economic justice, a deepened awareness of peoples outside the United States, and a sense of human interdependence. One also does well to heed the observation of William McGuire King, writing of the Methodist bureaucratic transformation:

> Whether this reorientation of denominational self-understanding was ultimately good or bad is a vital question, but one which cannot be answered on historical grounds alone. In yielding to a corporate self-understanding, denominations may have betrayed their religious mandate. Stripped of its spirit of boosterism, however, the corporate redefinition [of denominational life] was a sincere effort to translate the Christian ideal of an inclusive, serving community into a modern idiom. If the corporate ideal threatened to erode the transcendent ground of Christianity, it may also have helped to prevent Christianity from becoming merely a sectarian backwater in the floodplains of modernity.[46]

There were many ironies in the search for more efficient kingdom-building organizations. Not the least of these was a contradiction with the notion of efficiency itself. Those who espoused administrative reshuffling, promotional campaigns, and new forms of professional expertise argued that they were trying to provide unified, effective expression to Protestantism's or their denomination's common mind. In reality, the new agencies and specializations undermined unity as well as advancing it. Those who spent their careers working for national agencies of churches often acquired perspectives different from those whom they served. As the people with the "facts" about their specialized domains or, alternately, as the ones keeping a steady gaze on the entire mission of the church, they often viewed as narrow the outlook of parish ministers and their congregations. William Adams Brown alluded to this dynamic when he insisted that leaders of the churches must be the shapers of the common mind, not merely its reflectors. One promoter of the Presbyterian New Era campaign in 1920 made the same point more bluntly. Extolling denominational leaders as people of "high executive ability . . . comparable to that of the men who are managing big business" and calling the agencies they led "our eyes and hands and feet in building the Kingdom of God in this world," this Presbyterian warned against finding fault with them. If we in the pews, he suggested, think we could do their jobs better, "this feeling is due to our lack of information, if not to our lack of knowledge of our own limitations." It is not surprising that these attitudes provoked resentments among constituents who preferred to see the boards as servants rather than as masters. Traditions of localism, democratic control, and anti-elitism were sunk deep in American life, and these coexisted uneasily with centralized denominational control. John Higham's comments about the "experts" of the Progressive Era are equally applicable to the new class of agency leaders in the Protestant denominations: "Contrary to what the progressives supposed, technical organization is essentially undemocratic. Not equal rights but the hierarchical articulation of differentiated functions is its working principle. The more complex the knowledge required for maintaining a system, the further the professional expert is detached from the common life and the more the centers of power are hidden from public view."[47]

The dream of kingdom-building efficiency was also ironic in another sense. The ideal had arisen in the milieu of corporate business where efficiency could be measured by the volume of goods sold and profits earned. Yet churches traded in the intangibles of symbolic rewards less susceptible to precise computation. William Adams Brown had admitted as much when he declared in 1922 that "there is always something incalculable about religion." Yet, aside from periodic grumbling about the church being overrun by its machinery, few persons, if any, systematically explored the implications of this complaint. The failure to do so would have far-reaching consequences. With uncertainties and unresolved questions built into the search for an ill-defined efficiency, Protestants could never be sure whether they had completed the quest and thus returned again and again to the pursuit of an elusive goal.[48]

But the fundamental irony of this rage for rational control was that it was built in part on irrational longings and fears—or at least upon feelings transcending rationality. Although one might describe these motivations in timeless existential terms, their shape was conditioned by circumstances peculiar to the late nineteenth and early twentieth centuries: Protestant fears of the loss of cultural hegemony due to immigration, labor unrest, and unsettled gender roles; anxieties about maintaining personal agency and significance in the age of the machine and the corporation; and the corresponding dreams of unlimited possibility unleashed by technology and an economy of abundance. These atavisms were readily discernible in the lives and thought of many prominent figures around the turn of the century. They appeared in the work of psychologist G. Stanley Hall, who argued that to rear properly civilized men, one had to allow them as boys to be little savages. Theodore Roosevelt, whose mature political thought called for unprecedented control and management of national life, needed to immerse himself periodically in the primitive by ranching in the Dakotas, by leading troops into battle in Cuba, or, in the post-presidential years, by game-hunting on safari. The great religious crusades, the very ones promoting efficiency and organization, drew upon similarly elemental images: Foreign missions were an heroic endeavor, an opportunity to exert "a full-orbed manhood"; the Social Gospel took the Christian message into the gritty world "where sound the cries of race and clan"; the ecumenical movement conjured images of a powerful army moving "as one solid phalanx against every enemy of truth and righteousness." Yet what originated in deep longing or fear invariably ended up in the controlled atmosphere of committees and agencies.[49]

In itself, this result was scarcely exceptional. The postmillennial activists of the antebellum era had likewise built their voluntary societies and boards in an effort to create an ordered church and society. They often did so, however, by appealing to apocalyptic images of the End: the dread finality of death, last judgment, and damnation. But the new eschatology largely obliterated these somber associations with the End; in fact, it eliminated virtually all sense of a definitive End. Left with no way of adequately symbolizing an ultimate resolution of their elemental hopes and fears, the adherents of this eschatology had no choice but to return again and again, as if in an endless loop, as they tried to subject never-ending time to rational mastery.

Perhaps here is a clue to the frenetic, ceaseless activity that many have observed in twentieth-century ecclesiastical life. Of Methodist G. Bromley Oxnam (1891–1963), one of the leading Protestant figures at midcentury and a person styled by his biographer as "the paladin of liberal Protestantism," Robert Moats Miller writes: "Here is a powerful Methodist bishop who apparently had a minimal contemplative life. . . . Oxnam budgeted his time to the minute, but his total devotion to the gospel of salvation through good works left little time for private devotions. There is not the slightest hint in the record that he ever quietly sat still and practised the presence of God. . . . Like a shark, he felt he had to keep moving or would die. . . . Patently

Oxnam's New Jerusalem is a technocrat's heaven from which the Thomas Mertons would be exiled." We must be careful, of course, in generalizing too broadly from one life, but there was much indeed in the new eschatology to encourage the mentality of the shark who had to keep moving or die.[50]

Perhaps this eschatology also contained a hint of mainstream Protestantism's waning power in the twentieth century. To be sure, the prime sources of that change lay in demographic and cultural transformations over which Protestant leaders had little, if any, control. Nevertheless, to the extent that it had surrendered the grand and fearsome images of the End, mainstream Protestantism lost the capacity to satisfy those who longed for a faith with a more definitive vision of the Day of the Lord. Perhaps such persons found their way into dispensational fundamentalist congregations, into Pentecostalism, or into various sectarian groups. Perhaps also many who never left the mainstream churches experienced an attenuation or weakening of faith because mainline eschatology had become so amorphous.

To make these observations is not, of course, to suggest that mainstream Protestants would necessarily have succeeded better had they emulated the overly literal visions of the End proffered by Jehovah's Witnesses in their door-to-door visitation or had they offered a picture of the last things analogous to dispensationalism. Such a tactic would not have worked. For weal or woe, mainstream Protestantism had staked its life on the assumption that a measure of theological ambiguity was inevitable in the modern world. Had Protestants attempted to provide an eschatological scenario as hard or precise as the ones offered by their conservative critics, they would have compromised their own identities and thus probably would not have been very convincing. In any event, those who wished pre-critical absolutes would have more likely turned to groups that had far more practice in this art than mainline Protestants did. Moreover, one must romanticize neither the idea of the End nor those who hold it. People who have been certain, in Douglas W. Frank's words, that they have "a line on the future" often pay fearful costs for that confidence. Assurance that the End is nigh often brings with it profoundly dangerous baggage. The conviction tends toward the demonizing of opponents and toward the glorification of the divine violence which will supposedly usher in the new order. Adherents of such views all too easily assume the position of detached spectators, placidly awaiting the inevitable destruction, or more ominously, they may be tempted to shed the pose of bystander, to enter the arena, and to nudge history toward its appointed cataclysm. "The panoramas of destruction," A. G. Mojtabai has reminded us, "depicted in loving detail, with no human solution offered but flight from the world, are helping to create the conditions through which they become scenes from a self-fulfilling prophecy." In the aftermath of the apocalyptic violence at the

Branch Davidian Compound in Waco, Texas, and with growing numbers of armed militias preaching their own doomsday scenarios, Mojtabai's warning cannot be ignored.[51]

Yet if the dangers of taking the End too literally are self-evident, the story of mainline Protestant eschatology from the 1870s to the 1920s warns of another peril. It is also dangerous, albeit in a fashion far more subtle, to live without a sense of an End. Time with endless loops and summary courts in perpetual session—a world without End—may exact from the human spirit something as costly as any vision of the *Dies Irae*.

Epilogue

IN 1965, a young theologian published a study book for a series of conferences planned by the National Student Christian Federation. Within its first year, Harvey Cox's *The Secular City* sold over two hundred and fifty thousand copies and was reissued in a new edition. Eventually sales in all languages and editions reached nearly a million. At the heart of this best-seller was an affirmation that the present was pregnant with new possibilities. Calling upon Christians to forsake the metaphysical for the practical, Cox gloried in the achievements of a technocratic age and urged believers to pour their energies into the search for pragmatic solutions to the problems of urban civilization. In a chapter comparing the Kingdom of God to the ethos of the city, Cox declared: "The coming of the secular city is a historical process which removes adolescent illusions. Freed from these fantasies man is expected to assume the status of sonship, maturity, and responsible stewardship. His response to the call must include a willingness to participate in the constant improvisation of social and cultural arrangements which will be changed again and again in the future. The acceptance of provisionality is part of maturity." Although Cox did not advocate a return to the kingdom-building dreams of early-twentieth-century liberalism, his thought had significant resonances with those hopes. Once again one heard the notes of an eschatology centered upon the secular world, exalting open-ended forward movement ("constant improvisation"), and stressing the virtually limitless capacity of humans to engineer a more humane world.[1]

The success of Cox's book illustrates the fact that ideas seldom disappear completely or forever. After a period of neo-orthodox ascendancy in mainline Protestant seminaries, ideas associated with an earlier liberalism again received a hearing. Neo-orthodoxy itself, while far from disappearing, was losing its dominance. In part, it waned because it had never constituted a fully unified movement and had left many theological questions unanswered. From the beginning it was united chiefly by an awareness of crisis in Western culture, a sense of the inadequacy of liberalism, and a willingness to look seriously at classic Christian doctrines. Once the immediate sense of crisis faded after the Depression and the world war had been weathered, and after liberalism (at least in its more exuberant nineteenth-century forms) had passed from the scene, much of the common focus of the movement gradually disappeared. Moreover, the fact that the neo-orthodox conceived theology in dynamic rather than static terms created within the movement a principle of self-criticism and volatility conducive to further change. Already in the 1950s, there were hints among those influenced by neo-orthodoxy of a critique of conventional religiosity preparing the way for what Sydney Ahlstrom later called "The Radical Turn in Theology and Ethics." Although the revival of religion in the post–World War II era aided the movement superficially by promoting the sales of neo-orthodox books and by giving notoriety to its theologians (Reinhold Niebuhr, for example, appeared on the cover of *Time* magazine), the deeper thrust of the revival was in another direction. As church rolls burgeoned, as new church edifices rose across the suburbs of America, and as best-selling religious books presented a generally upbeat view, neo-orthodoxy's somber evaluation of the human condition had less appeal than it had in the 1930s. In any event, Protestant theology was moving in a new direction by the time Dwight D. Eisenhower left the White House in 1961.[2]

Harvey Cox's book caught the wave at full tide. In fact, the volume was, in the words of Robert S. Elwood, "the supreme icon" of "the hopeful, secular-as-sacred spirit of the early to mid-Sixties." Another expression of that mood was the so-called "death of God" theology that flourished briefly in those years under the tutelage of figures such as Thomas J. J. Altizer, William Hamilton, and Paul Van Buren. Members of a diverse movement whose adherents did not fully agree on the meaning of the deity's demise, the "death of God" theologians nevertheless shared a common optimism about the possibilities of life in this world. In an essay published in early 1966, Hamilton pointed to the success of President Johnson's reformist legislative program in the 1965 session of Congress and to the conviction of the Civil Rights Movement that "this world is the place, and now is the time, for the making of . . . long-overdue changes." Indeed, as he read the portents of his age, Hamilton concluded that "tragedy is culturally impossible" or—he added, hedging his bets—at least "unlikely." And his "worldly optimism" grew out of the confidence that human beings had it in their power to overcome the causes of human despair "whether those conditions be poverty, discrimination, or mental illness."[3]

The death-of-God was espoused by a handful of academics, at most. Yet the movement's significance cannot be assessed solely in terms of numbers.

These thinkers were symptomatic of a disposition widespread among mainstream Protestants even when the latter did not agree with the affirmations of Altizer, Hamilton, and company. The mood was one of activistic optimism, turning with renewed enthusiasm to the transformation of this world and seeking to create what an earlier generation would have called a kingdom "as wide as the earth itself." One of the most significant of these ventures was the engagement of major Protestant denominations with the Civil Rights Movement. Individually and through the National Council of Churches (the successor to the former Federal Council), Protestant denominations moved beyond their cautious antisegregation pronouncements of the 1950s to support civil-rights demonstrations, to lobby on behalf of the civil rights bills of 1964 and 1965, and to create new agencies designed to promote racial and economic justice. The most thorough student of these enterprises has called them a "revival of the Social Gospel, which had become the social creed of establishment Protestants in the early twentieth century." It was a revival manifest not only in the advocacy of civil rights but also in antiwar protest and in calls for greater economic justice.[4]

Protestant enthusiasm for the possibility of social transformation was in sync with broader trends in American life. It resonated with the great expectations generated by John F. Kennedy's summons to a New Frontier, with Lyndon B. Johnson's promise of a Great Society, and with the first phase of the Civil Rights Movement in the 1960s. Prior to the shift of emphasis from integration to black power in mid-decade, the movement stressed biracial cooperation and offered an optimism captured in the haunting words of the movement's best-known protest song: "We Shall Overcome." Sustaining the hopes for a boundless future was the extraordinary economic growth that had, with only minor interruptions, continued since World War II. With his typical pungency, President Johnson expressed to an aide what this abundance meant for the future. "Hell, we're the richest country in the world," LBJ declared, "the most powerful. We can do it all. . . . We can do it if we believe it."[5]

By the end of the 1960s and by the early 1970s, Johnson's confidence was shared by diminishing numbers of his fellow citizens. After the Civil Rights Movement turned toward black power, it became more controversial and alienated some erstwhile supporters. Debate over the war in Vietnam not only sorely divided the country but, for many, called into question America's former faith in its capacity to accomplish whatever it purposed. By the early 1970s, a combination of inflation and stagnating growth—"stagflation" as it became known—weakened the economic assumptions that had undergirded America's faith in unlimited progress. In the midst of these transitions, the mainline Protestant churches—many would soon be calling them oldline churches—were losing members and were often conflicted among themselves about the role they ought to play in society. Moreover, as mainstream churches tried to sort out their differences over social questions, they found themselves without a theological perspective powerful enough to contain their differences. A resurgent conservative evangelicalism, representing emphases which some thought had died with the fundamentalist controversy, exhibited new strength in mainline churches. Likewise, various theologies stressing, among other issues, liberation, black consciousness, and feminism gained power. Although it still had a few notable exponents, neo-orthodoxy no longer existed as a movement able to serve as a bridge between liberal and conservative concerns.[6]

Viewed in retrospect, much of the optimistic activism of the mainline churches in the early 1960s appears to have been what James F. Findlay Jr. has called "a last hurrah of the [Protestant] establishment." To be sure, many of the reformist energies unleashed in those years lived on in subsequent decades among those mainline Protestants who espoused causes such as liberation theology, feminism, environmentalism, the nuclear freeze, the sanctuary movement, or the rights of gays and lesbians. Generally missing from this activism, however, has been what was so conspicuous in the early 1960s: a buoyant confidence among the participants that they were riding the wave of the future. To change the metaphor, what Elwood called "the hopeful, secular-as-sacred spirit of the early to mid-Sixties" appears to have been not a second spring for the kingdom-building zeal of the early twentieth century, but perhaps an Indian summer.[7]

Yet even as ideas of building a kingdom "as wide as the earth itself" waxed and waned, another eschatological vision proved more durable. In 1970, Hal Lindsey published *The Late Great Planet Earth*. That work was a slick, popularized version of dispensationalism. The book predicts an imminent Rapture and an upward spiral of wickedness and international tension culminating in nuclear conflagration. This pattern is a predetermined one which no person can stop, but the impending disaster should occasion no alarm. At the height of human folly and catastrophe, Jesus will return to establish his millennial kingdom. Although Lindsey came closer to date-setting and to equating specific contemporary events with prophecy than nineteenth-century dispensationalists would have liked, his system was largely indebted to John Nelson Darby, Cyrus I. Scofield, and the scores of Bible schools through which the eschatology had been disseminated for more than a century. "By the mid-1990s," writes historian Paul Boyer, "the estimated total sales in successive editions and many translations [of *Late Great Planet*] stood in excess of twenty million copies." Lindsey was only one of the numerous expositors of prophecy who gained notoriety after the 1970s. Televangelists such as Jimmy Swaggart, Jack Van Impe, and Jerry Falwell also proclaimed a similar apocalyptic message over the airwaves. Nor was the interest in End times confined to sensationalist preachers on TV. The growing evangelical, fundamentalist, and pentecostal bodies, "discovered" by the secular media and by the mainline churches in the 1970s, were the very groups in which End time scenarios most often flourished. By the 1980s, the United States even had in Ronald Reagan a president deeply interested in the fulfillment of prophecy and in the Second Coming.[8]

Among allegedly secularized intellectuals, a different form of apocalypticism gained currency. Works such as Barry Commoner's *The Closing Circle* (1971) and Robert Heilbroner's *An Inquiry into the Human Prospect* (1974) foretold catastrophe of apocalyptic proportions unless humanity repented of unregulated economic expansion. Jonathan Schell's *The Fate of the Earth* (1982), perhaps the best representative of this genre, directed its warnings to the nuclear arms race. Though written from an avowedly secular standpoint, Schell's volume, too, was an eschatological tract, occasionally interspersing its warnings against nuclear destruction with metaphors of destruction derived from the Apocalypse. But unlike traditional visions of the terrors of the End, Schell's Armageddon, should it occur, would not be the prelude to a cosmic rebirth. "[E]xtinction by nuclear arms," wrote Schell, "would not be the Day of Judgment, in which God destroys the world but raises the dead and then metes out perfect justice to everyone who ever lived; it would be the utterly meaningless and completely unjust destruction of mankind by men." Unlike Lindsey, who took comfort in a foreordained plan and in a pattern of meaning transcending human purpose, Schell saw humans as the arbiters of their destiny and the sole determiners of meaning. "Mankind is to be thought of not as something that possesses a certain worth . . . —but as the inexhaustible source of all the possible forms of worth, which has no existence or meaning without human life." Thus for Schell, a nuclear Armageddon would be infinitely more terrifying than the traditional Day of Doom foretold by ancient prophets. It would be an anti-Apocalypse negating all meaning.[9]

Images of the End have also been prevalent in popular culture. For example, the movies *Omen* (1976), *Damien—Omen II* (1978), and *The Final Conflict* (1981) deal with the birth, childhood, and career of the Antichrist. *Independence Day* (1996) tells of sinister aliens, fantastic "beasts" like those in the Book of Revelation, who engaged the entire human race in a struggle for survival. Similarly, the public has been fascinated with groups who, for the sake of an apocalyptic dream of a better world, have been prepared to accept the destruction of their lives in this world: for example, Jim Jones's People's Temple (1978), David Koresh's Branch Davidians (1993), and Marshall Applewhite's Heaven's Gate (1997). Moreover, in the subculture surrounding the so-called militia movement, fears of a satanic New World Order, catalyzed by images drawn from the Apocalypse, have fueled resistance to the federal government. In short, the idea of the End has remained very much alive and well in popular culture, whether at its center or on its fringes.[10]

In sum, what mainstream Protestantism has been loath to supply is nevertheless abundant in many sectors of America. What are we to make of this fact?

We might take a clue from a book written a generation ago. In 1972, Dean M. Kelley, an executive of the National Council of Churches, published *Why Conservative Churches Are Growing*. He did so at the moment that the declining membership of mainstream churches was first becoming a subject of widespread discussion. In one of the less-noted passages of the book, Kelley hinted suggestively that perhaps mainstream churches had not understood as well as the stricter churches the nature of religion itself. He compared the religious urge to other basic human drives not easily tamed or subjected to rational order.

> Hunger, sex, and aggression are rude forces that often break out of the channels and institutions that are supposed, in this latter day, to make them less disruptive of society and less obnoxious to their neighbors. The craving for ultimate meaning . . . is likewise very deep and ancient in human experience, and so we should not be surprised if it, too, has its crude, fierce, and elemental aspects. . . .
>
> A human need whose fulfillment has sometimes entailed mutilations, human sacrifices, crusades, and inquisitions should not be classed with parlor games, literary teas, or other amiable indoor recreations.

Kelley, a Methodist minister working at the very citadel of the Protestant mainstream in the headquarters of the National Council of Churches in New York City, was scarcely advocating contemporary mutilations, human sacrifices, or inquisitions. He was, however, reminding his hearers that the drive for religious meaning is often an elemental longing and that those who seek to address the need ignore that fact at their peril.[11]

Kelley's observation applies with especial force to the last things. The idea of the End evokes primal terrors and fantasies—images of final reckonings, visions of lavish reward and punishment. Like the flame which draws the moth, the notion of the End is something to which people are attracted and from which they are repelled. While it is dangerous indeed to allow free reign to the fantasies and terrors of the End, neither is it wise to attempt to ignore or to suppress them entirely in favor of reveries of a bland, rationally mastered future. The idea of the End corresponds to something in the human spirit than longs for more than parlor games and amiable recreations.

NOTES

Preface

1. Edmund Gosse, *Father and Son: A Study of Two Temperaments* (New York: W. W. Norton, 1963; original edition, 1907), 231–32.

2. "History of Opinions Respecting the Millennium," *American Theological Review* 1 (November 1859): 655.

3. Frank Kermode, *The Sense of an Ending: Studies in the Theory of Fiction* (New York: Oxford University Press, 1966), 7.

4. Many eschatologies of Eastern religions, for example, see the End as part of a recurring cycle. After the destruction of the current world order and a return to primal chaos, the cosmos repeats the process. See Mircea Eliade, *The Myth of the Eternal Return,* tr. Willard R. Trask (New York: Pantheon, 1954). For an overview of the apocalyptic tradition and its many permutations, see *The Encyclopedia of Apocalypticism,* 3 vols., ed. John J. Collins, Bernard McGinn, and Stephen J. Stein (New York: Continuum, 1998).

5. Charles B. Strozier, *Apocalypse: On the Psychology of Fundamentalism in America* (Boston: Beacon Press, 1994), 2. Stephen D. O'Leary, *Arguing the Apocalypse: A Theory of Millennial Rhetoric* (New York: Oxford University Press, 1994), argues persuasively that apocalypticism constitutes an enduring rhetorical tradition focused on the themes of time and evil. This discourse, O'Leary contends, assumes that time must have an end that will eradicate the corruptions of a world gone awry.

6. Philippe Ariès, *The Hour of Our Death* (New York: Random House, 1981), 473.

7. George Cross, "Millenarianism in Christian History," *Biblical World,* 46 (July 1915): 3–4.

8. James T. Kloppenberg, *Uncertain Victory: Social Democracy and Progressivism in European and American Thought, 1870–1920* (New York: Oxford University Press, 1986), 65; John Patrick Diggins, *The Promise of Pragmatism: Modernism and the Crisis of Knowledge and Authority* (Chicago: University of Chicago Press, 1994), 20. The quotation from Fitzgerald is found in F. Scott Fitzgerald, *The Great Gatsby* (New York: Scribner's, 1953; original edition, 1925), 182.

9. Jackson Lears, *Fables of Abundance: A Cultural History of Advertising in America* (New York: Basic Books, 1994), 48.

10. William R. Hutchison, "Protestantism as Establishment," and Edwin Scott Gaustad, "The Pulpit and the Pews," in *Between the Times: The Travail of the Protestant Establishment, 1900–1960,* ed. William R. Hutchison (Cambridge: Cambridge University Press, 1989), 3–20, 21–47. On the evolution of terminology, I am indebted to Marianne Okkema Rhebergen, "'Mainstream' and 'Mainline': A Study in Emerging Terminology" (Ph.D. seminar paper, Princeton Theological Seminary, 1994).

11. Timothy P. Weber, *Living in the Shadow of the Second Coming: American Premillennialism, 1875–1982,* enlarged edition (Chicago: University of Chicago Press, 1983), 40; Paul Boyer, *When Time Shall Be No More: Prophecy Belief in Modern American Culture* (Cambridge: Belknap Press of Harvard University Press, 1992), 312; Robert T. Handy, *A*

Christian America: Protestant Hopes and Historical Realities, 2nd ed. (New York: Oxford University Press, 1984), 159–84.

12. James Turner, *Without God, Without Creed: The Origins of Unbelief in America* (Baltimore: Johns Hopkins University Press, 1985), xiii; William R. Hutchison, *Between the Times: The Travail of the Protestant Establishment, 1900–1960* (Cambridge: Cambridge University Press, 1989).

Introduction

1. Samuel Harris, *The Kingdom of Christ on Earth: Twelve Lectures Delivered before the Students of the Theological Seminary, Andover* (Andover, Mass.: Warren F. Draper, 1874), 23, 73, 136, 185, 234–35.

2. The relationship of the millennial-apocalyptic tradition to modern ideas of progress merits additional comment. Among others, Ernest L. Tuveson, Robert Nisbet, and Theodore Olson have argued that the apocalyptic sense of linear history is one of the intellectual roots of the concept of progress. I do not dispute the contention as long as one also acknowledges significant differences between the two perspectives. Most modern ideas of progress have stressed (1) that a pattern of improvement is discernible in history, (2) that this forward movement will continue in the future, and (3) that this amelioration is developmental—that is, it proceeds by stages, each one organically related to the one before it with the whole process governed by forces resident within history. By contrast, the apocalypticism of the book of Revelation (1) describes history as declension, (2) predicts further decline, and (3) declares that improvement will not derive from forces now visible in history but must await a supernatural abrogation of mundane time—in other words, the Second Coming and the overthrow of the present world. Ernest Lee Tuveson, *Millennium and Utopia: A Study in the Background of the Idea of Progress* (Berkeley: University of California Press, 1949), esp. 1–21; Robert Nisbet, *History of the Idea of Progress* (New York: Basic Books, 1980), 124–40; Theodore Olson, *Millennialism, Utopianism, and Progress* (Toronto: Toronto University Press, 1982), 3–10.

3. Perry Miller, *The Life of the Mind in America* (New York: Harcourt, Brace, and World, 1965), 79. Daniel Whitby, *A Paraphrase and Commentary on the New Testament,* 2 vols. (London: W. Bowyer, 1703); Tuveson, *Redeemer Nation: The Idea of America's Millennial Role* (Chicago: University of Chicago Press, 1968), 33–38; C. C. Goen, "Jonathan Edwards: A New Departure in Eschatology," *Church History* 28 (March 1959): 25–40; Sacvan Bercovitch, *The American Jeremiad* (Madison: University of Wisconsin Press, 1978), 98–99; James West Davidson, *The Logic of Millennial Thought: Eighteenth-Century New England* (New Haven, Conn.: Yale University Press, 1977), 255–97; Ruth Bloch, *Visionary Republic: Millennial Themes in American Thought, 1756–1800* (Cambridge: Cambridge University Press, 1985), 217.

4. Gordon S. Wood, "The Democratization of Mind in the American Revolution," in Library of Congress Symposia on the American Revolution, *Leadership in the American Revolution* (Washington, D.C., 1974), 63–89; Robert H. Wiebe, *The Opening of American Society: From the Adoption of the Constitution to the Eve of Disunion* (New York: Oxford University Press, 1984), 295. Otis is quoted in Nathan O. Hatch, "The Christian Movement and the Demand for a Theology of the People," *Journal of American History* 67 (December 1980): 546. See also Richard D. Brown, *Modernization: The Transformation of American Life, 1600–1865* (New York: Hill and Wang, 1976), 74–158; David Hackett Fischer, *The Revolution of American Conservatism: The Federalist Party in the Era of Jeffersonian Democracy* (New York: Harper and Row, 1965), 188–99; Charles H. Sellers, *The Market Revolution: Jacksonian America, 1815–1846* (New York: Oxford University Press, 1991), 229–355; Chilton Williamson, *American Suffrage: From Property to Democracy, 1760–1860* (Princeton: Princeton University Press, 1960), esp. 117–259 and 545–67; Gordon S. Wood, *The Radicalism of the American Revolution* (New York: Alfred A. Knopf, 1992), 229–335.

5. Stuart M. Blumin, *The Emergence of the Middle Class: Social Experience in the American City, 1760–1900* (Cambridge: Cambridge University Press, 1989), 66–191; Daniel Walker Howe, *The Political Culture of the American Whigs* (Chicago: University of Chicago Press, 1979), 96–122; Mary P. Ryan, *Cradle of the Middle Class: The Family in Oneida County, New York, 1790–1865* (Cambridge: Cambridge University Press, 1981); Sellers, *Market Revolution,* 237–68, 364–95.

6. Edwin Scott Gaustad, *Historical Atlas of Religion in America,* rev. ed. (New York: Harper and Row, 1976; original edition, 1962), 37–56; Nathan O. Hatch, *The Democratization of American Christianity* (New Haven, Conn.: Yale University Press, 1989).

7. Hatch, *Democratization,* 193–209; Richard L. Bushman, *The Refinement of America: Persons, Houses, Cities* (New York: Alfred A. Knopf, 1992), 313–52; Donald G. Tewksbury, *The Founding of American Colleges and Universities before the Civil War* (New York: Teacher's College, Columbia University, 1932); A. Gregory Schneider, *The Way of the Cross Leads Home: The Domestication of American Methodism* (Bloomington: Indiana University Press, 1993), 149–68; Charles I. Foster, *An Errand of Mercy: The Evangelical United Front, 1790–1837* (Chapel Hill: University of North Carolina Press, 1960), 121–22; Richard D. Birdsall, "The Second Great Awakening and the New England Social Order," *Church History* 39 (September 1970): 345–64.

8. Donald M. Scott, *From Office to Profession: The New England Ministry, 1750–1850* (Philadelphia: University of Pennsylvania Press, 1978), 51. I borrow the term "plebeian religion" from Paul E. Johnson and Sean Wilentz, *The Kingdom of Matthias* (New York: Oxford University Press, 1994), which offers a dramatic case in point. See also Byron Cecil Lambert, *The Rise of the Anti-Mission Baptists: Sources and Leaders, 1800–1840* (New York: Arno Press, 1980); and Teresa Anne Murphy, *Ten Hours' Labor: Religion, Reform, and Gender in Early New England* (Ithaca: Cornell University Press, 1992).

9. Robert Baird, *Religion in America,* ed. Henry Warner Bowden (New York, 1970; original edition, 1844), 202; Calvin Colton, *History and Character of American Revivals of Religion* (London: F. Westley and A. H. Davis, 1832), 4, 6; Charles Roy Keller, *The Second Great Awakening in Connecticut* (New Haven, Conn.: Yale University Press, 1942), 136–87; John B. Boles, *The Great Revival, 1787–1805: The Origins of the Southern Evangelical Mind* (Lexington: University of Kentucky Press, 1972), 184–186; William G. McLoughlin Jr., *Modern Revivalism: Charles Grandison Finney to Billy Graham* (New York: Ronald Press, 1959), 3–121; C. I. Foster, *Errand of Mercy,* esp. 156–222. See also Jon Butler, *Awash in a Sea of Faith: Christianizing the American People* (Cambridge: Harvard University Press, 1990), 164–93, 257–88; Donald G. Mathews, "The Second Great Awakening as an Organizing Process, 1780–1830: An Hypothesis," *American Quarterly,* 21 (spring 1969): 23–43. The deliberately promotional characteristics of the Great Awakening are well documented in Frank Lambert, *"Pedlar in Divinity": George Whitefield and the Transatlantic Revivals* (Princeton: Princeton University Press, 1994); and in Harry S. Stout, *The Divine Dramatist: George Whitefield and the Rise of Modern Evangelicalism* (Grand Rapids, Mich.: William B. Eerdmans, 1991).

10. Jonathan Edwards, *Apocalyptic Writings,* ed. Stephen J. Stein (New Haven, Conn.: Yale University Press, 1977), 24–48; *Proceedings of the First Ten Years of the American Tract Society, Instituted at Boston, 1814* (New York: Flagg and Gould, 1824), 102; William Cogswell, *The Harbinger of the Millennium* (Boston: Peirce and Parker, 1833), 299–300. See also Joseph Emerson, *Lectures on the Millennium* (Boston: Samuel T. Armstrong, 1818).

11. Henry F. May, *The Enlightenment in America* (New York: Oxford University Press, 1976), esp. 307–57; Donald Meyer, *The Instructed Conscience: The Shaping of the American National Ethic* (Philadelphia: University of Pennsylvania Press, 1977), 77–87; Mark A. Noll, "Common Sense Traditions and American Evangelical Thought," *American Quarterly* 37 (summer 1985): 216–38; Conrad Cherry, *Nature and Religious Imagination from Edwards to Bushnell* (Philadelphia, Pa.: Fortress Press, 1980), 85–133.

12. Joseph Bellamy, *Sermons on the Following Subjects, vis., The Divinity of Jesus Christ. The Millennium. The Wisdom of God, in the Permission of Sin* (Boston: Edes and Gill, 1758), 62–66; *Oberlin Evangelist,* December 6, 1843, p. 195. See also Mark Valeri, *Law and Providence in Joseph Bellamy's New England: The Origins of the New Divinity in Revolutionary America* (New York: Oxford University Press, 1994); Joseph A. Conforti, *Samuel Hopkins and the New Divinity Movement: Calvinism, the Congregational Ministry, and Reform in New England between the Great Awakenings* (Grand Rapids, Mich.: Christian University Press, 1981), 164–65. Stephen D. O'Leary, *Arguing the Apocalypse,* argues cogently that all millennial systems seek to explain the problem of evil.

13. [L. D. Barrows], "The Millennium and Second Advent," *Methodist Quarterly Review,* 58 (July 1876): 433–57. See also E. Benjamin Andrews, "The Missionary Future in the Light of Prophecy," *Baptist Quarterly,* 9 (October 1875): 430–50.

14. J. F. Maclear, "The Republic and the Millennium," in *The Religion of the Republic,* ed. Elwyn A. Smith (Philadelphia, Pa.: Fortress Press, 1971), 184; Revelation 11:15; Edwards, *Apocalyptic Writings,* 272–84; Bercovitch, *American Jeremiad,* 40–44; Nathan O. Hatch, *The Sacred Cause of Liberty: Republican Thought and the Millennium in Revolutionary New England* (New Haven, Conn.: Yale University Press, 1977), 21–54; Alan Heimert, *Religion and the American Mind from the Great Awakening to the Revolution* (Cambridge: Harvard University Press, 1966), 59–94; Sidney E. Mead, *The Nation with the Soul of a Church* (New York: Harper and Row, 1975), 71–73. For two accounts that emphasize ways in which Protestant hopes were *not* tied to American nationalism, see Mark Y. Hanley, *Beyond a Christian Commonwealth: The Protestant Quarrel with the American Republic, 1830–1860* (Chapel Hill: University of North Carolina Press, 1994); and Diana Hochstedt Butler, "The Church and American Destiny: Evangelical Episcopalians and Voluntary Societies in Antebellum America," *Religion and American Culture: A Journal of Interpretation* 4 (summer 1994): 194–219.

15. Samuel Harris, *Our Country's Claim* (Bangor, Maine: Wheeler and Lynde, 1861), 10.

16. Erskine Mason, *An Evangelical Ministry, the Security of a Nation: A Sermon, Preached in Behalf of the American Home Missionary Society, in the Bleecker Street Church, New York, January 2, 1848* (New York: W. Osborn, 1848), 23. See also Jesse T. Peck, *The History of the Great Republic, Considered from a Christian Stand-Point* (New York: Broughton and Wyman, 1868), 707–10; Joseph F. Berg, *The Stone and the Image; or, The American Republic, the Bane and Ruin of Despotism. An Exposition of the Fifth Kingdom of Daniel's Prophecy, and of the Great Wonder in Heaven of the Apocalypse* (Philadelphia, Pa.: Higgins and Perkinpine, 1856), 54, 114; *Christian Advocate and Journal,* November 20, 1862, p. 370, and November 27, 1862, 378; Hollis Read, *The Coming Crisis of the World; or, The Great Battle and the Golden Age* (Columbus: Follett, Foster and Company, 1861), 226–28, 233.

17. Bruce Kuklick, ed., *The Works of Samuel Hopkins,* 3 vols. (New York and London: Garland Publishing, 1987; original edition, 1865), 2:273, 274, 276, 287, 290–91; Joseph Brady, "The Magnetic Telegraph," *Ladies' Repository* 10 (February 1850): 61–62; Albert Barnes, *Life at Threescore and Ten* (New York: American Tract Society, 1871), 130–31. The instance of singing a hymn in response to the laying of the transatlantic cable is recounted in Meyer, *Instructed Conscience,* 123–24, See also Anthony F. C. Wallace, *Rockdale: The Growth of an American Village* (New York: Alfred A. Knopf, 1978), 401–74; Paul E. Johnson, *A Shopkeeper's Millennium: Society and Revivals in Rochester, New York, 1815–1837* (New York: Hill and Wang, 1978), 95–115; Howe, *American Whigs,* 150–80; For an example of critiques of secular progress and materialism, see Hanley, *Beyond a Christian Commonwealth.*

18. Sellers, *Market Revolution,* 211; Walter Clarke, "The Reign of the Saints," *The National Preacher* 4 (February 1861): 56–57. In making this observation, I do not wish to reopen what has become an often sterile debate as to whether evangelical Protestantism was

a liberating force or an instance of social control. Clearly, it was both. As Daniel Walker Howe has sagely commented, "Evangelical Christians were and are people who have consciously decided to take charge of their own lives and identities. The Christian discipline they embrace is both liberating and restrictive. Insofar as the discipline is self-imposed, it expresses the popular will; insofar as it is imposed on others, it is social control. . . . Liberation and control were thus two sides of the same redemptive process"; Howe, "The Evangelical Movement and Political Culture in the North during the Second Party System," *Journal of American History* 77 (March 1991), 1220.

19. J. B. Bury, *The Idea of Progress: An Inquiry into Its Origin and Growth* (London: Macmillan, 1920), 2; Bercovitch, *American Jeremiad,* 93–94; M. A. DeWolfe Howe, *The Life and Letters of George Bancroft,* 2 vols. (New York: Charles Scribner's Sons, 1908), 2:119; "The Signs of the Times," *Methodist Quarterly Review* 35 (July 1853): 427; Hanley, *Beyond a Christian Commonwealth,* 126.

20. George Duffield, *Dissertations on the Prophecies Relative to the Second Coming of Jesus Christ* (New York: Dayton, 1842), v, vi; Leonard Woods, *A Sermon Delivered at the Tabernacle in Salem, Feb. 6, 1812, on the Occasion of the Ordination of the Rev. Messrs. Samuel Newell, A. M. Adoniram Judson, A. M. Samuel Nott, A. M. and Luther Rice, A. B. Missionaries to the Heathen in Asia* (Boston: Samuel T. Armstrong, 1812), 24; Marie Caskey, *Chariot of Fire: Religion and the Beecher Family* (New Haven, Conn.: Yale University Press, 1978), 23; Lyman Beecher, *The Memory of Our Fathers. A Sermon Delivered at Plymouth, on the Twenty-Second of December, 1827* (Boston: T. R. Marvin, 1828), 12; "The National Crisis," *Christian Review* 26 (July 1861): 492.

21. Richard Hofstadter, *The Paranoid Style in American Politics and Other Essays* (New York: Alfred A. Knopf, 1965), 3; David Brion Davis, "Some Themes of Counter-Subversion: An Analysis of Anti-Masonic, Anti-Catholic and Anti-Mormon Literature," *Mississippi Valley Historical Review* 47 (September 1960): 205–24; John M. Werly, "Premillennialism and the Paranoid Style," *American Studies* 18 (spring 1977): 39–55; Timothy Dwight, *A Discourse on Some Events of the Last Century, Delivered in the Brick Church in New Haven, on Wednesday, January 7, 1801* (New Haven, Conn.: Ezra Read, 1801), 19–39; Read, *Coming Crisis of the World,* 74–75. See also Lyman Beecher, *Plea for the West* (Cincinnati: Truman and Smith, 1835).

22. "The Fulfilment of Prophecy," *Biblical Repertory and Princeton Review* 33 (January 1861): 84. For examples of differing interpretive approaches, see A. L. Crandall, *A Brief Explanation of the Book of Revelation in Chronological Order* (Troy, N.Y.: James M. Stevenson, 1841); and "Millennial Traditions," *Methodist Quarterly Review* 25 (July 1843): 421–46; Seth Williston, *Millennial Discourses; or, A Series of Sermons Designed to Prove That There Will Be a Millennium of Peace and Holiness; Also to Suggest Means for Hastening Its Introduction* (Utica, N.Y.: Roberts and Sherman, 1849); Heman Lincoln, "The Millennium of the Bible," *Christian Review* 28 (January 1863): 131–44; Moses Stuart, *A Commentary on the Apocalypse,* 2 vols. (Andover, Mass.: Allen, Morrill, and Wardwell, 1845), 1:158, 2:353–95.

23. Joseph F. Berg, *The Second Coming of Jesus Christ, Not Premillennial* (Philadelphia, Pa.: Perkinpine and Higgins, 1859), 282.

24. Stuart, *Commentary on the Apocalypse,* 1:478; *Independent,* December 19, 1861, 4.

25. M. T. Adam, *The Millennium: Being a Series of Discourses Illustrative of Its Nature, the Means by Which It Will Be Introduced, and the Time of Its Commencement* (New York: Robert Easter, 1837), 161; Timothy L. Smith, "Righteousness and Hope: Christian Holiness and the Millennial Vision in America, 1800–1900," *American Quarterly* 31 (spring 1979): 21–45; George M. Marsden, *Fundamentalism and American Culture: The Shaping of Twentieth-Century Evangelicalism, 1870–1925* (New York: Oxford University Press, 1980), 93–101; Davidson, *Logic of Millennial Thought,* 122–75.

26. *Oberlin Evangelist,* December 22, 1841, p. 204, and May 11, 1842, p. 76; John

Dowling, *An Exposition of the Prophecies, Supposed by William Miller to Predict the Second Coming of Christ in 1843. With a Supplementary Chapter upon the True Scriptural Doctrine of a Millennium prior to the Judgment* (Providence, R. I.: George P. Daniels, 1840), 162–63, 165. See also Michael Barkun, *Crucible of the Millennium: The Burned-Over District of New York in the 1840s* (Syracuse: Syracuse University Press, 1986); Ruth Alden Doan, *The Miller Heresy, Millennialism, and American Culture* (Philadelphia, Pa.: Temple University Press, 1987); Edwin Scott Gaustad, ed., *The Rise of Adventism: A Commentary on the Social and Religious Ferment of Mid-Nineteenth Century America* (New York: Harper and Row, 1974); Ronald L. Numbers and Jonathan M. Butler, *The Disappointed: Millerism and Millenarianism in the Nineteenth Century* (Bloomington: Indiana University Press, 1987); and David L. Rowe, *Thunder and Trumpets: Millerites and Dissenting Religion in Upstate New York, 1800–1850* (Chico, Calif.: Scholars Press, 1985).

27. Horace Bushnell, *Christian Nurture* (New Haven, 1916; original edition, 1847), 5–121 (the 1916 edition is a reprint of the 1861 edition, which expands considerably on the 1847 edition); Charles O. Jackson, ed., *Passing: The Vision of Death in America* (Westport, Conn.: Greenwood Press, 1977), 91–144; James J. Farrell, *Inventing the American Way of Death, 1830–1920* (Philadelphia, Pa.: Temple University Press, 1980), 74–98; David E. Stannard, ed., *Death in America* (Philadelphia: University of Pennsylvania Press, 1975), 49–91.

28. [Lyman Abbott et al.], *That Unknown Country; or, What Living Men Believe concerning Punishment after Death, Together with Recorded Views of Men of Former Times* (Springfield, Mass.: C. A. Nichols, 1890), 381; Gilbert Haven, *Christus Consolator; or, Comfortable Words for Burdened Hearts* (New York: Hunt and Eaton, 1893), 68, 170–71; William Newton Clarke, *Sixty Years with the Bible: A Record of Experience* (New York: Charles Scribner's Sons, 1909), 102; Anne M. Boylan, "The Role of Conversion in Nineteenth-Century Sunday Schools," *American Studies* 20 (spring 1979): 35–48.

29. Lewis O. Saum, *The Popular Mood of Pre–Civil War America* (Westport, Conn.: Greenwood Press, 1980), 74; William J. Gilmore, *Reading Becomes a Necessity of Life: Material and Cultural Life in Rural New England, 1780–1835* (Knoxville: University of Tennessee Press, 1989), 316, 323, 338; Bloch, *Visionary Republic,* 33.

30. W. N. Clarke, *Sixty Years,* 102.

31. Martin Marty, *The Modern Schism: Three Paths to the Secular* (New York: Harper and Row, 1969), 95–142, and David A. Martin, *A General Theory of Secularization* (New York: Harper and Row, 1978), 27–36, offer analyses congruent with my own in regard to the role of Protestantism during the years modern America was emerging.

32. James H. Moorhead, *American Apocalypse: Yankee Protestants and the Civil War, 1860–1869* (New Haven, Conn.: Yale University Press, 1978). See also George M. Fredrickson, *The Inner Civil War: Northern Intellectuals and the Crisis of the Union* (New York: Harper and Row, 1965); Anne C. Rose, *Victorian America and the Civil War* (Cambridge: Cambridge University Press, 1992). Jesse T. Peck, *The History of the Great Republic, Considered from a Christian Stand-point* (New York: Broughton and Wyman, 1868), provides an example of the postmillennial interpretation of American history in the aftermath of the war.

1. Prophecy, the Bible, and Millennialism

1. Theodore Tilton, *Independent,* October 1, 1862, 4.

2. "The Fulfilment of Prophecy," 84.

3. W. H. Oliver, *Prophets and Millennialists: The Uses of Biblical Prophecy in England from the 1790s to the 1840s* (Auckland: Auckland University Press, 1978), 13, observes: "The millennial dream is simple and infinitely malleable. Millennialism and prophecy were so readily available and useful because they were so entirely traditional and conventional at all social levels."

4. Kemper Fullerton, *Prophecy and Authority: A Study in the History of the Doctrine and Interpretation of Scripture* (New York: Macmillan, 1919), 199, 200, 202.

5. Robert K. Whalen, "Millenarianism and Millennialism in America, 1790–1880" (Ph.D. diss., State University of New York, Stony Brook, 1972), 120.

6. Stuart, *A Commentary on the Apocalypse,* 159, 163, 483, 474–90. For further information on Stuart, consult Jerry Wayne Brown, *The Rise of Biblical Criticism in America, 1800–1870: The New England Scholars* (Middletown, Conn.: Wesleyan University Press, 1969), 45–59, 94–110; and John H. Giltner, *Moses Stuart: The Father of Biblical Science in America* (Atlanta, Ga.: Scholars Press, 1988).

7. Stuart, *A Commentary on the Apocalypse,* 1:478, 481, 2:353, 480; Moses Stuart, *Hints on the Interpretation of Prophecy* (Andover, Mass.: Allen, Morrill, and Wardwell, 1842), 140.

8. Charles Hodge, *Systematic Theology,* 3 vols. (New York: Scribner, Armstrong, 1872–75), 3:790–91, 797, 830, 849, 858–59.

9. Joseph F. Berg, *The Second Advent,* 152, 161–62; Joseph F. Berg, *The Stone and the Image,* 25–26; *Christian Advocate and Journal,* November 20, 1862, 370; ibid., November 27, 1862, 378.

10. Doan, *The Miller Heresy,* makes a strong case that Millerism played a crucial role in forcing postmillennialists to define their principles of biblical interpretation.

11. In this and the three succeeding paragraphs, I am heavily indebted to Marsden, *Fundamentalism and American Culture,* 48–62; Ernest R. Sandeen, *The Roots of Fundamentalism: British and American Millenarianism* (Chicago: University of Chicago Press, 1970), 107–11; T. P. Weber, *Living in the Shadow,* 13–81; Whalen, "Millenarianism and Millennialism," 217–49.

12. Theodore Dwight Bozeman, *Protestants in an Age of Science: The Baconian Ideal and Antebellum American Religious Thought* (Chapel Hill: University of North Carolina Press, 1977), 124–59; George M. Marsden, "Everyone One's Own Interpreter? The Bible, Science, and Authority in Mid-Nineteenth Century America," in *The Bible in America: Essays in Cultural History,* ed. Nathan O. Hatch and Mark A. Noll (New York: Oxford University Press, 1982), 79–100.

13. Duffield, *Prophecies Relative to the Second Coming,* 63, 101, 104–5, 409.

14. Hodge, *Systematic Theology,* 3:844; Stuart, *Commentary on the Apocalypse,* 2:480; Stuart, *Interpretation of Prophecy,* 140; Berg, *The Second Advent,* 128–49.

15. "The Millennium of Rev. xx.," *Methodist Quarterly Review* 25 (January 1843), 87. See also the same article, 83–110; "Modern Millenarianism," *Biblical Repertory and Princeton Review* 25 (January 1853), 66–83; Berg, *The Second Advent,* 128–49; Hodge, *Systematic Theology,* 3:790–868.

16. E. B. Andrews, "The Missionary Future," 430–50.

17. "Millennial Traditions," 422, 435; [Barrows], "The Millennium and Second Advent," 440.

18. "Modern Millenarianism," 69; Daniel Buck, "The Millennium and the Advent," *Methodist Quarterly Review* 57 (July 1875): 403.

19. S. M. Merrill, *The Second Coming of Christ Considered in Its Relation to the Millennium, the Resurrection, and the Judgment* (Cincinnati, Ohio: Hitchcock and Walden, 1979), 13, 282.

20. Israel Warren, *The Parousia: A Critical Study of the Scripture Doctrines of Christ's Second Coming; His Reign as King; The Resurrection of the Dead; and the General Judgment* (Portland, Me.: Hoyt, Fogg, and Donham, 1879), 55–72, 88, 116. A similar argument was made by George Bush, *A Treatise on the Millennium; In Which the Prevailing Theories on That Subject Are Carefully Examined; and the True Scripture Doctrine Attempted to Be Elicited and Established* (New York: J. J. Harper, 1832). The appeal of Bush's work, however, was limited by his Swedenborgianism.

21. W. N. Clarke, *Sixty Years,* 102–4.

22. See, for example, J. Estlin Carpenter, *The Bible in the Nineteenth Century* (London: Longmans and Green, 1903); T. K. Cheyne, *Founders of Old Testament Criticism* (New York: Charles Scribner's Sons, 1893), 130 and passim; Werner Georg Kummel, *Das Neue Testament: Geschichte der Erforschung Seiner Probleme* (Freiburg: K. Alber, 1958). For biographical information on Hengstenberg, Keil, Delitzsch, and Lange, see *The New Schaff-Herzog Encyclopedia of Religious Knowledge,* ed. Samuel M. Jackson (New York: Funk and Wagnalls, 1908–1912), 3:397, 5:224, 6:305, 6:411. J. W. Brown, *Rise of Biblical Criticism,* does a good job of surveying developments before 1870, but unfortunately no comparable volume traces biblical studies in the United States in the important years after that date. Several synopses, however, have appeared as articles or chapters in books: e. g., Ferenc Morton Szasz, *The Divided Mind of Protestant America, 1880–1930* (Tuscaloosa: University of Alabama Press, 1982), 15–41; Ira V. Brown, "The Higher Criticism Comes to America, 1880–1900," *Journal of Presbyterian History* 38 (1960): 192–212; Norman H. Maring, "Baptists and Changing Views of the Bible, 1865–1918," *Foundations* 1 (July 1958): 52–78 and (October 1958): 30–61; Lefferts A. Loetscher, *The Broadening Church: A Study of Theological Issues in the Presbyterian Church Since 1869* (Philadelphia: University of Pennsylvania Press, 1954), pp. 18–29, 48–62; Grant Wacker, "The Demise of Biblical Civilization," in *Bible in America,* ed. Hatch and Noll, 121–38; Grant Wacker, *Augustus H. Strong and the Dilemma of Historical Consciousness* (Macon, Ga.: Mercer University Press, 1985); Robert W. Funk, "The Watershed of the American Biblical Tradition: The Chicago School, First Phase, 1892–1920," *Journal of Biblical Literature* 95 (1976): 4–22. Also useful are the volumes on individual scholars in the Biblical Scholarship in North America series sponsored by the Society of Biblical Literature: Roy A. Harrisville, *Frank Chamberlain Porter: Pioneer in American Biblical Interpretation* (Missoula, Mont.: Scholars Press, 1976); Roy A. Harrisville, *Benjamin Bacon Wisner: Pioneer in American Biblical Criticism* (Missoula, Mont.: Scholars Press, 1976); James I. Cook, *Edgar Johnson Goodspeed: Articulate Scholar* (Chico, Calif.: Scholars Press, 1981); William J. Hynes, *Shirley Jackson Case and the Chicago School* (Chico, Calif.: Scholars Press, 1981); James P. Wind, *The Bible and the University: The Messianic Vision of William Rainey Harper* (Atlanta, Ga.: Scholars Press, 1987). See also Mark S. Massa, *Charles Augustus Briggs and the Crisis of Historical Criticism* (Minneapolis, Minn.: Fortress Press, 1990).

23. Henry Preserved Smith, "Thirty Years of Biblical Study," *Biblical World* 39 (April 1912): 237; J. W. Brown, *Rise of Biblical Criticism,* 45–124; James H. Moorhead, "Joseph Addison Alexander: Common Sense, Romanticism and Biblical Criticism at Princeton," *Journal of Presbyterian History* 53 (spring 1975): 51–65.

24. Szasz, *Divided Mind of Protestant America,* 15–41; I. V. Brown, "The Higher Criticism Comes to America"; Warner M. Bailey, "William Robertson Smith and American Biblical Studies," *Journal of Presbyterian History* 51 (fall 1973): 285–308; Funk, "Watershed of the American Biblical Tradition"; Wind, *The Bible and the University;* Thomas W. Goodspeed, *William Rainey Harper: First President of the University of Chicago* (Chicago: University of Chicago Press, 1928).

25. Jon H. Roberts, *Darwinism and the Divine in America: Protestant Intellectuals and Organic Evolution, 1859–1900* (Madison: University of Wisconsin Press, 1988), 145, 156; see also Roberts, *Darwinism and the Divine in America,* 146–73; Lyman Abbott, *The Theology of an Evolutionist* (Boston: Houghton Mifflin, 1897), 9–10. On the ways in which liberal Protestants modified Darwin's hypothesis, see James R. Moore, *The Post-Darwinian Controversies: A Study of the Protestant Struggle to Come to Terms with Darwin in Great Britain and America, 1870–1900* (Cambridge: Cambridge University Press, 1979), 217–51. J. R. Moore, *The Post-Darwinian Controversies,* 252–98, also demonstrates that more conservative Christians, *if* they accepted the evolutionary hypothesis, found it easier than the liberals to endorse Darwin's version of it.

26. Archibald A. Hodge and Benjamin B. Warfield, "Inspiration," *Presbyterian Re-*

view 2 (April 1881): 238; Benjamin B. Warfield, "The Real Problem of Inspiration," *Presbyterian and Reformed Review* 4 (April 1893): 186. For more information on Princeton theologians, see Mark A. Noll, ed., *The Princeton Theology, 1812–1921: Scripture, Science, and Theological Method from Archibald Alexander to Benjamin Warfield* (Grand Rapids, Mich.: Baker Book House, 1983). Sandeen, *Roots of Fundamentalism,* 103–31, and Jack B. Rogers and Donald McKim, *The Authority and Interpretation of the Bible: An Historical Approach* (San Francisco: Harper and Row, 1979), have argued that the Hodge-Warfield understanding of inspiration represented an historical innovation. By contrast, John D. Woodbridge, *Biblical Authority: A Critique of the Rogers/McKim Proposal* (Grand Rapids, Mich.: Zondervan, 1982) emphasizes that positions similar to the Princeton view of inspiration were common and antedated the Princeton theology's formulation. While Woodbridge may be correct that something akin to inerrancy was widely assumed prior to the late 1800s, Sandeen, Rogers, and McKim are right in arguing that the theory had not been given the unambiguous clarity or prominence which the Princetonians bestowed on it.

27. Norman Fox, "The Extent of Inspiration," *Baptist Quarterly Review,* 7 (October 1885): 469–83; "The Inspiration of the Apostles," Fox, "The Extent of Inspiration., 8 (January 1886): 57. The entire series runs from page 48 to page 92. For Bushnell's views of language, see Horace Bushnell, "Preliminary Dissertation on the Nature of Language, as Related to Thought and Spirit," in his *God in Christ* (Hartford: Brown and Parsons, 1849).

28. "The Inspiration of the Apostles," in Bushnell, *God in Christ,* 80–81.

29. George T. Ladd, *What Is the Bible? An Inquiry into the Origin and Nature of the Old and New Testaments in the Light of Modern Biblical Study,* 5th ed. (New York, 1894), esp. 432–33, 439, 458–59; George T. Ladd, *The Doctrine of Sacred Scripture: A Critical, Historical, and Dogmatic Inquiry into the Origin and Nature of the Old and New Testaments* (New York: Charles Scribner's Sons, 1883).

30. Frank Hugh Foster, "The Argument from Christian Experience for the Inspiration of the Bible," *Bibliotheca Sacra* 49 (January 1883): 97–138.

31. For examples of some of the diversities, see S. T. Bowman, "Inspiration and Infallibility," *Methodist Review* 71 (March 1889): 169–85; Howard Osgood, "Jesus Christ: The Final Test of Biblical Criticism," *Baptist Quarterly Review* 9 (July 1887): 351–69; Ezra Gould, "The Extent of Inspiration," *Bibliotheca Sacra* 35 (April 1878): 326–52.

32. F. H. Foster, "Argument from Christian Experience," 136; Charles A. Briggs, *The Authority of Holy Scripture: An Inaugural Address* (New York: Charles Scribner's Sons, 1891), 35. For general comments on these issues, see William R. Hutchison, *The Modernist Impulse in American Protestantism* (Cambridge: Harvard University Press, 1976), 41–132.

33. F. H. Foster, "Argument from Christian Experience," 105; William Adams Brown, *The Essence of Christianity: A Study in the History of Definition* (New York: Charles Scribner's Sons, 1902), 283.

34. William H. Ryder, "The Fulfillment of Prophecy," *Andover Review* 13 (January 1890): 20–25. On the growth of liberalism at Andover, see Daniel Day Williams, *The Andover Liberals: A Study in American Theology* (New York: Kings Crown Press, 1941).

35. Charles A. Briggs, *Messianic Prophecy: The Prediction of the Fulfillment of Redemption through the Messiah* (New York: Charles Scribner's Sons, 1886), 34, 43, 44, 45.

36. J. W. Bashford, "Prophecy," *Methodist Review* 84 (May 1902): 345–55.

37. Fullerton, *Prophecy and Authority,* 197–98.

38. Arthur S. Peake, *The Revelation of St. John* (London: Primitive Methodist Publishing House, 1919), 368; Frederick C. Grant, "The Permanent Value of the Primitive Christian Eschatology," *Biblical World* 49 (March 1917): 157; Arthur Metcalf, "The Parousia versus the Second Advent," *Bibliotheca Sacra* 64 (January 1907): 54, 55, 59; A. B. Stormes, "The Heart of the Apocalypse," *Methodist Review* 84 (January 1902): 99, 107; "The Passing of Apocalypticism," *Biblical World* 36 (September 1910): 147–51.

39. Albert Schweitzer, *The Quest for the Historical Jesus* (New York: Macmillan,

1968; original edition, 1906); George D. Castor, "The Kingdom of God in Light of Jewish Literature," *Bibliotheca Sacra* 66 (April 1909); 352; Benjamin W. Bacon, "Jewish Eschatology and the Teaching of Jesus," *Biblical World* 34 (July 1909): 15–35; Harris Franklin Rall, *Modern Premillennialism and the Christian Hope* (New York: Abingdon, 1920), 56–74. For an example of a largely precritical reading of Matthew 24, see, for example, Cyrus Brooks, "An Inquiry into the Meaning of Matthew XXIV, 1–36," *Methodist Quarterly Review* 52 (July 1870): 350–65.

40. William B. Brown, *The Problem of Final Destiny: Studied in the Light of Revised Theological Statement* (New York: Thomas Whittaker, 1900), 298, 299; Rall, *The Coming Kingdom,* 26. On the influence of Ritschl, see W. R. Hutchison, *Modernist Impulse,* 122–32; Claude Welch, *Protestant Thought in the Nineteenth Century: Volume 2, 1970–1914* (New Haven, Conn.: Yale University Press, 1985), 1–30.

41. Metcalf, "The Parousia versus the Second Advent," 65.

42. Warren, *The Parousia;* Daniel Curry, "The Future of Christ's Kingdom," *Methodist Review* 69 (January 1887): 11–26; William E. Barton, "The Descent of the New Jerusalem," *Bibliotheca Sacra* 52 (January 1895): 29–47; G. L. White, "The Parousia of Christ," *Homiletic Review* 49 (January 1905): 37–40; and William S. Urmy, *Christ Came Again: The Parousia of Christ a Past Event, the Kingdom of Christ a Present Fact, with a Consistent Eschatology* (New York: Eaton and Mains, 1900).

43. Shirley Jackson Case, *The Revelation of St. John* (Chicago: University of Chicago Press, 1919), 407; Case, *The Millennial Hope* (Chicago: University of Chicago Press, 1918), 215–25.

44. W. N. Clarke, *Outline of Christian Theology,* 18th ed. (New York, 1909), 444, 446.

2. Millennial Dreams and Other Last Things

1. Peter Grant, *Light on the Grave,* 3rd ed. (New York: Virtue and Yourston, 1869), 71–72.

2. Russell E. Miller, *The Larger Hope: The First Century of the Universalist Church in America, 1770–1870* (Boston: Unitarian Universalist Association, 1979), 159–201; Gary Land, *Adventism in America* (Grand Rapids, Mich.: Eerdmans, 1986), 235–36; Klaus J. Hansen, *Mormonism and the American Experience* (Chicago: University of Chicago Press, 1981), 98–99; M. James Penton, *Apocalypse Delayed: The Story of Jehovah's Witnesses* (Toronto: University of Toronto Press, 1985), 14–15; Stephen Gottschalk, *The Emergence of Christian Science in American Religious Life* (Berkeley: University of California Press, 1973), 64–68.

3. William G. T. Shedd, *The Doctrine of Endless Punishment,* 2nd ed. (New York: Charles Scribner's Sons, 1887), 159.

4. Westminster Confession of Faith, chapter 10, section 3; Charles Hodge, *Systematic Theology,* 1:26. Loetscher, *The Broadening Church,* 39–47, 83–89, provides the standard account of the revision movement.

5. Charles Grandison Finney, *Finney's Lectures on Systematic Theology* (Grand Rapids, Mich.: n.d., reprint of 1878 edition), 7–11; J. E. Stebbins, *Our Departed Friends, or Glory of the Immortal Life* (Hartford, Conn: L. Stebbins, 1867), 477; H. Shelton Smith, *Changing Conceptions of Original Sin: A Study in American Theology Since 1750* (New York: Charles Scribner's Sons, 1955), 75–78; May, *The Enlightenment in America;* James Turner, *Without God, without Creed,* 142–43. For a succinct account of changing attitudes toward children, see Bernard Wishy, *The Child and the Republic: The Dawn of Modern American Child Nurture* (Philadelphia: University of Pennsylvania Press, 1968).

6. James Morris Whiton, *Is "Eternal" Punishment Endless? Answered by a Restatement of the Original Scriptural Doctrine* (Boston: Lockwood, Brooks, 1876), viii–ix; Frank Hugh Foster, *The Modern Movement in American Theology: Sketches in the History of American*

Protestant Thought from the Civil War to the World War (New York: Fleming H. Revell, 1939), 17–20. Geoffrey Rowell, *Hell and the Victorians: A Study of the Nineteenth-Century Theological Controversies Concerning Eternal Punishment and the Future Life* (Oxford: Clarendon, 1974), provides a helpful analysis of similar controversies in the British context.

7. *Progressive Orthodoxy: A Contribution to the Christian Interpretation of Christian Doctrines* (Boston and New York: Houghton, Mifflin, 1886), 109; Newman Smyth, ed. and trans., *Dorner on the Future State* (New York: Charles Scribner's Sons, 1883).

8. Williams, *The Andover Liberals*, 66–67.

9. Lyman Abbott, *Signs of Promise: Sermons Preached in Plymouth Pulpit, Brooklyn, 1887–9* (New York: Fords, Howard and Hulbert, 1889), 301; S. D. McConnell, *The Evolution of Immortality* (New York: Macmillan, 1901), 85, 186. The quote from Bacon is in an essay contained in *That Unknown Country or What Living Men Believe concerning Punishment after Death* (Springfield, Mass.: C. A. Nichols, 1891), 130. This massive volume, containing essays by fifty-one religious leaders of diverse theological persuasions, is an excellent guide to changing attitudes toward hell in the late nineteenth century.

10. *That Unknown Country*, 394–95; George A. Gordon, *Immortality and the New Theodicy* (Boston: Houghton, Mifflin, 1897), 78.

11. G. A. Gordon, *Immortality*, 100–101, 102–103.

12. *That Unknown Country*, 395, 396.

13. Ibid., 394; W. B. Brown, *The Problem of Final Destiny*, 282, 304, 316, 317; Charles Lewis Slattery, *The Gift of Immortality: A Study in Responsibililty* (Boston: Houghton Mifflin, 1916), 188–89.

14. *That Unknown Country*, 381, 860.

15. Ibid., 665, 168; E. D. Morris, *Is There Salvation after Death? A Treatise on the Gospel in the Intermediate State* (New York: A. C. Armstrong and Son, 1887), 209–10.

16. *That Unknown Country*, 816, 818.

17. See, for example, the essays in *That Unknown Country*, esp. 185, 219–20, 230, 430, 878; Morris, *Is There Salvation after Death?*, 191–92, 237–38; Shedd, *Doctrine of Endless Punishment*, 147, 155; S. D. Gordon, *Quiet Talks about Life after Death* (New York: Fleming H. Revell, 1920), 117–18.

18. *That Unknown Country*, 381; H. O. Rowlands, "The Present Drift in Eschatology," *Baptist Quarterly Review* 11 (October 1889): 411; Farrell, *Inventing the American Way of Death*, 95. On Universalism's decline, see R. E. Miller, *The Larger Hope*, 19–29. On D. L. Moody, see Jonathan M. Butler, *Softly and Tenderly Jesus Is Calling: Heaven and Hell in American Revivalism, 1870–1920* (Brooklyn: Carlson, 1991), 41–60.

19. George W. Shinn, "What Has Become of Hell?" in *Theology at the Dawn of the Twentieth Century: Essays on the Present Status of Christianity and Its Doctrines* (Boston: Sherman, French, 1907), 159–60; S. M. Vernon, *Probation and Punishment: A Rational and Scriptural View of the Future State of the Wicked* (New York: Wilbur B. Ketcham, 1886), 290.

20. Richard Baxter, *The Saint's Everlasting Rest*, ed. John T. Willinson (London: Epworth, 1962; original edition, 1650); Westminster Confession of Faith, chapter 32, section 1; William G. T. Shedd, *Sermons to the Spiritual Man* (London: Banner of Truth Trust, 1972; original edition, 1884), 78, 176; Rowell, *Hell and the Victorians*, 15. See also Colleen McDannell and Bernhard Lang, *Heaven: A History* (New Haven, Conn.: Yale University Press, 1988), 181–257.

21. William Branks, *Heaven Our Home*, 3rd ed. (Boston: Roberts Brothers, 1864), 5, 6; Adeline J. Bayard, *Views of Heaven* (Philadelphia, Pa.: American Sunday School Union, 1877), 7, 44–45.

22. Elizabeth Stuart Phelps, *The Gates Ajar* (Boston: Fields, Osgood, 1867); Elizabeth Stuart Phelps, *Beyond the Gates* (Boston: Houghton, Mifflin, 1885), 47.

23. Daniel R. Goodwin, *Christian Eschatology, or, Doctrine of the Last Things* (Phila-

delphia, Pa.: McCalla and Stavely, 1885), 37; Elizabeth Stuart Phelps, *Chapters from a Life* (Boston: Houghton, Mifflin and Company, 1896), 111–14, 118.

24. Phelps, *Chapters,* 129; David Gregg, *The Heaven-Life, or Stimulus for Two Worlds* (New York: Fleming H. Revell, 1895), 56, 57, 62–63; Lucy Larcom, *As It Is in Heaven* (Boston: Houghton, Mifflin, 1891), 27–28; George A. Gordon, *The Witness to Immortality in Literature, Philosophy, and Life* (Boston: Houghton, Mifflin, 1893), 238.

25. Levi Gilbert, *The Hereafter and Heaven* (Cincinnati, Ohio: Jennings and Graham, 1907), 181.

26. William Clarke Ulyat, *The First Years of the Life of the Redeemed after Death* (New York: Abbey Press, 1901), 58, 141; Charles Cuthbert Hall, *The Redeemed Life after Death* (New York: Fleming H. Revell, 1905), 49; S. D. Gordon, *Quiet Talks,* 41–42.

27. William Adams Brown, *The Christian Hope: A Study in the Doctrine of Immortality* (New York: Charles Scribner's Sons, 1923), 18; John Haynes Holmes, *Is Death the End?* (New York: G. P. Putnam's Sons, 1915), 295–96.

28. Jonathan Edwards, *Images or Shadows of Divine Things* (New Haven, Conn.: Yale University Press, 1948), 43; Davis W. Clark, *Man All Immortal; or, The Nature and Destination of Man as Taught by Reason and Revelation* (Cincinnati, Ohio: Poe and Hitchcock, 1864), 140, 141. The lines on the gravestones at the Rockingham, Vermont, meetinghouse were transcribed by the author.

29. See, Rowell, *Hell and the Victorians,* 18–23.

30. Edward Young, *The Poetical Works of Edward Young* (Boston: James R. Osgood, 1871), 13; Lewis French Stearns, *Present Day Theology: A Popular Discussion of Leading Doctrines of the Christian Faith* (New York: Charles Scribner's Sons, 1893), 521–22. See Isabel St. John Bliss, *Edward Young* (New York: Twayne, 1969), 154.

31. T. A. Goodwin, *The Mode of Man's Immortality: or the When, Where, and How of the Future Life,* 3rd ed. (New York: Fords, Howard, and Hulbert, 1879), v–vi, 168, 201–2, 233; Ivan Illich, *Medical Nemesis: The Expropriation of Health* (New York: Pantheon, 1976), 206.

32. Warren, *The Parousia,* 264–65; Urmy, *Christ Came Again,* 293, 294, 295.

33. W. B. Brown, *The Problem of Final Destiny,* 263–64, 266.

34. Newman Smyth, *The Place of Death in Evolution* (New York: Charles Scribner's Sons, 1897), vii–viii.

35. Ibid., 53.

36. Ibid., 92–93, 128, 132–33; Newman Smyth, *Modern Belief in Immortality* (New York: Charles Scribner's Sons, 1910), 54, 55, 56.

37. Smyth, *Place of Death,* 154, 155, 205.

38. "The Resurrection and Modern Thought," *Homiletic Review* 89 (April 1925): 318–20.

39. Stebbins, *Our Departed Friends,* 222; Farrell, *Inventing the American Way of Death,* 74–145; David Charles Sloane, *The Last Great Necessity: Cemeteries in American History* (Baltimore, Md.: Johns Hopkins University Press, 1991), esp. 44–64, 128–56; Stanley French, "The Cemetery as Cultural Institution: The Establishment of Mount Auburn and the 'Rural Cemetery' Movement," *American Quarterly* 26 (March 1974): 37–59.

40. Charles T. Russell, *Pastor Russell's Sermons* (Brooklyn: International Bible Student's Association, 1917), 589. Pratt is quoted in Hansen, *Mormonism and the American Experience,* 100–101; and Rutherford in Penton, *Apocalypse Delayed,* 57. See also Gottschalk, *Emergence of Christian Science,* 94–95; R. Laurence Moore, *In Search of White Crows: Spiritualism, Parapsychology, and American Culture* (New York: Oxford University Press, 1977), 3–129.

41. Ernest B. Gordon, *Adoniram Judson Gordon* (New York: Fleming H. Revell, 1896), 52.

42. R. L. Moore, *White Crows,* 100–101, 133–68.

43. "For What is Your Life?" *American National Preacher* 24 (1850): 99.

44. George Albert Coe, *The Religion of a Mature Mind* (Chicago: Fleming H. Revell, 1902), 185–86, 378.

45. Ibid., 263–64.

46. Theodore T. Munger, *On the Threshold,* rev. and enlarged ed. (Boston: Houghton Mifflin, 1891), 235; Washington Gladden, *Ruling Ideas of the Present Age* (Boston: Houghton Mifflin, 1898), 25, 27; Coe, *Religion of a Mature Mind,* 107.

47. Bushnell, *Christian Nurture.* On Bushnell, see Daniel Walker Howe, "The Social Science of Horace Bushnell," *Journal of American History* 70 (September 1983): 305–22; Bruce Kuklick, *Churchmen and Philosophers: From Jonathan Edwards to John Dewey* (New Haven, Conn.: Yale University Press, 1985), 161–70.

48. Ibid., 173–74; Horace Bushnell, *Nature and the Supernatural, as Together Constituting the One System of God* (New York: Charles Scribner, 1858).

49. William Adams Brown, *Christian Theology in Outline* (New York: Charles Scribner's Sons, 1906), 408–9, 410. See, for example, G. Stanley Hall, *Adolescence: Its Psychology and Its Relations to Physiology, Anthropology, Sociology, Sex, Crime, Religion, and Education* (New York: D. Appleton, 1908); Edwin Diller Starbuck, *The Psychology of Religion: An Empirical Study of the Growth of Religious Consciousness,* 4th ed. (New York: Charles Scribner's Sons, 1914); James H. Leuba, *A Psychological Study of Religion, Its Origin, Its Function, and Future* (New York: Macmillan, 1912); George Albert Coe, *The Spiritual Life: Studies in the Science of Religion* (New York: Eaton and Mains, 1900).

50. Stephen A. Schmidt, *A History of the Religious Education Association* (Birmingham, Ala.: Religious Education Press, 1983), 22–55; C. Howard Hopkins, *History of the Y. M. C. A. in North America* (New York: Association Press, 1951), 245–70; John Gardner Greene, "The Emmanuel Movement, 1906–1929," *New England Quarterly* 7 (September 1934): 494–532; Raymond J. Cunningham, *American Quarterly* 14 (spring 1962): 48–63. McComb is quoted from Elwood Worcester and Samuel McComb, *The Christian Religion as a Healing Power: A Defense and Exposition of the Emmanuel Movement* (New York: Moffatt, Yard, 1909), 63.

51. E. Brooks Holifield, *A History of Pastoral Care in America: From Salvation to Self-Realization* (Nashville, Tenn.: Abingdon Press, 1983), 159; Worcester and McComb, *Christian Religion,* 113; Gladden, *Ruling Ideas,* 29; Munger, *On the Threshold,* 139–40.

3. "A Summary Court in Perpetual Session"

1. W. N. Clarke, *Outline of Christian Theology,* 467.

2. Franz Kafka, "Reflections on Sin, Pain, Hope, and the True Way," in *The Great Wall of China: Stories and Reflections,* trans. Willa Muir and Edwin Muir (New York: Schocken Books, 1970), 169. For calling my attention to the Kafka citation, I am indebted to O'Leary, *Arguing the Apocalypse,* 2.

3. Karen Halttunen, "Early American Murder Narratives: The Birth of Horror," in *The Power of Culture: Critical Essays in American History,* ed. Richard Wightman Fox and T. J. Jackson Lears (Chicago: University of Chicago Press, 1993), 99–100.

4. Owen Chadwick, *The Victorian Church,* 2 vols. (New York: Oxford University Press, 1966), 1:527.

5. Vincent P. DeSantis, *The Shaping of Modern America, 1877–1916* (New York: Forum Press, 1977), 1; Nell Irvin Painter, *Standing at Armageddon: The United States, 1877–1919* (New York: Norton, 1987), xvii, xix; William Dean Howells, "A Sennight of the Centennial," *Atlantic Monthly* 38 (July 1876), 92–107; the observer of the Corliss Engine is quoted in Howard Mumford Jones, *The Age of Energy: Varieties of American Experience, 1865–1915* (New York: Viking, 1973), 142. My use of the phrase "divided mind" is informed by Szasz, *Divided Mind of Protestant America,* and by Peter Conn, *The Divided*

Mind: Ideology and Imagination in America, 1898–1917 (Cambridge: Cambridge University Press, 1983). My notion of the sharp polarities within late-nineteenth-century religion is also indebted to Paul A. Carter, *The Spiritual Crisis of the Gilded Age* (DeKalb: Northern Illinois University Press, 1971).

6. William H. Leach, *Land of Desire: Merchants, Power, and the Rise of a New American Culture* (New York: Pantheon Books, 1993), xiii. See also Jackson Lears, *Fables of Abundance.*

7. Painter, *Standing at Armageddon,* 141–69.

8. George M. Beard, *American Nervousness: Its Causes and Consequences* (New York: G. P. Putnam's Sons, 1881). See also Tom Lutz, *American Nervousness, 1903: An Anecdotal History* (Ithaca, N.Y.: Cornell University Press, 1991); and Donald Meyer, *The Postive Thinkers: Religion as Pop Psychology from Mary Baker Eddy to Oral Roberts,* reissue with new preface and conclusion (New York: Pantheon, 1980), 22–31.

9. Beard, *American Nervousness,* 97, 96–192; Lutz, *American Nervousness,* 63–98.

10. Daniel T. Rodgers, *The Work Ethic in Industrial America* (Chicago: University of Chicago Press, 1978); T. J. Jackson Lears, *No Place of Grace: Antimodernism and the Transformation of American Culture, 1880–1920* (New York: Pantheon, 1981); Robert H. Wiebe, *The Search for Order, 1877–1920* (New York: Hill and Wang, 1967), 11–110, 142; Alan Trachtenberg, *The Incorporation of America: Culture and Society in the Gilded Age* (New York: Hill and Wang, 1982), 3–10; William H. Jordy, *Henry Adams: Scientific Historian* (New Haven, Conn.: Yale University Press, 1952), 158–229.

11. Painter, *Standing at Armageddon,* xx, 15, 18, 47–50, 110–14, 121–25; Lawrence Goodwyn, *Democratic Promise: The Populist Moment in America* (New York: Oxford University Press, 1976), 3–86.

12. Goodwyn, *Democratic Promise,* 244–72.

13. John Higham, *Strangers in the Land: Patterns of American Nativism, 1860–1925,* 2nd ed. (New York: Atheneum, 1971), esp. 35–105, 131–157, 300–330; David H. Bennett, *The Party of Fear: From Nativist Movements to the New Right in American History* (Chapel Hill: University of North Carolina Press, 1988), 159–237; Joel Williamson, *The Crucible of Race: Black/White Relations in the American South since Emancipation* (New York: Oxford University Press, 1984).

14. James Bryce, *The American Commonwealth,* 3rd ed., 2 vols. (New York: Macmillan, 1904), 1:637; Paul Boyer, *Urban Masses and Moral Order in America, 1820–1920* (Cambridge: Harvard University Press, 1978), 130.

15. Barbara Welter, "The Cult of True Womanhood, 1820–1860," *American Quarterly* 18 (June 1966): 151–74; Nancy F. Cott, *The Bonds of Womanhood: "Woman's Sphere" in New England, 1780–1835* (New Haven, Conn.: Yale University Press, 1977); Kathryn Kish Sklar, *Catherine Beecher: A Study in American Domesticity* (New Haven, Conn.: Yale University Press, 1977); Colleen McDannell, *The Christian Home in Victorian America, 1840–1900* (Bloomington: Indiana University Press, 1986); Christine Stansell, *City of Women: Sex and Class in New York, 1789–1860* (New York: Alfred A. Knopf, 1986); Laurie F. Mafly-Kipp, *Religion and Society in Frontier California* (New Haven, Conn.: Yale University Press, 1994); Lori D. Ginzberg, *Women and the Work of Benevolence: Morality, Politics, and Class in the Nineteenth-Century United States* (New Haven, Conn.: Yale University Press, 1990), 36–66. For a survey and analysis of literature on this subject, see David G. Hackett, "Gender and Religion in American Culture, 1870–1930," *Religion and American Culture: A Journal of Interpretation* 5 (summer 1995): 127–57; and Linda K. Kerber, "Separate Spheres, Female Worlds, Woman's Place: The Rhetoric of Women's History," *Journal of American History* 75 (June 1988): 3–39.

16. Peter G. Filene, *Him/Her/Self: Sex Roles in Modern America,* 2nd ed. (Baltimore, Md.: Johns Hopkins University Press, 1986), 6–68; E. Anthony Rotundo, *American Manhood: Transformations in Masculinity from the Revolution to the Modern Era* (New York:

Basic Books, 1993), 209–21; Karen J. Blair, *The Clubwoman as Feminist: True Womanhood Redefined, 1868–1914* (New York: Holmes and Meier, 1980); Ruth Bordin, *Frances Willard: A Biography* (Chapel Hill: University of North Carolina Press, 1986); Aileen S. Kraditor, *The Ideas of the Woman Suffrage Movement, 1890–1920* (New York: Columbia University Press, 1965).

17. Filene, *Him/Her/Self,* 73; Mark C. Carnes, *Secret Ritual and Manhood in Victorian America* (New Haven, Conn.: Yale University Press, 1989), 39–127; Lynn Dumenil, *Freemasonry and American Culture, 1880–1930* (Princeton: Princeton University Press, 1984); Stuart McConnell, *Glorious Contentment: The Grand Army of the Republic, 1865–1900* (Chapel Hill: University of North Carolina Press, 1992).

18. Theodore Roosevelt, *The Strenuous Life: Essays and Addresses* (New York: Century, 1900), 3–4, 20; Rotundo, *American Manhood,* 222–46; John Higham, "The Reorientation of American Culture in the 1890s," in *The Origins of Modern Consciousness: Essays,* ed. John Weiss (Detroit, Mich.: Wayne State University Press, 1865), 46–47. For a provocative analysis of the ways in which discourse about civilization, race, and gender overlapped, see Gail Bederman, *Manliness and Civilization: A Cultural History of Gender and Race in the United States, 1880–1917* (Chicago: University of Chicago Press, 1995).

19. Henry George, *Progress and Poverty: An Inquiry into the Cause of Industrial Depressions, And of the Increase of Want with Increase of Wealth* (New York: John W. Lovell, 1879), 389–90, 396.

20. Mark Twain, *A Connecticut Yankee in King Arthur's Court* (New York: Charles L. Webster, 1889); Ignatius Donnelly, *Caesar's Column: A Study of the Twentieth Century* (Chicago: F. J. Schulte, 1891); Edward Bellamy, *Looking Backward: 2000–1887,* ed. Daniel H. Borus (New York: Bedford Books, 1995 [1888]), 129, 190. For another contemporary example of a literary foray into implicitly eschatological turf, see William Dean Howells, *The Altrurian Romances,* introduction and notes by Clara Kirk and Rudolf Kirk (Bloomington: Indiana University Press, 1968). See also W. Warren Wagar, *Terminal Visions: The Literature of Last Things* (Bloomington: Indiana University Press, 1982); and Frederic Cople Jaher, *Doubters and Dissenters: Cataclysmic Thought in America, 1885–1918* (London: Free Press of Glencoe, 1964).

21. George B. Tindall, ed., *A Populist Reader: Selections from the Works of American Populist Leaders* (New York: Harper Torchbooks, 1966), 90; Bruce Palmer, *"Man Over Money": The Southern Populist Critique of American Capitalism* (Chapel Hill: University of North Carolina Press, 1980), 136; Stanley Coben, ed., *Reform, War, and Reaction, 1912–1932* (Columbia: University of South Carolina Press, 1972), 7.

22. M. James Penton, *Apocalypse Delayed,* 13–46; Sandeen, *Roots of Fundamentalism;* T. P. Weber, *Living in the Shadow;* George M. Marsden, *Fundamentalism and American Culture* (New York: Oxford University Press, 1980), 43–71.

23. *Prophetic Studies of the International Prophetic Conference* (Chicago and New York: Fleming H. Revell, 1886), 174.

24. *God Hath Spoken* (Philadelphia, Pa.: Bible Conference Committee, 1919), 358–59.

25. *Victory in Christ: A Report of Princeton Conference* (Philadelphia, Pa.: Board of Managers of Princeton Conference, 1916), 87. See also Marsden, *Fundamentalism and American Culture,* 72–80, 93–101.

26. *The Victorious Life: Messages from the Summer Conferences* (Philadelphia, Pa.: Board of Managers of Victorious Life Conference, 1918), 141, 153–54.

27. Ibid., 339; Douglas W. Frank, *Less Than Conquerors: How Evangelicals Entered the Twentieth Century* (Grand Rapids, Mich.: William B. Eerdmans, 1986), 68. The possible overlap of Christian Science and perfectionist constituencies was revealingly attested when Charles Trumbull asked the audience at a Victorious Life conference: "how many of you who are here in this meeting have friends or members of your family circle who

are either interested in, or actually believing or thinking they are believing in, Christian Science?" At this question, the editor of the conference proceedings interpolated, "Almost every hand in the chapel went up." See *Victorious Life*, 173.

28. Josiah Strong, *Our Country: Its Possible Future and Its Present Crisis,* ed. Jurgen Herbst (1891 edition; Cambridge: Belknap Press of Harvard University Press, 1963), ix–xxvi, 253. The rhetorical strategy Strong employed shows the persistence of the pattern outlined by Bercovitch, *American Jeremiad.*

29. Strong, *Our Country,* 133–256.

30. Josiah Strong, *The New Era; or, The Coming Kingdom* (New York: Baker and Taylor, 1893), 30, 39, 231, 237.

31. Richard Wightman Fox, "The Culture of Liberal Protestant Progressivism, 1875–1925," *The Journal of Interdisciplinary History* 23 (winter 1993): 640, 645.

32. Josiah Strong, *Religious Movements for Social Betterment* (New York: Baker and Taylor, 1900). For an account of the development of Strong's career and thought, see Wendy Jane Deichmann, "Josiah Strong: Practical Theologian and Social Crusader for a Global Kingdom" (Ph.D. diss., Drew University, 1991).

33. Josiah Strong, *The New World-Religion* (Garden City, N.Y.: Doubleday, Page, 1915), 379–80.

34. Ibid., 380, 381.

35. Josiah Strong, *The Times and Young Men* (New York: Baker and Taylor, 1901), 179, 217, 239.

36. Colin T. Campbell, *The Romantic Ethic and the Spirit of Modern Consumerism* (Oxford: Basil Blackwell, 1987), 99–137; Max Weber, *The Protestant Ethic and the Spirit of Capitalism,* trans. Talcott Parsons (New York: Charles Scribners' Sons, 1958 [originally published in 1904–05 and revised by author in 1920]).

37. Leach, *Land of Desire,* 7.

38. Strong, *Our Country,* 26, 164, 165. For a thoughtful account of the implications of consumerism on another religious tradition, see Andrew Heinze, *Adapting to Abundance: Jewish Immigrants, Mass Consumption, and the Search for American Identity* (New York: Columbia University Press, 1990).

39. Strong, *New World-Religion,* 356; Ryder, "Fulfillment of Prophecy," 20–25; C. C. Hall, *Redeemed Life after Death,* 49; W. N. Clarke, *Outline of Christian Theology,* 446; Strong, *Our Country,* 9.

40. Coe, *Religion of a Mature Mind,* 264.

41. M. Weber, *Protestant Ethic,* 182.

4. A Kingdom "as Wide as the Earth Itself"

1. Stearns, *Present Day Theology,* 110, 123, 124, 125,

2. Albert Christ-Janer, Charles W. Hughes, and Carleton Sprague Smith, *American Hymns: Old and New,* 2 vols. (New York: Columbia University Press, 1980), 1:673.

3. Sydney E. Ahlstrom, *A Religious History of the American People* (New Haven, Conn.: Yale University Press, 1972), 857–72; Alfred D. Chandler Jr., *The Visible Hand: The Managerial Revolution in American Business* (Cambridge: The Belknap Press of Harvard University Press, 1977); Clyde W. Barrow, *Universities and the Capitalist State: Corporate Liberalism and the Reconstruction of American Higher Education, 1894–1928* (Madison: University of Wisconsin Press, 1990); Burton J. Bledstein, *The Culture of Professionalism: The Middle Class and the Development of Higher Education in America* (New York: W. W. Norton, 1976); Laurence R. Veysey, *The Emergence of the American University* (Chicago: University of Chicago Press, 1965).

4. Historians of individual denominations have examined the growth of organization and bureaucracy—e. g., Louis B. Weeks, "The Incorporation of American Religion: The Case of the Presbyterians," *Religion and American Culture* 1 (winter 1991): 100–118;

and Paul M. Harrison, *Authority and Power in the Free Church Tradition: A Social Case Study of the American Baptist Convention* (Princeton, N.J.: Princeton University Press, 1959). Ben Primer, *Protestants and American Business Methods* (Ann Arbor, Mich.: UMI Research Press, 1979); Valentin H. Rabe, *The Home Base of American China Missions, 1880–1920* (Cambridge: Harvard University Press, 1978); and Donald K. Gorrell, *The Age of Social Responsibility: The Social Gospel in the Progressive Era, 1900–1920* (Macon, Ga.: Mercer University Press, 1988), provide useful interdenominational surveys of the growth of religious organization, but more work on this important subject is needed.

    5. Christ-Janer et al., *American Hymns*, 1:538; William R. Hutchison, *Errand to the World: American Protestant Thought and Foreign Missions* (Chicago: University of Chicago Press, 1987), 118–21; Oliver W. Elsbree, *The Rise of the Missionary Spirit in America, 1790–1815* (Philadelphia, Pa.: Porcupine Press, 1980 [1928]); Patricia R. Hill, *The World Their Household: The American Woman's Foreign Mission Movement and Cultural Transformation, 1870–1920* (Ann Arbor: University of Michigan Press, 1984); C. Howard Hopkins, *John R. Mott, 1865–1955: A Biography* (Grand Rapids, Mich.: Eerdmans, 1979).

    6. Alexander Martin, "The Mission of the Republic," *Methodist Review* 71 (September 1889), 687.

    7. *The One Hundredth Anniversary of the Haystack Prayer Meeting* (Boston: American Board of Commissioners for Foreign Missions, 1907), 73, 80, 81, 100.

    8. Robert E. Speer, ed., *A Memorial of Horace Tracy Pitkin* (New York: Fleming H. Revell, 1903), 82.

    9. William T. Ellis, *Men and Missions* (Philadelphia, Pa: The Sunday School Times, 1909), 11, 39, 40, 46, 220.

    10. Ellis, *Men and Missions*, 44; Jane Hunter, *The Gospel of Gentility: American Women Missionaries in Turn-of-the-Century China* (New Haven, Conn.: Yale University Press, 1984), xiii. The female missionary is quoted in Hunter, *The Gospel of Gentility*, 51.

    11. William Newton Clarke, *A Study of Christian Missions* (New York: Charles Scribner's Sons, 1900), 52; *Ecumenical Missionary Conference: Report of the Ecumenical Conference on Foreign Missions, Held in Carnegie Hall and Neighboring Churches, April 21 to May 1* (New York: American Tract Society, 1900), 1:95. On the Watchword, its origins, and diverse interpretations, see Dana L. Robert, "'The Crisis of Missions': Premillennial Mission Theory and the Origins of Independent Evangelical Missions," in *Earthen Vessels: American Evangelicals and Foreign Missions, 1880–1980*, ed. Joel A. Carpenter and Wilbert R. Shenk (Grand Rapids, Mich.: Eerdmans, 1990), 29–46; W. R. Hutchison, *Errand to the World*, 99, 118–21.

    12. *Ecumenical Missionary Conference*, 1:95–103.

    13. Sidney L. Gulick, *The Growth of the Kingdom of God* (New York: Fleming H. Revell, 1898), 308, 318; James S. Dennis, *Christian Missions and Social Progress: A Sociological Study of Foreign Missions*, 3 vols. (New York: Fleming H. Revell, 1897–1906), 2:v, vi.

    14. W. R. Hutchison, *Errand to the World*, 62–90; Wayland is quoted on p. 84.

    15. W. R. Hutchison, *Errand to the World*, 91–124; Stearns, *Present Day Theology*, 124.

    16. Rabe, *Home Base of American China Missions*, 9–48, 141–191; W. R. Hutchison, *Errand to the World*, 99–102; Robert E. Speer, "A Few Comparisons of Then and Now," *Missionary Review of the World* (January 1928), 5; Primer, *Protestants and American Business Methods*, 127–48; Arthur Judson Brown, *One Hundred Years: A History of the Foreign Missionary Work of the Presbyterian Church in the U.S.A.* (New York: Fleming H. Revell, 1936), 59–60; Hill, *The World Their Household*, 93–122.

    17. Joan Jacobs Brumberg, *Mission for Life: The Story of the Family of Adoniram Judson* (New York: Free Press, 1980). On Mott, consult Hopkins, *Mott*. The description of Speer is from Richard W. Reifsnyder, "The Reorganizational Impulse in American Protes-

tantism: The Presbyterian Church (U.S.A.) as a Case Study, 1788–1983" (Ph.D. diss., Princeton Theological Seminary, 1984), 333.

18. Arthur Judson Brown, *The Why and How of Foreign Missions,* 3rd ed. (New York: Board of Foreign Missions of the Presbyterian Church in the U.S.A., 1908), 35, 39; W. N. Clarke, *Study of Christian Missions,* 134–35, 172, 226; Samuel B. Capen, *The Next Ten Years* (Boston: American Board of Commissioners for Foreign Missions, 1910), 10, 21–22, 30.

19. Standard works on the Social Gospel include Aaron Ignatius Abell, *The Urban Impact on American Protestantism, 1865–1900* (Cambridge: Harvard University Press, 1943); Robert D. Cross, ed., *The Church and the City, 1865–1910* (Indianapolis, Ind.: Bobbs-Merrill, 1967); James Dombrowski, *The Early Days of Christian Socialism in America* (New York: Columbia University Press, 1936); Robert D. Handy, ed., *The Social Gospel in America* (New York: Oxford University Press, 1966); C. Howard Hopkins, *The Rise of the Social Gospel in American Protestantism, 1865–1915* (New Haven, Conn.: Yale University Press, 1940); Henry F. May, *Protestant Churches and Industrial America* (New York: Harper and Row, 1949). These accounts have stressed the Social Gospel's role in providing a critique of unrestrained capitalism and its efforts to address the problems of urban America. Several recent works have illuminated other dimensions of the movement. Ronald C. White and C. Howard Hopkins, eds., *The Social Gospel: Religion and Reform in Changing America* (Philadelphia, Pa.: Temple University Press, 1976); Ronald C. White, *Liberty and Justice for All: Racial Reform and the Social Gospel, 1877–1925* (San Francisco: Harper and Row, 1990), and Ralph Luker, *The Social Gospel in Black and White: American Racial Reform, 1885–1912* (Chapel Hill: University of North Carolina Press, 1991) have explored the relationship of the movement to the problem of racial equality. Janet Forsythe Fishburn, *The Fatherhood of God and the Victorian Family: The Social Gospel in America* (Philadelphia. Pa.: Fortress Press, 1981) probes gender roles in the Social Gospel. Susan Curtis, *A Consuming Faith: The Social Gospel and Modern American Culture* (Baltimore, Md.: Johns Hopkins University Press, 1991), treats the movement as a promoter of the ethos of corporate consumerism. Donald K. Gorrell, *Age of Social Responsibility,* examines the institutionalization of the Social Gospel. Winthrop S. Hudson, ed., *Walter Rauschenbusch: Selected Writings* (New York: Paulist Press, 1984), emphasizes the wellsprings of piety that nourished the Social Gospel. A new synthesis, more comprehensive than can be offered in this brief section on the movement, is clearly needed.

20. Washington Gladden, *The Church and the Kingdom* (New York: Fleming H. Revell, 1894), 8, 13.

21. Edward S. Ninde, *The Story of the American Hymn* (New York: Abingdon, 1921), 382–85.

22. Walter Rauschenbusch, *Christianity and the Social Crisis* (New York: Harper Torchbooks, 1964 [1907]), ed. Robert D. Cross, 65. Sometimes the rejection of the old faith appeared to be born of trauma—e.g., Washington Gladden, *Recollections* (Boston: Houghton Mifflin, 1909), 59; on other occasions, as in Walter Rauschenbusch, *Christianizing the Social Order* (New York: Macmillan, 1912), 75, rejection was tempered by appreciation and nostalgia. The classic argument of the connection between the Social Gospel and antebellum evangelicalism is Timothy L. Smith, *Revivalism and Social Reform: American Protestantism on the Eve of the Civil War* (Nashville, Tenn.: Abingdon, 1957). For an analysis of pre–Civil War evangelicalism's ambiguous stand vis-à-vis social reform, see James H. Moorhead, "Social Reform and the Divided Conscience of Antebellum Protestantism." *Church History* 48 (December 1979): 416–30.

23. Richard T. Ely, *Social Aspects of Christianity and Other Essays* (New York: Thomas Y. Crowell, 1889), 53; Dores Robinson Sharpe, *Walter Rauschenbusch* (New York: Macmillan, 1942), 121.

24. Kloppenberg, *Uncertain Victory,* 65; Walter Rauschenbusch, *A Theology for the*

Social Gospel (Nashville, Tenn.: Abingdon, 1978 [1917]), 227; W. N. Clarke, *Outline of Christian Theology,* 446. Kloppenberg uses Ely and Rauschenbusch as two examples of Euro-American social democracy. For a brief series of biographical vignettes indicating the diversities within the Social Gospel, see Peter J. Frederick, *Knights of the Golden Rule: The Intellectual as Christian Social Reformer in the 1890s* (Lexington: University Press of Kentucky, 1976); see also note 19 supra.

25. Jacob H. Dorn, *Washington Gladden: Prophet of the Social Gospel* (Columbus: Ohio State University Press, 1968); Paul M. Minus, *Walter Rauschenbusch: American Reformer* (New York: Macmillan, 1988); Sharpe, *Rauschenbusch;* Louise C. Wade, *Graham Taylor: Pioneer for Social Justice, 1851–1938* (Chicago: University of Chicago Press, 1964).

26. Graham Taylor, *Religion in Social Action* (New York: Dodd, Mead, 1913), 6; Washington Gladden, *The Christian Pastor and the Working Church* (New York: Charles Scribner's Sons, 1898), 112–13.

27. Hall is quoted in Samuel Haber, *Authority and Honor in the American Professions, 1750–1900* (Chicago: University of Chicago Press, 1991), 285. William Rainey Harper, *Religion and the Higher Life: Talks to Students* (Chicago: University of Chicago Press, 1904), 44–45, 178–84. See also James P. Wind, *The Bible and the University,* 105–46; David A. Hollinger, "Justification by Verification: The Scientific Challenge to the Moral Authority of Christianity in Modern America," *Religion and Twentieth-Century Intellectual Life,* ed. Michael J. Lacey (Cambridge: Woodrow Wilson International Center for Scholars and Cambridge University Press, 1989), 116–35.

28. Benjamin G. Rader, *The Academic Mind and Reform: The Influence of Richard T. Ely in American Life* (Lexington: University of Kentucky Press), 12–82. Works stressing the religious origins—especially the millennial ones—of American social science include Jean B. Quandt, "Religion and Social Thought: The Secularization of Postmillennialism," *American Quarterly* 25 (October 1973), 390–409; and Dorothy Ross, *The Origins of American Social Science* (Cambridge: Cambridge University Press, 1991). See also Arthur J. Vidich and Stanford M. Lyman, *American Sociology: Worldly Rejections of Religion and Their Directions* (New Haven, Conn.: Yale University Press, 1985); and Bradley J. Longfield, "From Evangelicalism to Liberalism: Public Midwestern Universities in Nineteenth-Century America," *The Secularization of the Academy,* ed. George M. Marsden and Bradley J. Longfield (New York: Oxford University Press, 1992), 46–73.

29. Ely, *Social Aspects of Christianity,* 16, 17, 88.

30. Wade, *Graham Taylor,* 1–41; Abell, *Urban Impact,* 137–65; *The Open or Institutional Church League: Preliminary Conference* (Boston: Everett Press, 1894), 1–42; Elias B. Sanford, *Origin and History of the Federal Council of the Churches of Christ in America* (Hartford, Conn.: S. S. Scranton, 1916), 34–57, 146–59, 196–203. Thompson is quoted in Abell, *Urban Impact,* 156; Sanford, in Sanford, *History of the Federal Council,* 65.

31. Allen F. Davis, *Spearheads for Reform: The Social Settlements and the Progressive Movement, 1890–1914* (New York: Oxford University Press, 1967), 3–39; Mina Carson, *Settlement Folk: Social Thought and the American Settlement Movement, 1885–1930* (Chicago: University of Chicago Press, 1990), 10–50; Graham Taylor, *Pioneering on Social Frontiers* (Chicago: University of Chicago Press, 1930), 8–9.

32. Worth Marion Tippy, *The Church A Community Force: A Story of the Development of the Community Relations of Epworth Memorial Church, Cleveland, Ohio* (New York: Missionary Education Movement, 1914), 15–17, 30–31.

33. Samuel Zane Batten, *The Christian State: The State, Democracy and Christianity* (Philadelphia, Pa.: Griffith and Rowland, 1909), 11, 33, 288, 351–52, 362, 363. See, for example, Herbert Croly, *The Promise of American Life,* new foreword by Michael McGerr (Boston: Northeastern University Press, 1989 [1909]); and Walter Lippmann, *Drift and Mastery: An Attempt to Diagnose the Current Unrest,* rev. introduction by William E. Leuchtenburg (Madison: University of Wisconsin Press, 1985 [1914]).

34. Robert M. Crunden, *Ministers of Reform: The Progressives' Achievement in American Civilization, 1889–1920* (New York: Basic Books, 1982), 15; Carson, *Settlement Folk*, 122–60; A. F. Davis, *Spearheads for Reform*, 194–217.

35. A succinct analysis of these developments is contained in Gorrell, *Age of Social Responsibility*, 131–53.

36. Warren H. Wilson, *The Church of the Open Country* (New York: Missionary Education Movement, 1911); Warren H. Wilson, *The Church at the Center* (New York: Missionary Education Movement, 1914); Merwin Swanson, "The Country Life Movement and the Churches," *Church History* 46 (September 1977): 358–73; James H. Madison, "Reformers and the Rural Church, 1900–1950," *Journal of American History* 73 (September 1986): 645–68.

37. Warren H. Wilson, *The Second Missionary Adventure* (New York: Fleming H. Revell, 1915), 5, 8, 9.

38. Ibid., 12, 14, 21, 27–28, 29.

39. G. Taylor, *Religion in Social Action*, 201, 206, 221, 240–41.

40. Ibid., 205.

41. On the antebellum voluntary societies, see C. I. Foster, *Errand of Mercy;* Clifford S. Griffin, *Their Brothers' Keepers: Moral Stewardship in the United States, 1800–1865* (New Brunswick, N.J.: Rutgers University Press, 1960); Elsbree, *Rise of the Missionary Spirit in America;* Colin Brummitt Goodykoontz, *Home Missions on the American Frontier, with Particular Reference to the American Home Missionary Society* (Caldwell, Id.: Caxton, 1939); Lemuel Moss, *Annals of the United States Christian Commission* (Philadelphia, Pa.: J. B. Lippincott, 1868); C. Howard Hopkins, *History of the Y. M. C. A. in North America* (New York: Association Press, 1951); Ruth Bordin, *Women and Temperance: The Quest for Power and Liberty, 1873–1900* (Philadelphia: Temple University Press, 1981); and Michael Parker, *The Kingdom of Character: The Student Volunteer Movement for Foreign Missions, 1886–1926* (Lanham, Md.: University Press of American, 1998).

42. Philip D. Jordan, *The Evangelical Alliance for the United States of America, 1847–1900: Ecumenism, Identity and the Religion of the Republic* (New York: Edwin Mellen Press, 1982), esp. 143–90.

43. Ibid., 182. John A. Hutchison, *We Are Not Divided: A Critical and Historical Study of the Federal Council of the Churches of Christ in America* (New York: Round Table Press, 1941), 16–53; Samuel McCrea Cavert, *The American Churches in the Ecumenical Movement, 1900–1968* (New York: Association Press, 1968), 15–51; Sanford, *History of the Federal Council*, 87–243.

44. G. Taylor, *Religion in Social Action*, 205–06; Elias B. Sanford, *Federal Council of the Churches of Christ in America: Report of the First Meeting of the Federal Council, Philadelphia, 1908* (New York: Fleming H. Revell, 1909), 331; G. Taylor, *History of the Federal Council*, 92, 155; Graham Taylor, *Church Federation: Inter-Church Conference on Federation, New York, November 15–21, 1905* (New York: Fleming H. Revell, 1906), 434; Newman Smyth, *Passing Protestantism and Coming Catholicism* (New York: Charles Scribner's Sons, 1908), 27–28.

45. Charles S. Macfarland, *Christian Unity at Work: The Federal Council of the Churches of Christ in America in Quadrennial Session at Chicago, Illinois, 1912* (New York: Federal Council of Churches, 1912), 32.

46. Cavert, *American Churches in the Ecumenical Movement*, 54–58; J. A. Hutchison, *We Are Not Divided*, 34–53; Gorrell, *Age of Social Responsibility*, 131–53; Jean Miller Schmidt, *Souls or the Social Order: The Two-Party System in American Protestantism* (Brooklyn, N.Y.: Carlson Publishing, 1991); Bruce David Forbes, "William Henry Roberts: Resistance to Change and Bureaucratic Adaptation," *Journal of Presbyterian History* 54 (winter 1976), 405–21.

47. Sanford, *Federal Council, 1908*, 21, 229, 323; Macfarland, *Christian Unity at Work*, 27.

48. Sanford, *History of the Federal Council,* 132.

49. Charles S. Macfarland, *Christian Unity in the Making: The First Twenty-Five Years of the Federal Council of the Churches of Christ, 1905–1930* (New York: Federal Council of the Churches of Christ, 1948), 54, 55, 57, 63–64, 66–67, 78, 79, 84–85.

50. Charles S. Macfarland, *Spiritual Culture and Social Service* (New York: Fleming H. Revell, 1912), 17. The description of the pastor as "director general" is from John R. Mott, *The Pastor and Modern Missions: A Plea for Leadership in World Evangelization* (New York: Student Volunteer Movement for Foreign Missions, 1904), 52.

5. The Kingdom of God and the Efficiency Engineer

1. Elias B. Sanford, ed., *Federal Council of the Churches of Christ in America: Report of the First Meeting of the Federal Council, Philadelphia, 1908* (New York: Fleming H. Revell, 1909), 508–09.

2. Samuel Haber, *Efficiency and Uplift: Scientific Management in the Progressive Era* (Chicago: University of Chicago Press, 1964), ix.

3. Quotation from Robert H. Wiebe, *Search for Order, 1877–1920,* 59; see also Haber, *Efficiency and Uplift,* ix–x, 18–74. On progressivism, consult also David W. Noble, *The Progressive Mind, 1890–1917,* rev. ed. (Minneapolis, Minn.: Burgess, 1981); Wiebe, *Search for Order,* 164–223; Robert M. Crunden, *Ministers of Reform.* See also John M. Jordan, *Machine-Age Ideology: Social Engineering and American Liberalism, 1911–1939* (Chapel Hill: University of North Carolina Press, 1994), 21, 63.

4. R. O. Everhart, "Engineering and the Millennium," *Methodist Review* 96 (1914): 44.

5. For primary sources, see the seven volumes of *Messages of the Men and Religion Movement* (New York: Association Press, 1912); Clarence Barbour, ed., *Making Religion Efficient* (New York: Association Press, 1912); and *Extracts of Letters from Mr. Fred B. Smith Relating to the World Tour of the "Men and Religion Forward Movement" Team* (privately printed, 1913). See also Gail Bederman, "'The Women Have Had Charge of the Church Work Long Enough': The Men and Religion Forward Movement of 1911–1912 and the Masculinization of Middle-Class Protestantism," *American Quarterly* 41 (September 1989), 432–65; and Gary Scott Smith, "The Men and Religion Forward Movement of 1911–12: New Perspectives on Evangelical Social Concern and the Relationship Between Christianity and Progressivism," *Westminster Theological Journal* 49 (1987), 91–118. The quotation is from *The Church and the Press,* vol. 7 of *Messages,* 10.

6. *Congress Addresses,* vol. 1 of *Messages,* 3; Barbour, *Making Religion Efficient;* Bederman, "Men and Religion Forward Movement," 441, 444; G. S. Smith, "Men and Religion Forward Movement," 97; Fred B. Smith, *I Remember* (New York: Fleming H. Revell, 1936), 90–113.

7. *The Church and the Press,* 103–104.

8. *Social Service,* vol. 2 of *Messages,* 82, 101; *Christian Unity; Missions,* vol. 4 of *Messages,* 26; *Bible Study; Evangelism,* vol. 3 of *Messages,* 273.

9. *The Church and the Press,* 14–15, 28, 63, 101, 156.

10. Ibid., 80–83.

11. Ibid., 30, 99.

12. Ibid., 11; Bederman, "The Men and Religion Forward Movement," 453–54; G. S. Smith, "The Men and Religion Forward Movement," 109. The point that women have disproportionately predominated in church membership is made forcefully by Ann Braude, "Women's History *Is* American Religious History," in *Retelling U.S. Religious History,* ed. Thomas A. Tweed (Berkeley: University of California Press, 1997), 87–107.

13. Charles Grandison Finney, *Lectures on Revivals of Religion* (Cambridge: Belknap Press of Harvard University Press, 1960; original edition, 1835), ed. William G. McLoughlin, 33; James H. Moorhead, "Charles Finney and the Modernization of America," *Journal of Presbyterian History* 62 (summer 1984), 95–110.

14. Charles F. Thwing, *The Working Church* (New York: Baker and Taylor, 1888), 13; Washington Gladden, *The Christian Pastor,* 9–10; William Herbert Perry Faunce, *The Educational Ideal in the Ministry* (New York: Macmillan, 1908), v, 29; George Whitefield Mead, *Modern Methods in Church Work* (New York: Dodd, Mead, 1906), 355.

15. Frank Barkeley Copley, *Frederick W. Taylor: Father of Scientific Management,* 2 vols. (New York: Harper and Brothers, 1923), 1:40–91; Haber, *Efficiency and Uplift,* 5. Taylor's description of his father is found in Copley, 1:47.

16. Haber, *Efficiency and Uplift,* 9–30; Daniel T. Rodgers, *The Work Ethic in Industrial America* (Chicago: University of Chicago Press, 1978), 53–57; [Taylor Society, ed.] *Frederick Winslow Taylor: A Memorial Volume* (New York: Taylor Society, 1920), 4.

17. Haber, *Efficiency and Uplift,* 51–98.

18. Unnumbered page at the end of [Taylor Society], *Frederick Winslow Taylor.*

19. Shailer Mathews, *The Faith of Modernism* (New York: Macmillan, 1925), 178–79. On Mathews's life, consult Shailer Mathews, *New Faith for Old: An Autobiography* (New York: Macmillan, 1936); and Susan Curtis, *A Consuming Faith: The Social Gospel and Modern American Culture* (Baltimore, Md.: Johns Hopkins University Press, 1991), 48–59.

20. Shailer Mathews, *The Church and the Changing Order* (New York: Macmillan, 1907), 4, 5, 138, 148, 203–04, 209.

21. Ibid., 105.

22. Shailer Mathews, *Scientific Management in the Churches* (Chicago: University of Chicago Press, 1912), v, 16, 37, 44–45, 55–56, 57, 58, 60–61; Shailer Mathews, "Theological Seminaries as Schools of Religious Efficiency," *Biblical World* 47 (1916): 84.

23. S. Mathews, *Scientific Management,* 10, 13, 64.

24. Paul Moore Strayer, *The Reconstruction of the Church, With Regard to Its Message and Program* (New York: Macmillan, 1915), 2.

25. Ibid., 166, 170, 172.

26. Ibid., 150, 158, 163–64, 186, 252, 261.

27. Ibid., 229.

28. Edwin L. Earp, *The Social Engineer* (New York: Eaton and Mains, 1911), ix, xviii, xxii, 13.

29. Charles E. Carroll, *The Community Survey in Relation to Church Efficiency: A Guide for Workers in the City, Town, and Country Church* (New York: Abingdon, 1915), 3, 17, 18, 34–36.

30. Curtis, *Consuming Faith,* 234–35; Rolf Lundén, *Business and Religion in the American 1920s* (Westport, Conn.: Greenwood Press, 1988), 80–82. Christian F. Reisner's books include *Preacher-Persuader* (New York: Eaton and Mains, 1910); *Church Publicity: The Modern Way to Compel Them to Come In* (Cincinnati, Ohio: Methodist Book Concern, 1913); and *Disciple Winners* (Cincinnati, Ohio: Abingdon, 1930).

31. Reisner, *Preacher-Persuader,* 66; Reisner, *Church Publicity,* 59.

32. Reisner, *Church Publicity,* 161, 174, 176, 189, 190, 196, 258, 375.

33. Ibid., 367–68.

34. Ibid., 370; Reisner, *Disciple Winners,* 179.

35. Simon N. Patten, *The New Basis of Civilization* (New York: Macmillan, 1907), 127, 136–38, 164, 182.

36. John F. Kasson, *Amusing the Million* (New York: Hill and Wang, 1978), 105–6.

37. See, for example, Reisner, *Church Publicity,* 236–72.

38. McGarrah's books were published by Fleming H. Revell, New York.

39. Albert F. McGarrah, *Modern Church Management,* 7, 14; *Modern Church Finance,* 26–27.

40. McGarrah, *Modern Church Finance,* 35–45, 48, 49.

41. Ibid., 85–207.

42. McGarrah, *Modern Church Management,* 67, 69, 120–35, 154–63.

43. Ibid., 73–74, 195–204; McGarrah, *Modern Church Finance,* 210.

44. Harrison, *Authority and Power*, esp. 38–52; Winfred Ernest Garrison and Alfred T. DeGroot, *The Disciples of Christ: A History*, rev. ed. (St. Louis, Mo.: Bethany Press, 1958), 428–29; James H. Moorhead, "Presbyterians and the Mystique of Organizational Efficiency, 1870–1936," in *Reimagining Denominationalism*, ed. Robert Bruce Mullin and Russell E. Richey (New York: Oxford University Press, 1994), 264–87; William McGuire King, "Denominational Modernization and Religious Identity: The Case of the Methodist Episcopal Church" in *Perspectives on American Methodism: Interpretive Essays*, ed. Russell E. Richey, Kenneth E. Rowe, and Jean Miller Schmidt (Nashville, Tenn.: Abingdon, 1993), 343–55.

45. "Report on a Survey of Fifty-Eight Organizations of the Northern Baptist Convention" (privately printed, 1925), iii, quoted in Harrison, *Authority and Power*, 5; "Seventy-Second Annual Report of the Presbyterian Board of Ministerial Relief and Sustentation," in *Minutes of the General Assembly of the Presbyterian Church in the U.S.A.; Part II: The Reports of the Boards* (Philadelphia, Pa.: Office of the General Assembly, 1927), vii. For further information on the creation of the Presbyterian pension plan as an instance of organizational rationalization, see R. Douglas Brackenridge and Lois A. Boyd, *Presbyterians and Pensions: The Roots and Growth of Pensions in the Presbyterian Church (U.S.A.)* (Atlanta, Ga.: John Knox, 1988).

46. McGarrah, *Modern Church Finance*, 86.

6. Efficiency and the Kingdom in a World at War

1. Arthur S. Link, ed., *The Papers of Woodrow Wilson*, 69 vols. (Princeton, N.J.: Princeton University Press, 1966–1994), 41:522, 525. On the formation of Wilson's international vision, see Thomas J. Knock, *To End All Wars: Woodrow Wilson and the Quest for a New World Order* (New York: Oxford University Press, 1992).

2. George Creel, *How We Advertised America* (New York, 1920) quoted in Coben, 91, 93; Alan Dawley, *Struggle for Justice: Social Responsibility and the Liberal State* (Cambridge: Belknap Press of Harvard University Press, 1991), 172–217; the quotation from Dawley is on p. 189. See also Michael O'Malley, *Keeping Watch: A History of American Time* (New York: Viking Penguin, 1990), 273–77.

3. Robert A. Woods, "The Regimentation of the Free," *Survey* 40 (July 6, 1918), 395–99, quoted in Carson, *Settlement Folk*, 158; Haber, *Efficiency and Uplift*, 117–34; James Weinstein, *The Corporate Ideal in the Liberal State: 1900–1918* (Boston: Beacon Press, 1968), 214–54.

4. William Adams Brown, *The Church in America: A Study of the Present Condition and Future Prospects of American Protestantism* (New York: Macmillan, 1922), 101.

5. "The Clear and Urgent Duty of the Church in the Present World Crisis," *Homiletic Review* 73 (January 1917) 20–25.

6. Abraham Mitrie Rihbany, *Militant America and Jesus Christ* (Boston: Houghton Mifflin, 1917), 9; Charles E. Locke, "The New Day," *Methodist Review* 101 (July 1918): 580–88; Newell Dwight Hillis, *German Atrocities, Their Nature and Philosophy: Studies in Belgium and France during July and August of 1917* (New York: Fleming H. Revell, 1918). Sunday is quoted in Roger A. Bruns, *Preacher: Billy Sunday and Big-Time American Evangelism* (New York: Norton, 1992), 255. Ray H. Abrams, *Preachers Present Arms: The Role of the American Churches and Clergy in World War I and II, with Some Observations on the War in Vietnam*, rev. ed. (Scottsdale, Pa: Herald Press, 1969), is the standard account of clerical warmongering in World War I. For an analysis of a more restrained Christian response to the conflict, see John F. Piper Jr., *The American Churches in World War I* (Athens: Ohio University Press, 1985).

7. Harry Emerson Fosdick, *The Challenge of the Present Crisis* (New York: Association Press, 1917), 42, 44, 67.

8. Piper, *American Churches*, 51–56, recounts this episode.

9. Charles S. Macfarland, *The Churches of Christ in Time of War: A Handbook for*

the Churches (New York: Federal Council of the Churches of Christ, 1917), 130, 133, 136–37.

10. William E. Barton, "The Moral Meanings of the World War," *Homiletic Review* 79 (September 1918): 234–42.

11. W. F. McDowell, "The Church in a World at War," *Methodist Review* 101 (July 1918), 515; William Herbert Perry Faunce, *The New Horizon of State and Church* (New York: Macmillan, 1918), 70; Fosdick, *Challenge of the Present Crisis*, 72, 76; Link, *Papers of Woodrow Wilson*, 61:436.

12. Charles Reynolds Brown, "Moral and Spiritual Forces in the War," *Religion and the War*, ed. E. Hershey Sneath (New Haven, Conn.: Yale University Press, 1918), 20; Fosdick, *Challenge of the Present Crisis*, 98–99; Worth Marion Tippy, *The Church and the Great War* (New York: Fleming H. Revell, 1918), 14, 16–17.

13. Henry Churchill King, *For a New America in a New World* (Paris: The Young Men's Christian Association, 1919); Bennett, *The Party of Fear*, 183–84.

14. Samuel McCrea Cavert, "The Missionary Enterprise as the Moral Equivalent of War," *Biblical World* 50 (December 1917), 348; H. P. Almon Abbott, *The Religion of the Tommy: War Essays and Addresses* (Milwaukee, Wisc.: Morehouse Publishing, 1918), 9, 11–12; A. Eugene Bartlett, "The Creed of a Returned Soldier," *Homiletic Review* 77 (May 1919), 410–13.

15. Henry Hallam Tweedy, "The Ministry and the War," *Religion and the War*, 95, 96–97, 99, 100.

16. Luther Allan Weigle, "The Effect of the War upon Religious Education," *Religion and the War*, 114, 117, 118.

17. Abbott, *Religion of the Tommy*, 54, 56; Fosdick, *Challenge of the Present Crisis*, 82, 89–90.

18. Daniel Dorchester, "The Imponderables and a Better World Order," *Methodist Review* 102 (May 1919): 350–56.

19. Tippy, *The Church and the Great War*, 88–89, 121.

20. Hopkins, *History of the Y. M. C. A.* The quotation from Hopkins is on p. 456.

21. Quoted in Hopkins, *History of the Y. M. C. A.*, 509.

22. Piper, *American Churches*, 35–48; the quote from the commission's statement of purpose is on p. 37. For an account of the various denominational and interdenominational agencies with which the General War-Time Commission cooperated, see Margaret Renton, ed., *War-Times Agencies of the Churches: Directory and Handbook* (New York: General War-Time Commission of the Churches, 1919).

23. Piper, *American Churches*, 40–41, 109–10, 134–37. The quote from Piper is on p. 45.

24. Tippy, *The Church and the Great War*, 14, 17, 22, 94.

25. Bartlett, "Creed of a Returned Soldier," 413; King, *For a New America in a New World*, 59–60, 61; Piper, *American Churches*, 40, 118.

26. W. A. Brown, *Church in America*, 119; [Interchurch World Movement], *Speakers' Manual*, abridged ed. (New York: Interchurch World Movement of North America, 1920), 17–21. The standard account of the movement is Eldon Ernst, *Moment of Truth for Protestant America: Interchurch Campaigns Following World War I* (Missoula, Mont.: Scholars' Press, 1974).

27. [Interchurch World Movement], *Speakers' Manual*, 17; Ernst, *Moment of Truth*, 35–49.

28. [Interchurch World Movement] *World Survey: American Volume*, rev. preliminary ed. (New York: Interchurch Press, 1920), 56; Ernst, *Moment of Truth*, 91.

29. Ernst, *Moment of Truth*, 91. For the organizational structure of the movement, see [Interchurch World Movement] *Speakers' Manual*, 107–20.

30. John D. Rockefeller Jr., "Efficiency in the Lord's Business," *New Era Magazine*

26 (June 1920), 418–19. Rockefeller's article in the *Saturday Evening Post* is quoted from Raymond B. Fosdick, *John D. Rockefeller, Jr.: A Portrait* (New York: Harper and Brothers, 1956), 206. Fosdick, 207–12, treats Rockefeller's involvement in the IWM. On Rockefeller's role in mainstream Protestantism, see Albert F. Schenkel, *The Rich Man and the Kingdom: John D. Rockefeller, Jr., and the Protestant Establishment* (Minneapolis, Minn.: Fortress Press, 1995).

31. See, for example, [Interchurch World Movement] *World Survey: Foreign Volume* (New York: Interchurch Press, 1920), 204–17.

32. Rockefeller, "Efficiency in the Lord's Business," 418.

33. [Interchurch World Movement] *World Survey: American Volume,* 42.

34. Ibid., 70–71; Warren H. Wilson, "The Benefit to the Minister in the Interchurch Survey," *Homiletic Review* 78 (October 1919), 293.

35. [Interchurch World Movement] *World Survey: American Volume,* 221, 226, 227.

36. Ibid., 280–85, 295.

37. *Report on the Steel Strike of 1919* (New York: Harcourt, Brace and Howe, 1920), 11–19, 245–50. The quotations are from pp. 248, 250.

38. *Public Opinion and the Steel Strike* (New York: Harcourt, Brace, 1921), vi; Alva Taylor, "Mr. Rockefeller versus Judge Gary," *Christian Century* 37 (September 9, 1920), 18–19; Donald Meyer, *The Protestant Search for Political Realism, 1919–1941,* 2nd ed. (Middletown, Conn.: Wesleyan University Press, 1988), 58–64.

39. *Public Opinion and the Steel Strike,* 263, 265.

40. Ernst, *Moment of Truth,* 94–98; the quote from Ernst is on 98.

41. John E. Lankford, "The Impact of the New Era Movement on the Presbyterian Church in the United States of America, 1918–1925," *Journal of Presbyterian History* 40 (December 1962): 213–24; Lankford, "Methodism 'Over the Top': The Joint Centenary Movement, 1917–1925," *Methodist History* 2 (1963): 27–37; Garrison and DeGroot, *The Disciples of Christ,* 427. S. Earl Taylor and Halford E. Luccock, *The Christian Crusade for World Democracy* (New York: Methodist Book Concern, 1918), 182. The letter to Presbyterian youth groups is dated November 1, 1918, and signed by William Hiram Foulkes, general secretary of the New Era Movement; the accompanying pamphlet—*Comrades of the New Era*—bears no date. I am indebted to the Reverend Robert H. Stephens and to Mary Helen Stephens for sharing these last two documents.

42. David McConaughy, *Money the Acid Test* (Philadelphia, Pa.: Westminster Press, 1918), 185; Trachtenberg, *The Incorporation of America,* 135.

43. John Marshall Barker, *The Social Gospel and the New Era* (New York: Macmillan, 1919), 46, 32, 66, 74, 78.

44. Ibid., 62; [Interchurch World Movement] *World Survey: American Volume,* 44.

7. The Fundamentalist Controversy and Beyond

1. Ernst, *Moment of Truth,* 157–79.

2. I. M. Haldeman, *Why I Am Opposed to the Interchurch World Movement* (n.d., n.p.), reprinted in *The Fundamentalist Modernist Conflict: Opposing Views on Three Major Issues,* ed. Joel A. Carpenter (New York: Garland, 1988), 4, 17, 18, 46.

3. On Machen and Bryan, see D. G. Hart, *Defending the Faith: J. Gresham Machen and the Crisis of Conservative Protestantism in Modern America* (Baltimore, Md.: Johns Hopkins University Press, 1994); and Bradley J. Longfield, *The Presbyterian Controversy: Fundamentalists, Modernists, and Moderates* (New York: Oxford University Press, 1991), 28–76.

4. Marsden, *Fundamentalism and American Culture,* 153–64; Betty A. DeBerg, *Ungodly Women: Gender and the First Wave of American Fundamentalism* (Minneapolis, Minn.: Fortress Press, 1990), 99–117; Margaret Lamberts Bendroth, *Fundamentalism and Gender, 1875 to the Present* (New Haven, Conn.: Yale University Press, 1993), 54–72; Martin E.

Marty, *The Noise of Conflict, 1919–1941,* vol. 2 of *Modern American Religion* (Chicago: University of Chicago Press, 1991), 59–102. Siegfried quoted in Marty, 63.

5. See chapter 1.

6. Grant Wacker, "The Holy Spirit and the Spirit of the Age in American Protestantism, 1880–1910," *Journal of American History* 72 (June 1985), 45–62.

7. D. B. Pepper, "The First Resurrection." *Baptist Review* 2 (January–March 1880): 29; James F. Findlay Jr., *Dwight L. Moody: American Evangelist, 1837–1899* (Chicago: University of Chicago Press, 1969), 408–13.

8. "Address of Hon. Henry B. F. Macfarland," *Light on Prophecy: A Coordinated Constructive Teaching* (New York: Christian Herald, 1918), 71–72, 73; *Light on Prophecy,* 32; A. E. Thompson, "The Capture of Jerusalem," *Light on Prophecy,* 144; Reuben A. Torrey, *What the War Teaches, or The Greatest Lessons of 1917* (Los Angeles, Calif.: Bible Institute of Los Angeles, 1918), 13, 14.

9. *God Hath Spoken,* 342, 352.

10. Shirley Jackson Case, "The Premillennial Menace," *Biblical World* 52 (July 1918): 16–23.

11. Cortland Myers, "War on German Theology," *Light on Prophecy,* 176, 181; Harris H. Gregg, "Hath God Spoken?" *Light on Prophecy,* 29.

12. John M. MacInnis, "What Is Prophecy and Why Study It?" *Light on Prophecy,* 49; Mark Mathews, "The Doctrine of Our Lord's Return," *Light on Prophecy,* 66; T. P. Weber, *Living in the Shadow,* 40. See the Niagara Creed reproduced in Ernest L. Sandeen, *Roots of Fundamentalism,* 273.

13. See Virginia Lieson Brereton, *Training God's Army: The American Bible School, 1880–1940* (Bloomington: Indiana University Press, 1990) for a description of the separate world which millenarians had begun to create for themselves.

14. William B. Riley, *The Menace of Modernism* (New York: Christian Alliance, 1917), 86, 95.

15. George Ricker Berry, *Premillennialism and Old Testament Prediction: A Study of Interpretation* (Chicago: University of Chicago Press, 1929), 12; Herbert Willett, "Millenarian Misuse of Scripture," *Christian Century* 35 (August 22, 1918), 8; James H. Snowden, "Summary of Objections to Premillennialism," *Biblical World* 53 (March 1919), 172–73.

16. Herbert Willett, "The Kaiser's Number," *Christian Century* 35 (January 24, 1818), 5–6; Arthur Metcalf, "A Bible Class and the Second Advent," *Homiletic Review* 74 (November 1917), 360.

17. Fordyce H. Argo, "The Second Coming and the Kingdom," *Biblical World* 54 (March 1920), 156.

18. Shailer Mathews, *Will Christ Come Again?* (Chicago: American Institute of Sacred Literature, 1917), 2; Levi Gilbert, "Will Jesus Return in the Flesh?" *Methodist Review* 99 (March 1917), 255; George P. Mains, *Premillennialism: Non-Scriptural, Non-Historic, Non-Scientific, Non-Philosophical* (New York: Abingdon, 1920), 100; Herbert Willett, "Millennial Hopes and the War Mood," *Christian Century* 35 (March 14, 1918), 3.

19. Mathews, *Will Christ Come Again?,* 4, 6, 13–14, 16, 20, 21.

20. Harris Franklin Rall, *The Coming Kingdom,* 7–8, 26.

21. Mains, *Premillennialism,* 87, 92, 94, 148–49.

22. George Eckman, *The Return of the Redeemer* (New York: Abingdon, 1920), 257–58.

23. Harris Franklin Rall, "Methodism and Premillennialism," *Methodist Review* 103 (March 1920), 219; William E. Hammond, "The End of the World," *Biblical World* 51 (May 1918), 282.

24. Rall, *Modern Premillennialism and the Christian Hope,* 129, 131, 180ff.

25. G. Cross, "Millenarianism in Christian History," 3–4; Herbert Willett, "Is Christ Coming Again?" *Christian Century* 35 (September 5, 1918), 6.

26. Willett, "Is Christ Coming Again?" 6; Herbert Willett, "The Blessed Consummation," *Christian Century* 35 (May 9, 1918), 10; Mains, *Premillennialism*, 92.

27. Mathews, *Will Christ Come Again?* 21; Willett, "Is Christ Coming Again?" 8; Gilbert, "Will Jesus Return in the Flesh?" 257–58; Hammond, "The End of the World," 282.

28. James M. Campbell, *The Second Coming of Christ: A Message for the Times* (New York: Methodist Book Concern, 1919), 70, 96, 98.

29. Shirley Jackson Case, *The Millennial Hope: A Phase of War-Time Thinking* (Chicago: University of Chicago Press, 1918), 239; Rall, *Coming Kingdom*, 27.

30. William Jennings Bryan, *The Last Message of William Jennings Bryan* (New York: Fleming H. Revell, 1925), 53, 54; O'Malley, *Keeping Watch*, 307.

31. Edgar Y. Mullins, *Christianity at the Crossroads* (New York: George H. Doran, 1924), 30, 151.

32. Marsden, *Fundamentalism and American Culture*, 176–95.

33. Reuben A. Torrey, *The Power of Prayer and the Prayer of Power* (New York: Fleming H. Revell, 1924), 16; Martin Marty, *The Irony of It All, 1893–1919*, vol. 1: *Modern American Religion* (Chicago: University of Chicago Press, 1986), 215; Brereton, *Training God's Army*, 40; Joel A. Carpenter, *Revive Us Again: The Reawakening of American Fundamentalism* (New York: Oxford University Press, 1997); William Vance Trollinger Jr., *God's Empire: William Bell Riley and Midwestern Fundamentalism* (Madison: University of Wisconsin Press, 1990).

34. Gaustad, *Historical Atlas of Religion in America*, 122. See also Donald W. Dayton, *Theological Roots of Pentecostalism* (Metuchen, N.J.: Scarecrow Press, Inc., 1987); and Robert Mapes Anderson, *Vision of the Disinherited: The Making of American Pentecostalism* (New York: Oxford University Press, 1979).

35. Marty, *Noise of Conflict*, 214; Sanford, *Federal Council of the Churches of Christ*, 207; Robert A. Schneider, "Voice of Many Waters: Church Federation in the Twentieth Century," in *Between the Times: The Travail of the Protestant Establishment, 1900–1960*, ed. William R. Hutchison (Cambridge: Cambridge University Press, 1989), 95–121; James Alan Patterson, "The Loss of a Protestant Missionary Consensus: Foreign Missions and the Fundamentalist-Modernist Conflict," in *Earthen Vessels: American Evangelicals and Foreign Missions, 1880–1980*, ed. Joel A. Carpenter and Walter R. Shenk (Grand Rapids, Mich.: Eerdmans, 1990), 73–91.

36. Dorothy Bass, "Ministry on the Margin: Protestants and Education," in *Between the Times*, 48–71; R. Laurence Moore, "Secularization: Religion and the Social Sciences," in *Between the Times*, 235; Robert S. Lynd and Helen Merrell Lynd, *Middletown: A Study in Modern American Culture* (New York: Harcourt, Brace and World, 1929), 339. See also Stanley Coben, *Rebellion Against Victorianism: The Impetus for Cultural Change in 1920s America* (New York: Oxford University Press, 1991), 36–68.

37. Lynd and Lynd, *Middletown*, 370; R. L. Moore, "Secularization," 237–38. For an example of the way in which religion could remain vital though voluntary in higher education, see P. C. Kemeny, *Princeton in the Nation's Service: Religious Ideals and Educational Practice, 1868–1928* (New York: Oxford University Press, 1998).

38. William H. Leach, *How to Make the Church Go: A Desk Manual for the Every Day Use of the Modern Minister Executive* (New York: George H. Doran, 1922), 11–50, 104; Roger W. Babson, *Religion and Business* (New York: Macmillan, 1921), 17; Bruce Barton, *The Man Nobody Knows: A Discovery of the Real Jesus* (Indianapolis, Ind.: Bobbs-Merrill, 1924). See Leo P. Ribuffo, "Jesus Christ as Business Statesman: Bruce Barton and the Selling of Corporate Capitalism," *American Quarterly* 33 (summer 1981), 206–31. Harding is quoted in Rolf Lundén, *Business and Religion in the American 1920s*, 20–21. Barton's name later became part of the Republican trio of "Martin, Barton, and Fish" ridiculed by President Franklin Roosevelt.

39. W. A. Brown, *The Church in America*, ix.

40. Ibid., 19, 20, 21, 72–76. The study upon which Brown drew is *Religion among American Men: As Revealed by a Study of Conditions in the Army* (New York: Association Press, 1920).

41. W. A. Brown, *Church in America,* 122, 123–24, 133.

42. Ibid., 186, 251–52, 234–48.

43. Ibid., 151, 234, 279–326.

44. Reinhold Niebuhr, *Reflections on the End of an Era* (New York: Charles Scribner's Sons, 1934).

45. Edwin Lewis, *A New Heaven and a New Earth* (New York: Abingdon-Cokesbury, 1941), 106, 115–16. On the changed temper of Protestant theology, see Sydney E. Ahlstrom, "Continental Influence of American Christian Thought since World War I," *Church History* 27 (September 1958), 256–72; Deane William Ferm, *Contemporary American Theologians: A Critical Survey* (New York: Seabury, 1981); and W. R. Hutchison, *Modernist Impulse,* 288–311.

46. W. M. King, "Denominational Modernization and Religious Identity", 354–55.

47. "Boards and Agencies," *New Era Magazine* 26 (February 1920): 87; John Higham, "Hanging Together: Divergent Unities in American History," *Journal of American History* 61 (June 1974): 26.

48. W. A. Brown, *Church in America,* 11.

49. Ellis, *Men and Missions* (Philadelphia, Pa.: The Sunday School Times, 1909), 220; Ninde, *The Story of the American,* 382–85; Sanford, *Federal Council of the Churches.* On Hall and Roosevelt, see Bederman, *Manliness and Civilization,* 77–120, 170–216.

50. Robert Moats Miller, *Bishop G. Bromley Oxnam: Paladin of Liberal Protestantism* (Nashville, Tenn.: Abingdon, 1990), 185–86, 187.

51. Frank, *Less Than Conquerors,* 68; A. G. Mojtabai, *Blessèd Assurance: At Home with the Bomb in Amarillo, Texas* (Boston: Houghton Mifflin, 1986), 163. See also Robert Fuller, *Naming the Antichrist: The History of an American Obsession* (New York: Oxford University Press, 1995); Charles B. Strozier, *Apocalypse: On the Psychology of Fundamentalism in America* (Boston: Beacon, 1994); and Boyer, *When Time Shall Be No More.*

Epilogue

1. Harvey Cox, *The Secular City: Secularization and Urbanization in Theological Perspective,* rev. ed. (New York: Macmillan, 1967), 105.

2. Sydney E. Ahlstrom, "Neo-Orthodoxy Demythologized," *Christian Century* 74 (May 22, 1957): 649–51; Sydney E. Ahlstrom, "The Radical Turn in Theology and Ethics: Why It Occurred in the 1960s," *Annals of the American Academy of Political and Social Science* 387 (January 1970): 1–13; James Hudnut-Beumler, *Looking for God in the Suburbs: The Religion of the American Dream and Its Critics, 1945–1965* (New Brunswick, N.J.: Rutgers University Press, 1994).

3. Robert S. Ellwood, *The Sixties Spiritual Awakening: American Religion Moving from Modern to Postmodern* (New Brunswick, N.J.: Rutgers University Press, 1994), 131; Thomas J. J. Altizer and William Hamilton, *Radical Theology and the Death of God* (Indianapolis, Ind.: Bobbs-Merrill, 1966), 160, 164, 168, 169. Hamilton's essay appeared originally as "The New Optimism," *Theology Today* (January 1966).

4. James F. Findlay Jr., *Church People in the Struggle: The National Council of Churches and the Black Freedom Movement, 1950–1970* (New York: Oxford University Press, 1993), 224. For a different perspective on religious engagement with the struggle for racial equality, see Charles Marsh, *God's Long Summer: Stories of Faith and Civil Rights* (Princeton, N.J.: Princeton University Press, 1997). See also Michael B. Friedland, *Lift Up Your Voice Like a Trumpet: White Clergy and the Civil Rights and Antiwar Movements, 1954–1973* (Chapel Hill: University of North Carolina Press, 1998); and Jill Gill, "'Peace Is Not the Absence of War But the Presence of Justice': The National Council of Churches' Re-

action and Response to the Vietnam War, 1965–1972 (Ph.D. diss., University of Pennsylvania, 1996).

5. Johnson is quoted by Robert M. Collins, "Growth Liberalism in the Sixties," in *The Sixties: From Memory to History,* ed. David Farber (Chapel Hill: University of North Carolina Press, 1994), 19.

6. For a sample of the proliferating positions which replaced neo-orthodoxy, see Deane William Ferm, *Contemporary American Theologies II;* for an examination of the transformation in one tradition, see James H. Moorhead, "Redefining Confessionalism: American Presbyterians in the Twentieth Century," in *The Confessional Mosaic: Presbyterians and Twentieth-Century Theology,* ed. Milton J. Coalter, John M. Mulder, and Louis B. Weeks (Louisville, Ky.: Westminster/John Knox, 1990), 59–83. For an overview of the profound transformations in American expectations in the late 1960s and early 1970s, see James T. Patterson, *Grand Expectations: The United States, 1945–1974* (New York: Oxford University Press, 1996), esp. 593–790.

7. Findlay, *Church People,* 224. For examples of the continuing activist spirit, see Robert Booth Fowler, *The Greening of Protestant Thought* (Chapel Hill: University of North Carolina Press, 1995).

8. Paul Boyer, "The Growth of Fundamentalistic Apocalyptic in the United States," in *The Encyclopedia of Apocalypticism,* vol. 3, *Apocalypticism in the Modern Period and the Contemporary Age,* ed. Stephen J. Stein (New York: Continuum, 1998), 168. The entire essay, on which this paragraph draws, covers pp. 14–78.

9. Jonathan Schell, *The Fate of the Earth* (New York: Alfred A. Knopf, 1982), 127, 129. See also Michael Barkun, "Divided Apocalypse: Thinking About the End in Contemporary America," *Soundings* 66 (fall 1983): 257–80.

10. See the following essays in *Encyclopedia of Apocalypticism,* vol. 3, *Apocalypticism in the Modern Period,* ed. Stein: Stephen J. Stein, "Apocalypticism Outside the Mainstream in the United States," 108–39; Stephen D. O'Leary, "Popular Culture and Apocalypticism," 392–426; and Michael Barkun, "Politics and Apocalypticism," 442–60.

11. Dean M. Kelley, *Why Conservative Churches Are Growing: A Study of Sociology of Religion,* rev. ed. (New York: Harper and Row, 1977), 154–55.

INDEX

James H. Moorhead is the Mary McIntosh Bridge Professor of American Church History at Princeton Theological Seminary. He previously taught at North Carolina State University in Raleigh. The author of *American Apocalypse: Yankee Protestants and the Civil War, 1860–1869,* Mr. Moorhead is also senior editor of *The Journal of Presbyterian History.*